WHERE MORTAL
and
IMMORTAL MEET

Essays in Celebration of the Eighty-Fifth Anniversary of The Society of Friends of Glasgow Cathedral

EDITED BY ANDREW G. RALSTON

Foreword by Mark E. Johnstone

Introduction by James H. Macaulay

WIPF & STOCK · Eugene, Oregon

WHERE MORTAL AND IMMORTAL MEET
Essays in Celebration of the Eighty-Fifth Anniversary
of the Society of Friends of Glasgow

Copyright © 2021 Andrew G. Ralston. All rights reserved. Except for brief quotations in critical publications or reviews, no part of this book may be reproduced in any manner without prior written permission from the publisher. Write: Permissions, Wipf and Stock Publishers, 199 W. 8th Ave., Suite 3, Eugene, OR 97401.

Wipf & Stock
An Imprint of Wipf and Stock Publishers
199 W. 8th Ave., Suite 3
Eugene, OR 97401

www.wipfandstock.com

PAPERBACK ISBN: 978-1-7252-9951-1
HARDCOVER ISBN: 978-1-7252-9952-8
EBOOK ISBN: 978-1-7252-9953-5

OCTOBER 18, 2021

*Cover picture: A late eighteenth-century oil painting of Glasgow Cathedral and the Molendinar Burn by an unknown artist.
(Courtesy of the Trustees of the Macaulay Settlement).*

"Art, if one in spirit, takes many forms, Music, Poetry, Eloquence, Painting, Sculpture, Architecture, and others; but with one end, to discover and interpret the beauty of the world, to find the eternal amid the transient, the Spiritual in the Material. It connects the two worlds, drawing out all that is finest into one pure river of life. In this stream the Mortal and Immortal meet. . . .

Our Churches [should] be Sanctuaries where Art in its manifold and beautiful forms ministers to worship through the eye as well as the ear. Without and within, every part and every detail should be a setting forth in the language of art of Jesus Christ, the chief Corner Stone. Christ first, the ever open western door; and Christ last, the Holy Table in the East, the end, the sacrifice, the triumph, the holy place where the glory of the Lord shall be revealed."

(FROM "THE CHURCH AND THE ARTS,"
AN ADDRESS BY THE ARTIST SIR DAVID YOUNG CAMERON
TO THE CHURCH SERVICE SOCIETY IN 1941).

Contents

Notes on Contributors		ix
Acknowledgements		xv
Foreword by Mark E. Johnstone		xvii
Introduction by Dr. James H. Macaulay		xxi
	A History of the Society of Friends of Glasgow Cathedral ANDREW G. RALSTON	3
1	The Death of St. Kentigern of Glasgow DAVID MCROBERTS	43
2	The Earlier Cathedrals of Glasgow C. A. RALEGH RADFORD	53
3	King David I and the Church of Glasgow G. W. S. BARROW	61
4	The Diocese of Glasgow before the Wars of Independence: an Overview NORMAN F. SHEAD	75
5	Benefactions to the Medieval Cathedral and See of Glasgow NORMAN F. SHEAD	95
6	Jocelin, Abbot of Melrose (1170–74), and Bishop of Glasgow (1175–99) NORMAN F. SHEAD	112

7   Glasgow Cathedral and its Clergy in the Middle Ages   136
    Ian B. Cowan

8   The Blacader Choir Screen and the Crossing Area in Glasgow Cathedral   144
    David McRoberts

9   Archbishop Robert Blackadder's Will   152
    John Durkan

10 The Tombs of St. Kentigern and Bishop Wishart in the Lower Church   163
    E. L. G. Stones

11 "Their Own Parish Kirk": Jurisdictional Jealousy and Sacramental Spaces Across the Reformation Divide   181
    Daniel MacLeod

12 Archbishop Spottiswoode and the See of Glasgow   197
    James Kirk

13 The Glasgow Assembly of 1638   218
    Roger A. Mason

14 The Western Towers of Glasgow Cathedral   241
    James H. Macaulay

15 The Makers of the "Munich Glass": the Munich Royal Glass Painting Works   258
    Elgin Vaassen

16 "Reverent and Cultured Ritual": Worship in Glasgow Cathedral, 1865–1915   275
    Andrew G. Ralston

Bibliography   303

Index   315

Notes on Contributors

Professor G. W. S. Barrow FBA (1924–2013)

Educated at the University of St. Andrews and Pembroke College, Oxford, Geoffrey Barrow began his career as a lecturer at University College, London and subsequently became Professor of Medieval History in Newcastle upon Tyne and Professor of Scottish History at St. Andrews. His final appointment was as Sir William Fraser Professor of Scottish History and Palaeography at the University of Edinburgh. His special interest was in aspects of feudalism and governance in medieval Scotland. He is the author of *Robert Bruce* and one of the founder members of the Conference of Scottish Medievalists.

Dr. Ian B. Cowan (1932–90)

Ian Cowan taught at the University of Glasgow for twenty-eight years and was a key figure in developing the Scottish History Department. His main research interest lay in the medieval church and for many years he made regular trips to work in the Vatican Archives. He is the author of *The Scottish Reformation: Church and Society in Sixteenth-century Scotland* (1982) and a selection of his other writings was edited by James Kirk and published as *The Medieval Church in Scotland* in 1995.

Dr. John Durkan (1914–2006)

John Durkan was a Glasgow schoolteacher of Irish descent who built up a formidable reputation as a scholar of the Renaissance and Reformation period. He was a founding member of the SCHA (Scottish Catholic Historical Association) and served on the editorial boards of both the SCHA journal *The Innes Review* and the Scottish Church History Society's journal *Scottish Church History*. The Universities of Glasgow and Edinburgh both awarded him honorary doctorates. He was a Senior Honorary Research Fellow of Glasgow University. Among his numerous publications was *Scottish Schools and Schoolmasters 1560–1633*.

Monsignor David McRoberts (1912–78)

Born in Wishaw, David McRoberts trained for the priesthood in the Scots College at Rome during the 1930s. He served as a curate in Partick and in 1945 was appointed Professor of Church History at St. Peter's College, Bearsden. Between 1951 and 1978 he was editor of *The Innes Review*. One of his most important contributions to scholarship was his work on collating pre-1855 baptismal and marriage records from Catholic churches. The University of Glasgow awarded him an honorary degree of D.Litt in 1970.

Dr. C. A. Ralegh Radford (1900–98)

Educated at Exeter College, Oxford, Ralegh Radford was an archaeologist, historian and author of many guide books and surveys of ancient buildings for the Ministry of Works (formerly the Office of Works), including a guide to Glasgow Cathedral. He published widely in scholarly journals. He specialized in the early medieval period and undertook many excavations including those at Glastonbury and Tintagel. He was awarded the OBE in 1947.

NOTES ON CONTRIBUTORS

Professor E. L. G. Stones FBA (1914–87)

Lionel Stones was educated at the University of Glasgow and Balliol College, Oxford. After war service in the Royal Signals he became a lecturer at Glasgow in 1945 and was Professor of Medieval History there between 1956 and 1978. He was editor of *Anglo-Scottish Relations 1174–1328* and (with Grant G. Simpson) *Edward I and the Throne of Scotland* (two volumes).

Professor James Kirk

A specialist in Reformation History, James Kirk was educated at Edinburgh University and joined the Department of Scottish History in the University of Glasgow in 1972. He was appointed to a personal chair in Scottish History in 1999. His works include *Patterns of Reform* and (with John Durkan) *The University of Glasgow 1451–1577*. He was also the editor of *The Books of Assumption of the Thirds of Benefices: Scottish Ecclesiastical Rentals at the Reformation.*

Professor Roger A. Mason

Roger Mason is Emeritus Professor of Scottish History at the University of St. Andrews and a specialist in the late medieval and early modern period. He is founding director of the St. Andrews Institute of Scottish Historical Research, a former editor of the *Scottish Historical Review* and general editor of the ten volume New Edinburgh History of Scotland published by Edinburgh University Press.

Dr. James H. Macaulay

James Macaulay is a former senior lecturer at the Mackintosh School of Architecture in Glasgow and former chairman of the Society of Architectural Historians of Great Britain and the Architectural Heritage Society of Scotland. He is the author of various books including a biography of Charles Rennie Mackintosh (2010) and has for many years served as Chairman of the Society of Friends of Glasgow Cathedral.

Dr. Daniel MacLeod

Daniel MacLeod is the Director of the Jesuit Centre for Catholic Studies at St. Paul's College, University of Manitoba, where he has been working since 2014. He earned a PhD in History from the University of Guelph where he studied in the Centre for Scottish Studies. His research examines Christianity in early-modern Scotland with a particular focus on Catholicism and the Society of Jesus. In 2014 he edited *Keeping the Kirk: Scottish Religion at Home and in the Diaspora* and has published on Scottish conceptions of time in the Reformation-era, Scottish Jesuit St. John Ogilvie, and lay religious experiences in sixteenth- and seventeenth-century Glasgow. He lives in Winnipeg, Manitoba, Canada with his family.

Dr. Andrew G. Ralston

A graduate of the University of Glasgow and Balliol College, Oxford, Andrew Ralston is a former teacher who has published many educational textbooks for schools and historical works including *Opening Schools and Closing Prisons: Caring for Destitute and Delinquent Children in Scotland, 1812–1872* (2017) and a biography of Dr. Nevile Davidson, *A Life to be Lived* (2019). He is an elder of Glasgow Cathedral and a member of the Council of the Society of Friends.

Norman F. Shead

A graduate of Glasgow University, Norman Shead was Principal Teacher of History at Hutchesons' Grammar School between 1979 and 1998. He contributed the chapters on Medieval Glasgow in *The Scottish Medieval Town* and *A Tale of Two Towns: a History of Medieval Glasgow*. He is one of the editors of Walter Bower's *Scotichronicon* (general editor D. E. R. Watt) and editor of *Scottish Episcopal Acta* (two volumes).

Dr. Elgin Vaassen

Elgin Vaassen studied art history and archaeology at the universities of Bonn, Zürich, and Würzburg. Her PhD thesis was a study of fifteenth-century manuscripts and incunabula. She has subsequently spent nearly forty years researching nineteenth-century stained glass and is the author of two books on the subject: *Bilder auf Glas. Glasgemälde zwischen 1780 und 1870* (1997) and *Die kgl. Glasmalereianstalt in München 1827–1874. Geschichte-Werke-Künstler* (2013).

Acknowledgements

THE PRODUCTION OF THIS book would not have been possible without the help of many people and I would particularly like to express my thanks to the following:

Dr. James Macaulay, Chairman of the Society of Friends[1] of Glasgow Cathedral, who provided the initial idea, supplied a number of illustrations and gave permission to reproduce material previously published as pamphlets or in annual reports by the Society of Friends (chapters 2, 3, 7, 8, 12, 13, 14, and 15);

Heather Beadling, Glasgow Cathedral administrator, and Professor Ronnie Baxendale, joint session clerk of Glasgow Cathedral, for assistance with access to archive material;

Henty and Alan Diack and Liz and Charles Scott for sharing memories of their involvement in various appeals undertaken by the Society of Friends;

Ailene Hunter for helping with proof-reading;

Steven J. Branford for checking sections of text in Latin;

Douglas Annan for permission to reproduce the photographs of Sir D. Y. Cameron and Rev. Dr. William Morris;

The National Portrait Gallery, London, for permission to reproduce the photographs of Lord Bilsland and Sir Albert Richardson;

The University of Strathclyde for permission to reproduce the photographs of Sir Graham Hills and Sir John Arbuthnott;

---

1. For the avoidance of doubt, it may be worth pointing out that the Society of Friends of Glasgow Cathedral has no connection with the Religious Society of Friends (Quakers). The Cathedral congregation is part of the Church of Scotland but the Society of Friends of Glasgow Cathedral is a non-denominational organization whose primary purpose is the "care of the Cathedral and its preservation for posterity." The building belongs neither to the congregation nor to the Society of Friends but is maintained and managed on behalf of the State by Historic Environment Scotland (HES).

Glen Collie, joint session clerk of Glasgow Cathedral, for photographs of the Cathedral interior;

Andrew Forbes for the photograph of Dr. James Macaulay;

David Palmar (www.photoscot.co.uk) for converting slides into digital images;

Gregor Smith, RSW, for drawings of the thirteenth-century chapter seal (chapter 10);

Professor Julia Barrow for permission to reproduce the text of her late father's lecture on "David I and the Church of Glasgow" (chapter 3);

Professor Roger A. Mason for permission to reproduce the text of his lecture on "The Glasgow Assembly of 1638" (chapter 13);

Professor Brian D. Spinks for reading chapter 16 on nineteenth-century liturgical developments in draft form;

Dr. John Reuben Davies and the Council of the Scottish Catholic Historical Association (SCHA) for permission to reproduce articles previously published in *The Innes Review* (chapters 1, 5, 6, 9, and 10);

Emeritus Professor W. Ian P. Hazlett for his ongoing advice and encouragement and for putting me in touch with Dr. Daniel MacLeod, who contributed chapter 11;

Norman F. Shead, who not only contributed chapters 4, 5, and 6 but meticulously checked footnotes and references in the whole volume and ensured the bibliography was complete. These tasks turned out to be the most time-consuming aspects of the whole project as in several cases new editions of medieval sources have appeared since the chapters were originally written. Norman's input into this book has therefore been far greater than originally envisaged. Few historians have such an encyclopedic knowledge of the medieval Scottish church and I am extremely grateful for all his help. Any errors are, of course, my own responsibility.

A.G.R.

Foreword

As the great west door of Glasgow Cathedral is eased open and the setting sun warms the ancient flagstones, someone stepping across the threshold may be tempted to ask: "What purpose does this thirteenth-century cathedral have in a twenty-first-century city?"

Entering this ancient building, the visitor crosses from the secular to the sacred. Visitor numbers confirm that, even in a diverse and modern city, this is something that remains important to visitors: in one recent year the cathedral attracted in excess of 500,000 visitors whereas the nearby Provand's Lordship, the city's oldest house, drew in fewer than 100,000. The pilgrimage made to Glasgow Cathedral by digitally connected international travelers is clearly significant—even if too many Glaswegians still repeat the mantra "I have never been inside."

What, then, is the purpose of this cathedral?

The open door and the welcome afforded by the members of the Society of Friends of Glasgow Cathedral strengthens the cathedral's role in offering hospitality. In the early days of the cathedral, the buildings in the surrounding complex catered to both spiritual and physical needs. Today, hospitality remains the duty of the host and the expectation of the guest. We must help inform the pastoral care of those who seek refuge, asylum, shelter, and safety. We have a responsibility through heritage and vision to represent the Christian duty of care to all who visit this city.

In the lower church, at the heart of the cathedral, lies the tomb of St. Mungo, Patron Saint of Glasgow, and it was within this forest of pillars that fifteenth-century scholars connected with their students. The papal bull of Nicholas V enhanced the status of the cathedral by establishing the university. Educational opportunity and intellectual inquiry played a key part in the cathedral's early history and we continue to maintain connections with the schools and higher education institutions within the city.

The creative industries, too, have often found an encouraging patron in the church. In a city teeming with music, dance, literature, art, radio, and TV the cathedral must continue to touch the creative nerve of the artist. Through the use of space and an understanding of the human condition we can inform complex matters of the soul. The ancient story of the cathedral acts as a source of creativity and inspiration while its venerable walls provide an ideal setting for cultural events and festivals.

The story of Glasgow has also been measured by the evolution of particular commercial activities and industries. Medieval pilgrimages had a significant economic dimension. In more recent times the Tobacco Lords or figures like Charles Tennant, the Scottish chemist with his industrial bleaching powder in St. Rollox, were important. Today the economic and commercial impact of the cathedral is recognized, even though tourism may have largely replaced manufacturing industry. As we look to the future, interested stakeholders—Historic Environment Scotland, Glasgow Life, the cathedral congregation, The Society of Friends—and others will be working together to develop the overall visitor experience in this part of the city. This is the industrial capital the cathedral contributes to its environment and place in the heart of many Glaswegians.

Thus, throughout the centuries, the cathedral has been central to hospitality, education and industry in the city, evolving to meet the needs of each era. But its fundamental purpose remains unchanged: its lofty spire directs the eye of the viewer beyond the everyday to higher things of the spirit. The essays in this book stress this continuity in purpose, from the time of Mungo himself, through the medieval period, the Reformation and the Victorian era up to the present day, reminding us of the original vision of St. Mungo which still lies behind all we do: "let Glasgow flourish by the preaching of the Word and the praising of His Name."

It has been important to identify the person qualified to appraise, digest, edit, and present the academic and literary contribution many have made in respect of the cathedral and its history. The ideal person to carry out this task was Dr. Andrew Ralston who has already used his experience of academic research to write numerous books, including biographical studies of two former cathedral ministers, most recently *Nevile Davidson: A Life to be Lived*. As an elder of the cathedral and a member of the Council of the Friends, he is well-acquainted with the importance of the crucial work of both, as well as the links between them. Andrew brings a theologically informed approach. This reveals his own faith and the zeal he has for the witness of Glasgow Cathedral to the city and beyond.

As minister of Glasgow Cathedral I am pleased to commend this volume to those who have an interest in and love for this ancient building and for all that it has stood for over so many centuries.

Rev. Mark E. Johnstone
Minister
Glasgow Cathedral

Introduction

THIS BOOK HAS TWO purposes. The first is to trace the history of the Society of Friends of Glasgow Cathedral which over the past eighty-five years has sought to improve "the adornment and furnishing of the cathedral" especially by overseeing the installation of "stained glass of worthy quality."

The second purpose reflects another key objective of the Society, "the encouragement of research into the history of the cathedral," and with this in mind the book brings together a selection of essays on various aspects of the cathedral's past. Some of these were originally delivered by eminent historians in the form of lectures to the Friends; others were published in annual reports or in *The Innes Review* and some were specially written for the present volume, based on new research.

A volume of this kind is long overdue. *Where Mortal and Immortal Meet* represents the first attempt to present a scholarly overview of the cathedral's history since Scottish historian and literary critic George Eyre-Todd (1862–1937) compiled *The Book of Glasgow Cathedral: A History and Description* more than 120 years ago. The cover was by the noted decorative artist and book designer Talwin Morris (1865–1911), a friend of Charles Rennie Mackintosh. This volume is highly prized, not only as a source of information but as a collectors' piece, and has for long been the standard work on the cathedral.

Since the publication of Eyre-Todd's book in 1898, much has of course changed with regard to Glasgow Cathedral. The furnishings and stained glass have little in common with those of the late Victorian era. A great deal of research has since been carried out into the history of the cathedral, but the fruits of this scholarship are largely to be found in back-numbers of scholarly journals which are not easily available to a wider readership. While various publications on the cathedral exist (guidebooks for visitors, or studies of specific aspects such as stained glass, archaeological finds, biographies of ministers, etc) there has been no comprehensive volume since Eyre-Todd.

The Society of Friends is very grateful to Dr. Andrew Ralston for all his work in editing this book. We are confident that it provides a compendium of knowledge about the cathedral's history which will be an invaluable resource both for future generations of historians and for all those who have a love for one of Scotland's most significant architectural treasures.

Dr. James H. Macaulay
Chairman
The Society of Friends of Glasgow Cathedral

PART ONE

A History of the Society of Friends
of Glasgow Cathedral

A History of the Society of Friends of Glasgow Cathedral

Andrew G. Ralston

Rev. Dr. A. Nevile Davidson (1899-1976). Founder of the Society of Friends; Chairman, 1936-67; President, 1967-76. Photo: Glasgow Cathedral.

THE WEATHER WAS TYPICALLY dull and drizzly on the morning of January 30, 1935 when thirty-six-year-old Nevile Davidson walked towards Glasgow Cathedral on one of the most important days of his life. He was about to be inducted as minister of "the mother church of Glasgow" and, as he saw the great spire come into view he said that "an overwhelming sense of responsibility swept over me, followed by a silent but intense prayer that I might be given the much needed strength to be equal to it."[1] Over the next thirty-two years he proved that he was indeed equal to the task. He was a highly effective minister to his parish and the wider city, a leading figure in the national church, and a pioneer of ecumenical co-operation and religious broadcasting. Yet it is his role in founding a Society of Friends for the purposes of "the adornment and furnishing of the cathedral, the installation of stained glass of worthy quality, the safeguarding of the cathedral's amenity, the beautifying of its surroundings and the encouragement of research into the history of the cathedral"[2] that has proved his greatest legacy. A recent biography, *Nevile Davidson: A Life to be Lived*,[3] traces his life and work in depth but the full story of the Society of Friends remains to be told.

"AN OPPORTUNITY WHICH MIGHT NEVER RECUR": THE FORMATION OF THE SOCIETY OF FRIENDS, 1936–39

After successful ministries at St. Mary's, Aberdeen and St. Enoch's, Dundee, Davidson had received "a call I could not refuse" to become minister of Glasgow Cathedral, "a church which for stateliness, size and architectural beauty can hold its own with almost any of the great cathedrals across the Border."[4] Though the son of a United Free Church minister, Nevile Davidson was a High Church "Scoto-Catholic" presbyterian, a group characterized by one ecclesiastical historian as being "devoted to seemliness and dignity in worship, and by no means averse from a little pomp and circumstance."[5] There could hardly be a better setting for such a ministry than Glasgow Cathedral.

But the new minister did not like what he saw inside the building which he considered to be "entirely unworthy" of its external grandeur. "The pews and organ gallery are of clumsy Victorian design," he wrote. "The chapels are bare, damp and with one exception unfurnished; and

---

1. Davidson, *Beginnings but No Ending*, 30.
2. Society of Friends of Glasgow Cathedral Annual Report [hereafter SoFGC], 1959, 4
3. Ralston, *Nevile Davidson*.
4. *Glasgow Herald*, March 14, 1936.
5. Cheyne, *The Transforming of the Kirk*, 195.

the nineteenth-century stained-glass windows belong to a period when that art was at a low ebb."[6]

Nevile Davidson was by no means the first to remark on this state of neglect. On his first visit to the cathedral in 1927, Rev. James Bulloch, who later became one of Davidson's assistants, remembered "the atmosphere of Victorian gloom" that pervaded the place; "a hand laid on Archbishop Law's tomb left a visible imprint in the deposit of grime."[7] Another visitor entering the building in 1932 was struck by the fact that the resting place of Glasgow's patron saint, St. Mungo, was not properly marked, the sole provision for tourists being a "chart of the cathedral hung in an inconspicuous corner of the nave" which he only discovered on his way out.[8]

The interior of the cathedral became a matter of controversy on the very day of Nevile Davidson's induction when, at a kirk session luncheon afterwards attended by the Lord Provost and other civic figures, Rev. Dr. Charles Warr of St. Giles' Cathedral, Edinburgh, provocatively stated that "the whole of the magnificent interior" should be opened up by removing the stone screen or pulpitum dividing the nave from the quire—a feature dating from the early fifteenth century and reckoned to be the only one of its type left in any secular (i.e. non-monastic) church of the pre-Reformation period in Scotland. This immediately put the new incumbent in an awkward position and he was forced to dissociate himself publicly from the suggestion made by his clerical friend and mentor from Edinburgh (whose influential backing had been one of the reasons why he got the job in the first place!) A few weeks later, during a visit to the cathedral by members of the Glasgow Elders' and Office-bearers' Union of the Church of Scotland, Davidson took the opportunity to make clear that "no-one who knew the history of the cathedral and who knew anything of medieval architecture could ever contemplate for a moment such an act of sacrilege as the removal of the rood screen."[9]

Warr's intervention was nevertheless significant in that it ignited debate and contributed to a growing feeling within the city that it was high time something was done to improve the cathedral's furnishings. The state of the stained glass windows was of particular concern. Between

---

6. *Glasgow Herald*, March 14, 1936.
7. Davidson, *Beginnings but No Ending*, viii.
8. *Glasgow Herald*, April 11, 1932.
9. *The Scotsman*, February 25, 1935.

1856 and 1864 windows in the quire and nave had been replaced with the then-fashionable Munich glass. According to Iain Macnair's history of the windows, these had aroused controversy right from the start "as their strength and glow of intense color were seen to be 'disturbing and distracting elements.'"[10] By the 1930s, however, the windows were a source of controversy for precisely the opposite reason: a combination of poor manufacture and years of atmospheric pollution meant that the intense color had given way to a "dim religious light," suffusing the interior with an atmosphere of melancholy.

The process of installing one new window was in fact already under way. A Glasgow stockbroker, Ronald W. Mowat, died in 1929 and left a proportion of his estate to the cathedral amounting to £3737 for the erection of a stained glass window in memory of himself and his wife and sons. Finding an appropriate space for the window caused some difficulties and the kirk session minutes for March 1931 record a simple if drastic solution: it was proposed to remove a window in the nave that had been erected in memory of someone else, James Buchanan, a Glasgow merchant who had founded the Buchanan Institution for destitute boys in the mid-nineteenth century. In the absence of any living descendants, the kirk session approached the Trades and Merchants Houses and the Buchanan Trust, none of whom, it seems, were able to provide any further information. A somewhat uneasy arrangement was reached in October 1931 when the Trades House stated that, while "deprecating" the removal of the window, they did not propose to raise any objection, provided that an inscription on the new window made it clear that it replaced Mr. Buchanan's.[11] It appears that endowing a window in memory of an individual is no guarantee that it will remain *in situ* for ever. The new window, on the theme of Moses's leadership, was by the foremost Scottish stained glass designer of the day, Douglas Strachan, and it set a precedent for what would follow by showing the standard of workmanship that was now available. In his dedicatory prayer in February 1936, Nevile Davidson voiced the hope that the new window "might bring refreshment, delight and heavenly thoughts to all who looked upon it."[12]

In other ways, too, the tide was flowing in the direction of those who favored an upgrade of the cathedral. Not only did 1936 mark the 800th

10. Macnair, *Glasgow Cathedral: the Stained Glass Windows*, 3. For the history of the mid-nineteenth-century glazing, see Fawcett, *Glasgow's Great Glass Experiment*.

11. Glasgow Cathedral Kirk Session Minutes, Vol. 604, 50.

12. *The Scotsman*, February 24, 1936.

anniversary of the dedication of an earlier cathedral building in the reign of King David I in 1136 but the city was looking ahead to a huge influx of visitors to the Empire Exhibition to be held at Bellahouston Park between May and October 1938. Hitherto, Glasgow was seen as a grimy, industrial city rather than a tourist destination but the Exhibition drew in more than twelve million visitors and many of them took the opportunity to visit other local places of interest, not least the cathedral and the adjacent Provand's Lordship, the oldest house in Glasgow and originally part of the cathedral's complex of buildings.

All that was needed was a visionary figure who could pull these forces together. That figure was Nevile Davidson and, barely four months into his ministry, he had met with the city's Lord Provost, Sir Alexander Swan, with a view to holding a public meeting for the purpose of the formation of a Society of Friends with the aim of improving "the adornment and furnishings of the cathedral."

There was a precedent for such an organization and in a sense, the story of the Society of Friends really begins, not in Glasgow, but Dunblane as it was here that Rev. J. Hutchison Cockburn, the minister of Dunblane Cathedral, formed a Society of Friends in 1930. This was apparently the first time the idea had been applied to a Scottish cathedral, following a model already used in Canterbury and York. The plan was welcomed by those interested in preserving Dunblane's heritage: by October the society was able to hold its first annual festival and the number of members grew steadily, reaching 750 by 1938.[13] Nevile Davidson was one of them.

A dignified, patrician figure with aristocratic connections to the Agnews of Lochnaw Castle, Wigtownshire and the Kinnaird family of Rossie Priory, Perthshire, Davidson mixed easily with the great and the good and by the time of the public meeting to launch the Glasgow Society in October 1936 he had on board a wide variety of prominent individuals and public bodies such as the Trades and Merchants Houses. He had even secured the agreement of the Duke and Duchess of York—soon to

---

13. Cockburn and Davidson were each members of the other's society. In October 1958 Cockburn, "having retired, found himself unable to continue his membership" of the Glasgow society but the Council unanimously decided to elect him as an Honorary Member. Nevile Davidson remained closely involved with the Dunblane society in the 1960s. In October 1967 he addressed the thirty-eighth Annual Festival on "the Legacy of Leighton" (i.e. Robert Leighton, Bishop of Dunblane, 1611–84) and on that occasion he was described as having "recently retired as Minister of Glasgow Cathedral, which had closer associations than any other with Dunblane." (Society of Friends of Dunblane Cathedral, 10 (1967) Pt. II, 31).

be King George and Queen Elizabeth—to be the Society's first members and patrons, which he described as a "very happy augury" for the success of the new venture.

Equally fortunate was the willingness of two of the most respected benefactors of the city of Glasgow to serve as vice-chairmen of the Society: Sir James MacFarlane (1857–1944), the cathedral's senior elder and chairman of the biscuit makers MacFarlane Lang and Co., and Sir John Stirling-Maxwell (1866–1956), philanthropist and former Conservative MP. Sir John was one of the founders of the National Trust for Scotland and after his death Pollok House and much of the surrounding estate was donated to Glasgow Corporation, while Sir James served for many decades as chairman of the Board of Managers of the Royal Infirmary and gave land at Canniesburn, Bearsden for a new hospital to help reduce the pressure on the main institution.

The first meeting of the Friends was chaired by Lord Provost Swan himself and right from the start the various strands of the cathedral's role—spiritual, civic, and aesthetic—were stressed. As Swan pointed out, a key principle was that "the cathedral did not belong so much to the congregation as to the entire city." The resolution to institute the Society was moved by the painter and etcher Sir David Young Cameron (1865–1945), a son of the manse and a well-known figure in artistic circles. He delivered a passionate if at times idiosyncratic speech in which he interpreted the moves to improve the cathedral as not merely a plan to improve the furnishings of the building but as something "prophetic of a desire to return to the greater things of life."

> Let Glasgow seize that opportunity which might never recur . . . and fashion its cathedral into a shrine of exceeding beauty, alluring and leading towards the pathway where "truth is beauty and beauty is truth."

As an artist, Cameron set out a vision of the new Society. It should be

> guided and inspired by the thought that many worshiped in large part through the eye rather than through the ear. The Church today only appealed to those who hear and never to those who see. The early Church understood that better than we did, hence we found that from the very earliest all that was finest and most significant in the Arts had a place in temples and places of worship.

In a final flourish, Cameron looked forward to "a great universal revival of the Church as a place of appealing beauty... when all the Arts would contribute their parts in the mighty chorus. I see our cathedral once again glorious, a rhapsody of praise."[14] Sadly, Cameron died in 1945 and would not see the fruits of his vision.

Sir D. Y. Cameron (1865–1945). Photo courtesy of Annan Photographs.

The Society had the active support of leading figures in the political, cultural, and business worlds but it also depended on the involvement of ordinary Glaswegians who could join on payment of five shillings (25 pence) per annum. By the time of the first Annual Meeting (or "Festival" as it was then called) in January 1937, 577 had signed up and they in turn were constantly encouraged to recruit more. In addition, the Constitution of the Society ensured that, initially at least, there was a significant representation of both the kirk session and ordinary membership of the cathedral congregation.[15]

---

14. *Glasgow Herald*, October 31, 1935. Cameron developed these romantic notions further in an article entitled *The Church and the Arts*, published in the Church Service Society Annual for 1941. "Once the Church was the chiefest friend of all the Arts and the Arts found their utmost joy in the service of the Church. That was the golden age. May not that come again?" To Cameron, this "golden age" occurred in the Middle Ages which he believed were "the highest revelation of this Beauty spiritualized."

15. The size of the ruling Council was reduced from forty-eight to twenty-four members in 1957 to make it a more workable body.

The idea of restoring the cathedral's interior had thus aroused keen interest in the city—but that did not mean everything would go smoothly. Everybody had an opinion on what form the improvements should take and various interest groups were not slow to stake their claims. In spite of weighty matters like a general election campaign, rearmament, and the rise of Nazism, there was no shortage of letters to the *Glasgow Herald* during 1936 on the subject of remodeling the cathedral, giving a foretaste of the issues that the Friends would have to thrash out over the years to come. The combative Thomas Innes of Learney who, as Lord Lyon between 1945 and 1969, would have responsibility for regulating heraldry, weighed in by demanding to know what was going to happen to the donors' coats of arms if windows were replaced. Not mincing his words, he wrote that "it will be a dastardly shame and insult to the memory of those distinguished citizens . . . if their armorial bearings are now to be ruthlessly 'dashed out of' the cathedral windows as if they had been traitors."[16] This led "one whose ancestor lies in the cathedral yard" to retort that "Church windows are understood to be to the glory of God but those at present are more to the glory of those who presented them, judging by the blatantly large and obtrusive coats of arms upon them."[17] One minister inquired why a General Assembly Committee on "Artistic Questions" should have input on such matters rather than Glasgow presbytery; someone else thought stained glass artists from Glasgow should be doing the work and not those from Edinburgh or England; still another considered that the new windows should "reflect the spirit of St. Mungo" (whatever that may mean). It was already clear that the Friends would only be able to please some of the people some of the time.

Undeterred, Davidson and his supporters forged ahead and by the time of the first Annual Festival, held in the cathedral on St. Mungo's Day, January 13, 1937, there was already much progress to report. The Blacader Aisle which protrudes from the south side of the cathedral had, for the first time in almost four hundred years, been restored for use as a place of worship and daily services were soon to take place in it (though problems of dampness would still be encountered for many years to come). The Friends had also gifted 400 chairs for the furnishing of the nave enabling a series of informal "People's Services" to be held there during the winter. Plans were being considered for an ambitious scheme to "remove

---

16. *Glasgow Herald*, March 3, 1935.
17. *Glasgow Herald*, March 7, 1935.

the cumbrous and unsightly Victorian woodwork from the quire screen; and to replace the narrow, crowded pews by carved oak stalls of seemly design and comfortable dimensions."[18] Furthermore, the Society had the external surroundings of the cathedral under consideration and had a vision of a "tree-lined avenue or processional way" leading to the west door. But the priority was the replacement of the stained glass, beginning with the ten large windows in the quire. Donors for seven of these had already come forward and artists would be commissioned as soon as the Office of Works gave the go ahead. By 1938, the cathedral was ready to welcome visitors to the Empire Exhibition; the building had been thoroughly cleaned inside, a guide book prepared and signs put up, together with a memorial listing the bishops, archbishops, and ministers of the cathedral over the previous 800 years, and a competition was being devised inviting ideas for a redesign of the chancel area with stalls on medieval lines.

An impressive enough list of achievements for a Society that had only been founded two years earlier—but Nevile Davidson felt that more could have been done. A hint of future tension can been seen from his remark to the 1938 Annual Festival that the Office of Works had still not given its approval in spite of having had the plans for almost a year. Being Crown property,[19] the cathedral building was at that time maintained by the Office of Works, the equivalent body today being Historic Environment Scotland (HES). This relieves the congregation and the Society of Friends of responsibility for the burden of maintaining the fabric, but plans for replacing the glazing required to be approved by the Office of Works and the Royal Fine Art Commission for Scotland, all of which took up much time and involved patient negotiation.

In any event, the plans of the Society of Friends ground to a sudden halt in September 1939 with the outbreak of war. The competition for furnishing the quire was postponed, but Herbert Hendrie of Edinburgh College of Art continued to work on several of the windows which were put in storage until after the war. However, one of Hendrie's windows was dedicated on May 5, 1940: "Christ and the World's Work" in the north aisle of the quire, donated by Sir John Stirling-Maxwell to replace an earlier one presented by his great uncle and aunt, Sir John and Lady Matilda Maxwell. While the threat of damage during wartime was real,

18. SoFGC, 1937, 9.

19. For an explanation of the varying claims of Town Council and Crown to ownership of the Cathedral up to the nineteenth century, see Eyre-Todd, *The Book of Glasgow Cathedral*, 174–75.

the Society had nevertheless decided to go ahead with this installation on the grounds that seeing it in position would be of great assistance to artists working on the other windows.[20]

"A VERY COMPREHENSIVE PROGRAM OF WORK": CATHEDRAL IMPROVEMENTS, 1946–61

After the war, the Society's activities resumed, albeit slowly. In May 1946 the two windows made by Hendrie six years earlier were dedicated, an event attended by Sir John Stirling-Maxwell in his bath chair on account of his deteriorating health. Later that year window designs by three new artists were chosen. The Annual Festival continued each January on St. Mungo's Day, usually consisting of a service at the saint's tomb, an AGM and, in the evening, a concert or recital which was sometimes broadcast on the radio. However, a 1947 report from the Ancient Monuments Board states that "friction and confusion have arisen owing to lack of proper coordination between (a) the Ministry, (b) the Friends of the Cathedral and (c) the Minister of the Cathedral, and it is vital that no effort should be spared to remove causes of misunderstanding." 1948 was deemed "a disappointing year," with official restrictions on many schemes which were consequently "still held in suspense."

It was not until 1949 that the restoration program recommenced with new vigor. A meeting in the Central Hotel on May 6, 1950 unanimously agreed that

> the attention of the Committee should be concentrated on the Quire and Transepts, with the exception of the Cameronian Window in the south-west corner of the Nave and the Great West Window of the Nave for which negotiations should now be instituted by Lord Bilsland with the Lord Provost as the leading representative of the Corporation of Glasgow.

The achievement of these aims was to a great extent due to the contribution of two significant figures who between them had the very different skills required to make the project a reality: Lord Bilsland, President of the Society of Friends, and Professor Albert Richardson.

---

20. *Glasgow Herald*, May 6, 1940.

Steven, 1st Baron Bilsland (1892–1970), President of the Society of Friends, 1947–67. Photo ©National Portrait Gallery, London.

Steven, 1st Baron Bilsland, could draw on a lifetime's experience of business and public service. The Cambridge-educated son of former Glasgow Lord Provost, Sir William Bilsland, he inherited the family bakery business, but his dismay at the waste of human potential in the depression of the inter-war years led him to devote his career to stimulating the Scottish economy and, in addition to a host of directorships and philanthropic roles, he served for more than thirty years as President of the Scottish Council for Development and Industry. He had been a member of the Council of the Society of Friends since its formation in 1937 but his contribution as President between 1947 and 1967 was crucial as he patiently led negotiations with individual donors, military authorities, and public bodies, each of whom had their own specific desires.

Glasgow Corporation required particularly careful handling. Things began well, with Nevile Davidson reporting to the sixteenth annual meeting in January 1952 that the City had made a "magnificent offer" to donate the Great West Window which "would form a permanent symbol of the link between Church and City." The joint committee approved of the minister's idea of the Creation as a suitable theme and four artists were invited to submit designs for a fee of £50 each. After some delay, the commission was eventually given to Francis Spear, who lived in Reigate, Surrey and taught at the Royal College of Art in London.

A depiction of the Creation would necessarily include representations of Adam and Eve and one obvious decision had to be made at the start: would they be shown as they were before or after they sinned? Mr. Spear helpfully produced two alternative versions of his design, showing the figures naked and clothed. "After considerable discussion, the committee decided [on September 23, 1955] that the nude figures be retained." However, when the design was presented to "a sub-committee of the finance committee of Glasgow Corporation" there was some criticism of the fact that the artist was neither a Glaswegian nor a Scot and that the Corporation's coat of arms did not feature in the design. Eighteen months later, a contract had still not been signed as the Corporation was unhappy that there was no provision for insuring the window. In turn, the artist "had become perturbed" and stated that "he could not continue work on the window unless by May 31, 1957 a contract with the Ministry of Works or the Society of Friends had been concluded." Once again, the committee placed its faith in Lord Bilsland, in conjunction with the Honorary Treasurer, to sort the matter out, giving him "discretionary power to enter upon a Contract with the Artist on the Society's behalf."[21]

Even when all these issues had been dealt with and the window installed, problems persisted. After inspecting the window in October 1958, the committee decided that certain aspects did not look quite right: "the figures of Adam and Eve were too muscular. The tonality of the glass might with advantage be reduced and a lighter tint given to Eve . . ." and so on. Fortunately, the artist turned out to be accommodating and readily agreed to make alterations, with certain panels being temporarily replaced with clear glass while the changes were made. "Lord Bilsland assured the Committee that there had been no pressure on Mr. Spear and there was no question of yielding by him. He would go so far as to say that Mr. Spear would like to lighten the window and had said the alterations must be made."[22]

The diplomacy exercised by Bilsland when handling the Corporation and the artists was equally necessary when it came to the armed services. The windows of the north and south transepts, by William Wilson and Gordon Webster, commemorate those who lost their lives in the 1939–45

---

21. SoFGC Minutes, May 17, 1957.
22. SoFGC Minutes, December 15, 1958.

war and it has been suggested that on account of these "Glasgow Cathedral can lay claim to being Scotland's national memorial to the Second World War."[23] This phase of the window replacement program involved Lord Bilsland in protracted collective and individual discussions with the twelve Scottish Regiments, the Royal Air Force, Royal Navy, Royal Naval Volunteer Reserve, and the Merchant Navy, who did not always appreciate the complexity of the process and sometimes expressed frustration at the seeming lack of progress, becoming, as Bilsland tactfully said of the RAF at one point, "somewhat restive." With his own military record in the 8th Battalion of the Cameronians (Scottish Rifles) during World War I and his current position as an Honorary Colonel, he would have been listened to with respect by the military top brass.

If patience and tact characterized the contribution of Lord Bilsland, the second key figure during the 1950s was of a completely different caliber. Professor, later Sir, Albert E. Richardson (1880–1964), Professor of Architecture at the University of London and later President of the Royal Academy, was appointed as an "artistic consultant" on the recommendation of the Ancient Monuments Board. This was something of a gamble, for although Richardson's eminence and expertise were not in doubt, he was reputed to be "a difficult character—bombastic, self-centered, a reactionary conservative who hated Modernism as much as he loathed modern society"[24]—and that was in the opinion of one of his admirers. To Richardson, the celebration of progress at the 1951 Festival of Britain was more like "the festering of Britain" and he thought the design for the new Coventry Cathedral was so "frightful to look upon" that he never visited the city again. There are many tales of his eccentricity: his home at Avenue House, Ampthill, Bedfordshire was crammed with antiques and for a long time he resisted having electricity installed. He not only loved Georgian architecture but liked to dress up in full period outfit and be carried to dinner parties in a sedan chair.[25]

23. MacNair, *Stained Glass*, 20.

24. https://adriantinniswood.wordpress.com/2013/09/19/albert-richardson/

25. For more examples of Richardson's quirky views and behavior, see the biography written by his grandson, Simon Houfe, *Sir Albert Richardson: the Professor*.

Sir Albert E. Richardson (1880–1964). Photo ©National Portrait Gallery, London.

For nearly a decade Richardson's advice to the Society of Friends on the artistic merit of proposed designs was decisive and it would not be going too far to suggest that both the glazing and the furnishing of the cathedral reflect his tastes. He regularly traveled to Glasgow for meetings of the joint committee made up of representatives of the Friends, the Ministry of Works and the Ancient Monuments Board. Considering that the professor worked on the principle that "it was for the committee to state what treatment was desired and for the artist to submit to direction and discipline"[26] conflict was unavoidable. Minutes of meetings do not generally make for lively reading but it is not necessary to read between the lines to detect the opinionated professor's dominance of the proceedings. Time and again, we read that Richardson made a suggestion and the committee agreed. The artists' designs were placed under very close scrutiny with surprisingly detailed modifications being demanded. On almost every occasion, it seems, the professor had the last word. Artists were summoned to the cathedral to show their designs—ostensibly so that they could see each others' work and understand "the degree of correlation which was essential"[27] though it appears that at times they were treated as students undergoing an examination. Regarding the drawings

26. SoFGC Minutes, November 12, 1956.
27. SoFGC Minutes, December 15, 1950.

for the North Transept window by William Wilson of the Edinburgh College of Art, "Professor Sir Albert Richardson advised that Mr Wilson ought to subdue some of the excitement in his design."[28] Another design in the Blacader chapel was criticized on the grounds that "the figure representing a 'sinner' was 'too doleful.'"[29]

Sadie McLellan (Mrs Pritchard), who taught for a time at the Glasgow School of Art, seems to have had a particularly hard time. She was working on a window depicting St. Mungo's childhood for the south aisle of the quire, but certain aspects did not meet with Richardson's approval:

> Mrs Pritchard's attention had been directed to the position in the arms of his mother of St. Mungo as an infant. . . . As drawn one could mistake it for the Madonna and Child and it was only after lengthy discussion on the legendary aspect of the one and the factual aspect of the other that Mrs Pritchard agreed to consider some means by which the depiction would be identified with St. Mungo and not Our Lord.[30]

Mrs Pritchard again fell foul of the professor in 1952 with her design for "Christ and the World's Beauty" in the north aisle. He did not admire the "claw-like" appearance of the hands and feet and considered that the figure of Christ was "excessively untraditional." Two years later, the argument had still not been settled and Sadie had had enough. "The artist had declined to make any further alteration to the figure" and requested a fee of £150–£200 for her abandoned work. But she had "a strong and determined personality"[31] and was not prepared to go quietly. She and her husband Walter, also a lecturer at the Art School, asked for a meeting with Lord Bilsland and showed him correspondence which made it clear that her design had been accepted. Once again, Bilsland's skills of people management came into play. "Statements had been made which were, I'm afraid, much more specific in this respect than had been authorized," he told the committee, and recommended that Mrs Pritchard should be given another opportunity of amending her drawing.[32] This was agreed to and by September the committee was unanimous that her latest version

28. SoFGC Minutes, November 12, 1956.
29. SoFGC Minutes, May 17, 1957.
30. SoFGC Minutes, December 15, 1950.
31. *Glasgow Herald,* February 24, 2007.
32. SoFGC Minutes, July 21, 1954.

"expressed the beauty and spiritual quality which it had always been desired to achieve."[33]

Needless to say, there was no hint of any of these disagreements when the window was dedicated the following year. Nevile Davidson praised it as "rich in color and charming in design" and believed that it was "perhaps the finest example yet seen of her craftsmanship."[34]

The early 1960s marked the end of the first chapter of the Society's history and the 1961 annual report drew a line under the previous twenty-five years by referring to the "completion last year of the very comprehensive program of work which has occupied the Society since its formation."[35] The windows were of course the most important aspect of this, and Davidson quoted with pride a remark made to him by Dr. Eric Milner-White (1884–1963) who, as Dean of York, had overseen the replacement of windows at York Minster: "I expect you know that you now have here in your cathedral the most comprehensive and representative collection of modern stained glass anywhere in Britain."[36] A full description of all the windows, and the artists who made them, can be found in the book written in 2009 by the cathedral's librarian and archivist, the late Iain Macnair[37] and in the latest edition of the guidebook *A Walk Through Glasgow Cathedral*.

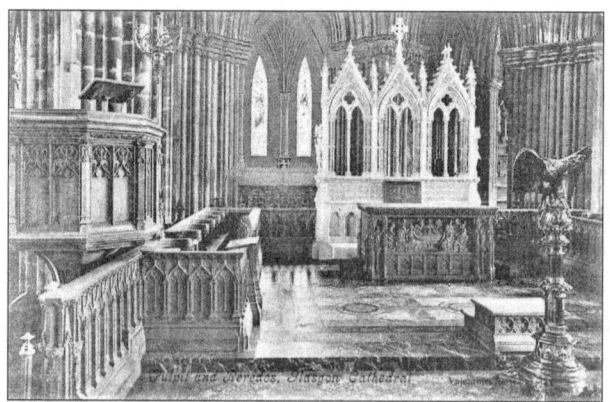

Chancel with reredos, from a Valentine's postcard of 1893.
Image courtesy of the University of St. Andrews Library, ID JV-18140.

33. SoFGC Minutes, September 14, 1954.
34. *Glasgow Herald*, September 5, 1955.
35. SoFGC Annual Report, 1961, 5.
36. Davidson, *Reflections*, 55.
37. Macnair, *Stained Glass*.

In addition to the windows, the furnishings of the cathedral had been transformed. Refinishing of the pews required much trial and error, various experiments with wax and staining being undertaken. An appeal was made to the various incorporated bodies of the city, schools and other institutions who were invited to contribute to the cost in return for having their heraldic arms displayed on the pew ends. There was a good response to this, but once again delicacy was required in dealing with "the important matter of precedence of the various bodies and organizations" who had sponsored pews.[38] The chancel area also took on a very different look. Since 1893 a reredos of Caen stone and alabaster had sat behind the communion table; Nevile Davidson had never liked it and was pleased to record in his diary on February 8, 1945 that the "unsuitable Victorian reredos was at last removed."[39] The pulpit was replaced by one which had originally been used by the congregation of the Barony which met in the Lower Church between 1595 and 1798. It had once been occupied by Zachary Boyd (1585–1653), preacher, devotional writer, and Vice-chancellor of the University of Glasgow and Davidson "felt very honored and excited as I stood and preached from it" for the first time in November 1952. Wylie and Lochhead, cabinetmakers, donated the Royal Pew and, more controversially, a carved cross was positioned on the central pillar behind the Chancel. Responding to expressions of "marked reluctance or antagonism" to this idea, Davidson took pains to stress that it was a cross and not a crucifix, while Sir Albert Richardson noted that it was customary in Lutheran churches to have hanging crosses of a similar style.

The activities of the Society of Friends during the 1950s encompassed practical as well as aesthetic matters. Things like the condition of the graveyard and the replacement of railings and gates all came within the remit of "beautifying the surroundings" of the cathedral. The ever-present problems of heating and drafts, too, were endlessly discussed, though to this day a solution has proved elusive. £1,000 was spent on red leather covered doors at each side of the quire and it is amusing to note that Richardson, who supposedly hated all things modern, suggested that "the space above the doors might be filled by transparent plastic material like the window in the cockpit of an aeroplane,"[40] though eventually glass was used for this purpose. Of course, not every idea worked: experiments

---

38. SoFGC Minutes, November 4, 1957.
39. For details, see Macaulay, *Charles Rennie Mackintosh*, 95.
40. SoFGC Minutes, November 4, 1957.

in lime washing sections of the interior walls were unsuccessful; the suggestion of installing a revolving door between quire and nave was quickly rejected, while Nevile Davidson's dream of a peal of bells rather than a single "mournful" one came to nothing after years of discussion, mainly because of structural concerns related to the weight of bells.

Now that the quire had been refurnished, the lower church brought back into use, and the windows reglazed, it appeared that "the period of intensive renovation of the cathedral has passed but no less important is the rather less spectacular but necessary work of caring for and preserving the fabric of the ancient building."[41] Sir Albert was no longer needed in his advisory capacity and at his final meeting in March 1960 he was profusely thanked for his "invaluable services" and presented with a Georgian silver salver.

Meanwhile, the structural maintenance required by such an ancient building was endless and major tasks such as the replacement of the copper sheeting of the roof between 1962 and 1965 were undertaken at the expense of the Ministry of Works. For a time the Society was mostly concerned with contributing decorative gifts and furnishings. A chancel carpet commissioned from the famous Glasgow Templeton's factory and many other items were gifted by Charles Hepburn (1891–1971), a former Artillery Captain and patron of the arts who made his fortune in the whisky blending and broking firm Hepburn and Ross of "Red Hackle" fame. On selling the business in 1959 for a reputed £2 million, he distributed much of the proceeds in benefactions to city institutions such as the Cathedral, Glasgow University, the High School, and Calderpark zoo.[42]

"ADVANCES MUST BE MADE": MUSIC AND TOURISM, 1961–86

With so much work having already been carried out by the Friends by 1960, it was perhaps inevitable that several consecutive annual reports thereafter intimated that no major projects were currently being undertaken. Frequent references to "slender funds" and ritual appeals for more members to be recruited suggest that to some extent the Society was marking time. There was, moreover, a tendency to look back to past achievements, an outline of these being published to mark the thirtieth

41. SoFGC Annual Report, 1963, 5.
42. *Glasgow Herald*, July 17, 1971.

anniversary of the Friends. The impression of having reached the end of an era was further reinforced in 1967 when Lord Bilsland demitted office as President and Nevile Davidson retired as minister, his place as Chairman of the Council being taken by his successor, Dr. William J. Morris. Lord Bilsland, whose "restless energy" had enabled the Society to achieve so much since its foundation, died in December 1970 but Dr. Davidson's involvement continued as he now took over as President, remaining in that role until his death in 1976.

Rev. Dr. W. J. Morris, Minister of Glasgow Cathedral, 1967—2005, and Chairman of the Society of Friends, 1967-2003.

And yet, as was the case with Mark Twain, any rumors of the death of the Society were much exaggerated. "No organization can exist in a healthy condition if it contents itself by taking a long, lingering look at its past achievements," warned Davidson and Morris in their 1969 report. "Advances must be made; new objectives must be attained."

Two such objectives, one short term and one long term, emerged that very year, and the Society found a new sense of purpose and energy. The most urgent task was that the cathedral's four-manual pipe organ required major overhaul. The original instrument was built by Henry ("Father") Willis and inaugurated on Easter Day 1879 by the cathedral organist Dr. A. L. Peace, the first permanent organ installed in the building since the time of the Reformation. It was rebuilt and enlarged by Willis and Sons in 1903 and 1931 but over the ensuing four decades dirt, temperature variations and dampness had inevitably taken their toll. In conjunction with the kirk session, the Society of Friends secured the services of Dr. Francis Jackson, organist of York Minster who, with the cathedral organist John R. Turner, submitted a detailed report on the maintenance work required and suggested various tonal changes to enhance the sound. There was no time to lose, for Jackson and Turner reckoned "the blowing apparatus could fail at any time."[43] This work was entrusted to J. W. Walker and Sons of London at a cost estimated in 1969 to amount to the "staggering figure" of £30,000. At the same time, the installation of modern sound amplification and concealed lighting in the quire was under consideration and a joint committee was set up to launch an appeal with a target of £50,000. The opportunity was soon taken to widen the scope of the appeal by including a further, longer-term aspiration: the establishment of an endowment fund to maintain the standard of choral music in future years, with the result that the target was revised upwards to £70,000. The equivalent sum today would be something like £874,000. Once again, key figures in public life came forward to show their support for the cathedral and there was no shortage of business expertise to call upon: the prominent industrialist and politician Viscount Weir of Eastwood took on the role of Chairman of the Appeals Committee which included representatives from bodies such as the Trades and Merchants Houses, the Universities, and Glasgow Chamber of Commerce, all of whom had valuable contacts in business and public life. A specialist company, Richard Maurice Fund Raising Ltd., was appointed, with Lt. Col. A. J. Noble as Campaign Director. No wonder the President and Chairman thought that "1971 is going to be a really exciting year."[44]

Things moved quickly and by the end of the year the Appeals Committee was already in a position to disband, having achieved its target. The largest contribution was a sum of £10,000 from Glasgow Corporation, again reinforcing the close link between the cathedral and the city fathers. For the most part, the planned works had been completed too, thanks to the offer of a loan of £17,000 which had allowed the organ renovation to start before all the funding was in place. However, the improvements to the quire lighting turned out to be more complicated than expected: "it was far from easy to design the lighting for such a large building as the quire so as to show up its beautiful structure, literally in

43. SoFGC Minutes, March 12, 1970.
44. SoFGC Annual Report, 1970, 7.

a new light," reported Davidson, adding that "vulgarity had at all costs to be avoided."[45] It was not until June 1973 that this work was "virtually complete."

The work of the Society inevitably followed a cyclical pattern over the years, with the completion of major schemes being followed by quieter periods. Thus, by 1974 it was reported that "current activity has rather been behind the scenes."[46] Naturally, innovations continued such as the introduction of a lecture on an aspect of the cathedral's history at annual meetings from 1972 onwards and there were always various projects of fabric improvement on the go, among the various achievements of the decade being the restoration of regimental colors, a new bookstall, installation of improved lighting and memorial windows for Lord Bilsland (in the eastern ambulatory chapel of St. Stephen and St. Lawrence) and Dr. Davidson (in the chapel of St. Peter and St. Paul in the lower church). A particularly large legacy from a member of the Society, Robert Love, allowed the St. Kentigern Tapestry to be commissioned and this was dedicated in November 1979 in the presence of HRH Princess Margaret, considerably improving the appearance of the Lower Church around the tomb of the saint.

The investment in choral music was starting to pay off: by 1973, music in the cathedral was reckoned to be at "an extremely high level of performance" and a broadcast of choral evensong on radio and a live color transmission of a morning service on Scottish Television were well received. In addition, John Turner and the choir had produced a record of "Music from Glasgow Cathedral" on an Easter theme, including the *Hallelujah Chorus*. The expenditure on the organ enabled greater use to be made of the instrument for recitals, the organization of these being in the hands of another Friends' sub-committee which arranged thirteen recitals during 1974–75, eight of them "in a lighter vein" over the summer months, helping to attract many tourists to the cathedral.

This was only one aspect of the Society's response to the needs of tourists, something that would become an increasingly important theme from this stage onwards. In addition to the new recording of music, items for sale from the bookstall in the nave now included postcards, color transparencies, Christmas cards, and an official guidebook written by C. A. Ralegh Radford and published by HMSO (Her Majesty's Stationery

---

45. SoFGC Annual Report, 1972, 5.
46. SoFGC Annual Report, 1974, 4.

Office). Towards the end of the decade, reports make reference in general terms to the desirability of members of the Friends volunteering to help with the bookstall, to welcome visitors and to answer questions, but it was not until 1980 that steps were taken to formalize a system of guides. According to the 1980 Annual Report, "The necessity to tighten up security in the cathedral has meant that during the last few years the custodians have been unable to act as guides. Our members are therefore being invited to act as guides during the months June to September. There will be an introductory meeting to assist those whose knowledge of the cathedral is somewhat scanty."[47] Support for this scheme was promising in the first year and a similar invitation was made for the following summer. The need to recruit more, and younger, members (meaning people under fifty) was an oft-repeated refrain at annual meetings and in 1982 an event was held to show the public something of the recent achievements of the Society such as the St. Kentigern tapestry consisting of an illustrated talk, musical entertainment, a buffet meal and, of course, an invitation to join the Society. Such initiatives led to an increase in membership over the next couple of years until numbers started to tail off again. 1982 also saw improved access to the building for disabled visitors and a further expansion of the range of items for sale to tourists which now included "guidesheets in foreign languages . . . leather goods and Caithness Glass tableware with the image of the cathedral engraved." The bookstall was now running at a profit, some of which was donated to the kirk session to assist with the general running expenses of the cathedral. Yet, in spite of twenty-five members acting as volunteer guides, during 38% per cent of summer opening times no-one was available and in future the plan was "to have at least two people on duty so that if a visitor wishes to be shown something in the church there is no need to close the bookstall."[48] Guiding took on a still higher profile in 1983 when nearly 100 people responded to a letter published in the *Glasgow Herald* asking for volunteers which enabled a full rota of guides to be drawn up and, in turn, led to significantly increased sales at the bookstall.

All this required organization and by the early 1980s the Society of Friends gave the impression of operating on a distinctly more businesslike footing. There were now separate committees dealing with publicity (management and stocking of the bookstall, advertising, and guiding),

47. SoFGC Annual Report, 1980, 5.
48. SoFGC Annual Report, 1982, 4.

recitals and events, while the existing executive committee acted as a liaison body between the cathedral and the Crown Department which was responsible for the maintenance of the building.

"NOTHING MORE. NOTHING LESS": A VISITOR CENTRE FOR GLASGOW CATHEDRAL, 1986-93

An artist's impression of the planned Visitor Centre used in the various publications produced in connection with the appeal.

The Society was now moving into another cycle of intensive activity, in preparation for the celebrations of the 850th anniversary of the cathedral in 1986, a year which by happy coincidence also marked the golden jubilee of the Friends. The Annual Report for 1984 states that "So much of the work is interlinked and involves contact with outside organizations that it was clear that there must be a central office to coordinate the work. . . . It was therefore decided to appoint an Administrator to work part-time as required."[49] A full program of cultural events was envisaged for 1986, arranged by a new festival committee. Major musical performances included a sell-out performance of Handel's *Messiah* on New Year's day, Thomas Wilson's *St. Kentigern Suite* and, most ambitiously, Kenneth Leighton's opera *Columba*, based on the life of the Irish missionary saint credited with spreading the Christian faith in Scotland, with libretto by the poet Edwin Morgan who would later become Scotland's first "Scots Makar" or national poet. Staging a full-scale opera in a medieval cathedral presented many practical challenges but critics deemed

49. SoFGC Annual Report, 1984, 6.

the end result "imaginative and truly worthy of the setting—all parts of the cathedral being used to great dramatic effect."[50] In addition, there was a civic reception, a midsummer party, and a buffet lunch after the Thanksgiving Service attended by the Queen and Prince Philip. Princess Margaret performed the opening ceremony at a very successful Festival of Flowers which attracted 12,000 visitors. A particularly imaginative idea to make younger Glaswegians aware of their heritage was a schools' art competition on the theme of "Glasgow Cathedral Through the Ages" which ran during December. All of this cost money, of course, but the estimated £14,000 cost of the year-long series of events was covered by a generous bequest from cathedral member William Martin.

As a result of the Festival, it was felt that the cathedral had become better known. Yet by this time the Society of Friends had already begun work on its biggest ever project: the creation of a new visitor center. With the increasing numbers visiting the cathedral, the desirability of a base for the Friends with proper retail space, tea room, etc. had long been talked about. For its part, the cathedral kirk session was also looking for bigger premises for its organizations, an office and a flat for an assistant minister, the current church halls (Cathedral House) being inadequate. The architectural historian Dr. James Macaulay, Chairman of the Friends' Council and a well-known expert involved in a variety of heritage organizations, recalls a moment of inspiration which he had at a service in the cathedral on New Year's Eve 1982. Opposite the cathedral, beside the oldest house in Glasgow known as Provand's Lordship, there was a vacant plot of land and Dr. Macaulay and the cathedral minister, Rev. Dr. William Morris, wrote to the Town Clerk, Steven Hamilton, with the idea that this space might be used as a base for the Friends. Provand's Lordship was in need of renovation and the Society was invited to become involved in discussions about the building's future with Glasgow District Council who owned the buildings and who were open to considering proposals. Nothing came of the Provand's Lordship scheme, partly because the Royal Infirmary used the open ground as a car park and was unwilling to part with it, but the Society's plan for a visitor center fitted in well with the wider vision of the District Council for a redevelopment of the cathedral square and its environs. Until the 1960s the cathedral had been surrounded by dilapidated and overcrowded tenements and when these were demolished "the areas in the immediate vicinity suffered from

---

50. *Glasgow Herald*, February 6, 1986.

a lack of initiative due to uncertainty over roads proposals and related matters. As a result, sites have been left vacant, the residential population has virtually disappeared and a general air of decline has set in."[51]

By early 1985 a new idea was being discussed: a complex in Cathedral Square on the site once occupied by the Bishop's Castle in the Middle Ages. While still intended as a facility for the Society of Friends and the congregation, the center would now form part of a bigger multi-agency venture led by the District Council which also included representatives of the Scottish Development Agency (SDA), a body set up in 1975 to encourage economic development, and the Scottish Tourist Board.[52] A £14 million plan was drawn up that envisaged not only a cathedral visitor center but a complete redevelopment of the precinct area to include a new housing development, stone-cleaning of the Royal Infirmary, and conversion of the Barony Church into a ceremonial hall for Strathclyde University. A key part of the plan would be a new tourist attraction in the form of a "multi-media educational experience" on the history of Glasgow to be called "the Glasgow Ark," run by the company which operated the successful Jorvik Centre in York. There would be new approach roads and underground car parking was under consideration.

This ambitious program was in turn part of a still bigger process of urban regeneration as Glasgow sought to shed its negative image as a city blighted by poverty and crime in favor of promoting its cultural and artistic heritage in a post-industrial era. The re-branding was kick-started in the early eighties by the "Glasgow's Miles Better" campaign, followed by the Garden Festival of 1988 which brought tens of thousands of visitors to the city. The hope was to transform the cathedral precinct area in time for 1990, Glasgow's year as European Capital of Culture when an even greater influx of tourists was expected.

The building as envisaged by architect Ian Begg was to be of five stories on an L-shaped layout, built "in the traditional Scottish manner in natural stone." The ground floor would consist of a cloistered passage through the garden to the restaurant, shop, and tourist information center. Excavated remains of the Bishop's Castle would be visible. On the first floor would be the principal hall and another restaurant, with a gallery and music room on the floor above, further meeting rooms and offices on the third floor, and a flat and service area on the top.

51. *The Society of Friends of Glasgow Cathedral Precinct Project: Report and Business Plan* [1987].
52. The equivalent bodies today are Scottish Enterprise and VisitScotland.

The Society of Friends undertook to build and manage the center and incorporated two new companies for these purposes: Glasgow Cathedral Precinct Ltd to handle planning and construction and its subsidiary, Glasgow Cathedral Precinct (Management) Ltd, to look after operational matters. Dr. Macaulay was the chairman of the parent company and Peter Rintoul the administrative secretary. Like another of the directors, cathedral session clerk and lawyer Thomas Fergus,[53] Peter Rintoul had worked for Scottish Industrial Estates[54] under the President of the Friends, the late Lord Bilsland. Rintoul came from a wealthy background (as a student at Cambridge he used to drive around in a Bugatti) and he and his wife were very active in the Society. Apparently, Lord Bilsland had summoned his protégé one day and simply told him: "Peter, you'll take over as the secretary of the Society of Friends"—a task which he faithfully carried out for thirty-three years.

Left to right: Dr. James Macaulay with Jean and Peter Rintoul at a Garden Party, Holyrood Palace, Edinburgh in the 1980s. Photo courtesy of J. Macaulay.

The task of raising the estimated building costs of £3.5 million was not left to the Society alone. On January 13, 1987—St. Mungo's Day—Lord Provost Robert Gray hosted a lunch at the City Chambers for thirty of the city's most prominent businessmen and, under his chairmanship, a fund-raising committee was set up, consisting of members of the Friends

---

53. Tom Fergus also served as Hon. Secretary of the Society of Friends from 1954 until 1968.

54. This body merged with the SDA (Scottish Development Agency) in the 1970s.

and the congregation, local councillors, representatives from the universities, and captains of industry, all of whom were then expected to encourage their respective organizations and colleagues to support the venture. The Society of Friends and the congregation were tasked with raising £250,000 which was achieved over the next few years by a whole range of special events, many organized by Mrs Jean Morris, wife of the minister, and a team of enthusiastic ladies.

A special brochure encouraging people to donate or take out covenants carried a message from the Lord Provost: "This Appeal is to help the Society of Friends of Glasgow Cathedral to build the new Centre. Nothing More. Nothing Less. The Friends will turn the dream into a reality."

But soon the dream became more like a nightmare. The efforts of the fund-raising committee, led by a salaried Project Director, Moira MacAskill, were initially promising, with some substantial high-profile donations being received from corporate bodies. Glasgow District Council gave £500,000 and Strathclyde Regional Council promised a similar sum.[55] However, Mrs MacAskill had to remind committee members of some basic principles such as "charity begins at home"—meaning that members should themselves make a financial commitment to the project—and "people give to people"—in other words, members should make personal approaches to their business contacts. Some of the committee were doing neither of these things and quite a few were not attending the meetings. There was a steady trickle of resignations and those present at a meeting in February 1988 decided that "the recruitment of new blood was essential."

Worse was to come. The business plan for the center was predicated on significant numbers of visitors using the catering facilities, not only those coming to the cathedral[56] but also those visiting the proposed Glasgow Ark which, it was hoped, might attract 750,000 visitors each year. This was seen as an "anchor project for the overall development of the Square"[57] and when the planned attraction was first relocated to

---

55. As a result of local government reorganization in Scotland, Strathclyde Region, covering a large area of the west of Scotland, was formed in 1975. The region was subdivided into nineteen districts, one of which was Glasgow District Council.

56. At that time around 100,000 per annum, a figure that had steadily increased to over 400,000 by the time of the 2020 Coronavirus lockdown.

57. Letter from Arthur Young Management Consultants, to Peter Rintoul, July 5, 1988.

the south side of the city and then abandoned altogether, the visitor center cafe and restaurant became a much less attractive commercial proposition and catering tenders proved hard to come by. Hoped-for SDA support was also less certain, on the grounds that the Agency had already committed itself to financing other aspects of the precinct development. Each setback in turn led to another: the initially enthusiastic Tourist Board now said it "might consider a contribution at a later stage," being unconvinced that a proper funding deal for the center was in place. An approach by the Lord Provost to central government was similarly rebuffed. A gloomy prognosis was presented to the fund-raising committee on April 12, 1988: the total raised so far was only about £1.1 million and "the appeal would not raise £3.5 million." Nevertheless, arrangements for the Prince of Wales to lay the foundation stone had already been made, and this duty was duly carried out on April 29 on the same day that he performed the opening ceremony for the Glasgow Garden Festival, accompanied by Princess Diana.

This was merely a symbolic beginning, as another year would pass before construction began. In the interim, the directors of the Cathedral Precinct Company obtained tenders from six contractors and as the full funding was still not in place they managed to arrange a loan facility with the Clydesdale Bank. After much thought, the directors pressed ahead and signed a contract with Balfour Beatty for the first phase of construction, though they made it clear that they would first seek money from the Appeal Fund before drawing on the bank loan.[58] By this stage the news on the financial front was slightly better: nearly £2 million had been raised, including the initial £500,000 from the District Council and the £500,000 promised by Strathclyde Regional Council which had now handed over the first installment of £100,000. The remainder came from corporate bodies, trusts and individual donations via covenants and other tax-efficient means, while the sale of the old Cathedral House building raised £80,000.

Now that building work had started, the pressure on the fund-raising committee to find the remaining £1.5 million further intensified. A different approach was now adopted with the launch of a new appeal in an attempt to persuade ordinary citizens to contribute. Recognizing that asking for money for a building lacked the emotive dimension of humanitarian charitable causes, the committee came up with the theme

58. Minutes of Fund Raising Committee, April 28, 1989.

of "Say Thanks to Old Glasgow" and placed advertisements couched in more personal language, urging citizens to "write themselves into history" by donating: "Many thousands of people are enjoying the "Miles Better" Glasgow.... But here's a thought. Had it not been for *old* Glasgow (the bit that first flourished around the cathedral) there would be *no* Glasgow."

At the same time, the committee redoubled its efforts to come up with new ideas. Some were extremely successful, such as the Theatre Royal Gala Evening of opera and ballet in October 1989 in the presence of HRH the Princess Margaret, Countess of Snowdon, where there was "a real sense of occasion, with lots of long dresses and dinner jackets and champagne (donated by a sponsor) flowing during the interval."[59] However, other ideas—a charity concert by Cliff Richard, an invitation to the pop group "Wet Wet Wet," a football match between Rangers and Celtic, a lottery, and even an appeal to other local churches for donations—smacked of desperation. Meanwhile, costs continued to escalate. A dire warning from the Directors of the Precinct Company dated December 1989 stated that they found themselves "in an exceedingly difficult position." There were only six months left to find the £1 million to pay for phase one of the building (the outer shell) and, even assuming that significant interest charges could be avoided, total costs were now likely to be £4 million. Attempts to increase the commercial viability of the center by including more retail outlets or franchising catering facilities were fruitless. Discussions took place with a company interested in turning the upper floors into hotel accommodation but, quite apart from planning and financial considerations, this had to be rejected as donors would understandably resent that fact that they had contributed to the costs of a building whose purpose had then been changed.

In July 1990, having exhausted every possible avenue, the fund-raising committee bowed to the inevitable:

> The only money now coming into the Appeal consisted of small donations, covenanted contributions from private individuals and companies and the interest on sponsorship money on special deposit; no major fund-raising events or initiatives were planned for the near future; there was no likelihood of further contributions being given by the public sector ... and in the light of these facts the committee needed to acknowledge that

---

59. *Glasgow Herald,* October 11, 1989.

they were most unlikely to be able to raise the money needed to complete the construction of the shell of the Visitor Centre.

That left only one solution: the committee approached the District Council in the hope of a rescue package. In September the Council agreed to provide the £1 million required to complete phase one, with the result that ownership of the partly completed building passed from the Precinct Company to the local authorities. When completed, the center would still accommodate "the basic needs of the Friends of the Cathedral"[60] but would then function as "a Visitor Centre/Museum run by the Museums and Art Galleries Department." Mrs MacAskill was thanked for her "unstinting work" and the fund-raising committee disbanded.

An August 1990 report to the District Council compiled by the Town Clerk and Chief Executive outlined the three criteria that would determine the future use to be made of the building: it would

> serve the purposes and provide accommodation for cathedral-related activities as originally intended and thus keep faith with those organizations, individuals and companies which made donations; attract tourists and complement the other elements of the Precinct Project; and provide a properly run and professionally managed venue to interpret the history of the cathedral area.

The end result was the St. Mungo Museum of Religious Life and Art which, when it opened in 1993, was described by Julian Spalding, Director of Glasgow Museums, as unique in its combination of "aesthetic, international and local perspectives. As far as we know, there is no museum anywhere so wide-ranging in its approach to religion."[61] The idea was to "reflect the central importance of religion in human life" through a multi-faith approach, with a special emphasis on local aspects, from the story of St. Mungo onwards. The curators recognized the difficulty in representing in visual form a subject which, by definition, dealt with non-material beliefs and values, particularly in the case of world religions such as Judaism and Islam which forbid or discourage the making of images. Many objects stored in the city's collections could now be exhibited in a thematic way and for some years Salvador Dali's famous painting *Christ of St. John of the Cross* took pride of place before it returned to the renovated Kelvingrove Art Gallery in 2006.

---

60. Minutes of Fund Raising Committee, November 8, 1990.
61. *The St. Mungo Museum*, 6.

The Friends and the congregation were still required to contribute £350,000 to the fitting out of the premises, but much of this had already been donated for specific features and furnishings and the total was reached by April 1991. Work on the interior began on March 30, 1992 and the various cathedral organizations were able to occupy part of the building the following January. The Lord Provost opened the museum on April 2 and this was followed by an "official" opening ceremony by HRH Princes Anne, in June. Glasgow Cathedral now had the hall and office space that it had long desired, but had given up the planned living accommodation for an assistant minister on the top floor. This was not a huge inconvenience, as recent assistance of this kind had been from part-time and retired clergy who did not require to live on site, but the loss of potential sources of income in the form of the cafe and shop was a far bigger blow, as these were of course now run for the benefit of the Museums Department. The Society has had to be content with a bookstall within the nave of the cathedral.

The trials and tribulations of the visitor center project resulted in the most difficult years the Society of Friends had ever experienced. Inevitably, there was at times a certain amount of tension between the various individuals and organizations involved, and no doubt many a sleepless night for the fund-raisers. But the last word should perhaps be left to Peter Rintoul who wrote in September 1990 that "In a few years time all these financial problems will have been forgotten and everyone will admire the marvelous building and the tenacity and enterprise of those who built it."

"IT IS NOT OUR INTENTION TO REMAIN STATIC": TOWARDS THE MILLENNIUM—AND BEYOND

By the early 1990s the Society of Friends was, understandably, suffering from fund-raising fatigue. But another problem was already looming: the "Father" Willis pipe organ was again in urgent need of attention. There had been some embarrassing moments during services and recitals and the congregation had "lived in dread of a total breakdown during broadcast or television events . . . in front of the world." Frequently the organist, John Turner, had been compelled to nurse the instrument through an important service. During a meal at the Rintouls' home at which James Macaulay and fellow Society members Alan and Henty Diack were present, the conversation turned to the state of the organ and the feeling was that the Society should take up the cause.

However, this suggestion was not universally welcomed. Dr. Morris was not in favor of another large-scale fund-raising venture, and he insisted that members of the congregation should not be asked to give yet more money. There had already been an expensive rebuild of the organ in the seventies but the results were mixed, as some of the work carried out at that time had proved unreliable[62] and some of the original Willis pipework had, regrettably, been removed. Nevertheless, a new committee was set up, chaired by Iain McGlashan, a generous supporter of the cathedral, with the Diacks as treasurers and the support of three distinguished patrons who added their weight to the cause: Sir Alexander Gibson, principal conductor of the Royal Scottish National Orchestra, Sir Graham Hills, Principal of Strathclyde University and Dr. (later Sir) Philip Ledger, Principal of the Royal Scottish Academy of Music and Drama, and President of the Royal College of Organists. Alan Diack researched suitable grant-awarding bodies and local businesses which could be approached for support and as a result the target of £350,000 was reached without the need for a general public appeal, though of course many people did contribute—and there were even some cathedral members who expressed disappointment that they had not been approached. For their remarkable efforts, Alan and Henty Diack were each awarded an MBE.

Asking for money was not the Society's only activity in these years. One prominent member recalls that, apart from a cup of tea at the annual general meeting, there were few regular social gatherings in connection with the Society. To encourage existing members to feel more involved, and to bring along their friends, Mrs. Jean Rintoul took on the new role of Membership and Social Secretary in 1991. Various memorable events were held, such as an "At Home" in the cathedral in November 1992 at which, according to the annual report, "there were many invited guests representing organizations and companies in the City and all were in evening dress, with a substantial number of the gentlemen in highland dress. After the reception and buffet, there was a concert by four members of The Royal Scottish Academy of Music and Drama which concluded with a rendering of the famous Widor 'Toccata' played on the organ by John Turner. The evening was brought to a close by the switching on of the cathedral floodlights by

---

62. According to a short booklet, *The Father Willis Organ of Glasgow Cathedral*, compiled by John R. Turner.

Forbes Macpherson, Chairman of the Glasgow Development Agency."[63] Similar "At Homes" were held in subsequent years.

In the 1990s a pattern of annual activities emerged which has remained substantially the same to to this day. The ever-increasing importance of tourism to Glasgow has been reflected in the number of volunteer guides working with the Society (seventy in 1995) and in the production of new printed material, most recently in 2018 with a redesigned foldout leaflet translated into thirteen languages, including Chinese and Japanese. The winter series of historical lectures continue on a regular basis. These lectures fulfill one of the Society's primary objectives, "the encouragement of research into the history of the cathedral" and a selection of them forms the basis of part two of the present volume. Equally popular have been the annual coach trips to destinations as varied as Abbotsford House, Rosslyn Chapel, Scone Palace, Balcarres (the seat of the Earl of Crawford and Balcarres), St. Andrews, Hopetoun House and, closer to home, the Abbey and Coats' Memorial Church in Paisley and Windyhill, the Charles Rennie Mackintosh-designed house at Kilmacolm.

Over the decades the emphasis of the Friends has gradually shifted from large-scale capital ventures to supporting ongoing activities, particularly musical ones. For many years it was the tradition to hold a performance of Handel's *Messiah* on New Year's day and there was an events committee which arranged many concerts and organ recitals. Music in the cathedral received a particular boost in 2000 when a friend of the cathedral, Miss Pat Cullen, left what was reckoned to be the most generous bequest ever made to the Society amounting to over £98,000. An annual Pat Cullen Recital was held for a number of years, the inaugural one being given by Jennifer Bate, an organist of international repute. In 1998 the Society added to its support for the cathedral choir by contributing to the establishment of choristerships, and made further donations thereafter. A more recent innovation has been a Cathedral Festival, a series of artistic, musical and other cultural events held over several days. First organized in 2016, the Festival has seen highlights such as a Charles Rennie Mackintosh exhibition (2018) and the world premiere of *Dhātu* by Edwin Hillier (2019), the winner of the Electroacoustic/Sound Artwork category in the fourth annual Scottish Awards for New Music. The musical director of the festival is the cathedral's director of music, Andrew

---

63. SoFGC Annual Report, 1992, 6–7.

Forbes, who at the time of his appointment to that role in 2014 at the age of twenty-one was the youngest person to hold such a post in the UK.

Left to right: Andrew Forbes (Festival Artistic Director), Rachel Thomas (Business Manager) and James Macaulay.

While supporting music in the cathedral, catering for visitors and encouraging historical research have been the main concerns of the Society of Friends in recent years, there have still been occasional opportunities to make significant contributions to the beautification of the building. When the original vision of refurnishing and reglazing the choir was achieved in the early 1960s, Nevile Davidson stated that it was deliberate policy not to renovate the nave in a similar manner. "It seemed selfish that every window in a cathedral church should be filled with stained glass at the same time," he said. "There might well be brilliant artists in a future generation for whose work room should be available."[64] Thirty years later, that future generation had arrived and the approach of the millennium offered an appropriate occasion to consider a major new installation. Under the convenership of Mr. Ian Smail, a new committee was formed to plan for a new window in the nave. Looking to the future, the chosen theme was initially "Youth," later changed to "Growth," and the window was partly financed by the three city schools which annually hold their services of thanksgiving and commemoration at the cathedral, namely The Glasgow Academy, Hutchesons' Grammar and the High School of Glasgow, and partly by a generous bequest. The artist chosen was John K. Clark of the Glasgow School of Art, part of his remit being that "the work should be modern and

64. Davidson, *Beginnings*, 54.

of our time and should be different from the other windows in the cathedral." Clark developed the theme of growth via a symbolic representation of the parables of the sower and the mustard seed, incorporating numerous quotations from Scripture, which he said, made the window "one of the most technically difficult works" he had ever made. On the suggestion of Historic Scotland, the colors blue and white predominate. The window was unveiled on June 3, 1999 by HRH the Princess Royal.

The most recent stained glass window in the cathedral dates from October 2018 and is dedicated to the Very Rev. William J. Morris, minister from 1967 until 2005, the costs once again being largely covered by a generous donation. This time, the artist was Emma Butler-Cole Aiken who took her inspiration from the Tree of Jesse, the father of King David in the Old Testament who is mentioned in the genealogy of Jesus in the New Testament. Again, the work depends on symbolism, as the artist herself has explained. "The dynamic splash of colorful semi-abstract trees represents life flowing from the beginning of time and culminating in Christ while the red represents the redeeming sacrifice of Christ."[65]

Other improvements to the building in recent decades have included the restoration of regimental colors and flags (rededicated in March 1998) and the renovation of the long disused thirteenth-century lower chapter house where there is now a seventeenth-century refectory table and set of King Charles II chairs gifted by the family of Joseph Paton, 1st Baron Maclay. In 2007 the idea of the Friends having their own base re-emerged in the form of a feasibility study into the possibility of the Society managing the St. Mungo Museum—effectively a return to the original intention when the building was constructed. This, however, was rejected by the city's recently established Culture and Sport Trust which felt it could use its own expertise for the purpose. Since then, there have been protracted discussions about the possible use of the empty gatehouse at the entrance to the Necropolis as a base for the Society's activities, but in spite of various business plans any progress on this has been held up by uncertainties surrounding longer term Council plans for the cathedral precinct, the future of the Museum of Religion and the intentions of Historic Scotland. With the cathedral now being one of the most visited tourist sites in Scotland, it is clear that the Society will still have a valuable role to play in future, but the number of stakeholders involved adds to the complexity of planning and decision making.

---

65. *Glasgow Cathedral Chronicle,* October 2018.

Sir Robin McLellan, President, 1977–88. Photo: Glasgow Cathedral.

Sir Graham Hills, President, 1988–95. Photo: University of Strathclyde.

Sir John Arbuthnott, President, 1995–2003. Photo: University of Strathclyde.

Dr. James Macaulay, Chairman, 2003 onwards. Photo: Andrew Forbes.

We cannot finish this survey of the activities of the Society of Friends without paying tribute to the dedication of so many people who served on the various committees, as office-bearers, as volunteer guides and in many other capacities. The impossibility of mentioning them all makes it invidious to single out individuals. Prior to the second World War there was a preponderance of titled persons on the Society's Council, and initially no fewer than five distinguished figures were listed as joint Honorary Presidents, including the Lord Provost of the City. Sir Steven Bilsland had been involved as a Council member from the very start and in 1947, now elevated to Lord Bilsland of Kinrara, he was elected to the position of President, a role in which he was no mere figurehead, overseeing the glazing program and actively managing the Society's affairs until he demitted office in 1967. In that year Nevile Davidson, who had been Chairman since 1937, retired as minister and took over as President until his death in 1976.

Dr. Davidson was succeeded by Sir Robin McLellan (between 1977 and 1988) who had been deputy chairman of the British Airport Authority with responsibility for Scotland, Sir Graham Hills (1988–95), Principal of the University of Strathclyde and his successor in that role, Sir John Arbuthnott (1995–2003). After 2003 significant changes to legislation governing Scottish charitable bodies were on the horizon and the Friends adopted a new constitution. Administration was simplified, the "multiplicity of committees which operated independently" reduced, and the "confusing and potentially conflicting positions of President and Chairman" merged.[66] Since 2003 the Chairman of the Council of the Society has been Dr. James Macaulay, formerly senior lecturer at the Mackintosh School of Architecture in Glasgow, who in the course of a distinguished career has also been chairman of the Society of Architectural Historians of Great Britain and the Architectural Heritage Society of Scotland.

Shakespeare wrote that "There is a tide in the affairs of men which, taken at the flood, leads on to fortune." Over the past eight decades, the priorities of the Society of Friends of Glasgow Cathedral have evolved but it has always shown itself ready to take advantage of opportunities to further its aims and has provided the vision which has enabled ambitious projects to be achieved in spite of challenging circumstances. There is every reason to believe that it will continue to do so.

---

66. SoFGC Annual Report, 2001, 5.

APPENDIX: OFFICE-BEARERS OF THE SOCIETY OF FRIENDS, 1936–2001

Honorary Secretary:

John Murdoch (1936–49)
J. G. Harvey (1950–54)
Thomas Fergus (1954–68)
Peter Rintoul (1969–2001)
Madeleine Thomson (2002–5)
Ian H. White (2005–8)
Alison Gifford (2009–)

Honorary Treasurer:

Colonel Norman MacLeod (1937–55)
W. I. French (1956–70)
Hew C. Davidson (1971–76)
William R. Weir (1977–92)
Mark Eden-Bushell (1993)
Gordon Smith (1994–2002)
Henty Diack (2002–8)
Leslie J. McIntyre (2008–21)

(Dates quoted from annual reports)

PART TWO

Essays and Lectures
on Glasgow Cathedral

1

The Death of St. Kentigern of Glasgow

David McRoberts

Glasgow Cathedral is dedicated to St. Kentigern, also known as St. Mungo, first bishop of the ancient British kingdom of Strathclyde. He is believed to have been buried on the site of the Cathedral around 612. In this chapter,[1] Monsignor David McRoberts examines the account of Kentigern's life and death written in the twelfth century by a monk called Jocelin[2] and argues that, in spite of layers of legendary material, it is possible to "catch a fleeting glimpse of a real person."

---

1. Originally published in *Innes Review* 24 (1973) 45–50.

2. The name is variously spelt Jocelin or Jocelyn; for the sake of consistency, throughout this book Jocelin is used as this is closest to the Jocelinus referred to in the contemporary documents.

St. Mungo: detail of a window by William Wilson installed in the south aisle of the Quire of Glasgow Cathedral in 1954. Photo: Glen Collie.

IN THE WHOLE RANGE of medieval hagiography it would be difficult to find an episode more curious than the description of the death of St. Kentigern given in the legend of that saint, which was commissioned by bishop Jocelin for his cathedral at Glasgow sometime in the last quarter of the twelfth century and which was written by the bishop's namesake Jocelin, who is usually described as a Cistercian monk of Furness Abbey in Lancashire but about whose life little is known with any certainty.[3]

In brief outline, Jocelin's story relates how St. Kentigern had reached extreme old age (he assures us that Kentigern was actually 185 years old) and warned by increasing infirmity he prepared for death. The saint received the last sacraments, gathered his monks around him and delivered the conventional exhortation that such circumstances demanded in hagiographical biographies. Some of the saint's disciples, saddened at the prospect that their beloved master should depart alone, leaving them bereft of his guidance, expressed their ardent desire to accompany him. Forthwith an angelic messenger appeared and announced that, since Kentigern's life had been one long martyrdom, God had decreed that his departure from this world should be easier and gentler than was normal

---

3. See McFadden, "*The Life of Waldef* and its author Jocelin of Furness." One might add that there would appear to be some link between Jocelin and the abbey of Melrose. Two of the four *vitae* known to have been written by Jocelin are connected with Melrose: the life of Waldef is the life of an abbot of Melrose and the life of Kentigern was commissioned by Jocelin, bishop of Glasgow, who had been abbot of Melrose.

for mortal men. The following day therefore a warm bath should be made ready, the aged saint should be placed in it and he would fall asleep in the Lord and all the brethren who would bathe in the water while it was still warm would accompany their bishop into the realms of glory. The next day (it was the octave day of the feast of the Epiphany, when Kentigern had been accustomed to hold the annual baptismal ceremony) the warm bath was prepared, Kentigern was assisted into it and there he passed peacefully away. All the disciples who subsequently entered the bath while the water remained warm, also went to their reward. Afterwards the body of the holy bishop was interred at the right hand of the altar and the brethren who died with him were buried in the cemetery of the church.

This extraordinary story of ecclesiastical suttee is not one of the usual stock episodes which hagiographers borrowed freely from one another. It is reminiscent, as Jocelin points out (and who should know better), of the Gospel account of the Pool of Bethesda, but apart from that similarity, it appears to be peculiar to Jocelin's life of St. Kentigern. As far as I am aware, no one has ever attempted to give any explanation of this curious story and the following interpretation is suggested with some diffidence.

To begin with, we must note briefly the date and the purpose of Jocelin's life of St. Kentigern.[4] Jocelin, who was commissioned to write this legend of the patron saint of Glasgow, was no ordinary hack writer but well-known *littérateur,* whose work in this very specialized literary genre was apparently both popular and admired in the late twelfth century. Jocelin took his commission seriously and did some original research on his subject. For example, he either visited St Wilfrid's church at Ripon, or at least made inquiries there, so as to have a correct description of the reputed *bachall*[5] of St. Kentigern which was preserved in that church.[6] He claims to have sought out, on bishop Jocelin's orders, an earlier account of the saint's life.[7] He made use of two earlier biographies, one the official life used in Glasgow, "quam vestra frequentat ecclesia,"[8] and the other, a small book, provincial in style and lacking elegance of diction, "stilo

---

4. Forbes, *Jocelin's "Life of St. Kentigern,"* 159–242. Quoted hereafter as *Vita.*
5. i.e. crozier (from the old Irish, from the Latin "baculum").
6. *Vita,* 184 and 232.
7. *Vita,* 159.
8. *Vita,* 160.

Scottico dictatum... per totum soloecismis scatentem."[9] Using this source material, Jocelin had all the available traditional information about Kentigern, some of it no doubt authentic historical material deriving from seventh-century sources. Some of this authentic information Jocelin has incorporated in his life of St. Kentigern but that was not his main purpose in writing. His purpose was to compile an account of the saint that would edify those who read it or listened to it. Just as a nineteenth-century novelist, writing a "historical novel," or a twentieth-century film producer, making a "historical film," is concerned primarily with entertaining his audience and has no particular interest in accuracy of historical detail so, in the same way, a twelfth-century hagiographer, who was concerned not with the entertainment but with the edification of his audience, took similar liberties with historical facts and, in addition, in order to impress his readers with his hero's sanctity, the hagiographer normally padded out his narrative with miracles of all sorts, borrowed from the Scriptures and from other sources, not excluding pagan mythology.

In particular, Jocelin was much concerned with literary style. Literary style in the leisurely twelfth century consisted largely in the imitation of the diction and composition of approved Latin stylists, in the use of rare and abstruse Latin words and, above all, in overloading the narrative with phrases from the Vulgate, the Latin translation of the Bible, by which means the author was able to display his profound knowledge of Holy Writ. This use of Scripture, which to modern taste is excessive and utterly boring, had effects which the modern scholar does not immediately appreciate. Educated men in the Middle Ages were steeped in the phraseology of the Vulgate and to couch a narrative in the familiar phrases of the Scriptures was to surround it automatically with an aura of sanctity. Also, the reader would be immediately aware of the Scriptural circumstances in which the phrase was originally used and, by association, this would enrich the narrative with additional imagery and meaning. To take an example: when, in his prologue, Jocelin says that, acting under the bishop's command, he searched for an earlier account of Kentigern's life, he uses phrases built up from the *Song of Songs*: "circuivi enim per plateas et vicos civitatis, juxta mandatum vestrum, querens vitam Sancti Kentegerni descriptam, quam diligat anima vestra,"[10] which to an ear attuned to the Vulgate, would emphasize the eagerness with which he conducted his

9. *Vita*, 160.
10. *Vita*, 159.

search. More important however was the fact that the hagiographer was writing a *legenda,* something to be read aloud in the monastic refectory or in the liturgy of the church and the sonorous cadences of the Vulgate Latin were perfectly suited to this purpose.

Keeping such considerations in mind, we turn to Jocelin's account of the death of St. Kentigern.[11] The narrative is typical hagiographical material in its abundance of miracles and in its overwhelming Scriptural phraseology, but there are occasional sentences which clearly derive from the earlier life which Jocelin is elaborating. These phrases probably derive ultimately from some factual account of St. Kentigern's death similar to the seventh-century narrative of the death of St. Columba of Iona which is preserved in Adamnan's life. The most important of these surviving phrases concerns the day on which the saint died: "cumque illucesceret dies Dominice apparitionis octavus, in quo singulis annis sacro baptismate consuerat abluere multitudinem populi, ipse pontifex almus"—and there dawned the octave day of the Lord's Epiphany, a feast day on which the dearly beloved bishop had been wont, each recurring year, to baptize with his own hands a great number of people.[12] This phrase has been preserved intact from an earlier source because it provides the basic reason for Kentigern's feast day being held annually on January 13. This phrase tells us that Glasgow was one of those churches of the north-west of Europe where, during the Dark Ages, the annual baptismal ceremony was held, not on the normal occasion during the Easter Vigil, but on the feast of the Epiphany (a feast which was associated with the baptism of Christ in the Jordan).[13] This statement is early and not an invention of Jocelin because, by his day, the custom of having baptisms on the Epiphany was quite obsolete and this reference to it must have seemed to him a regrettable aberration quite as irregular as Kentigern's episcopal consecration which also he relates without approval.

The information that Kentigern died at the time when he was wont to conduct the annual baptismal service seems to provide the key to this whole curious episode. The original narrative has apparently been

---

11. *Vita,* 235–43.

12. *Vita,* 238.

13. Baptisms on the feast of the Epiphany seem to have been common in Spain (Migne, *Patres Latini,* XIII, 1134) and North Africa (*Patres Latini,* LXIII, 216). The practice was condemned by Pope Leo I and by the Council of Gerona in 617. Glasgow must have retained the practice to an exceptionally late date, possibly because of the long episcopate of St. Kentigern.

a description of Kentigern's last baptismal service and Jocelin has metamorphosed the narrative to make his saint depart this life in a blaze of miracles. We shall try to recover the outline of the original narrative, remembering that the several incidents mentioned by Jocelin must originally have had their place in the context of a baptismal service.

Reconstructing the probable sequence of events of the original narrative, one would assume that there had been some introductory description of the advanced years and the decrepitude of the saint. This survives at the beginning of Chapter XLII and at least one item of that description is original, the reference to the bandage tied round St. Kentigern's head and under his chin to support his lower jaw because his facial muscles had now become too weak to hold his mouth closed.[14] Jocelin did not invent this because it makes his hero cut a rather pathetic and undignified figure and anyhow his imagination did not run along such lines.

Making our way through Jocelin's Scriptural verbiage, we come to the dying saint's conventional farewell exhortation to his brethren. During this part of the narrative, Jocelin tells us that Kentigern gathered himself into that splendid stone bed of his: "in lectulo suo illo nobili lapideo se collegit."[15] This phrase arouses suspicion. If Kentigern had a stone bed, it was presumably a penitential affair of simple construction. Here quite obviously we have a phrase surviving from the original narrative which is manifestly out of place in Jocelin's refurbished account of the saint's death. If we reject Jocelin's meaning of the word "lectulus," as a bed or couch, and take one of its less usual meanings, namely a seat or chair, then it is possible to give this phrase a more reasonable signification. The original narrative has described how the decrepit old bishop, at the beginning of the annual baptismal ceremony, took his seat "in lectulo suo illo nobili lapideo," on his splendid stone *cathedra* to deliver the final catechetical instruction to the group of catechumens who were about to be baptized. In other words the episcopal throne in the cathedral church of Glasgow was a handsome stone chair, which was the normal type of early episcopal throne.[16] Jocelin has already referred to this episcopal chair when he spoke of Kentigern's cathedral church of the Holy Trinity at Glasgow, in which stands the episcopal throne: "in qua episcopalis

---

14. *Vita*, 235.

15. *Vita*, 236.

16. The ancient "frid stool" at Hexham is an obvious example. See Radford, "The Bishop's Throne in Norwich Cathedral," 115–32.

collocatur cathedra."[17] The conventional farewell exhortation which Jocelin provides presumably replaces an earlier homily in which may have been preserved some phrases of St. Kentigern's last sermon to the faithful of Glasgow.

Ignoring the request of St. Kentigern's brethren to accompany the saint into eternity, which is part of Jocelin's remodeling of the passage and which has some reminiscence of the death of St. Martin of Tours, and leaving out the angelic promise of paradise to those who bathed in the saint's bath while the water remained warm, which is an adaptation of the Pool of Bethesda theme, we come to the bath with its warm water. Here again we have an item in the story which must have come from an earlier narrative. Left to his own unaided imagination, Jocelin would not have invented this bath of warm water. Jocelin's purpose was to impress the reader with Kentigern's heroic sanctity. In a welter of Scriptural phrases, he has already spoken at great length of Kentigern's feats of austerity and in particular of his custom of reciting the complete psalter while standing immersed in icy-cold water.[18] Left to himself, Jocelin would undoubtedly have avoided such an anti-climax as this and would have had the saint depart this life, in freezing water, in an excess of heroic asceticism. But the bath of warm water was apparently a well-established feature of the story of the saint's death and Jocelin has to accept it and make the best of it.

However, the bath which fits so incongruously into Jocelin's description of the saint's death is a normal feature of the baptismal ceremony that we are trying to reconstruct. Having finished his address to the catechumens, Kentigern ordered the bath, that is the font, to be prepared "balneum fieri impetravit."[19] There is no difficulty from the Latin text. Throughout this passage, three words are used for the "bath"; "lavacrum," "vasculum," and "balneum," all of which have general sense of a receptacle for water used for washing and can be translated either as "bath" or "font." In fact "lavacrum" is used earlier in the life for a baptismal font. The baptismal font of Glasgow in the early seventh century would be in some building adjacent to the cathedral church after the manner of contemporary Gallic or North African churches. The actual font would be a stone-lined cistern, located in the floor of the baptistery, with steps by which the bishop and the catechumens could descend into the water. Mid-January

17. *Vita*, 233.
18. *Vita*, 184–85.
19. *Vita*, 237.

is never very warm in Glasgow and, to make the ceremony more bearable for the frail old bishop, warm water was poured into the stone font. Some phrase to this effect was presumably in one of the sources and became the basis for Jocelin's angel ordering the warm-water bath "ut mitiorem ceteris hominibus habeas mortis exitum," that you (Kentigern) may have a gentler road to eternity than is the common lot of mortal men.[20]

At two earlier stages in the life, Jocelin refers briefly to Kentigern baptizing and those descriptions help us to fill in the parts of the ceremonial that he has omitted at this point to make room for his fanciful miracles. On both of these occasions we seem to be dealing with the early baptismal rite which Jocelin has merely incorporated from his sources.[21] Speaking of Kentigern's general missionary activity in Strathclyde, we are told: "qui vero vitali unda nondum regenerati fuerant, sicut cervi sitibundi, ad fontem vivum baptismi, estuanti desiderio, concurrerunt," and those who, up till then, had not been reborn in the life-giving water, now throng, like harts parched with thirst, to the living fountain of baptism.[22] In this phrase we have an allusion to the psalm: "Quemadmodum desiderat cervus ad fontes aquarum," which was normally sung in the churches of western Christendom as the catechumens went in procession to the baptistery after the bishop had delivered his homily. Again, in the description of Kentigern's pastoral work at Hoddam, reference is made to the other ceremonies which immediately preceded and followed the actual baptism On this occasion, when Kentigern sat in his episcopal chair, in the open air, to instruct the catechumens, Jocelin tells us that the ground rose up into a hillock so that all could see him and then "certatim omnes ergo, viri cum mulieribus, senes cum junioribus, simul in unum dives et pauper, ad virum Dei concurrentes fidei regulis imbuuntur; catezizati abrenuntiant sathane et omnibus pompis et operibus ejus, ac in nomine Sancte Trinitatis lavacro salutari abluuntur; sicque crismate sacro et oleo liniti, corpori ecclesie associati, membra Christi efficiuntur"—they came eagerly, thronging to the man of God, men and women, old and young, rich and poor together, to be instructed in the teachings of the faith: once instructed, they renounced Satan and all his works and pomps then in the name of the Blessed Trinity they were cleansed in the saving water

---

20. *Vita*, 237.

21. For early baptismal rites, see Cabrol et Leclerq, *Dictionnaire d'Archéologie chretienne et de Liturgie:* "Baptême."

22. *Vita*, 192.

and, anointed with holy chrism and oil, they were incorporated into the church and made members of Christ.[23]

At the end of his life, when bishop Kentigern performed the baptismal ceremony for the last time, the font was prepared, then the catechumens, the clerics and the bishop went in procession to the baptistery, singing the psalm: "Quemadmodum desiderat cervus ad fontes aquarum." The frail old saint, after he had blessed the water with the sign of the cross, was helped down into the font by his clerics: "ingreditur sanctus, manibus eorum gestatus, in vasculum aqua calida plenum, ab eo prius signo salutari sanctificatum."[24] The clerics stood around the font: "circumstans corona fratrum,"[25] and the catechumens went down one by one to be baptized. The strain was too much for the aged bishop and he collapsed. Jocelin's narrative would suggest that he died there and then in the font but, for the moment, we will merely say that the saint collapsed and that his clerics helped him out of the font: "discipuli videntes que fiebant, elevantes sanctum corpus de lavacro illo."[26]

On the two earlier occasions where baptism has been referred to in Jocelin's narrative, the catechumens are described as eagerly thronging towards the waters of baptism. I suggest that some such conventional phrase was repeated here in this part of the narrative with possibly an added reason being given for their eagerness, namely their desire to be baptized before the water became too cold. Some such statement may have given Jocelin the idea for his Bethesda-type miracle. Further, just as in the description of the baptism at Hoddam, where an earlier writer has used some of the commonplace doctrinal phrases with regard to the theology of baptism, so we can imagine some such phrases being used here, stating that those who received baptism before Kentigern's collapse brought the ceremony to an end were set free from the yoke of sin and became "cives sanctorum et domestici Dei," fellow citizens with the saints and members of the household of God. It seems likely that Jocelin has taken some ideas of this kind, which were meant to be taken in a spiritual sense, and has interpreted them crudely to mean that those who entered the font died and went straight to heaven. Jocelin moreover has applied this crude concept to the saint's disciples instead of to the newly baptized

23. *Vita*, 217.
24. *Vita*, 238.
25. *Vita*, 238.
26. *Vita*, 238.

neophytes and this has been done in order to build up his Bethesda-type miracle out of a straightforward description of St. Kentigern's last baptismal service.

If this reconstruction of the episode is accepted, it might conceivably raise the question of the exact date on which St. Kentigern died. The year is not in question because we have no reason to doubt the date 612, which is given in the *Annales Cambriae*.[27] The annual baptismal ceremony however, which we have described, would take place on the actual feast day of the Epiphany, January 6, and not on the octave day of the feast, January 13. Thus, if Jocelin's narrative is accepted with its implication that Kentigern actually died in the font, then the date of death would be that of the feast and not of the octave day. However, even though Jocelin is more interested in miracles than in historical accuracy, he does mention the octave day as the day of death presumably because it was the date given in his source and, in any case, he could not very well alter the generally accepted date of the saint's feast day.

We might suppose then that the sequence of events was that St. Kentigern collapsed during the ceremony on the feast of the Epiphany and was carried off to bed by his friends and that he actually survived until the octave day when he eventually died. The simple explanation would be that Jocelin telescoped the events in the interests of his miracle-story. The subsequent burial of the saint in the church alongside the altar is part of the authentic history and can be paralleled from contemporary accounts of other founders of churches in the Dark Ages.

Jocelin's narrative no doubt impressed medieval people but it fails to carry any conviction to modern minds. The interpretation which I have suggested is presented as an attempt to recover the original narrative which has been obscured by Jocelin's fanciful treatment of the events. Behind Jocelin's parade of bogus miracles and Scriptural verbosity, we do seem to catch a fleeting glimpse of a real person, the venerable figure of bishop Kentigern who, even in extreme old age, shows that devotion to the welfare of his flock and that forcefulness of character which have impressed his name permanently and indelibly on the church of Glasgow.

---

27. The *Annales Cambriae* ("Annals of Wales") is a collection of chronicles put together from a variety of sources, the earliest being a twelfth-century copy of an earlier original.

2

The Earlier Cathedrals of Glasgow

C. A. RALEGH RADFORD

Between the twelfth and fourteenth centuries Glasgow Cathedral was built in four successive phases: Bishop John's work (dedicated 1136); Bishop Jocelin's work (dedicated 1197); Bishop Walter's work (started after c. 1200), and Bishop Bondington's work, (completed c. 1300).[1] In this chapter, Dr. C. A. Ralegh Radford discusses the development of the architecture and the ecclesiastical life of these earlier buildings.[2]

GLASGOW CATHEDRAL IS ONE of the greatest buildings of medieval Scotland. The church was conceived and largely carried out in the thirteenth century in the Gothic style; it belongs to an age when Scotland was still part of an architectural and cultural province which not only covered the whole of this island but extended beyond the English Channel. Glasgow represents the full development of the medieval secular cathedral. The secular cathedral was then the normal form on the continent, but in England and Scotland many of the cathedrals were served by monastic chapters or chapters of Canons Regular. Others, like Glasgow, remained chapters of secular canons and the intimate links within this group are

---

1. Driscoll, *Excavations at Glasgow Cathedral*, 7.
2. This chapter is based on an address delivered at the Annual General Meeting of the Society of Friends in 1974.

emphasized by the adoption in Glasgow and other Scottish cathedrals of the Use of Sarum, the most widely recognized medieval order of service designed in the first place for the secular cathedral at Old Sarum.[3]

Unlike Athena, Glasgow Cathedral did not emerge fully equipped from the head of Zeus, or, more prosaically, from the mind of Bishop William de Bondington and his architect. It rather represents the result of a long historical process, not every stage of which can be illustrated in Glasgow itself, but most of which can be understood by the study of comparable buildings. To trace the whole of this long process would take a great deal of time. The purpose of this address is therefore to examine the position of ecclesiastical Glasgow at certain periods prior to the emergence of the present building in the mid-thirteenth century.

It will be convenient to turn first to the seventh century, the period following the death of St. Kentigern, our founder. Glasgow was then a British monastery, the seat of a community of clergy, the *clas* of Welsh tradition or, to use a more formal Latin term, the *classis monastica*. This community lived according to a monastic rule derived ultimately from the practices of the Egyptian desert. It was responsible for the pastoral care of the surrounding countryside; it wielded considerable political power; it possessed rights of sanctuary, which made the monasteries of this type suitable foci for the development of trade and commerce. The point is well illustrated by the story of the harvest feast at Clonmacnois. The writer is concerned to stress the miraculous element; the excellence of the wine is due to divine favor. Almost by chance he slips in the more prosaic observation "for by chance merchants from Gaul had that day filled the great wine jars of the monastery." Clonmacnois lies far up the Shannon, above the falls, and cannot have been the most accessible of Irish monasteries.

The best description of a monastic city of this type is to be found in the life of St. Brigid, written by the monk Cogitosus in the second quarter

---

3. "'The Sarum Use' is the name applied to the particular rendering of divine worship in the English Church that was developed at Salisbury, in Wiltshire, from the early thirteenth century and then gradually spread to become at least by the fourteenth century the finest local expression of the Western or Roman Rite in England up to the Reformation. 'Sarum' is the abbreviation for Sarisburium, the Latin word for Salisbury, which was and is both a city and a diocese in south central England. The Use of Sarum, then, was a rather exuberant, elaborate, beautiful, and especially well arranged adaptation of the Western or Roman Rite that was gradually adopted by most of the rest of England as well as much of Wales, Scotland, Ireland, and even some places on the continent." (J. Robert Wright, http://anglicanhistory.org/essays/wright/sarum.pdf)

of the seventh century. He relates a miracle concerned with the building of a new church to accommodate the increasing number of worshipers. It is not the miracle that is of interest, but the incidental description of the church and the city in which it was set. The following translation omits passages of purely homiletic interest.

> A miracle [was] observed during the restoration of the church ... in which those two glorious bodies rest, that is to say, Archbishop Conlaed and the wonder-working Brigid. To the right and the left of the richly decorated altar, they are placed in shrines adorned with gold and silver and precious stones, with crowns of gold and silver hanging above and pictures on carved and painted panels. And out of the old structure a new one is born; that is a church. As the number of the faithful of both sexes was increasing, a church of spacious size and menacing height was quickly completed and adorned with painted woodwork. Under the single roof of the same building are three ample oratories separated by walls of planking. One wall, decorated with painted pictures and hung with linen curtains, stretches from side to side across the eastern part of the building; at each end is a door. That on the right gives access to the sanctuary of the altar, where the Bishop with the community under his rule and those appointed to celebrate the holy mysteries celebrate the sacrifice of the Lord. And by the door on the left enter the Abbess with her virgins and the faithful widows so that they may enjoy the feast of the body and blood of Jesus Christ. And another wall stretches from the west wall of the church to the transverse wall, dividing the space into two equal parts. And the church has many windows and on the right side a decorated portal, through which the priests and the faithful people of the male sex enter the church; and on the left side is another portal, through which the virgins and the congregation of faithful women are accustomed to enter. And thus in one large basilica a very great congregation worships Almighty God, in different orders, but with one spirit, being divided according to order and rank and sex into different places separated by walls.... And who can describe the great beauty of this church and the innumerable wonders of this city? If indeed it be right to call city that place which is enclosed by no circuit of walls; it rather received the name city from the assembly of many men, innumerable peoples living together therein. Very great is this city and metropolitan; in its suburbs, within the limits marked out by St. Brigid herself, no earthly foe nor hostile onslaught

need be feared, it is a safe city of refuge for all fugitives from the whole land of the Irish. In it are laid up the treasures of kings and the splendors of its decorated roofs appear most beautiful.[4]

To the modern reader the "three spacious oratories under a single roof" and the "large basilica" conjure up the picture of a spacious church, perhaps a building on the scale of the nave of this cathedral. But all things are relative. Cogitosus was comparing the new church of Kildare with the tiny oratories, many of which survive as ruins on the western coasts and islands of Scotland and Ireland. By this standard a church of fifty feet by twenty feet would be large and these are the dimensions of the comparable cathedrals of Clonmacnois and Glendalough as rebuilt in stone three hundred years later, in the tenth century. With some adjustments this is the picture of seventh-century Glasgow: a small cathedral, probably wooden built, set in a city which was the home of a community of clergy and acted as a magnet for many peoples, including the traders, whose presence in Britain and Ireland at this date is attested by the imports of pottery from distant Africa and Asia Minor. Without undue exaggeration the origin of that trade and commerce, which has so long been the pride of Glasgow, may be traced back to those distant days.

The Carolingian Renaissance looked back to the glories of Imperial Rome. The Holy Roman Empire of Charlemagne was founded as a deliberate act of policy; its influence extended into every field of ecclesiastical and secular activity. Ecclesiastical reform was largely in the monastic field with an emphasis on the Benedictine ideal of the monastic family replacing that of the monastic city. In architectural terms this meant the extension of the idea of the great church, a development also favored by the revival of Roman models. Once the new ideas were established the Benedictines became regarded as the true monks and the terms monk and monastery became confined to the Benedictine Order and the reformed orders, like the Cistercians, which took their origin from the Rule of St. Benedict. The older communities, like Glasgow, were eventually denied the title of monk and became canons. A few houses of canons, living a common life on the Benedictine model became Canons Regular, but the majority, if they survived as communities became churches of secular canons, each living in his own house. In Scotland St. Andrews was re-established as a cathedral with a chapter of Canons Regular, but

---

4. For a fuller version of this passage see de Paor, *St. Patrick's World*, 222–23.

most of the cathedrals remained houses of secular canons; these included Glasgow.

England and still more Scotland lay on the periphery of the Carolingian reform and the Benedictine ideal of the monastic family and its expression, the great church, was long in penetrating. The early cathedrals of Winchester and North Elmham in Norfolk well illustrate the small size of the older pre-Conquest cathedrals; in scale they are small parish churches. But by 1000 there were between twenty and thirty Benedictine communities, mostly in southern England and the architectural evidence for churches on a grander scale is beginning to emerge. Sherborne in the early eleventh century had a cathedral, served by a chapter of Benedictine monks, with an aisled nave, crossing and transepts closely related to the present plan and preceded by a spacious western annex with a tower, the plan of which has been recovered by excavation. The size of the eastern arm is unknown; it was certainly much smaller than at present. The culmination of the process in pre-Conquest England is the Confessor's church at Westminster, which was comparable in size with the present abbey.

But the Benedictine ideal of the monastic family and its expression in the great church has its influence on the older communities. In the tenth and eleventh centuries the old minsters of England began to adopt a larger type of church, cruciform in plan, with the quire of the community placed in the crossing and separated from the nave occupied by the lay congregation. The east end and the transepts held shrines or formed separate chapels. St. Mary in Castro at Dover is the English church which best represents this development; it is an early example of tenth-century date. But the plan can be recovered in a number of churches including Stow in Lincolnshire and Great Paxton in Huntingdonshire. The last named is of particular interest today in view of its Scottish connections; it also illustrates the complexity of these developments. Great Paxton, together with Toseland and a number of other villages, formed a large estate. Toseland recalls the name of the last Danish Earl, together with the place name element *lundr*, meaning a heathen temple. This was replaced by a Christian church, which was rebuilt in the eleventh century, perhaps by Earl Waltheof, perhaps by his widow the Countess Judith, who was holding the estate in the late eleventh century. The church was cruciform with a spacious aisled nave of four bays, a fine example of the type. The estate came by inheritance to King David I of Scotland, with the title Earl of Huntingdon. It was intended to convert the older community into a cell of Augustinian Canons Regular and make it dependent on Holyrood. But the intention was not carried through and Great Paxton became a normal, but rather wealthy, parish church with the dependent chapels, like Toseland, slowly asserting independent parochial rights.

The cruciform minster church of pre-Conquest England was still in favor far into the twelfth century. It also became the architectural model for the older Celtic communities, which were being transformed into churches of secular canons. This was the development of Bangor Cathedral in North Wales in the second quarter of the twelfth century. At the same date there is evidence that Whithorn Cathedral followed the same line under Bishop Gillealdan, before it was reformed with a Chapter of Praemonstratensian Canons Regular. There is evidence of a similar development which is set out in the Bulletin of the Friends of Dunblane Cathedral; there the date is c.1150. The same result is evident, after a more complex development, in the little church of St. Mary of the Rock, the seat of the older Culdee community of St. Andrews, which long survived the establishment of the Chapter of Canons Regular. But perhaps the most significant because the most easily understood is the "small but elegant" cathedral of the north at Dornoch, built soon after 1200. As planned this cruciform church had an aisleless nave.

In an article contributed by Professor Stones and myself to the *Antiquaries Journal*, a plan of this type was suggested for the early twelfth-century cathedral of Glasgow, built by Bishop John and consecrated in 1136.[5] The plan and position may be accepted in view of the later development and the relation to the tomb of St. Kentigern. But it may well be that the scale is too small and that there should be an aisled nave of more than the three bays indicated. Were it not for the adjectives "small" and "narrow" used at the time when Bishop Jocelin "gloriously enlarged" the cathedral, it would be tempting to think in terms of St. Osmund's late eleventh-century cathedral at Old Sarum with its short aisled eastern arm, its transeptal towers and its aisled nave of eight bays. But this cathedral stands at the end of one and a half centuries of the evolution of the great church in southern England and it would be rash to try to see a similar development in less than half of that time, which is all that had elapsed since St. Margaret initiated the reform movement in Scotland.

With the final stage, immediately preceding the present cathedral, the story moves on to firmer ground. The cruciform church of the late

---

5. Radford and Stones, "The Remains of the Cathedral of Bishop Jocelin at Glasgow," 220–32.

eleventh and twelfth centuries was soon shown to be inadequate; a comparison with the great churches arising in the houses of the Canons Regular and the monasteries was scarcely complimentary to the cathedrals which remained secular. The principal defects were at the east end. This provided inadequate access to the relics, which were attracting pilgrims in ever greater numbers and made insufficient provision for the chapels and altars required for services desired by individuals or corporations such as the guilds. But the nave was also proving insufficient for the growing congregations. The first difficulty was the more pressing as shrines and altars had necessarily to be under cover, while an occasional service could be held in the open if the numbers were too great for the church.

At Glasgow Bishop Jocelin conceived the plan, which led to a cathedral adequate for these purposes. The cathedral, which he "gloriously enlarged," was consecrated in 1197. The architectural evidence, slight as it is, shows that the consecration in that year was concerned only with the new east end. The lower walls of the existing aisled nave, which are older than the present superstructure, date from after 1200.

Normally the twelfth-century extension of a church implies an aisled eastern arm and an ambulatory enclosing it together with eastern chapels opening out of the ambulatory. An eastern transept with further chapels was sometimes added, but this is a rather later development. Where, as at Glasgow, the configuration of the ground precluded the full realization of the concept, the necessary provision could be made in two stages, with a raised presbytery and chapels above a lower church. The early wall shaft still in position in the south aisle of the present cathedral, shows that Bishop Jocelin's east end was in two stages and that it had an eastern transept of at least two bays projecting beyond the line of the present side walls. The tomb of St. Kentigern was incorporated in the east end of the lower church, probably with the main altar or a shrine for the relics immediately above. The eastern transepts would provide chapels on both stages. The great extension of the aisled nave to approximately its present dimensions followed in the years after 1200.

Glasgow by this date—c.1220—had assumed a form comparable to the lesser English cathedrals of the twelfth century and the painted voussoir[6] which has been preserved shows that the building was of very high quality. The solution reached in the east end may be compared with the late twelfth-century extension of Rochester. It marks a considerable

---

6. A wedge-shaped element used to construct a vault or arch.

advance over the uncompleted extension of Old Sarum, as conceived in the first quarter of the century by Bishop Roger.

But by the time it was completed the church begun by Bishop Jocelin of Glasgow was already out of date. The new cathedral of Salisbury, begun about 1220 on a new site, untrammeled by earlier structures, represents a church designed for the full round of services laid down in the Use of Sarum, the earliest extant version of which dates from the last years of the earlier cathedral at Old Sarum, now a ruin on the hill two miles north of the city. It was under this inspiration that Bishop William de Bondington designed the present east end of Glasgow in the second quarter of the thirteenth century. But this is a theme beyond the scope of this address and at this point the story must close.

This short address has attempted, in very summary form, to indicate the main stages in the historical development of the early cathedrals of Glasgow and to show how they fit into the general picture of architectural change. If the first part rests very largely on conjecture and analogy, it does, at least, emphasize the British and Celtic elements in the story, a theme which has been illustrated in the literary field by Professor Kenneth Jackson, in his analysis of the elements which make up the Life of St. Kentigern.[7] In the later stages it may have seemed to harp unduly on Old Sarum and Salisbury. The excuse, if such is needed, must be that a cathedral—or for that matter any church—is a functional building. The Use of Sarum was eventually adopted at Glasgow and it is only to be expected that the cathedral where this was evolved would influence the requirements of Glasgow. But Glasgow is not a copy of the English cathedrals. It is an original concept worked out to provide for the same needs but adapted to fit the topographical conditions of a difficult site. This is true not only of the final stage, but also at an earlier date.

---

7. Jackson, "The sources for the Life of St. Kentigern," 273–357.

3

King David I and the Church of Glasgow

G. W. S. BARROW

One historian has written that "the munificence to the church in the twelfth century looks like the biggest investment in non-material activity that western Europe has seen."[1] In Scotland, King David I, who reigned from 1124 until 1153, took his sacred duty to support the church more seriously than any other Scottish king before or since. In this chapter (based on a lecture originally delivered to the Society of Friends in 1994) Professor Geoffrey Barrow outlines how David established law and order in his kingdom, endowed many churches, defined the area covered by the diocese of Glasgow, and supported the building of the Cathedral.

1. Donaldson, *The Faith of the Scots*, 27.

King David I of Scotland as depicted in the Kelso Abbey charter. Image courtesy of the Duke of Roxburghe and the National Library of Scotland.

"The Lord, who wishes no-one to perish, deigned to visit with his mercy these unhappy people living without reason, like beasts, in their accursed country. For in the time of Henry king of England, while Alexander king of Scots reigned in Scotland, God sent to them David, brother of the king of Scotland, to be their ruler and leader. He was able to punish them for their shameless and wicked practices and, through the honesty and unbending severity of his character, to bridle their outrageous rebelliousness."[2]

IN THESE WORDS, A member of the cathedral establishment of Glasgow, about the middle of the twelfth century, summarized the benefits which David, youngest son of Malcolm III and Saint Margaret, was believed to have conferred upon the diocese of Glasgow in the years before he succeeded to the throne. As we might put it, David restored law and order. The comment, sincere and heartfelt as we may suppose it to be, puts us in mind of the harsh side of life in twelfth-century Scotland and of an aspect of David's character more somber than our familiar image of a generous, open-handed welcomer of strangers and multiple founder of religious houses, the "sair sanct for the Croun" of James I's reported outburst. A

2. *Registrum Episcopatus Glasguensis* [hereafter *Glas. Reg.*], i, 4.

writer of about the second generation succeeding David's own praised the king because "prudently taking thought for the future he equipped his realm with castles and weaponry."[3] Long before his grandson Malcolm IV high-handedly transferred to his barons and knights, Flemings for the most part, the lands in the Middle and Upper Wards of Clydesdale which had belonged to the old church of St. Mungo) since time immemorial, David had established men of military power and expertise in a wide arc of fiefs which protected Glasgow from the south and west—Renfrew, Mearns and Strathgryfe, Kyle Stewart, Annandale, Eskdale, Ewesdale, and Liddesdale. He himself held on to Renfrew for many years, allowing ample time to build the first castle there and to found the burgh on his own demesne lands before all this was "mediated" to his steward Walter son of Alan. He also retained Rutherglen, and not so many miles further away lay the royal residences of Irvine, Cadzow, and Lanark, first and last of which acquired castles during the twelfth century. Only towards the north, the very airt from which in later ages plundering raids of wild highlanders came to be feared and expected, does David not seem to have provided any shield. In his days the earls of Lennox, of whom we have no record, must have been loyal supporters of the crown and obedient sons of Holy Mother Church.

The extensive distribution of Scottish Cumbria (the kingdom or province was never called Strathclyde in the twelfth century) among the king's powerful feudatories, whose castle-centered fiefs were interspersed with districts of similar size kept in royal hands, would have given the southern hinterland of Glasgow political cohesion in a high degree even without the developments of the next reign. By the time Malcolm IV had set up the artificial knight-service baronies of upper Lanarkshire, and had bestowed upon David Olifard the lands beside the Clyde which came to form the great lordship of Bothwell, the organization of Scotland's Middle West could compare favorably with the best regulated districts of the realm and, indeed, with well governed regions of other feudal kingdoms such as England or France.[4] When in 1164 Somhairle MacGillebrigte king of Argyll, with a formidable fleet, sailed up the Clyde to Renfrew in furtherance of we know not what schemes of plunder and revenge he was confronted by the common army of north Cumbria stiffened by a handful of knights and sergeants provided by the Steward, the

3. Anderson, *The Chronicle of Melrose* [hereafter *Chron. Melr.*], 32; cf. xxv–mcvi.

4. For the background see Barrow, *The Anglo-Norman Era in Scottish History*, especially 30–117.

bishop of Glasgow and (presumably) the Crown. The host of Argyll was decisively defeated and Somhairle himself slain.[5] Almost a century later, history repeated itself. Another vast fleet from the western isles, this time under the personal command of the king of Norway Haakon IV Haakonson, crossed from Brodick to the Great Cumbrae and sent strong detachments over to the mainland at Largs. Once again the common army of Cunningham and Renfrew and the feudal levies of the Stewart and his baronial neighbors proved equal to the occasion and repulsed the invaders.[6] Clearly, south-western Scotland, the old kingdom of Strathclyde or Cumbria as re-organized by David I and his grandsons was a part of the medieval Scottish realm which could give a good account of itself.

Law and order undoubtedly formed a part of King David's objectives, but they were far from being the whole story. No king of Scots, before or since his time, has held a higher view of the sacral role of kingship or taken more seriously the legitimate ruler's duty to uphold the church and her clergy and to maintain the whole body of the faithful firmly within the Christian fold. The seventeen-year reign of his brother Alexander I gave to David what must have seemed to him a providential opportunity to apply his religious principles in practical terms. His brother—reluctantly, we are told—had allowed him rule over a broad tract of southern Scotland, on the east the lands between Lammermuir and the Tweed, in the center the whole of Tweeddale and Teviotdale, and on the west the whole of ancient Cumbria with perhaps no more than a light overlordship over the kings of Galloway and lords of Nithsdale.[7] Within this broad territory the ecclesiastical policy even of so zealous a reformer as David would of necessity be molded by existing dependencies and boundaries, yet there can be no denying that he regarded the church of Cumbria as falling specially under his protection and patronage. Although he never styled himself "King" before his accession to the Scottish throne, there can be no doubt whatever that his position as ruler of Cumbria was kingly. The territory was called a *regio*[8] in a period when that word was commonly understood to be synonymous

---

5. Anderson, *Early Sources*, ii, 254–58; *Regesta Regum Scottorum* [hereafter *RRS*], i, 15, 20.

6. Reid, *Scotland in the Reign of Alexander III*, 118–23, 137–40.

7. Anderson, *Scottish Annals*, 193; Barrow, *Anglo-Norman Era*, especially chapters II–IV.

8. *Glas. Reg.*, i, 3.

with *regnum* "kingdom,"⁹ and David's authority and powers in this *regio* were those of a king. It behoved the ruler (*princeps*)¹⁰ of this suppressed or eclipsed kingdom to exalt its chief church. The easternmost part of David's great lordship, almost wholly in what became Berwickshire, lay in the diocese of the bishop of the Scots who had his seat at St. Andrews. There is little evidence that David had any prolonged dealings with this bishop before his accession to the Scottish throne, although he was careful to protect the rights of the monks of Saint Cuthbert, i.e. Durham Cathedral Priory, who already possessed large landed estates benorth Tweed, especially the sizable shire of Coldingham.¹¹ Tweeddale proper, however, and Teviotdale—i.e. approximately the later counties of Peebles, Selkirk, and Roxburgh—were never in St. Andrews diocese and their earliest ecclesiastical status is quite obscure. At the beginning of the twelfth century the Norman archbishop of York, Thomas II, had attempted to claim Teviotdale for the diocese of Durham, and indeed the Durham tradition was that Teviotdale had been allowed to slip from Durham's grasp when the powerful Ranulf Flambard, made bishop of Durham in 1099, was in exile following his disgrace at the beginning of Henry I's reign.¹² In fact it seems most improbable that any of the bishops of Durham ever exercised jurisdiction in Teviotdale. Their aggressive claim, typically Norman, was no doubt founded upon the ancient connection between Melrose and Holy Island and the fact that a ninth-century bishop of Holy Island had given his monks a church he had founded at Jedworth (Jedburgh), together with the secular settlement there *(villa)* and at "the other Jedworth (Jedburgh)."¹³

Whatever the truth of this may be, it is certain that David rejected Durham's pretensions and put Teviotdale and Tweeddale firmly under the control, ecclesiastically speaking, of the bishop of Cumbria, i.e. the bishop of Glasgow. The inquest which he caused to be held to ascertain what were the immemorial landed possessions of St. Mungo's church lists nine properties in Tweeddale and Teviotdale: the lands of

9. E.g., *Chron. Melrose*, 128; Potter, *Gesta Stephani*, 36; Bain, *Calendar of Documents*, no. 2160.

10. *Glas. Reg.*, i, 4.

11. Raine, *The History and Antiquities of North Durham*, Appendix, nos. XCIX–CII. For David's continued support for Durham after his accession see Raine, nos. XII–XXV.

12. Anderson, *Scottish Annals*, 129n, 133n.

13. Anderson, *Scottish Annals*, 160 and n.

Stobo, Eddleston, Ancrum, Tronie(hill), Lilliesleaf and Ashkirk, and the churches of Peebles (a parish then including Manor), Traquair and Morebattle, each endowed with a ploughgate of arable.[14]

It is of course possible that David would like to have gone further than this and created a wholly new see based upon some old-established church, e.g. Jedburgh, located in that naturally favored area where the valleys of Tweed and Teviot meet. There is no doubting David's attachment to the district; it was largely due to him that Roxburgh grew rapidly to a position of such importance and that the Augustinian canons of Jedburgh flourished under his benevolent patronage. Moreover, when David—as was bound to happen—came to introduce into his own land a congregation of one of the newest religious orders, the monks from Thiron-le-Cardais (Tiron) north of Chartres, the spot selected for their settlement was Selkirk. Selkirk, of course, lay within, or perhaps just on the eastern edge of, "the Forest," *par excellence*, of southern Scotland and David may have felt this was an appropriate *locale* for monks coming from the forest of Le Perche. From our point of view what matters is that Selkirk was well within the Tweeddale-Teviotdale region which David assigned to the bishopric of Glasgow. Even when, in 1128, the Tironensians transferred to Kelso, on the left bank of the Tweed and therefore in the diocese of St. Andrews, the splendid abbey which they built there remained in close association with the king's burgh and castle of Roxburgh. The bishop of St. Andrews, no doubt prompted by the king, explicitly permitted the abbot of Kelso to apply for chrism and holy oil to any bishop in Scotia or Cumbria—i.e. to the bishop of Glasgow, if desired, and certainly not to the bishop of Durham.[15]

It must be said firmly at this point that there is absolutely no evidence that David would have divided the diocese of Cumbria or transferred its see from Glasgow to Teviotdale.

The renown of St. Mungo and his shrine beside the Molendinar Burn was too well established to be passed over. This holy place must therefore be enlarged and exalted. The inclusion of Teviotdale and Tweeddale amounted to a very sizable enlargement, but it has to be set in the balance against the loss, which took place in at least two stages, of English Cumbria, i.e. the later counties of Cumberland (less the South Tyne district of Alston) and Westmorland. In 1092 King William II Rufus

14. *Glas. Reg.*, i, no. 1 (4–5). The most probable date for the Inquest seems to be either 1120–21 or 1123–24.

15. *Liber Sancte Marie de Calchou*, i, III–IV; *RRS*, i, no. 131 (193).

seized Cumbria as far north as Esk and Solway.[16] This left the ecclesiastical status of the country between the Esk and the Westmorland Fells undetermined. It has been thought that in the Conqueror's reign the bishop of Durham had exercised jurisdiction in Gilsland, admittedly something of a border zone between Cumberland and Tynedale.[17] It is now certain that the source involved refers to Athelwold bishop of Carlisle, not to Æthelwine bishop of Durham (died 1071–72).[18] Before 1114, the archbishop of York consecrated a Cumbrian priest named Michael bishop of Glasgow.[19] Although the choice of title may be important as a pointer to the geographical extent of the Cumbrian diocese, it seems likely that Michael performed his episcopal functions only in English Cumbria, and he conferred orders and was ultimately buried at the church of Morland, five miles north-west of Appleby.[20]

David seems to have recognized Michael as bishop, but on Michael's death and while the see of York was vacant he acted swiftly and positively. His chaplain, who witnessed as such a confirmation issued by David for the Cluniac priory of St. Andrews at Northampton c. 1114,[21] was a monk (*vir religiosus*) named John, who had been David's tutor (presumably in the 1080s or 1090s) and seems to have been strongly attracted by the Tironensian model of the Benedictine life.[22] This was the man chosen by David to be bishop of the chief church of his kingdom of Cumbria. The story put about in York circles and believed, at least momentarily, at the papal curia in 1122, that John was formally elected in the chapter of York and that his consecration at the hands of the pope was requested by that chapter, sounds like an attempt by York to assert authority over John

---

16. Barrow, *The Kingdom of the Scots*, 144.

17. Summerson, H. "Old and New Bishoprics: Durham and Carlisle" in Rollason, *Anglo-Norman Durham*, 369–80 [hereafter Summerson, "Durham and Carlisle"], 370–71.

18. The source which had sometimes been taken to be evidence that Bishop Æthelwine of Durham had exercised jurisdiction over Gilsland is shown to belong to c. 1150–56, and to refer to Bishop Athelwold of Carlisle, by H. Summerson in *Transactions of the Cumberland and Westmorland Archaelogical and Antiquarian Society*, new ser., 95 (1995) 85–91.

19. Dowden, *The Bishops of Scotland*, 294–95; Watt, *Series Episcoporum*, 54–55.

20. Dowden, *Bishops of Scotland*, 294.

21. *RRS*, i, no. 1.

22. Dowden, *Bishops of Scotland*, 295; Watt, *Series Episcoporum*, 55–58; Barrow, *Kingdom of the Scots*, 203–4.

after the event.[23] By whatever body of clergy he was elected, John was certainly chosen by his lord David and consecrated, not by an archbishop of York but by the outspokenly Gregorian reforming pope Paschal II, at an unknown date between 1114 and January 1118.[24]

As far as English Cumbria was concerned David bided his time and (as far as we know) made no protest when Augustinian canons were installed in the church of Carlisle in 1122 nor, more crucially, when Henry I established his chaplain Athelwold (or Athelulf) as bishop of Carlisle in 1133, thereby creating a new English diocese.[25] His Inquest of c. 1120–24 reported no ancient endowments of Glasgow in English Cumbria, even although, as is well known, the area contains several Kentigern or Mungo dedications.[26]

We know that such dedications were taken seriously in the twelfth century as evidence that a church or parish either formed part of the possessions of Glasgow or at least fell within its jurisdiction. It seems more likely, e.g., that the Tweeddale dedications to Mungo came first and the claims on behalf of Glasgow followed, rather than that once Glasgow's ownership was established the Mungo dedication was quickly applied as a species of name-tag. One of the most curious of Glasgow documents to survive from the first half of the twelfth century is a grant by the bishop of St. Andrews to Herbert bishop of Glasgow (John's successor) of the parish church of Lochwharret (now Borthwick in Midlothian).[27] This church had already been given by David I, inadvertently, to the Augustinians of Scone. Now, clearly at the prompting of the king after he had had second thoughts, aided and abetted by his son Henry, effectively assistant-king, Lochwharret was "restored" to Glasgow and the anomaly was regularized by the simple device whereby Bishop Herbert presented the prior of Scone to Bishop Robert as parson (or rector) of the church.[28] It cannot

---

23. Lawrie, *Early Scottish Charters*, no. 44.

24. Watt, *Series Episcoporum*, 55.

25. Summerson, "Durham and Carlisle," 373–74.

26. Arnold-Forster, *Studies in Church Dedications*, ii, 231, lists eight dedications to Kentigern in Cumberland and one (Simonburn, St. Mungo) in Northumberland.

27. *Glas. Reg.*, i, no. 11.

28. *Glas. Reg.*, i, no. 11. The words "a priore de Scona quem tradente nobis prefato Herberto episcopo in personam eiusdem ecclesie suscepimus" have been imperfectly rendered by Lawrie, *Early Scottish Charters*, 186.

be a coincidence that Lochwharret was dedicated to Kentigern or Mungo and figures in the legendary material concerning the saint.[29]

By 1120, therefore, or thereabouts, David had done two things for the church of Glasgow which were of decisive importance. He had effectively defined the diocese within the boundaries it was to retain, with only minor adjustments, until the sixteenth century—stretching from north of Loch Lomond to Sprouston on the south-eastern Borders, from Carrick in the south-west to Carnwath, Dunsyre and West Linton in the north-east. He had provided this large and potentially rich diocese with a pastor who must be reckoned one of the outstanding prelates of medieval Scotland. It only remained to honor St. Mungo by building a cathedral church worthy of what was to become the second diocese of the Scottish church and realm, and arrange for this church to be served by an adequate body of clergy.

Building the new cathedral in the twenties and thirties when the only closely comparable structures then going forward in Scotland were the abbey churches of Dunfermline, Holyrood, and Kelso[30] may well have posed problems in connection with the supply of quarrymen, carters, stone-masons and stone carvers, many of whom will have been induced to come to Glasgow from distant sites where work was completed or labor was being shed. It must also have been a question of liquid funds, for the provision of which neither the dense cluster of estates in and around the city itself nor the far-flung lands in Clydesdale, Tweeddale, Teviotdale, and Dumfriesshire may have been ideally suited. Nor could the profits of trade have helped very significantly in these early days when the burghs utilizing the water and land routes of the Clyde valley were all in the hands of the crown or its chief feudatories. The offerings of the faithful, including no doubt a stream of pilgrims, will have formed an important element in the financing of wages and purchase of building materials. While we can hardly escape the conclusion that the bishop would have had to borrow money to maintain the pace of work needed to

---

29. Jackson, "The sources for the life of St. Kentigern," 337–39. Jackson was unaware that at the end of the twelfth century Lochwharret (Borthwick, Midlothian) belonged to a family using the surname "of Lyne" originating in Stobo in Tweeddale, where the church, a possession of the see of Glasgow, bore a dedication to Kentigern (see Harvey, *Calendar of Writs*, nos. 7, 4).

30. Fawcett, *Scottish Medieval Churches*, 30–37; Cruden, *Scottish Medieval Churches*, 26–54, 102.

justify the dedication of 1136,[31] when presumably the choir and crossing at least had been completed, we see that as early as c. 1114 David made over to Glasgow an annual payment of five pounds in sterling money from his newly acquired estate of Hardingstone beside Northampton.[32] The land had come to David as a result of his marriage and he tells us that he consulted his wife and obtained her permission for the gift, made "for the construction and renewal" of the cathedral. It seems unlikely that this annual cash offering was the only one made whether by David or by lesser laymen, though it is the only one of which record survives from earlier than 1136.

Establishing a body of resident clergy was also, to some extent, a matter of money or at least of resources in kind which could be consumed directly or sold for cash. Here again the benefactions of David, in this case both before and after he became king of Scotland, were of fundamental importance. They included Govan; lands in the king's sizable estate of Partick, some of which were given by the king in direct endowment on the occasion of the dedication in 1136, some of which (yielding an annual rent of one merk of silver), the king had previously allotted to Ascelin, Bishop John's archdeacon; the church of Cadzow; the eighth penny of all his profits of justice throughout Cumbria whether they were rendered in coined money or in kind; and the tenth part of the substantial revenue *(cáin)* in cattle and pigs payable to the king in Strathgryfe, Cunningham, Kyle, and Carrick, to be received in all years save those in which the king traveled through those districts and consumed his revenues on the spot.[33]

What kind of clerical establishment is likely to have been envisaged by David and his bishop for the first church of Cumbria and second church of the realm? At the end of their illuminating paper of 1964 on the great re-build of Glasgow by Bishop Jocelin (c. 1197), Dr. Ralegh Radford and Professor Lionel Stones surely point their readers in quite the wrong direction when they portray the early twelfth-century church of Glasgow as a corporation of quasi-monastic clergy living communally, "the successor of a British monastic community of the type known as *clas*," found

---

31. Professor A. A. M. Duncan has kindly informed me, in a letter, that the date of "July 7" usually given for the 1136 dedication of Glasgow Cathedral is quite unsafe.

32. *Glas. Reg.*, i, no. 2.

33. The documentary evidence for these endowments appears in *Glas. Reg.*, i, 3,6,7,8,9,10.

widely throughout pre-Norman Wales.[34] Such it may indeed have been in former times, but surely not when reconstituted and literally rebuilt by David and Bishop John. All their known contacts and models for a major task of this sort lay in England and on the continent, especially in northern France. David himself had traveled in Normandy and northern France perhaps frequently as a youth and once or twice after he had gained his Cumbrian lordship and English earldom.[35] Bishop John visited the papal curia on at least two occasions and once journeyed to Jerusalem to be the guest there of the Patriarch Gormond.[36] In 1138 the bishop, deeply affected by the hostile pressure applied to him by the papacy and the archbishop of York, went into retreat at the monastery of Tiron, an experience which resulted, on his return to Scotland, in the founding of a daughter-house of Kelso much closer to Glasgow at Lesmahagow.[37]

These men were not interested in the ancient *clas* churches of Wales or Cornwall, nor would they readily look to Bangor as an exemplar for their new cathedral. The churches they would look to, however overambitious it might seem and however drastically they might have to scale down their own domestic version, were the secular cathedrals burgeoning in Norman England and in their longer-established counterparts in northern France. In particular, for all that John himself was a monk, they would eschew the peculiarly English (tenth-century) notion of filling their cathedral with Benedictine monks. Instead, a decent though modest college of secular canons was sought, on the model of Bayeux, York, Lincoln, and Salisbury, but of course a great deal smaller. In these and similar churches the archdeacon (*oculus episcopi*, "the bishop's eye") played a leading role: an archdeacon of Glasgow, the first in Scotland, appears by 1127, and bore a Norman personal name.[38] Again, in these churches a dean was beginning to make an appearance about the last decade of the eleventh century. There does not seem to have been a dean of Glasgow before Bishop John's death, but there was one by the mid-1160s.

---

34. Radford and Stones, "The Remains of the Cathedral of Bishop Jocelin at Glasgow," 231–32. What record tells us of the cathedral foundation of Glasgow from the 1130s onward contrasts markedly with the contemporary situation at, e.g. Llandaff, for which see Crouch, *Llandaff Episcopal Acta*, xxviii–xxxi.

35. Barrow, *Kingdom of the Scots*, 175, 202–23.

36. Watt, *Series Episcoporum*, 56.

37. Watt, *Series Episcoporum*, 56; Barrow, *Kingdom of the Scots*, 176.

38. Shead, *Fasti Ecclesiae Scoticanae Medii Aevi Ad Annum* 1638 [hereafter *Fasti*], 218.

A precentor *(cantor)* was a feature of the York and Sarum colleges by 1093 and 1122 respectively[39] and Simon "styled cantor of the church of Glasgow" was author of a letter addressed to the dean and a fellow canon, again in the 1160s.[40]

In John's time there is evidence for six resident canons at Glasgow, supported by prebends.[41] We cannot rule out the existence of further canons not so supported. No doubt they were closely subordinate to the bishop, but the important point is that he had already begun to create prebends, i.e. estates or incomes permanently allocated for the support of resident canons. The creation of prebends was characteristic of Salisbury, Lincoln, and other English secular cathedrals from the beginning of the twelfth century, but, as Dr. Diana Greenway has emphasized, it was a slow, gradual process.[42] At Glasgow the six prebends for which there is evidence before 1147 were Glasgow itself (i.e. the parochial incumbency), Govan, Renfrew, Barlanark, one further unnamed prebend, and a ploughgate in Glasgow to which King David seems to have added the church of Cadzow.[43] Confirmation that there were six prebends in Bishop John's time is provided by the statement that his successor Herbert created a new prebend—presumably that to which the name Provan became attached?—out of one measured ploughgate of arable in Glasgow together with the seventh part of the benefices accruing to the common fund which used formerly to be divided among six canons.[44] This may seem a far cry from Old Sarum where, as the Scottish chronicle of Holyrood—probably incorporating notes made at Merton in Surrey—tells us, in 1089 the first bishop of Salisbury, Osmund, constituted thirty-six canons.[45] But

---

39. Edwards, *English Secular Cathedrals*, 160; Clay, "The early Precentors," 116. See Table 2, 84 in the article of Greenway, cited below, n. 40; Le Neve, *Fasti Ecclesiae Anglicanae*, 13.

40. *Registrum S. Marie de Neubotle*, no. 3.

41. *Glas. Reg.*, i, no. 28: (1) parish of Glasgow, (2) and (3) churches of Govan and Renfrew, (4) a ploughgate of arable in Glasgow with the church of Cadzow, (5) Barlanark, and (6) teinds of fermes in cheese and flour etc., due to the bishop's cellar, and the teind of the eighth penny of the king's pleas.

42. Greenway, "The False *Institutio* of St. Osmund," in Greenway (ed.), *Tradition and Change*, 88–90; Barrow, J. "Cathedrals, Provosts and Prebends," 536–64, especially 555–60.

43. *Glas. Reg.*, i, no. 28.

44. *Glas. Reg.*, i, no. 28.

45. *Chron. Melr.*

what is relevant for us is that what happened at Glasgow was fashioned in a similar mold.

In a paper published in 1985,[46] Dr. Greenway has demonstrated conclusively that the so-called *Institutio* of Saint Osmund of Salisbury, dated to 1091, is in fact a forgery or rather a compilation of several periods, none earlier than the 1150s or 1160s. Before that, as a papal letter of 1146 shows us, Sarum enjoyed "reasonable customs," called "reasonable" precisely because they were unwritten and therefore needed the approval of some external referee.[47] Now, in another papal letter of 1173 which Dr. Greenway does not mention, Pope Alexander III confirmed to the clergy of Glasgow Cathedral "the reasonable customs and liberties which Herbert of good memory, lately your bishop, introduced into your church following the pattern of the church of Salisbury."[48] Herbert, previously a Tironensian monk at Kelso, reigned at Glasgow from 1147 to 1164, precisely the period when, as Dr. Greenway has shown, the "reasonable" or unwritten customs of Sarum began to be set down in permanent written form.[49] Allowing for time-lag we might suppose that Bishop Herbert adopted what were understood to have been the Sarum customs during the earlier decades of the twelfth century. He may already have begun to do this before the death of David I in 1153, but perhaps a more probable period would be the years of peace which followed the accession of Henry II as king of England in 1154. This introduction of explicitly Sarum customs by Bishop Herbert does not mean that before his time the cathedral fluctuated rudderless, or was guided merely by the bishop's whim. Once again the indefatigable Pope Alexander III comes to our aid, for we still have his letter (March 7, 1161) confirming to Solomon the dean and the chapter—as it is now called for the first time—of Glasgow "all the old and reasonable customs which King David I and Bishop John established in their church."[50] Thus the two stages in the creation

---

46. Greenway, "The False *Institutio*," 77-101.

47. Greenway, "The False *Institutio*," 80 and n. 15; Holtzmann, *Papsturkunden in England*, no. 53, 210 (1146): "alias antiquas et rationabiles ecclesie vestre consuetudines et libertates."

48. *Glas. Reg.*, i, no. 28 (26), March 25, 1173.

49. Greenway, "The False *Institutio*," 80, 92-94.

50. *Glas. Reg.*, i, no. 23: "omnes antiquas et rationabiles consuetudines." The dates of papal letters addressed to Scotland have been taken from, or checked against, Somerville, *Scotia Pontificia*. But in the case of *Glasgow Registrum*, i, no. 23 (= Somerville, *Scot. Pont.*, no. 73) the date given in *Glasgow Registrum*, i, cvi, 1161, is to be preferred to the date of 1175 given in Somerville, *Scot. Pont.*

of a college, eventually a chapter, of secular canons at Glasgow would have been, first, an empirical and eclectic beginning under Bishop John when there were certainly canons and prebends, when the canons divided the common fund among themselves and when the archdeacon dominated the cathedral establishment; and, second, a more precisely defined reorganization under Bishop Herbert with a larger number of prebendary canons, a dean and a cantor, and an archdeacon whose role is now seen as belonging more specifically to the diocese at large than to the government of the cathedral clergy. Incidentally, if the supposed foundation charter of Bishop Osmund of Salisbury is to be trusted,[51] the Glasgow customs were superior in one respect. Whenever a prebendary of Glasgow died the whole income from his vacant prebend would go to the poor for one year,[52] at Old Sarum only one third of the income from a deceased canon's prebend would be devoted to charity, the remaining two thirds being divided among the surviving canons. If St. Osmund's charter is as much a forgery as his Institution, then it may be that the original Salisbury custom had been the same as at Glasgow but had been made stingier during the course of the twelfth century.

The twelfth century was an age of rapid change and comparatively steady expansion, demographically and economically. It would not be long before the new church built for St. Mungo by King David and Bishop John, even with the additions made by Bishop Herbert, would appear "small and cramped" (to quote a description from one of William the Lion's charters).[53] The episcopate of Bishop Ingram saw an enlargement and consolidation of the liberties of the cathedral and bishopric; the succeeding episcopate of Bishop Jocelin saw a further enlargement of the chapter foundation and the first stage of an ambitious rebuilding of the cathedral on a grander scale than anything envisaged by Bishop John. But none of that later development can take from Bishop John and from his pupil, master and patron David son of Malcolm the credit for re-establishing and in many respects newly creating the cathedral church of Glasgow. It would not be easy to exaggerate the contribution made by that church to the life of Scotland during the four and a half centuries from the time of King David to the Reformation.

51. Greenway, "The False *Institutio*," 98, clause [45].

52. *Glas. Reg.*, i, no. 23 (1161): for later arrangements, modified by Bishop Jocelin (1176–77), see *Glas. Reg.*, i, no. 47.

53. *Glas. Reg.*, i, no. 76; *RRS*, ii, no. 316.

4

The Diocese of Glasgow before the Wars of Independence: an Overview

Norman F. Shead

Norman Shead has compiled a two volume collection of "Scottish Episcopal Acta" which brings together all the surviving documents issued by, or in the name of, the Scottish bishops up to c. 1240. Drawing on these and other contemporary sources, he shows how, by the late thirteenth century, the bishops of Glasgow had secured independence from the archbishop of York and, with the other Scottish bishops, had become part of a unique institution: a national church directly dependent on the papacy. This chapter also examines the contributions of cathedral canons, archdeacons, deans and other clergy to the running of the diocese of Glasgow.

BISHOPS[1]

An inspection of the careers of the thirteen bishops and bishops-elect (four were not consecrated) before the Wars of Independence[2] reveals

---

1. Unless otherwise stated, references to the bishops are from Dowden, *The Bishops of Scotland* and, for the twelfth century, Watt, *Series Episcoporum*. For a list of bishops see the Appendix below.
2. I omit Robert Wishart, for he was so heavily involved in the war.

that there were essentially two "qualifications" for the post. One was to be an archdeacon and the other was to have a connection to the king. These "qualifications" are readily explained. Archdeacons were deputies of the bishop, familiar with diocesan administration, carrying out visitations of parishes and holding courts for cases involving clergy and, in some cases, lay people. Since bishops ranked as great men of the kingdom, it is understandable that the king expected to have his say in choosing them: the election of Jocelin, abbot of Melrose, as bishop of Glasgow in 1174 took place at Perth, which may be interpreted as allowing the king to influence the result. Jocelin was only one of two religious elected to the see; the other was Herbert abbot of Kelso, elected in 1147, but the fashion in the twelfth century for religious as bishops did not last.[3]

Seal of Bishop Walter de St. Albans (1208–32) from Robert Renwick's "Glasgow Memorials."

A connection with the king was also important. We do not know the antecedents of Michael, chosen by Earl David (later King David I) when David became ruler of Cumbria, but he was certainly David's choice. John was David's chaplain.[4] Ingram was chancellor to Earl Henry and later to the king himself. Floris was King William's nephew and Walter de St. Albans the king's chaplain. The bishop who does not fit into this pattern,

3. Shead, *Scottish Episcopal Acta* [hereafter *SEA*] i, xxix.
4. Barrow, *The Charters of King David I*, 33 and no. 2.

though he was an archdeacon, is John de Cheam. He was nominated by the pope (he was a papal chaplain) and happened to be at the Curia when the vacancy occurred and the election was disputed. King Alexander III was offended, both by the interference with the royal prerogative and by the intrusion of an Englishman, and it was some time before Cheam was accepted.

A major issue was the claim of the archbishops of York to be the metropolitan of the Scottish bishops. The archbishops' ambition is understandable, for they had only three suffragans, Galloway, Durham and, after 1133, Carlisle. Up to the 1170s the papacy sided with York.[5] Ingram as archdeacon (the see was vacant) led a delegation to reject the claims of Archbishop Roger and appeal to the papal court. The capture of King William at Alnwick (1174) and the subsequent Treaty of Falaise/Valognes (1175) seemed the best chance the archbishop had to assert his authority over the Scottish bishops. A major obstacle to that was the new bishop of Glasgow, Jocelin. Glasgow clergy saw the diocese as the surviving remnant of the old kingdom of Cumbria and different from the other dioceses in the kingdom.[6] By a series of papal bulls Jocelin secured personal and then diocesan independence from all ecclesiastical authority except that of the papacy.[7] Jocelin consulted the papacy frequently, seeking support on the organization of the diocese.[8]

It is reasonable to suppose that once a chapter had been established the bishops were elected by it, but evidence is lacking. Herbert is described as "elect of Glasgow" in 1147,[9] but what form the election took is unknown. A papal letter to the dean and chapter about Ingram's consecration suggests that he had been elected by them.[10] Jocelin's election at Perth was presumably carried out by a delegation of canons representing the chapter. In 1173 Pope Alexander III granted a privilege to the dean and canons of Glasgow which included the right, along with the religious men of the city, to choose the bishop.[11] Who the religious men of the city were, and how they exercised their right is unknown. Michael

---

5. Somerville, *Scotia Pontificia, Papal Letters to Scotland before the Pontificate of Innocent III*, [hereafter *Scot. Pont.*], e.g. nos. 1, 4–10, 15–18.
6. Broun, "The Welsh identity of the kingdom of Strathclyde," 140–45.
7. Broun, *Scottish Independence*, 135–46.
8. *SEA*, i, Lost Acts nos. 56–58.
9. *Charters David I*, no. 159.
10. *Registrum Episcopatus Glasguensis* [hereafter *Glas. Reg.*], i, no. 18.
11. *Scot. Pont.*, no. 67.

was consecrated by the archbishop of York, but thereafter, and especially once David had become king, York was avoided. John (during a convenient vacancy at York), Herbert and Ingram were consecrated by popes, and Jocelin by the archbishop of Lund at the major Cistercian abbey of Clairvaux at the pope's behest. Walter de St. Albans was the first bishop of Glasgow to be consecrated in Scotland. The only enthronement to be recorded was that of John de Cheam (1260).[12]

Seal of Bishop William de Bondington (1232/3–58) from Robert Renwick's "Glasgow Memorials."

Bishops had both ecclesiastical and secular responsibilities. There were the standard duties of ordination, consecration of churches, holding ecclesiastical courts and carrying out visitations of the enormous diocese. There were also duties for the king: those bishops who were also chancellor, keeper of the great seal, such as William de Bondington, had to be frequently in attendance on the king. Bishops were often at court, attested royal charters, acted as ambassadors and offered advice on matters of state: Ingram advised King William against going to war in 1174; John de Cheam was a witness to the Treaty of Perth concluded with King Magnus of Norway in 1266.[13]

12. Anderson, *Early Sources*, ii, 598.
13. Anderson, *Early Sources*, ii, 278 n.1 and 655–56.

As to the origins of the bishops, Michael was a Briton, that is from the old kingdom of Cumbria, and Floris was Dutch. Walter de St. Albans and John de Cheam had names from places in England. William de Bondington may have originated in Berwickshire. Herbert, given his connection with the abbey of Tiron, Ingram (Enguerrand) and William Malveisin had French names, though they need not have come directly from France. Jocelin may have come from Lanarkshire where he certainly had relatives.[14]

At some date in the twelfth century a ringwork castle was constructed to the west of the cathedral. The bishop would have had a timber hall and buildings within the castle.[15] A group of acta of Walter de St. Albans, given at Ancrum in 1231 and 1232,[16] suggests that the bishop already had a house there. Excavation has revealed what seems to be the site of the house and found some fine ashlar work.[17] The castle at Glasgow was altered in the late thirteenth century when a long rectangular stone hall was built (cf. Rait and Acton Burnell) with the west end in the ditch of the castle, thus making the castle less easily defended.[18] After 1286 the bishop began building at Carstairs.[19] These residences provided convenient bases for visitations of the diocese.

CATHEDRAL CLERGY

Once cathedral building began, certainly by 1114 x 1124 when Earl David and Countess Maud granted 100 shillings from lands in Northamptonshire,[20] it was necessary to staff the cathedral. The number of clergy was presumably modest to begin with, and it is not until Herbert's episcopate that named canons occur, when three are named.[21] Since many have no surname, it is difficult to follow their careers. However, Herbert and Hugh Mortimer became deans of the cathedral and

---

14. See Norman Shead's account of the life of Jocelin in Chapter 6 of the present volume.

15. Yeoman, *Medieval Scotland*, 88.

16. *SEA*, ii, nos. 94, 99, 105, 106.

17. Maldonado, "The Archaeology of Ancrum," 10-12. I am grateful to Alistair Munro of Ancrum for providing me with a copy of this work.

18. Yeoman, *Medieval Scotland*, 94.

19. *Origines Parochiales Scotiae* [hereafter *OPS*], i, 125.

20. *Charters David I*, no. 3.

21. *Glas. Reg.*, i, no.16.

Simon de Biggar precentor. Abel de Gullane became archdeacon and then bishop of St. Andrews and Robert de Prebenda bishop of Dunblane.[22] Recruitment of graduates was slow to develop. Master John (1161 x 1162) was not followed by another graduate until Master Ralf de Malveisin in the early thirteenth century and by Masters Abel de Gullane and Gamelin in the 1230s and 1240s. By 1180 there were at least seven canons and the archdeacon.[23] In 1248 there were nine prebends and five dignities.[24] A document of 1259 lists the dean, two archdeacons, precentor, treasurer, chancellor and sacristan and seven canons.[25] The document of 1248 seems to be an "official" list, but that of 1259 may not be a complete tally of members of the chapter.

Revenues for the members of the chapter were derived from a common fund and from prebends for specific dignitaries and canons. The institution of prebends began with Bishop John,[26] and by 1164 there were seven prebends. Those were the parish of Glasgow (which eventually came to be called Glasgow Primo); the churches of Govan and Renfrew; Barlanark; an unnamed prebend endowed with farm produce and profits of royal justice; a prebend supported by land in Glasgow and one-seventh of the common fund of the canons. It seems likely that the seventh prebend was the church of Cadzow (Hamilton), first mentioned in 1172/3.[27]

It may be that the creation of dignities began with Bishop Herbert. Certainly, the first known dean, Salomon, occurs in 1161[28] and had been both clerk and chaplain to the bishop.[29] The dean's duties normally included presiding at meetings of the chapter, but there is no specific evidence at this early date. Bishop William de Bondington granted the chapter the right to elect the dean.[30] The first known chanter or precentor, Simon, occurs in only one document, which can be dated 1179 x 1221,[31] though it may date to the late twelfth century on the basis of wording.

22. Shead, *Fasti Ecclesie Scoticanae Medii Aevi Ad Annum 1638*, [hereafter *Fasti*], 194, 200, 384, 371, 99.

23. *SEA*, i, no. 93.

24. Bliss, *Calendar of Entries in the Papal Registers* [hereafter *CPL*], 257.

25. *Glas. Reg.*, i, no. 208.

26. *Glas. Reg.*, i, no. 66

27. *Glas. Reg.*, i, no. 28.

28. *Fasti*, 194.

29. *SEA*, i, no. 72; Barrow, *Regesta Regum Scottorum* [hereafter *RRS*], i, no. 131.

30. *Glas. Reg.*, i, no. 205.

31. *Registrum S. Marie de Neubotle*, no. 3.

As defined in 1259, his duties were the direction and rule of the choir.[32] The first known treasurer, John de Roxburgh, occurs in 1195 x 1196.[33] His duties involved the ornaments and treasures of the cathedral and the necessities of worship: lights, incense, bread and wine.[34] The first chancellor, Richard, occurs 1247 x 1258, but apparently there was no chancellor as late as 1249.[35] His duties should have included direction of a school,[36] but there is no evidence of one in Glasgow at that date. The first subdean, who undertook the duties of the dean in the latter's absence, seems to have been appointed between 1258 and 1266.[37]

The cathedral kept records of its documents, though not consistently. The work of several scribes, what became the Registrum Vetus consisted of unbound or only partially bound gatherings until they were bound into a register around 1300.[38] Bishops Herbert and Jocelin commissioned lives of St Kentigern.[39] It seems likely that it was Jocelin who collected the cathedral's relics of St. Thomas Becket, though they are not recorded till 1432.[40] That there were side altars in addition to the high altar is shown by the endowment by Alexander sheriff of Stirling of a chaplain to serve the altar of St. Serf (1214 x 1226).[41]

Statutes were important in providing a constitution for the clergy serving the cathedral. A papal bull of 1161 refers to "the ancient and reasonable customs which King David or John sometime bishop of Glasgow introduced in your church."[42] Nothing more is known of these customs. Bishop Herbert introduced "customs and liberties" in the manner of those of Salisbury Cathedral, according to a bull of 1172.[43] Precisely what

32. *Glas. Reg.*, i, no. 211.
33. *Fasti*, 208.
34. *Glas. Reg.*, i, no. 211.
35. *Fasti*, 204.
36. *Glas. Reg.*, i, no. 211.
37. *Fasti*, 212.
38. Tucker, *Reading and Shaping Medieval Cartularies*, chapter 3. This brief reference does not do justice to Dr. Tucker's remarkable original analysis of the scribes and the development of the Register.
39. Forbes, *Lives*.
40. Duncan, "St. Kentigern at Glasgow in the Twelfth Century" in Fawcett, *Medieval Art and Architecture*, 11–12.
41. *Glas. Reg.*, i, no. 121.
42. *Glas. Reg.*, i, no. 23.
43. *Glas. Reg.*, i, no. 28.

those were is also unknown, for at that date the fully developed customs of Salisbury had not achieved their final form.[44] William de Bondington granted the chapter the liberties and customs of Salisbury,[45] and a letter from the dean and chapter of Salisbury describing their constitution was copied and appears in the Registrum Vetus.[46] In a chapter act, however, the canons reserved the right to make changes if the whole chapter or a majority of the members agreed to do so.[47] The only set of regulations recorded in the Register is that of John de Cheam, issued with the consent of the chapter. These dealt with provision of vicars by the canons, residence at the cathedral and an annual chapter meeting to discuss cathedral business.[48]

In 1259 and 1268 the canons agreed that, if one of their number were elected bishop, he would remove "palatium suum ... extra castrum" (his palace outside the castle) and use the land for dwellings for the canons within one year of election. If the site proved to be too small, he was to find another site for the remaining canons, also within one year.[49] As no canon became bishop on either occasion, presumably the plan did not go ahead. In 1270 the subdean gave a house in Glasgow to a deacon vicar and a subdeacon vicar of the cathedral.[50] It is possible that in this period the vicars lodged with the canons.[51]

Since parochial and other duties might take canons away from the cathedral, they had substitutes, the vicars of the choir, so that the daily round of services could be maintained. They were already well established by 1201 x 1202 when eleven are named and told by Bishop William Malveisin that they had no voice in chapter unless proceedings affected them.[52]

44. Edwards, *The English Secular Cathedrals*, 319, 320.
45. *Glas. Reg.*, i, no. 208.
46. *Glas. Reg*, i, no. 211.
47. *Glas. Reg.*, i, no. 208.
48. *Glas. Reg.*, i, no. 212*.
49. *Glas. Reg.*, i, nos. 208, 213.
50. *Glas. Reg.*, i, no. 220.
51. Edwards, *English Secular Cathedrals*, 274-75.
52. *Glas. Reg.*, i, no. 98.

ARCHDEACONS AND DEANS OF CHRISTIANITY

The archdeacon is the first of the dignitaries to appear on record (1126/7).[53] Possibly the archdeacon presided over the chapter before there were deans; there is no evidence of this, but someone had to preside and there are examples from other cathedrals.[54] The first archdeacon, Ascelin, witnesses over a dozen surviving charters,[55] but Glasgow is mentioned only once,[56] while later in the century Simon is called archdeacon of Teviotdale, which suggests that the title had not been finally settled. The archdeacon's experience as the bishop's agent was all the more important during a vacancy in the see or when the bishop was absent: Bishop John was in Rome and Jerusalem 1122–1123, in Rome 1125–1126 and at the abbey of Tiron in France 1136(?)–1138.[57]

It is not possible to say if the archdeacon had a seat in the chapter for much of this period. The English evidence is that no dignitary without a prebend was allowed to attend chapter meetings,[58] and the archdeacon of Glasgow had no prebend until the episcopate of William de Bondington. Ian Cowan suggested that the Scottish bishops were finding seats in their chapters for archdeacons in the thirteenth century.[59] It seems likely that it was the size of the diocese which prompted the creation of a second archdeaconry, that of Teviotdale (1238). It is possible that the archdeacons were two of the five dignitaries mentioned in 1249.[60]

In the twelfth century the archdeacon had no prebend. Ascelin drew his revenues from land and the church of Old Roxburgh.[61] Financial arrangements were made for the archdeacon by Bishop Walter de St. Albans.[62] During the episcopate of William de Bondington the church of Peebles was assigned to the archdeacon of Glasgow as his prebend.[63]

---

53. *Fasti*, 218.
54. Edwards, *English Secular Cathedrals*, 98.
55. E.g. *SEA*, i, nos. 75, 76, 124, 131.
56. Lawrie, *Early Scottish Charters*, no. CXXI.
57. Watt, *Series Episcoporum*, 56–57.
58. Edwards, *English Secular Cathedrals*, 252.
59. Cowan, "The Organisation of Scottish Secular Cathedral Chapters" [hereafter Cowan, *Organisation*] in Kirk, *The Medieval Church in Scotland*, 80.
60. *CPL*, i, 257.
61. *Glas. Reg.*, i, no. 3; *RRS*, i, no. 114.
62. *SEA*, ii, no. 106; *Glas. Reg.*, i, no.147.
63. *Glas. Reg.*, i, no. 204.

Whether similar arrangements were made for the archdeacon of Teviotdale in this period is unknown.

The Lateran Council of 1179 ordered archdeacons to restrict their retinue to seven persons.[64] The archdeacon had his own household: there are references to his clerk, his chaplain and his official,[65] and of course his own seal.[66] His duties as the bishop's agent are listed in the thirteenth-century statutes of the Scottish Church.[67] An act of Malcolm IV enjoining obedience to the archdeacon shows the latter acting in that capacity (1165).[68] In 1201 archidiaconal visitation was assumed to be normal practice.[69] During a visitation the archdeacon expected to be comfortably accommodated; parish priests might be forced to erect a manse for that purpose,[70] though a sum of money, the procuration, came to be demanded instead of accommodation.[71] He held courts: e.g. in a case involving Melrose Abbey, Archdeacon Simon acted as judge and administered to the parties the oath to keep the final settlement.[72] He was expected to be present at the annual diocesan synods: Simon is recorded attending one at Peebles.[73]

Deans of Christianity had responsibility for smaller areas. The first recorded dean was Aldred during John's episcopate.[74] Evidence for deans is scanty and there are big gaps in our knowledge. The death of William dean of Cunningham in 1211 was noted in the Chronicle of Melrose.[75] Such a record is unusual, but the explanation is that in the same year William had been one of the judges delegate in a case involving the abbey.[76] The titles used by deans varied: Aldred is once called dean of Roxburgh, but his three successors appear as dean of Hassendean, Roxburgh and Ancrum, which suggests that their titles were derived from

64. Moorman, *Church Life in England*, 121.
65. *SEA*, i, no. 65; *Glas. Reg.*, i, no. 143; Patrick, *Statutes*, 52.
66. E.g. *SEA*, ii, no. 100.
67. Patrick, *Statutes*, 12–15, 18, 52.
68. *RRS*, i, no. 258.
69. *Glas. Reg.*, i, no. 93.
70. Patrick, *Statutes*, 12.
71. Dowden, *The Medieval Church in Scotland*, 218.
72. *SEA*, i, no. 103.
73. *Glas. Reg.*, i,. no. 103.
74. *Charters David I*, no. 34.
75. Anderson, *Early Sources*, ii, 388.
76. Ferguson, *Medieval Papal Representatives in Scotland*, 220.

their parishes. From the mid-1220s their successors are called deans of Teviotdale.[77] A charter of Bishop Jocelin lists six deans,[78] which suggests that a full system of deaneries was in being by the 1190s. It is not certain if the dean was appointed by the bishop or the archdeacon. At least one deanery seems to have been subject to considerable lay influence: the deanery of Lennox coincided with the earldom.[79] The first known dean bore the same name as the earl, Maldouen, and the other two of that earl's time, Luke and Michael, may be identified with Luke, the earl's clerk, to whom the earl granted land, and Michael the clerk, who witnessed two of the earl's charters.[80] References to a former dean of Cunningham and a former dean of Luss show that the post was not held for life.[81]

As with the archdeacon, the dean's duty of visitation was assumed in 1201 to be normal practice.[82] The thirteenth century statutes ordered archdeacons and deans to investigate the cohabitation of clerics and women. The statute which ordered that confessors be appointed in every deanery lest the clergy "be ashamed to confess to the dean" suggests that the dean had acted as confessor to the clergy of his deanery.[83] Late thirteenth-century statutes show the dean instituting clerics to churches in the diocese.[84] A brief glimpse of the dean's activities is provided by the chance survival of a single sheet of parchment which may be a leaf of a register kept by the dean: the dean of Lanark was investigating the right of presentation to the church of Covington.[85] The dean was also used to collect money: the statutes ordered that money collected for the building of Glasgow Cathedral should be handed over to the deans, and in 1288 the deans were ordered to secure the payment of papal taxation in their deaneries.[86] The dean also presided at chapters of the deanery, though there is no evidence as to how often these met.

77. *Fasti*, 235–36.

78. *SEA*, i, no. 94.

79. Morgan, "The Organisation of the Scottish Church in the twelfth century," 144.

80. Shead, "The administration of the diocese of Glasgow," 145; Neville, *Native Lordship*, 157–58.

81. *Glas. Reg.*, i, no. 139; *Cartularium de Levenax* (Maitland Club, 1833), 31.

82. *Glas., Reg.*, i, no. 93.

83. Patrick, *Statutes*, 14–15, 13.

84. *Glas. Reg.*, i, nos. 225, 242.

85. Shead, "Administration of the diocese," 147–48.

86. Shead, "Administration of the diocese," 148.

PARISHES

The development of a regular pattern of parishes took place over a long period. It simply did not exist at the beginning of the twelfth century, but was well developed by the end of the thirteenth, when 225 can be identified.[87] It is possible that in the early twelfth century there were large districts served by minsters staffed by a group of clergy. There is some evidence that Hoddam and Applegarth were the sites of such minsters, and it is possible that Stow, Old Roxburgh, Mow, and Jedburgh fulfilled the same function. This gradually gave place to conventional parish churches with the construction and endowment of churches by landowners, both lay and ecclesiastical: Peebles, Traquair and Morebattle seem to have been on episcopal estates.[88] At least eight churches in the earldom of Lennox were in the earl's gift.[89] Walter son of Alan, the Steward, could speak of granting all the churches of Strathgryfe, except Inchinnan to Paisley Abbey.[90] Patronage was a possession which could be granted in the same way as land: in 1249 the patronage of Ecclefechan was given by Robert of Dundonald to the Bruce family.[91]

Scanty records mean that many churches are known only from incidental references. It is therefore impossible to describe the growth of the parochial system in the diocese, but some glimpses can be obtained. The church of Carnwath was built on the estate of William Somerville within the parish of Libberton. It probably gained parochial status during Ingram's episcopate when it was granted to the see, and its independent status was confirmed by Pope Urban III in 1186.[92] Wiston is an example of the early type of parish with wide jurisdiction, for it had three dependent chapels, Symington, Roberton and Crawford John.[93] "Coincidence between the parish and ... the vill[94] appears to have been very high; seventeen of the thirty parishes between Eaglesham and the watershed of

---

87. *Atlas of Scottish History to 1707*, 351.

88. Cowan, *Organisation*, 3, 5; *Glas. Reg.*, i. no. 1.

89. *Liber S. Marie de Calchou*, i, no. 181; *Glas. Reg.*, i, no. 108; *OPS*, i, 40, 43, 30, 46; *Registrum Monasterii de Passelet* [hereafter *Pais. Reg.*], 158, 209.

90. *Pais. Reg.*, 5.

91. Bain, *Calendar of Documents*, i, no. 1763.

92. *Glas. Reg.*, i, nos. 51, 52.

93. *SEA*, i, nos. 105, 90.

94. *Vill* refers to a rural land unit (such as a township) under the feudal system. The equivalent Scots term is *toun*.

the Clyde and Tweed were probably of that type."[95] The founder's name was often incorporated in the name of the parish: so Houston was Villa Hugonis, and Simon Lockhart's name is preserved in two Symingtons, one in Lanarkshire and one in Ayrshire. In the 1180s Pope Urban III instructed Bishop Jocelin to cause churches and chapels to be built to cater for the spiritual needs of his people,[96] an order that was almost certainly intended by Jocelin to clear the way for a building program. Bagimond's Roll of the 1270s, though incomplete, shows that a regular parochial system was in existence by the later thirteenth century.

Each parish should have had the services of a rector, but it was not necessarily the case that there would be only one cleric in the parish. The statutes decreed that larger churches should also have a deacon and subdeacon, presumably so that High Mass could be celebrated. "Chaplain" denoted the least important cleric in the parish; the statement that incumbents might give chaplains a gift of old clothes suggest that many were very poor.[97] Sometimes the incumbent was not in a position to discharge his duties: Roger vicar of Kilbarchan was only in deacon's orders[98] and therefore could not celebrate mass. This situation explains the statute ruling that every parish church should have an incumbent who could discharge the cure of souls and that deacons should not hear confessions or administer the sacraments.[99]

The granting of churches to religious houses began at an early date: for example, Bishop John's grant of the church of Sprouston to Kelso Abbey.[100] By the end of the thirteenth century over half the parishes in the diocese had been appropriated. Again scantiness of record presents problems: some are not recorded until they are listed in Bagimond's Roll in the 1270s. Where a parish church was appropriated to a religious house or prebend of a cathedral, the community or canon was technically the rector of the parish; the priest in the parish was therefore a vicar (deputy). Monks were to present priests to the bishop for the cure of souls in such churches. Pope Alexander III directed a bull on this subject to the

---

95. Morgan, "The Organisation of the Scottish Church," 141 and n. 2.
96. *Glas. Reg.*, i, no. 67.
97. Patrick, *Statutes*, 58, 53–54.
98. *Pais. Reg.*, 163.
99. Patrick, *Statutes*, 11, 54–55.
100. *SEA*, i, no. 28.

heads of religious houses in the diocese of Glasgow.[101] The Augustinian and Premonstratensian canons were permitted by their orders to serve their own churches, though it was not common practice. It was rare for a monk to act as parish priest, but in 1277 Sweetheart Abbey was allowed to serve the parish in which it was situated.[102]

In the twelfth century the practice arose whereby the bishop "ordained" a vicarage in an appropriated church, setting aside a suitable portion of the revenues for the vicar, thus creating a life-long tenure or "perpetual vicarage". The Lateran Council of 1215 ordered non-resident rectors to arrange the institution of perpetual vicars, who were to have an adequate share of the parish revenues.[103] The agreement made by Bishop Walter de St. Albans with Kilwinning Abbey allowed the bishop to remove a vicar if he proved unsatisfactory, did not reside in the parish, or failed to pay the abbey its share of the parish revenues.[104]

The thirteenth century statutes enacted that vicars should have a sufficient and decent maintenance "since those who serve the altars should live by them." The vicar's stipend, after all burdens had been met, was to amount to ten merks if the revenues of the parish were adequate. In wealthier parishes the stipend was to be in proportion to the resources and burdens of the parish.[105] Walter de St. Albans was very active in making agreements about vicarages with religious house,[106] but in 1258 the pope complained that vicarages had not been established in some churches.[107]

RELIGIOUS HOUSES[108]

The considerable variety of religious houses in Scotland is reflected in the diocese of Glasgow. The diocese contained three major monasteries: Melrose (Cistercian), founded by David I (1136/7), Paisley (Cluniac)

---

101. *Glas. Reg.*, i, no. 27.
102. Cowan, *Organisation*, 65–66, 74.
103. Hartridge, *A History of Vicarages*, 9.
104. *SEA*, ii, no. 111.
105. Patrick, *Statutes*, 11–12.
106. *SEA*, ii, nos. 92, 107, 110, 111, 113.
107. *Glas. Reg.* i, no. 209.
108. Unless otherwise stated, references in this section are to Cowan, *Medieval Religious Houses Scotland* and Shead, *Heads of Religious Houses in Scotland*.

founded by Walter son of Alan, the Steward, who brought monks from Wenlock, perhaps via a short-lived priory at Renfrew, and which was elevated to the status of abbey in 1220, and Jedburgh (Augustinian), founded by David I and Bishop John. Three others were Crossraguel (Cluniac), founded from Paisley in the mid- or late-thirteenth century, Kilwinning (Tironensian), founded in the later twelfth century possibly by Richard de Moreville, and Holywood (Premonstratensian), whose founder and date of foundation are unknown, but whose first known abbot occurs in 1225. A final flourish was the founding of Sweetheart (Cistercian) by Devorgilla Balliol in the 1270s.

Selkirk (Tironensian) was lost to the diocese when the community moved to Kelso in the diocese of St. Andrews. An attempt by Walter son of Alan, the Steward, to found a Gilbertine house at Dalmilling in the early thirteenth century was unsuccessful. Three smaller houses were at Lesmahagow, where David I and Bishop John granted land in 1144 so that Kelso Abbey could create a priory there, Blantyre, founded by Earl Patrick II of Dunbar and Countess Euphemia in the 1240s as a dependency of Jedburgh Abbey, and Canonbie, also a dependency of Jedburgh and always small, founded by Turgis de Rosdale and confirmed by King William in the later 1160s. The sole nunnery was Lincluden (Benedictine), founder and date of foundation unknown, but perhaps founded by Fergus lord of Galloway in the mid-twelfth century. The prioress occurs in 1296. Although the founding and spread of the orders of friars were an important development in the Western Church in the thirteenth century, only five houses are certainly known in the diocese of Glasgow in that first century of growth. The Dominican friary in Glasgow was founded by the bishop (probably William de Bondington) and the chapter. Its church was under construction in 1246; it and Ayr were the only friaries in the diocese to have left collections of muniments. Since the Dominicans were noted preachers, that is presumably why they came to Glasgow. King Alexander II favored the Dominicans and founded the house in Ayr. The founders of the Franciscan friaries at Dumfries (founded before 1266) and Roxburgh (in existence by 1235) are unknown. The one Carmelite friary, at Irvine (possibly in existence before 1293), seems to have been founded by one of the Fullers of Fullerton. Friaries were normally based in centers of population, where their preaching and example would be most influential.

It is impossible to say how many hospitals there were in the diocese in this period because most are known only from an incidental reference.

Eleven hospitals can be identified as being in existence in this period, but there may have been more. Nor is it possible to identify what type of hospital they were. The term covered houses for travelers, pilgrims, the sick and the poor. What seems to be the best documented, a house for guests (probably pilgrims) coming to the church of Kilpatrick, had ceased to exist by 1233.[109]

THE CHURCH OF GLASGOW AND THE PAPACY

For much of the twelfth century papal letters to Scotland included instructions to the bishops to accept the authority of the archbishop of York; some were addressed specifically to John.[110] Ingram was consecrated bishop by Pope Alexander III and seems to have pressed the claims of the Scottish bishops to independence of York; at any rate, thereafter Alexander was more sympathetic to the Scots' case.[111] Despite the recalcitrance of the Scottish bishops, John, Herbert and Ingram were consecrated by popes and Jocelin by the archbishop of Lund at the pope's instruction. John de Cheam's consecration at the Curia in 1259 was by then an exception to consecration in Scotland.

The papacy provided benefits, for example, by confirming the possessions of the see[112] and providing advice and support.[113] In 1175 Pope Alexander III granted the church of Glasgow the status of "specialem filiam nostram nullo mediante" (our special daughter no-one coming in between). When the privilege was renewed in 1179 the phrase had become "specialem nullo mediante Romane ecclesie filiam" (special daughter of the Roman church no-one coming in between). The first formula might be taken to mean that Glasgow's special status held good only during the pontificate of Alexander III. The second, however, was general and did not apply to one pontificate. Two successive popes confirmed this status in 1182 and 1186. This foreshadowed the bull *Cum universi* which extended the principle to the whole Scottish Church, thus

---

109. Neville, *Native Lordship*, 174; the evidence is translated by T. O. Clancy in Boardman, *Saints' Cults*, 39–40.

110. E. g. *Scot. Pont.*, nos. 8, 10, 15, 17.

111. Watt, *Series Episcoporum*, 59–60.

112. E.g. *Glas. Reg.*, i, 28, 32.

113. E.g. *SEA*, i, Lost Acts nos. 56–67.

rendering it unique in Western Christendom.[114] This in effect made the pope the metropolitan of the Scottish bishops; however, as he could not realistically visit Scotland regularly, his authority had to be delegated to legates, as in 1201 and 1221 when legates held councils and conducted business. The solution was the setting up of a provincial council by Pope Honorius III in 1225.[115] The idea was perhaps that of the bishops of St. Andrews and Glasgow.[116]

Another advantage was that the pope could issue dispensations, providing exemptions from canon law. Although pluralism had been condemned by the Third Lateran Council (1175), it was possible to secure a dispensation: in 1248 Abel, a canon of Glasgow and one of the king's clerks, was permitted to hold an additional benefice.[117] Illegitimacy and being too young were barriers to ordination to the major orders. That too could be overcome: Ralph de Somerville, an acolyte, was granted a dispensation that, despite his illegitimacy and being only nineteen, he might be promoted to all orders in the Church and hold the church of Linton, to which he had been presented.[118]

A closer connection to the papacy also had disadvantages. One was an increased burden of work. In addition to attendance at occasional General Councils, such as the Fourth Lateran Council, which Walter de St. Albans attended, bishops and other clergy might be called on to act as papal judges delegate. Judges delegate adjudicated in matters brought before the papal Curia, and had either to report back or to settle the case. Bishop Jocelin and the prior of Paisley adjudicated in a dispute between Kelso Abbey and Simon Lockhart. It was not, however, only bishops who were employed in this way: Archdeacon Simon, Dean Hugh de Mortimer, William dean of Cunningham and the rector of Lilliesleaf acted in a variety of cases.[119] After 1225 there was also attendance at the annual Provincial Council.

From the pontificate of Innocent IV the practice of papal provision, whereby the pope requested a benefice for a papal clerk, became commonplace. Since the clerk drew the stipend of the benefice, it cost the

---

114. Broun, *Scottish Independence*, ch. 5, gives an admirably clear exposition.
115. *SEA*, ii, lv.
116. Watt, *Medieval Church Councils*, 45.
117. Theiner, *Vetera Monumenta*, no. CXXXIV.
118. *CPL*, i, 315.
119. Ferguson, *Medieval Papal Representatives in Scotland*, 210, 220, 216.

papacy nothing and thus helped to staff the growing papal civil service.[120] In the 1230s William de Bondington was ordered to provide a suitable benefice for Master Peter, chamberlain of the cardinal of Santa Maria in Cosmedin; in the 1240s Gerard of Rome was a canon of Glasgow. In 1248 the pope conceded that, as the church of Glasgow had made provision in its chapter for four Italians, it would not be required to make provision for more until one of them had died.[121]

The Fourth Lateran Council made compulsory the collection of money for a crusade. Collections for that purpose continued throughout the thirteenth century. The duty was often carried out by papal legates, though in 1246 Bishop William de Bondington and the bishop of St. Andrews were appointed collectors. The best remembered collector was Boemundo de Vezza, remembered in Scotland as Bagimond.[122] His importance to historians lies in what came to be called Bagimond's Roll: though incomplete it provides the first clear evidence for the parochial structure of the diocese of Glasgow.[123] The clergy were rather resistant to the demand for a tenth of ecclesiastical revenues for a six year period to fund a crusade, imposed by the Second Council of Lyon in 1274,[124] but papal taxation, like the desire for a crusade, did not go away.

CONCLUSION

By the late thirteenth century the bishops of Glasgow had secured independence from the archbishop of York and, with the other Scottish bishops, had become part of a unique institution: a national church directly dependent on the papacy. It was no longer necessary to seek consecration abroad: since 1208 consecration in Scotland had become the norm. After 1225 the Scottish bishops had the authority of a Provincial Council and could issue statutes. The bishops remained great men of the kingdom and the king continued to expect a say in their choice.

From very modest beginnings in the early twelfth century, the cathedral had a full complement of dignitaries: the "four square" constitution

---

120. *SEA*, ii, lii.
121. *SEA*, ii, liii.
122. *SEA*, ii, lvii–lviii.
123. Dunlop, *Bagimond's Roll*; Cowan, "Two Early Taxation Rolls"; Watt, "Bagimond di Vezza."
124. *SEA*, ii, lviii.

of dean, precentor, chancellor, and treasurer. Like them, the canons were provided with prebends and had vicars to deputise for them in their absence in order to maintain the daily round of services. The chapter constituted a corporate body with its own seal[125] to authenticate its own acts.

The bishops of Glasgow had created a fully functioning diocesan structure. There was a network of parishes. After 1238 there were two archdeacons to help the bishop in visitations of a large diocese, stretching from the northern end of Loch Lomond to the border with England. At least from the 1190s, there was a body of deans of Christianity to assist the bishop and archdeacons. All needed clerks, parchment, and seals to record their work.

The variety of religious orders in the diocese reflected that in the kingdom. David I preferred the new "reformed" orders of monks and canons rather than the long established Benedictines, but he had no obvious favorite. Friaries and hospitals were cheaper to found than monasteries. Three of the new orders of friars were established in the diocese, one in Glasgow itself and founded by the bishop and chapter. Though it is impossible to say how many, a number of hospitals had been set up. Relations between the bishop and religious houses were not always harmonious. Visitation, hospitality dues, the creation of vicarages could all be contentious, and Melrose and Holywood were beyond the bishop's reach because the Cistercian and Premonstratensian Orders had their own internal systems of inspection.

The twelfth and thirteenth centuries saw closer relations with the reformed papacy. Although King Macbeth had visited Rome,[126] the earliest recorded communication from the papacy to Scotland belongs to 1100 x 1101.[127] The new emphasis on the authority of the papacy from the middle of the eleventh century probably explains why Scotland began to receive papal letters and bulls. Consecrations, instructions and confirmations followed. The supreme benefit of communication with the papacy was the granting of the status of "special daughter" not only to the church of Glasgow but also to the whole Scottish Church. Additional responsibilities followed: bishops and other clerics of the diocese acted as papal judges delegate; bishops of Glasgow attended General Councils in 1215 and 1274. There were, however, the problems of papal provisions and

---

125. The earliest example dates from the early 1190s: *Glas. Reg.*, ii, plate v, no. 1.
126. Anderson, *Early Sources*, ii, 588.
127. *Scot. Pont.*, no. 1.

papal taxation. Well before the end of the thirteenth century close relations with the papacy were the norm: the Scottish Church, including the see of Glasgow, was fully integrated into the Western Church.

APPENDIX: THE BISHOPS AND BISHOPS-ELECT OF GLASGOW

Michael 1109 x 14
John 1114 x 1118–47
Herbert 1147–64
Ingram 1164–74
Jocelin 1175–99
Hugh de Roxburgh elect 1199
William Malveisin 1199/1200–2 (translated to St. Andrews)
Floris elect 1202–7
Walter de St. Albans 1208–32
William de Bondington 1232/3–58
Nicholas de Moffat elect 1259
John de Cheam 1259–68
Nicholas de Moffat elect 1268–70
William de Wishart elect 1270–71 (translated to St. Andrews)

5

Benefactions to the Medieval Cathedral and See of Glasgow[1]

NORMAN F. SHEAD

Records have survived detailing the possessions of the see of Glasgow between the twelfth and sixteenth centuries. From the time of King David I, benefactions such as land, teinds (i.e. tithes), and chantry altars and chaplains to pray for departed souls provided valuable sources of income. In this chapter, Norman Shead shows how the nature of these gifts developed over the centuries.

THE TWO VOLUMES ENTITLED *Registrum Episcopatus Glasguensis*, printed by the Maitland and Bannatyne Clubs in 1843, contain over five hundred documents bearing on the history of the cathedral and see of Glasgow. These documents are drawn from two chartularies and many original charters, most of the latter in eighteenth-century transcripts, and cover the whole period from the twelfth century to the sixteenth. In addition, there exist the protocol book of Mr. Cuthbert Simson, clerk to the chapter at the beginning of the sixteenth century, and a rental of certain lands belonging to the see, also dating from the sixteenth century. As a result, there is considerable material on the possessions of the see, and this

---

1. The author is grateful to the late Professor E. L. G. Stones for many helpful suggestions and comments on this chapter.

material may have survived because, when the records were removed to France in 1560, it was thought desirable to preserve title deeds as a basis for future possible claims.[2] Thus, although not all the printed documents relate to benefactions, enough have survived to make a detailed study of this subject possible in respect of the cathedral and see of Glasgow.

The goodwill of David I towards the Church found active expression, even before his accession, in the *Inquisitio David*.[3] Designed to define the possessions of the see of Glasgow, the inquisition was carried out within a few years of the restoration of the see, and certainly before 1124, when David became king. Even at that early date the lands of the see were extensive, and those names which can be identified show that they lay scattered throughout the diocese.[4] The difficulty of identifying the place names, in itself a mark of authenticity, is accentuated by the fact that many of the lands, notably those in Clydesdale, passed into secular hands in the twelfth century, a development which marks the spread of feudalism in the area as an act of royal policy.[5] The problems in discussing this development derive largely from the vagueness of surviving documents as to the extent of land. Lilliesleaf, for example, belonged to Glasgow at the time of the *Inquisitio*, but by the reign of Malcolm IV, if not earlier, land in Lilliesleaf had passed to the Abbey of Kelso,[6] and we find David I granting Lilliesleaf to Walter of Ryedale.[7] The latter document seems likely to be part of the policy of feudalization at the expense of the lands of the see. One charter of Malcolm IV[8] admits that the king had granted to his barons and knights lands from which the see had once drawn rents and *cain*. It was remarkable effrontery on the king's part to seek absolution for all royal transgressions against the church of Glasgow by presenting to it Kinclaith (Glasgow Green), which it had possessed at the time of the *Inquisitio* and which had, therefore, been taken from it in the intervening half century. Not all land passed from the see by royal "transgression." The church land in Annandale was granted to Robert Bruce the younger by Bishop John as a fief although, as David I himself was a

---

2. Simpson, "The Archives of the Medieval Church of Glasgow."
3. Barrow, *The Charters of King David I* [hereafter *Charters David I*], no. 15.
4. Barrow, "The Beginnings of Feudalism," 11, n. 1.
5. Barrow, "The Beginnings of Feudalism," 11–12.
6. Barrow, *Regesta Regum Scottorum*, [hereafter *RRS*], i, no. 131.
7. *Charters David I*, no. 177.
8. *RRS*, i, no. 265.

witness, royal prompting might be suspected.⁹ It is not impossible that the loss of the lands in Clydesdale came about in the same way. The loss of these lands probably explains the subsequent disputes over land and patronage. Bishops Ingram and Jocelin both came into conflict with the Bruce family over lands in Annandale,¹⁰ and Jocelin with Roger Valognes over the church of [East] Kilbride.¹¹ The bishops had to vindicate their claims to Hoddom on two separate occasions.¹² A dispute concerning the patronage of Hassendean between Jocelin and King William ended in both parties renouncing their claims in favor of Melrose Abbey.¹³ John, lord of Wilton, made good his claim to the patronage of the church of Wilton only by promising the bishop five merks of silver annually.¹⁴

Compensation for loss of territory was found in the numerous and generous benefactions made to the diocese. An important form of gift was possession of a church. The *Inquisitio* lists only three churches, namely those of Morebattle, Traquair, and Peebles, but a comparison of that document with successive papal confirmations of the possessions of the see shows that, when churches were built on the diocesan lands, their patronage remained in the bishop's hands, for example, Dryfesdale, Castlemilk, Hoddam, Ashkirk, Lilliesleaf, Ancrum, and Stobo.¹⁵ Hamilton and Old Roxburgh came from kings;¹⁶ Robert, bishop of St. Andrews, gave the church of Borthwick,¹⁷ but this grant was ineffective, as David I granted it to Scone Priory.¹⁸ Churches in Dumfriesshire came from Robert Bruce the younger,¹⁹ Carnwath from William Somerville,²⁰ two churches from earls of Lennox,²¹ Dalziel from the abbey of Paisley,²² and the church of

9. Shead, *Scottish Episcopal Acta* [hereafter *SEA*], i, no. 68.
10. *SEA*, i, no. 108.
11. *SEA*, i, no. 107.
12. *SEA*, i, no. 108; *Glas. Reg.*, i, no. 98.
13. *SEA*, i, nos. 94, 95.
14. *Glas. Reg.*, i, no. 100.
15. *Glas. Reg.*, i, nos. 26, 32.
16. *Charters David I*, no. 200; *RRS*, i, no. 114.
17. *SEA*, i, no. 124.
18. *RRS*, i, nos. 57, 243.
19. *SEA*, i, no. 108.
20. *Glas. Reg.*, i, no. 52.
21. *Glas. Reg.*, i, nos. 101, 108.
22. *Glas. Reg.*, i, no. 112.

Kirkbride in Nithsdale from a woman, Affrica of Nithsdale.[23] The names of some of the donors are, however, unknown, for our knowledge of Glasgow's possession of churches often depends on papal confirmations. It is not known, for example, who granted Durisdeer to Glasgow.[24] The value placed on the patronage of a church is indicated by an agreement over the church of Straiton. John, son of the earl of Carrick, granted the patronage of that church to the bishop of Glasgow; if he failed to make good his right to the patronage, John was to give land worth one hundred shillings a year instead.[25] It should be added that there were special circumstances in this case, for the earl had already granted Straiton to Paisley Abbey.[26] A case of the indirect acquisition of a church is that of Strathblane. It was annexed to the hospital of Polmadie,[27] presumably granted to it by one of the earls of Lennox since they claimed to present to the hospital[28] and had at one time been the patrons of Strathblane church.[29] The hospital and annexed church briefly formed a prebend from 1427–28 until the creation of the collegiate church of Dumbarton, when both were annexed to it.[30] There is no record of the direct granting of a church or patronage to Glasgow between 1244 and 1429.[31] An undated document of Bishop John Cameron, ascribed by Cosmo Innes to c. 1430, records the erection of six prebends, Cambuslang, Tarbolton, Eaglesham, Luss, Kirkmahoe, and Killearn, each with the approval of the local lord.[32] In the circumstances it may not be unreasonable to attribute these benefactions to the prompting of Bishop Cameron, an energetic bishop, who issued the fullest extant statutes for the cathedral,[33] and who wished to enhance its dignity by adding to the number of canons "ad . . . augmentacionem cultus divini."[34] These were the last examples of "external" grants

23. *Glas. Reg.*, i, no. 142.
24. Listed as a prebend in 1401. *Glas. Reg.*, i, no. 320.
25. *Glas. Reg.*, i, no. 187.
26. *Pais. Reg.*, pp. 427–28.
27. *Glas. Reg.*, ii, no. 338.
28. Cowan, *Medieval Religious Houses*, 152.
29. *OPS*, i, p. 46.
30. Cowan, "The Organization of Secular Cathedral Chapters," in Kirk, "The Medieval Church in Scotland," 85.
31. *Glas. Reg.*, i, nos. 187 and ii, 335, 336.
32. *Glas. Reg.*, ii, no. 340.
33. *Glas. Reg.*, ii, no. 341.
34. *Glas. Reg.*, ii, no. 344.

of churches; the last grant, the addition of the church of Glencairn to the canons' revenues, was made by Bishop William Turnbull.[35] This was a controversial benefaction. While the patron, Alexander Cunningham of Kilmaurs, was a ward of the king, Turnbull appointed Thomas McGuffock as rector; McGuffock then agreed to Turnbull's plan to annex its revenues to the mensa of the canons.[36] On the bishop's death, Cunningham tried to regain the parish, and attempts were made to seize the church and its property.[37] On the other hand, Turnbull seems to have alienated the church of Lilliesleaf for the benefit of a relative, Robert Turnbull, and the chapter had to petition Pope Sixtus IV in order to recover it.[38] This case provides an example of the process of formal possession of a church. A canon, Mr. John Brown, was appointed procurator on behalf of the dean and chapter;[39] he then "took real possession of the church of Lilliesleaf by entering the main door with the key of the same, touching the baptismal font and also the chalice, books and other ornaments . . . as is customarily done in such cases."[40]

The possession of churches brought valuable revenues to the see in the shape of teinds. Normally included in grants among "all the rightful pertinents"[41] of the church, the teinds were sometimes mentioned separately, for example, when the churches of Cardross and of Kirkbride (Nithsdale) were given to Glasgow.[42] A patron might grant the teinds alone, as William Somerville did on one occasion.[43] For the period when such benefactions were most numerous, the twelfth and thirteenth centuries, the types of teind reflect a predominantly rural economy. As defined by successive royal acts enjoining their payment, they consisted of corn, flax, wool, cheese, butter, lambs, calves, piglets, horses, and foals.[44] David I granted to Glasgow all the teinds of his orchards, and of fat from the slaughtering of his animals in Teviotdale.[45] He also granted all the

35. *Glas. Reg.*, ii, nos. 357, 358, 376.
36. Durkan, *William Turnbull*, 28.
37. Durkan, *William Turnbull*, 53.
38. *Glas. Reg.*, ii, no. 423.
39. *Glas. Reg.*, ii, no. 424.
40. *Glas. Reg.*, ii, no. 425.
41. For this phrase see e.g., *Glas. Reg.*, i, no. 101.
42. *Glas. Reg.*, i, nos. 108, 142.
43. *Glas. Reg.*, i, no. 16.
44. *RRS*, i, no. 258; *RRS*, ii, nos. 179, 507.
45. *Charters David I*, no. 42.

teinds of his cain in cattle and pigs in Renfrewshire and Ayrshire, and one-eighth of the profits of justice throughout Cumbria.[46] One-eighth was a generous fraction, since one-tenth was much more common.[47] Even these latter emoluments were not always paid in coin and, if we follow Bishop Dowden's interpretation of the phrase *aut in denariis aut in pecunia* as "either in money or cattle" would include the goods of the convicted.[48] The resistance which might be offered to the payment of teinds is shown by two documents, in which the lord of Carrick and the earl of Lennox admit their liability to teinds, and promise to compel their vassals and tenants to pay, confiscating their goods in the last resort.[49] There was a decline in gifts of churches or teinds from about the middle of the thirteenth century. A form of substitute may be seen in the diversion to the see of revenues from a vicar's portion, for example, the four merks from the vicarage of Dalgarno granted by the abbot and convent of Holyrood in 1328.[50] The last example of an augmentation of the revenues of the see before the Reformation was the union of the perpetual vicarage of Dalziel to the mensa of the vicars choral in 1556.[51] This was not, however, a common type of gift.

The possession of land was, of course, a valuable source of income, and gifts of land continued regularly up to the sixteenth century. It is impossible to calculate the amount of land held by the see, for boundaries were rarely defined in documents, reliance being placed on perambulation by those trustworthy men who were likely to know the precise limits.[52] Occasionally a detailed description is included in a document[53] or recorded as a note in a register.[54] Isabella Valognes gave the land of Dalquhairn "as it is today or as it may be extended by the inspection (*per visum*) of trustworthy men."[55] Even the area of land is not always specified: often the form adopted is "the land of Auchincarroch" or "the holding lying on the western side of the High Street of Glasgow . . . between

   46. *Charters David I*, no. 57, 58.
   47. Stuart, *Exchequer Rolls*, i, lviii.
   48. Dowden, *Church*, 176, n.
   49. *Glas. Reg.*, i, nos. 139, 141.
   50. *Glas. Reg.*, i, no. 279.
   51. *Glas. Reg.*, ii, no. 525.
   52. E.g. *SEA*, i, no. 103.
   53. E.g. Theiner, *Vetera Monumenta*, no. CLXXXIX; *Melr. Lib.*, no. 298.
   54. E.g. *Glas. Reg.*, i, nos. 103, 104.
   55. *Glas. Reg.*, i, no. 199.

the holdings of Alexander Thomson to the south and John Currie to the north"[56] rather than "fifteen librates" or "three acres" of land.[57] No doubt an adequate description in the Middle Ages, names alone now give little indication of extent. Land granted to the Church was normally held in free alms, that is, free from all forms of service or burden.[58] The earliest grants bear such phrases as *in perpetuam elemosinam*;[59] the fully developed formula *in liberam puram et perpetuam elemosinam* does not occur in grants to Glasgow before 1200.[60] King William granted to Glasgow certain lands "free quit and absolved from every service and custom and secular exaction and the claim of all men."[61] The land granted by Isabella Valognes was to be held "without any intrinsic or forinsec service, and without any exaction or demand."[62] Some donors, however, insisted on their rights. Malcolm IV, granting Kinclaith, specified the obligation of military service in the royal army.[63] It may be suspected that this was the price which the see had to pay to recover territory which had once belonged to it. When granting land some individuals undertook to perform the feudal duties attached to it. Robert Line promised to be "responsible to the King for all services, customs and secular exactions and all forinsec service" due from the land of *Scrogges*.[64] Traditional grants of land virtually disappeared after the thirteenth century. The grant made by William Douglas, lord of Liddesdale, of "all that carucate of land which I had and held of Thomas Wishart in the *vill of Parva Nudref*" about the middle of the fourteenth century,[65] has an old-fashioned air when compared with other fourteenth-century benefactions. The see acquired virtually no land in that century, and when grants of land were resumed in the next century they were nearly all within towns. James II granted a holding in

56. *Glas. Reg.*, i, no. 177; ii, 485.

57. *Glas. Reg.*, i, nos. 199, 16.

58. Dowden, *Church*, 155.

59. *Charters David I*, no. 56.

60. *Glas. Reg.*, i, no. 115. For its use in a gift of money, also post-1200, see *Glas. Reg.* i, no. 92.

61. *RRS*, ii, no. 106.

62. *Glas. Reg.*, i, no. 199. For these forms of service see Poole, *The Obligations of Society*, 5.

63. *RRS*, i, no. 265.

64. *Glas. Reg.*, i, no. 88.

65. *Glas. Reg.*, i, no. 290.

Stirling which had been forfeited by Robert Livingstone,[66] and the archdeacon of Argyll one in Dumbarton.[67] The majority of such holdings lay in Glasgow; that these normally included buildings is shown by a document of 1494 which refers to "tenementum . . . noviter edificatum" and "tenementum edificatum per magistrum Thomam Forsyth."[68] Such tenements were acquired in Deanside;[69] in the Drygate;[70] in Royal Street (*via regia*), later called High Street (*magnus vicus*), defined as extending from the cathedral church to the market cross;[71] in the street of the rats (*vicus ratonum*), "commonly called Rottenrow";[72] and in the *via communis*.[73] Bishop John Laing bought a tenement in Edinburgh from a burgess of the town, granted it to the see, and secured a confirmation of the grant by James III.[74]

The total revenue of the see in 1561 was calculated to be £987-8-7.[75] The wealth of the see, however, was not calculated solely in terms of money from land, as the calculation of 1561 allows for renders in kind, and there were in addition specific grants of money. The latter were normally for some purpose connected with the cathedral's construction or upkeep,[76] the maintenance of the clergy,[77] and the provision of lights.[78] The earliest of these was David I's grant of 100/- from Hardingstone (Northants).[79] A grant of 2/- from the tax of the burgh of Renfrew by Walter son of Alan, prescribed Easter as the time of collection,[80] but thereafter Pentecost and Martinmas were the normal times of collection,[81] a fact confirmed by a document of 1446 which speaks of "the two customary times of the year,

66. *Glas. Reg.*, ii, no. 355.
67. *Glas. Reg.*, ii, no. 471.
68. *Glas. Reg.*, ii, no. 468.
69. *Glas. Reg.*, ii, no. 346.
70. *Glas. Reg.*, ii, no. 468.
71. *Glas. Reg.*, ii, nos. 367, 446.
72. *Glas. Reg.*, ii, no. 369.
73. *Glas. Reg.*, ii, no. 471.
74. *Glas. Reg.*, ii, nos. 411, 417, 419.
75. *Glas. Rent.*, 23 note.
76. *Charters David I*, no. 3.
77. *RRS*, ii, no. 426.
78. *RRS*, ii, no. 261.
79. *Charters David I*, no. 2.
80. *Glas. Reg.*, i, no. 20.
81. *Glas. Reg.*, i, nos. 31, 92, 121, 175, 184, 203.

namely at the feasts of Pentecost and of St. Martin in winter."[82] Money specifically for the building of the cathedral was obtained by a general appeal on two occasions. Towards the end of the twelfth century Bishop Jocelin established a fraternity under royal patronage for this purpose.[83] About the middle of the following century contributions for rebuilding the cathedral were treated as a matter of national importance: this good cause was to be publicized during mass in every parish church on Sundays and feast days from the beginning of Lent until Low Sunday, and an indulgence was offered to those who contributed to the scheme.[84] By the end of the fifteenth century the cathedral was receiving eighteen stones of wax for lights.[85] Grants might include common pasture or fishing rights; a developed formula of the twelfth century included rights "in wood and plain, waters and fishing rights, fields and pastures."[86] In the thirteenth century the bishop obtained a peat moss to supply fuel for his house at Ancrum.[87] There are two examples, one in the twelfth century and the other in the thirteenth, of the granting of serfs to Glasgow; in one case the serf, Gillemachoi of Kinclaith, was accompanied by his children.[88] Other, less tangible, concessions, which were of great economic value, were the creation of the burgh of Glasgow and the granting of an annual fair,[89] both at the instigation of Bishop Jocelin. Alexander II granted freedom of movement for trade to the bishop's burgesses or vassals, a concession which, as the rubric to this charter in the *Registrum Vetus* ("that the men of the bishop of Glasgow shall be free from toll throughout Scotland") shows, was prized as freeing them from toll.[90] The royal officers in Rutherglen were forbidden to levy tolls or customs in Glasgow, and the men of Dumbarton inhibited from preventing the men of the bishop of Glasgow from going to and from Argyll with merchandise.[91] In the late 1170s Bishop Jocelin decreed that if a canon died intestate

82. *Glas. Reg.*, ii, no. 348.
83. *RRS*, ii, no. 316.
84. Patrick, *Statutes*, 25.
85. *Glas. Reg.*, i, nos. 49, 98, 117, 136, 321; ii, 407, 427.
86. *Charters David I*, no. 56.
87. *Glas. Reg.*, i, no. 115.
88. *RRS*, ii. no. 192; *RRS*, iii, no. 106.
89. *RRS*, ii. nos. 190, 308.
90. *RRS*, iii, no. 283. I am grateful to Professor Keith Stringer for allowing me to see the texts of *RRS*, iii in advance of publication.
91. *RRS*, iv, pt. I, no. 272.

his books and vestments should pass to the cathedral.[92] There is no record of this provision being put into effect, but it may be surmised that some of the items listed in the cathedral inventory of 1431–32 came in this way, and certainly several books were bequeathed to the cathedral.[93] In 1320 Walter son of Gilbert gave a complete set of vestments for celebrant, deacon and sub-deacon, the chasuble, tunicle and dalmatic being of green cloth of Tars, a rich oriental fabric; in addition there were two altar cloths with silk frontals, three choir copes and surplices, a corporal and a sudary, a silver gilt chalice, two cruets, and a silver thurible. All these were to be used at the altar of the Blessed Virgin Mary in the lower church, but surprisingly the donor and his heirs retained some control over his gifts, which might be used in the chapel of St. Mary at Maychan on four important feasts in the year and in the chapel of St. Thomas the Martyr in Glasgow on the feasts of his martyrdom and his translation.[94] In 1430 Alan Stewart, lord of Darnley, gave a set of priest's vestments, the chasuble being of red velvet, with two embroidered altar cloths, a frontal and a pall. He, too, retained an interest, though less well defined, in his donations.[95] In 1401 Bishop Matthew de Glendonwyn decreed a taxation of the prebends to provide vestments and other ornaments for the cathedral,[96] and the inventory of 1431–32 catalogs vestments, ornaments, relics, jewels and books belonging to the cathedral. The only recorded addition to the cathedral vestments after this date is the gift of a cope for the chaplain serving the altar of St. Michael (1495).[97]

In the early thirteenth century three or five merks per annum seem to have been regarded as adequate provision for maintaining inferior clergy of the cathedral.[98] King William gave three merks to maintain a deacon and sub-deacon in the time of Bishop Jocelin but subsequently raised the sum to six merks;[99] to this Alexander II added four merks annually.[100] A group of documents relating to the 1360s and 1370s shows

92. *SEA*, i, no. 85.
93. *Glas. Reg.*, ii, no. 339. The inventory is discussed by Dowden in "Inventory of ornaments, etc.," 280–339.
94. *Glas. Reg.*, i, no. 267.
95. *Glas. Reg.*, ii, no. 337.
96. *Glas. Reg.*, i, no. 320.
97. *Glas. Reg.*, ii, no. 454.
98. *Glas. Reg.*, i, nos. 121, 184.
99. *RRS*, ii, no. 426.
100. *Glas. Reg.*, i, no. 175.

that by that period the usual sum had risen to ten or twelve merks;[101] unfortunately, it became common thereafter to endow chaplains with land in Glasgow, the annual revenue from which was unspecified in the documents, and thus it is impossible to continue a comparison beyond the 1370s. In a document dating from 1480, however, the dean and chapter agreed that in future vicars choral who received £5 per annum should have their stipends doubled.[102]

Many of the documents of the fifteenth and early sixteenth centuries relate to the endowment of chantry altars or chaplains, but the practice had begun much earlier. The thirteenth century was "the time when chantries began to be important, at any rate in Britain,"[103] and Alexander III endowed a chaplain to celebrate solemn mass and other divine offices at the altar of St. Kentigern for his ancestors. Robert Lauder, the father of Bishop William, provided for two anniversary services, one for himself and his wife and the other for his son the bishop, to be celebrated in the choir of the cathedral "with the vigil of the dead and sung mass."[104] Another example is that provided by George Hutchinson's foundation of an anniversary in 1471. On the feast of St. Catherine the martyr, the vicars were to sing the dirge of nine lessons; bells were to be rung, both in the church and through the town (presumably before the funeral procession); the hearse was to be lighted by candles in the choir. On the following day, the feast of St. Gregory, the requiem mass was to be sung. After the first washing of hands the celebrant was also to say the *De profundis* with the customary prayers and to urge the people to say the Our Father and Hail Mary for the departed.[105]

The most detailed example has survived in a document[106] not included in the *Registrum Episcopatus Glasguensis*. In 1539 Mark Jamieson, subsequently vicar of Kilspindie, made extensive arrangements for services on behalf of the souls of his uncles John and Alexander Paniter, the former of whom had been master of the song school and organist in the cathedral. Every evening the master of the song school and six, or at least

---

101. *Glas. Reg.*, i, nos. 297, 302, 308, 315.
102. *Glas. Reg.*, ii, no. 426.
103. Wood-Legh, *Perpetual Chantries*, 5.
104. *Glas. Reg.*, ii, no. 324.
105. *Glas. Reg.*, ii, no. 395; cf. no. 392.
106. *Glasgow Protocols*, iv, 116–23. The whereabouts of this document is not now known.

four, boys were to sing *Ave gloriosa*[107] and to say the psalm *De profundis* with the appropriate collect, while a wax taper burned before the altar of Our Lady in the lower church. If this duty were neglected three nights running, the vicar pensioner was to secure two celebrations of the requiem mass by the two priests of St. Mungo's altar. On the first of June each year the vicar pensioner was to arrange thirty-six celebrations of mass at the six altars in the lower church by vicars of the choir, who were to find substitutes if they had the duty of saying any other mass, and by the two chaplains of the altar of Our Lady, the two chaplains of St. Mungo's altar, the chaplain of St. Peter's altar and the vicar pensioner *in rure*. These celebrations were to be accomplished in two days, and the vicar pensioner was to organize the attendance of twenty-four poor householders who were to pray for the souls of the Paniters. Six poor scholars were to keep the six altars and to assist at the celebrations, during which two wax tapers were to burn above John Paniter's tomb, which was situated beside that of Bishop Laing. St. Mungo's bell was to be rung through the town on the night before, and on the morning of, these celebrations. The same arrangements were to obtain on the feast of Sts. Cosmas and Damian. Finally, each Sunday after saying mass, the vicar pensioner, vested in an alb, was to say the psalms *Miserere mei deus* and *De profundis* at the tomb of John Paniter, and to pray for the souls of John and Alexander. This benefaction was to be put into effect only on the founder's death, but long before that event the Church had undergone the religious revolution of 1560 which, by forbidding the celebration of mass, nullified chantry foundations.[108]

The motives for which these benefactions were made are mentioned in some charters. Usually they were made for the souls of deceased relatives or ancestors, and the donor's soul and those of his successors were also included, for "at the basis of all medieval pious foundations there lies the idea of continuous intercession for the living and the departed."[109] The most complete example is contained in a charter of Alwin, earl of Lennox, who recorded the gift of the church of Campsie "for the souls of King David and Earl Henry and King Malcolm and for the health of my

---

107. The printed version is *"ane gloriosa."* Professor Stones suggested that this is a misreading of *ave gloriosa*. The likelihood of this is shown by the phrase "unam antiphonam gloriose Virginis Marie" viz. "Ave Gloriosa vel Salve Regina . . . " in *Glas. Reg.*, ii, 505.

108. *Glasgow Protocols*, iv, 121 note.

109. Hamilton Thompson, *The English Clergy*, 132.

lord King William and my lady Queen Ermengarde and my lord Alexander their son and all their ancestors, and for our health and that of all our heirs, and for the souls of all our ancestors and successors."[110] Guilty consciences, however, prompted a number of benefactions. Malcolm IV granted Kinclaith for remission and absolution of all royal transgressions against the church of Glasgow.[111] King William gave *Balain*, confessing that he, and his men acting on his behalf, had committed excesses against the see after the death of Bishop Ingram,[112] perhaps a reference to some abuse of the King's right to the temporalities of the see during a vacancy. John, son of Duncan, earl of Carrick, granted *Hachinclohyn* in reparation for injuries done to churches in the diocese during the "war in Galloway."[113] John de Vaux gave five marks annually for the maintenance of a chaplain in the cathedral "on account of a certain offence committed by us."[114]

The founding of chantries merely expressed in the most formal way the donor's belief that "he and his should be remembered daily at that altar, and that the salvation of their souls and their deliverance from the cleansing fires of purgatory should be constant topics of prayer."[115] In 1494 the subdean of Glasgow founded a new chaplaincy at the altar of St. John Baptist "because we believe sins to be banished, the pains of purgatory to be mitigated, and the souls of the departed more frequently to be set free from those pains and translated to the joys of paradise, by pious prayers and especially by continual celebrations of masses in which the Son of God is offered to the Father for our sins."[116]

The most striking feature which emerges from an analysis of benefactions to the see in the twelfth century is the predominance of royal gifts. Up to 1165 seven out of nine or ten[117] were from the king, and six of these were from David I.[118] This trend continued until c. 1200, all but one[119] of King William's gifts being before that date. Royal grants included

110. *Glas. Reg.*, i, no. 101.
111. *RRS*, i, no. 265.
112. *RRS*, ii, no. 192 .
113. *RRS*, iii, no. 301.
114. *Glas. Reg.*, i, no. 184.
115. Hamilton Thompson, *The English Clergy*, 132.
116. *Glas. Reg.*, ii, no. 468.
117. The gift of Walter, son of Alan, can be dated only as ante-1177.
118. *Charters David I*, nos. 3, 56, 34, 200, 57, 58.
119. *RRS*, ii, no. 261.

one carucate from the royal demesne at Roxburgh, a toft in Dumfries, and one toft in each of the royal burghs of Montrose, Forfar and Stirling.[120] Other benefactors before 1200 were mainly noblemen: William Somerville, Walter, son of Alan, the Steward, and a royal bastard Robert of London.[121] There was only one ecclesiastical donor, namely Robert bishop of St. Andrews, and one man of humbler rank, probably a knight, Ralph Nanus. The thirteenth century contrasts remarkably with the twelfth in this respect. Royal action was generally confined to the confirmation of previous grants[122] or to extending secular support to the bishop.[123] Alexander II granted to the see the privilege of possessing its lands round Glasgow in free forest.[124] His only tangible gifts were four merks annually from the ferme of the royal demesne at Hamilton, and the land of Mosplatt.[125] The same characteristic is discernible in the reigns of Alexander III and John: there were confirmations,[126] and the repetition of royal support for the bishop of Glasgow and his men, for example, in a brieve directed to the burgh of Dumbarton.[127] but only one really new gift, namely, the grant by Alexander III of 100/- from Rutherglen to maintain a priest in the cathedral.[128] King John's only benefaction to the see was to turn his mother's gift of land in Ayrshire into a holding in free forest.[129] Donors in the thirteenth century included the earls of Lennox and Buchan,[130] other noblemen,[131] men of lesser social degree,[132] a sheriff,[133] the abbots of Kilwinning and Paisley,[134] and several noble widows.[135] There was, however, a distinct decline in benefactions to the see after c. 1230. During the war

120. *Charters David I*, no. 42; *RRS*, ii, nos. 216, 210, 283, 325.
121. *Glas. Reg.*, i, nos. 16, 52, 20, 49.
122. *RRS*, iii, nos. 80, 81, 102.
123. *RRS*, iii, nos. 107, 283
124. *RRS*, iii, no. 258.
125. *RRS*, iii, nos. 293, 256.
126. *RRS*, iv, pt I, nos. 17, 108.
127. *RRS*, iv, pt I, no. 272.
128. *RRS*, iv, pt I, no. 148.
129. *Glas. Reg.*, i, no. 250.
130. *Glas. Reg.*, i, nos. 101, 108, 117.
131. *Glas. Reg.*, i, nos. 100, 184, 203.
132. *Glas. Reg.*, i, nos. 88, 115, 184.
133. *Glas. Reg.*, i, no. 121.
134. *Glas. Reg.*, i, nos. 98, 112.
135. *RRS*, iv, pt. 1, no. 108.

of independence there was virtually none, and certainly no church or land was added to the see.

Recorded benefactions to the see in the fourteenth century are surprisingly few, the last quarter of the century being virtually blank. Of the kings, only Robert I was mindful of the interests of the see, but many of his charters are simply the renewal of grants by his predecessors,[136] a fact which suggests that the war had interrupted customary payments. The king's only new grant to the see, was to allow the prebend of Barlanark to be held in free warren,[137] a concession requiring no expenditure on the part of the Crown. The donors of the fourteenth century were drawn from the same categories as those of the thirteenth, including the abbot of Holyrood, the earl of Strathearn, and two noble widows.[138] The lesser landowners had, however, become the most frequent benefactors of the see.[139]

Royal benefactions returned in the fifteenth century with James II, who was a canon of the cathedral.[140] Apart from founding the university in collaboration with Bishop Turnbull,[141] James granted to the see a tenement in Stirling and to the bishop the holding of the city, barony and bishop's forest in regality.[142] An ostensible benefaction by James II, the granting to Bishop Turnbull of £100 a year from "the farms, revenues and profits of all royal lands in Bute, Arran, Cowal with the great burgh customs of Ayr, Irvine, and Dumbarton,"[143] was in fact merely a method of repaying a loan of 800 merks from the bishop.[144] Two confirmations by James III[145] and a grant of land by James IV completed royal benefactions; the latter cost the king nothing, for the land in question had been surrendered into the king's hands on the same day by John, lord Semple.[146] The pattern of the fourteenth century is repeated in the first

136. *RRS, v,* nos. 50, 52, 53, 54.
137. *RRS, v.,* no. 209.
138. *Glas. Reg.,* i, nos. 279, 302, 277, 321.
139. *Glas. Reg.,* i, nos. 267, 275, 290, 297, 308, 315.
140. *Glas. Reg.,* ii, no. 356. The custom whereby rulers might be canons is paralleled in France, Spain, and the Empire. Dowden, *Church,* 85.
141. Durkan, *William Turnbull,* 36–38.
142. *Glas. Reg.,* ii, nos. 355, 356.
143. *The Register of the Great Seal,* ii, no. 542.
144. Durkan, *William Turnbull,* 48.
145. *Glas. Reg.,* ii, nos. 407, 419.
146. *Glas. Reg.,* ii, no. 482.

three-quarters of the fifteenth. The lesser landowners again predominate, partly because five representatives of this group were involved in the erection of six prebends during the episcopate of John Cameron, with whom possibly lay the initiative for this action. The last magnate to make a grant to the see was Archibald, earl of Douglas, who agreed to the erection of the church of Cambuslang into a prebend (1429).[147] There are no benefactions by abbots, but several members of the chapter make their appearance, usually as benefactors of the cathedral or its clergy and often in connection with the endowment of chantries.[148] Two burgesses made grants of revenue from land in the city.[149] Land in Edinburgh was bought by the bishop and chapter, and the chaplain of the altar of Sts. Stephen and Laurence bought annual revenues of 5/- and 2/- from two Glasgow couples in 1487.[150] From the mid-1470s the benefactors are almost exclusively clerics: several canons of Glasgow, a canon of Ross, archdeacons of Argyll, Glasgow, and Whithorn, two deans, a chancellor and a sub-dean of Glasgow, and the vicar of Cadder.[151] Archbishop Robert Blacader built the altar of the glorious Virgin Mary of Pity on the south side of the entrance into the choir, and endowed a chaplaincy at it. The ascription of the northern altar, that of the Holy Name, to the archbishop depended on an incorrect text in the *Registrum Episcopatus Glasguensis*; a better text, preserved in the *Register of the Great Seal*, shows that he merely repaired the altar and endowed a third chaplaincy at it, and that it had existed before his episcopate.[152] It might be added in support of this that the surviving western faces of the altar platforms display differences of detail in ornamentation, and that one has five panels and the other six, although they are very similar in general appearance. He founded two other chaplaincies: the first of the glorious Virgin Mary of Consolation at the altar of St. John the Baptist in the nave, and the second in honor of St. Kentigern at the altar founded by his brother, Sir Patrick Blacader of Tulliallan, near the tomb of the saint in the lower church.[153] The clerical character of these benefactions in the last three-quarters of a century of

147. *Glas. Reg.*, ii, nos. 340, 335.

148. *Glas. Reg.*, ii, nos. 346, 348, 369, 379.

149. *Glas. Reg.*, ii, nos. 386, 395.

150. *Glas. Reg.*, ii, nos. 447, 449.

151. *Glas. Reg.*, ii, nos. 446, 455, 476, 480, 481, 454, 485, 451, 468, 473, 495, 489.

152. *Glas. Reg.*, ii, no. 482. See McRoberts, "The Blacader Choir Screen" (Chapter 9 of the present volume).

153. *Glas. Reg.*, ii, nos. 482, 486.

the life of the medieval diocese of Glasgow was undoubtedly a symptom of the ills affecting the Scottish Church in general: if goodwill on the part of the laity remained it was no longer expressed in frequent benefactions, and more and more of the Church's revenue was directed towards multiplying chaplaincies and obit services.

It is possible that declining lay benefactions were due to a decline in the cult of St. Kentigern. The cult was stimulated in the twelfth century by the commissioning by Bishop Herbert and Bishop Jocelin of lives of the saint,[154] and was presumably connected with the construction and rebuilding of the cathedral. There is no evidence of national interest in local Scottish saints, such as Kentigern, in the fourteenth century.[155] In the fifteenth century there seems to have been a revival of interest in Scottish saints, and it is possible that an attempt was made in Glasgow to revive the cult of St. Kentigern: in 1420 Bishop Lauder sought permission to move the feretory of the saint to another part of the cathedral, and Archbishop Blacader's proposed two-story addition to the south transept was almost certainly intended as a setting for the shrine.[156] The only king known to have made an offering at the shrine was Edward I of England;[157] the Treasurer's Accounts and the Exchequer Rolls reveal no royal offerings at Glasgow, though James IV often made gifts to Whithorn. The shrine of St. Kentigern does not feature very prominently in the late medieval religious life of Scotland and this suggests that attempts to revive the cult were not wholly successful: perhaps it is symbolic that Blacader's extension to the south transept was never completed.

---

154. Forbes, *Lives of St. Ninian and St. Kentigern*.

155. McRoberts, "The Scottish Church and Nationalism," 8. This view has now been superseded: see Ditchburn, "The 'McRobert's Thesis'" in Boardman, *The Cult of Saints*.

156. McRoberts, "The Scottish Church and Nationalism," 9–10.

157. *Glas. Reg.*, ii, no. 548.

6

Jocelin, Abbot of Melrose (1170–74), and Bishop of Glasgow (1175–99)

NORMAN F. SHEAD

Guidebooks to Glasgow Cathedral talk about how the twelfth-century bishop Jocelin "gloriously enlarged" the cathedral. Today, only one remaining fragment of this building remains (in the lower church) but, as Norman Shead explains, Jocelin made his mark in many other ways. He not only defended the independence of his church from the Archbishop of York by securing a papal bull declaring that Glasgow was directly subject to the Pope, but secured from King William I the status of burgh for Glasgow and the right to hold a fair annually in July, which is still a public holiday in the city today.

Seal of Bishop Jocelin (1175-99) from Robert Renwick's "Glasgow Memorials."

THE YEAR 1999 SAW the eight hundredth anniversary of the death of one of the most influential figures in the history of Glasgow: Jocelin, bishop from 1175 to 1199. Yet, as far as I know, the event passed entirely unremarked. The founder of the burgh of Glasgow and initiator of Glasgow Fair (still observed, though in a rather different way) is commemorated in Glasgow by one place-name, Jocelyn Square. Even the celebration in 1975 of the eight hundredth anniversary of Glasgow's burgh charter (1175 x 1178) concentrated on the charter rather than its recipient. However, in his time Jocelin was a figure of national importance, active in defending the independence of the Scottish Church against the claims of the English Church and in serving both king and pope. He therefore deserves to be better known.[1]

FAMILY AND EARLY CAREER

As is the case with most people of the twelfth century, the year of Jocelin's birth is unknown. There are, however, two clues which might allow an

---

1. I am grateful to Professor A. A. M. Duncan for reading and commenting on a draft of this article. He has saved me from at least one blunder; I must take responsibility for errors that remain. My debt to his published work will be clear from the following footnotes.

approximate date to be suggested. The first is a letter written by Abbot R. of Melrose, presumably Ralf, abbot from 1194 to 1202 and later bishop of Down, and presumably composed on Jocelin's death in 1199.[2] I suggest that this letter was to be circulated among Cistercian houses with the intention of having Jocelin's name inserted in their mortuary rolls, especially as it is specific about the date of his death. It also gives us most of the little personal information that we have about Jocelin himself. The second clue is provided by the Cistercian rules about age of admission to the novitiate. Ralf says that Jocelin was *inpubes* when he came to Melrose.[3] Although this must be an imprecise guide to Jocelin's age,[4] Ralf's purpose was to illustrate Jocelin's enthusiasm for joining the Cistercian order; it may therefore be assumed that Jocelin came to Melrose about the age that Cistercian customs allowed admission to the novitiate. He came in the time of Abbot Waltheof (1148–59);[5] he received the habit as a novice on March 17 in an unspecified year about fifty years before 1199, and was professed as a monk on March 29 after a year of probation as a novice.[6] His arrival at Melrose may be placed therefore about 1149 or 1150. Since no-one could be admitted to the novitiate before the age of fifteen,[7] and if Jocelin became a novice in 1149, his year of birth seems to have been 1134 or thereabouts.

The name Jocelin was not uncommon in the twelfth century, and not only among clerics; this suggests that this was his baptismal name rather than one taken on entering the religious life. It, and the names of his brothers, Henry and Helia[8] and of his nephew, also Helia,[9] suggest a family of Anglo-French origin or a "native" family which had adopted more fashionable names. The grant of the church of Dunsyre to Kelso Abbey by his brother Helia[10] shows a family settled in lowland Scotland. Although Abbot Ralf stresses Jocelin's youth, he does not suggest an arduous long journey to bring Jocelin to Melrose; if there had been such

2. Printed in Forbes, *Lives of St Ninian and St Kentigern*, 308–12 [hereafter Letter]. For text, translation and commentary see Knott, *Apologia for Bishop Jocelin*.
3. Letter, 310.
4. Cf. Clanchy, *Abelard*, 173–74.
5. Letter, 310.
6. Letter, 312.
7. Canivez, *Statuta Capitulorum*, i. 31.
8. *Liber S. Marie de Calchou* [hereafter *Kel. Lib.*], ii, 414, 356.
9. *Liber Sancte Marie de Melros* [hereafter *Melr. Lib.*], i, 70.
10. *Kel. Lib.* ii, 356.

a journey, Ralf would surely have used it to emphasize further Jocelin's desire to become a Cistercian.

Very little is known of Jocelin's sojourn in Melrose Abbey. A close relationship with Abbot Waltheof developed and the abbot gradually committed to him virtually the whole administration of the monastery.[11] Presumably what is referred to here is Jocelin's promotion as prior, the office which he held when elected abbot in 1170.[12] That he became prior during Waltheof's time is all the more likely since relations with Abbot William, Waltheof's successor, were not good.[13] Since Waltheof died in 1159, Jocelin must have obtained the office of prior at a very early age.

It is understandable that Jocelin was keen to see Waltheof canonized (though ironically he never was).[14] Apart from the affection between the two men, it would do much for the reputation and income of the abbey. Miracles were needed. The hagiographer Jocelin of Furness records several examples of cures at Waltheof's tomb.[15] The numbers visiting the tomb in search of cures grew, and Abbot William, worried about disturbance to the life of the community, ordered that the sick should be kept away from the tomb.[16] It would be surprising if this policy did not bring the abbot into conflict with Jocelin and perhaps also with the convent in general. It may well have been this situation which caused William to resign. The speed with which Jocelin was elected to succeed him—on the same day, April 22, 1170[17]—supports such an opinion.

It has been argued that Jocelin's time as abbot had an important influence on the abbey's chronicle: that he commissioned that part of the chronicle covering 731 to 1170 and that he entrusted a monk called Reinald with the keeping of the contemporary annals.[18]

However, the only public action of Abbot Jocelin which has been recorded was a grand ceremony on June 22, 1171.[19] Jocelin intended to

11. Letter, 310.

12. Anderson, *The Chronicle of Melrose* [hereafter *Chron. Melrose*], 38.

13. McFadden, *Life of Waldef,* [hereafter *Life*], 341. The discovery of another manuscript of the *Life* (Madrid, Biblioteca del Palacio Real, II, 2097, folios. 41v–68) points to the need for a new edition. I am grateful to Professor Robert Bartlett for this reference.

14. Farmer, *The Oxford Dictionary of Saints*, 430.

15. *Life*, 334–40.

16. *Life*, 341.

17. Anderson, *Chronicle of Melrose* [hereafter *Chron. Melr.*], 38.

18. Duncan, "Sources and Uses of the Chronicle of Melrose," 150.

19. *Chron. Melr.*, 39.

replace the stone marking Waltheof's grave, which was situated at the entrance to the chapter house,[20] with a finer one of marble. There was a large gathering of prelates for the occasion, the main figures being Bishop Ingram of Glasgow and four abbots; only one of the abbots was named, Hardred of Calder, but another was the abbot of Kelso,[21] whom we know to have been John (1161–80). While the community watched, the stone was removed and the corpse, subjected to a vigorous physical inspection by the bishop, was found to be incorrupt, a sure sign of sanctity.[22] What Jocelin may have done to promote Waltheof's canonization during his remaining three years as abbot is quite unknown; any campaign on Waltheof's behalf was cut short by Jocelin's election as bishop of Glasgow on May 23, 1174.[23] Thereafter, to the regret of Waltheof's biographer,[24] he turned his attention to St. Kentigern and Glasgow.

ECCLESIASTICAL AND SECULAR POLITICS

Jocelin's election as bishop of Glasgow took place at Perth. According to the Melrose Chronicle, he was elected by the clergy, by popular demand and with the assent of the king.[25] The pope was told that he had been elected by the dean and chapter;[26] if so, then the election was probably formally made by *compromissarii*[27] so that the whole chapter did not have to travel to Perth. The choice of Perth was surely to allow the king to oversee the election.[28] The role of the people, if indeed the phrase was not simply a formality based on older canon law, can only be guessed at, especially as the influence of lay people other than the ruler was frowned on in the later twelfth century. Pope Alexander III wrote: "although for the election of a bishop the favor and assent of the prince should be requested, yet laymen should not be admitted to the election. But the election is to be held by the canons of the cathedral church and

---

20. *Chron. Melr.*, 87.
21. *Life*, 341–42.
22. *Life*, 232–33.
23. *Chron. Melr.*, 41.
24. *Life*, 344.
25. *Chron. Melr.*, 41.
26. Somerville, *Scotia Pontificia*, [hereafter *Scot Pont.*], no. 69.
27. Duncan, *Scotland: the Making of the Kingdom*, 277 n. 38.
28. Dowden, *The Bishops of Scotland*, 298.

the religious men from the city and diocese."[29] The king was therefore expected to have a say, at least. The *acta* of King William do not confirm his presence in Perth on the date of the election, but several acts show that the king was there at some time or times in the 1170s.[30] The choice of Jocelin might be attributed to his connection with Waltheof, the king's half-uncle. Cistercian bishops were rare in both England[31] and Scotland. Jocelin was only the second Cistercian to become bishop of a Scottish see (Simon de Tosny, a relative of the king, was elected bishop of Moray in 1171). However, Jocelin's election cannot be ascribed to a partiality for the Cistercian order on the part of the king, for only two more Cistercians were elected during William's long reign: Reinald to Ross in 1195[32] and Adam, abbot of Melrose, to Caithness in 1213.[33] Moreover, William's major monastic foundation, Arbroath, dedicated to St. Thomas Becket, was not Cistercian.[34] However, the king's choice may have been influenced by support for Becket on the part of the Cistercian order in general and by a number of abbeys in particular,[35] and by Cistercian propaganda in favor of his canonization.[36]

A Cistercian abbot had to seek the approval of the Cistercian General Chapter, before he could accept election,[37] and was required to attend the annual meeting of the Chapter, held in September.[38] Thus there are two reasons to suppose that in September 1174 Jocelin was at Citeaux. It is therefore possible that, as has been asserted,[39] Jocelin was present at Clairvaux on 13 October, 1174 when the newly enlarged monastic church was dedicated and St Bernard's body temporarily reburied

---

29. Morris, *The Papal Monarchy*, 224.

30. Barrow, *Regesta Regum Scottorum, vol. ii*, [hereafter *RRS*, ii], nos. 138, 148–53.

31. There were only two in twelfth-century England: Knowles, *Monastic Order*, 710.

32. On Reinald see Watt, *Series Episcoporum*, 73–74.

33. Shead, *Fasti* [hereafter *Fasti*], 77.

34. Queen Ermengarde was involved in the foundation of the Cistercian house of Balmerino, but as joint founder with her son, Alexander II, and not until the 1220s.

35. Barlow, *Thomas Becket*, 144–45, 157, 184.

36. Morris, *Papal Monarchy*, 235.

37. *Letter*, 310 cf. Canivez, *Statuta Capitulorum*, i, 22.

38. Hourlier, *Le Chapitre General*, 65, 66–67. I owe this reference to Professor Dauvit Broun.

39. Duncan, "St Kentigern at Glasgow Cathedral," 10.

pending a more worthy tomb.[40] By 16 December, 1174 Jocelin had confirmation of his election from Pope Alexander III, who ordered that if Jocelin could not come to the pope he should nevertheless be consecrated.[41] At Clairvaux, appropriately a Cistercian house, he was consecrated by Eskil, archbishop of Lund and papal legate.[42] Consecration by the pope or a papal legate marked twelfth-century bishops of Glasgow out from other Scottish bishops.[43] Glasgow seems to have been regarded as an entity different from the other sees under the rule of the king of Scots.[44] The ground of that difference, certainly as Glasgow clerics saw it, was that the bishops of Glasgow were the successors of the bishops of the defunct kingdom of Cumbria, geographically and politically between England and Scotland, "ethnically distinct," in which the bishop had been the source of royal power.[45] The date of Jocelin's consecration is unknown, but must have fallen between December 16, 1174 and March 15, 1175 when the pope addressed him as bishop rather than as elect.[46] Jocelin was reported by the pope on April 10, 1175 as having returned to Scotland,[47] and was at Melrose on May 23 to bless his successor as abbot.[48]

Jocelin was soon involved in two important issues: the freedom of the Scottish Church from subjection to the archbishop of York, and the king's quarrel with the papacy over the bishopric of St. Andrews.[49] As a result of his capture at Alnwick in July 1174, King William was obliged

---

40. Vacandard, Vie de Saint Bernard, ii, 549. The body of Malachy of Armagh (not yet canonized), beside whom Bernard had chosen to be buried, was moved at the same time: C. Waddell, "The Two Malachy Offices from Clairvaux," 131.

41. Scot Pont., no. 63.

42. Chron. Melr., 31.

43. Watt, Series Episcoporum, passim. Even though the evidence for consecrations is incomplete, it is clear that there is no parallel.

44. Scot Pont., no. 8.

45. Broun, "The Welsh Identity of the Kingdom of Strathclyde," and the remark by Ralph d'Escures, archbishop of Canterbury, to Calixtus II in 1119 that the bishop of Glasgow "est antiquorum Britonum episcopus": Raine, Historians of the Church of York, ii, 241.

46. Scot. Pont., no. 74. Both the Holyrood Chronicle, which began the year on December 25, and the Melrose Chronicle place the consecration in 1175: Anderson, A Scottish Chronicle, 24, 159; Chron. Melr., 41.

47. Scot. Pont., no. 75.

48. Chron. Melr., 41.

49. On both see Barrell, "The Background to Cum Universi" and Broun, "The Church and the origins of Scottish independence."

to accept the Treaty "of Falaise." The king had to agree that the Scottish Church should be subject to the English church. Although the language was ambiguous ("as it should do"; "which it lawfully should"), the king also had to agree that the bishops who were not present when the treaty was made should swear allegiance to Henry II.[50] As a result, Jocelin and other Scottish notables, both clerics and laymen, were obliged to take an oath of fealty to Henry II and his son, the Young King, at York on August 10, 1175.[51] In January 1176 the Scottish king and prelates were summoned by Henry II to a council at Northampton.[52] To Henry's demand that they should be subject to the English Church, the Scots prelates replied that they had never been subject to the English Church. Roger of Pont l'Eveque, the archbishop of York, brandishing papal bulls, retorted that the bishop of Glasgow specifically, and certain other bishops of Scotland had been subject to him.[53] Jocelin, however, had a trick up his sleeve: a bull of Alexander III of April or February 1175 declaring the church of Glasgow to be "our special daughter with no intermediary";[54] he therefore argued that Glasgow was subject to no bishop or archbishop, whatever might have been the case in the past.[55] Exempt status was not new in Scotland, for in 1165 Abbot John of Kelso had secured the same privilege for his house,[56] the first Scottish prelate to do so. Although *nullo mediante* was the commonest formula used by Pope Alexander to define the exempt status of monasteries, the phrase *filia specialis* was also used.[57] This was a rare privilege for an individual see outside Italy.[58] Jocelin significantly did not argue that this privilege extended to all the Scottish bishops, for it applied solely to Glasgow. The day was saved, however, by a dispute between the archbishops of Canterbury and York over their respective claims over the Scottish Church,[59] a dispute perhaps quite deliberately engineered by Canterbury to undermine York's position. Thus

50. Stones, *Anglo-Scottish Relations 1174–1328*, no. I.
51. Lawrie, *Annals of the Reigns of Malcolm and William* [hereafter *AMW*], 201–2.
52. *AMW*, 206–7.
53. *AMW*, 207.
54. *Scot. Pont.*, no. 76.
55. *AMW*, 207.
56. *Scot. Pont.*, no. 59.
57. Robinson, *The Papacy*, 234–45.
58. One in Germany, one in France and four in Spain: see Grant, *Medieval Scotland*, 140 note 2.
59. *AMW*, 207–8.

the council broke up, and the Scots bishops quickly sent messengers to the pope.[60] Although the bull *Super anxietatibus* of July 30, 1176 does not contain the phrase *filia specialis*, it denounced Henry II's attempts to secure the subjection of the Scottish Church as an affront to God and the papacy and as an impertinent lay interference in ecclesiastical affairs, and declared that the obedience of the Scottish bishops was due to the pope alone until York could prove his right. Significantly, the text of the bull was preserved in the register of Glasgow Cathedral.[61] The Scots could brand Henry II as the author of the Constitutions of Clarendon and the murderer of Becket,[62] and Archbishop Roger as the martyr's "most relentless enemy."[63] Even then the Scots' position may not have been secure: it has been suggested that Jocelin secured a renewal of the *filia specialis* bull in 1179 because King William's quarrel with the papacy threatened a review of policy by the pope,[64] or by the Third Lateran Council.[65] Jocelin thought it prudent to have this exempt status confirmed by Lucius III in 1182 and by Urban III in 1186.[66] There is no record of subsequent confirmations: the next pope, Gregory VIII, lived rather less than two months after his election, and there would have been no time to ask him to renew the privilege, but there is no record of a renewal by Clement III (1189-91): the danger seemed to have passed.[67]

The dispute over the bishopric of St. Andrews between the elected John the Scot and the king's nominee, Hugh, which began in late 1178 or early 1179, led King William into confrontation with the papacy and to the excommunication of the king and an interdict on the kingdom. The deaths of Pope Alexander and of Archbishop Roger of York, one of those who had excommunicated the king, made compromise easier. In 1182 Jocelin was chosen, along with the abbots of Melrose and Kelso and the prior of Inchcolm, and possibly the abbot of Dunfermline, to go to Rome

---

60. *AMW,* 208.

61. *Registrum Episcopatus Glasguensis* [hereafter *Glas. Reg.*], i, no. 38 = *Scot. Pont.,* no. 80.

62. Duncan, *Scotland,* 264.

63. Knowles, *Episcopal Colleagues,* 14.

64. *Scot. Pont.,* no. 110; Barrell, "The Background to *Cum Universi,*" 120-2.

65. Durkan, "Glasgow Diocese," 101.

66. *Scot. Pont.,* nos. 111, 135.

67. This seems to support Dr. Barrell's suggestion that it was Clement III rather than Celestine III who first issued the bull *Cum Universi.*

and plead the king's case.[68] They came to the new pope, Lucius III, during the brief time when he was in Rome itself (November 1181–March 1182),[69] and at the Lateran palace secured absolution for the king and the lifting of the interdict,[70] though the bull subsequently recording these events had to be issued at Velletri.[71] "How they argued, what bags of gold they may have opened, we do not know."[72] If gold changed hands, it is unlikely that the pope was aware of it, since he had been one of only two cardinals reckoned by Becket not to be open to bribery.[73] Perhaps Jocelin and the abbot of Melrose spoke as Cistercians to another Cistercian (if indeed Lucius was a Cistercian, for the point is uncertain).[74] Jocelin and the abbot of Kelso took the opportunity to secure a restatement of their churches' direct dependence on the papacy.[75] The Scots prelates returned with a gift from the pope for King William, the golden rose which Lucius carried on Laetare Jerusalem Sunday and which he would normally have presented to the prefect of Rome: no doubt it was his hasty departure from Rome which gave him the opportunity of sending it to the king.[76] This was not, however, the end of the dispute over St. Andrews: in 1186 Jocelin and the abbots of Melrose, Newbattle and Dunfermline, on the authority of Pope Urban III, excommunicated the intransigent Bishop Hugh,[77] and papal letters continued to be addressed to Jocelin and other prelates until Hugh's death in 1188.[78] At one point in the negotiations about the conflicting claims to St. Andrews, it was proposed that the rival bishops should give up St. Andrews, and have Glasgow and Dunkeld instead. It has to be assumed that Jocelin would have been translated to

---

68. *Chron. Melr.*, 44
69. Kelly, *The Oxford Dictionary of Popes* [hereafter *ODP*], 180.
70. *AMW,* 243.
71. *Scot. Pont.*, no. 110.
72. Duncan, *Scotland,* 272.
73. *ODP,* 180.
74. Robinson, *The Papacy,* 212.
75. *Scot. Pont.*, nos. 111, 112.
76. *Chron. Melr.*, 44; cf. Duncan, *Scotland,* 272–73. On it as presented to the prefect see Patrick, *Statutes,* 291. On the subject generally see Burns, "Papal gifts to Scottish Monarchs," especially 151–59.
77. *AMW,* 262, cf. 260. *Scot. Pont.*, no. 141.
78. *Scot. Pont.*, nos. 142, 150, 152.

St. Andrews;⁷⁹ what part Jocelin played in these negotiations and what he thought of the proposal are unknown.

Jocelin continued to be close to the king. He witnessed twenty-four of William's *acta* in the twenty-four years that he was bishop, the fourth most frequent attestation by a prelate after Andrew, bishop of Caithness, a courtier bishop who was probably more at court than in his diocese,⁸⁰ Archibald, abbot of Dunfermline, active in royal government for twenty years,⁸¹ and Matthew, archdeacon of St. Andrews and subsequently bishop of Aberdeen.⁸² Jocelin accompanied King William to the English court in 1186, and it is reasonable to assume that he was consulted on the question of the king's marriage to Ermengarde de Beaumont.⁸³ It is not known if Jocelin took part in the expedition against Roland of Galloway shortly after, but he was at Carlisle when Roland submitted and used the threat of excommunication to bind Roland to the agreement reached at the English court.⁸⁴ Jocelin accompanied William to Woodstock for the king's wedding to Ermengarde, blessed the couple in their chamber, and was one of the company which escorted the new queen to Scotland.⁸⁵ It seems likely that Jocelin traveled south with the king when he met Richard I in April 1194; he was certainly a witness to the arrangements made at Northampton by Richard for William's company when the king of Scots traveled within England.⁸⁶ When the king's heir, Alexander, was born in 1198, Jocelin baptized him, apparently at Haddington.⁸⁷ The birth, after twelve years of marriage without a son, may have seemed like a miracle, and was perhaps attributed to the intercession of Jocelin's predecessor, St. Kentigern, whose intercession some five hundred years earlier had brought about another royal birth, also long-awaited.⁸⁸ It would, however, be wrong to think that relations between king and bishop were

---

79. Duncan, *Scotland*, 273.

80. Broun, "The seven kingdoms in De Situ Albanie: a record of Pictish political geography or imaginary map of ancient Alba?" in Cowan, *Alba*, 29 and 28 n. 21.

81. *RRS*, ii, 57.

82. See *RRS*, ii, 57, ad indicem.

83. *AMW*, 265, 266.

84. *AMW*, 264.

85. *AMW*, 266–67; *Chron. Holyrood*, 170.

86. *AMW*, 291–92.

87. *AMW*, 313.

88. Duncan, "St. Kentigern," 13.

always smooth. In the 1190s they were in dispute over the parish church of Hassendean, which the bishop granted to his old abbey, Melrose.[89]

GLASGOW: BURGH AND CATHEDRAL

Jocelin certainly made considerable efforts to enhance the reputation of Glasgow and its patron, St. Kentigern. What Glasgow consisted of before Jocelin's time is a matter for conjecture.[90] In addition to a cathedral, there were, according to the Life of St. Kentigern by Jocelin of Furness, a freestanding cross, a tomb in a grove of trees, and a cemetery. To these may be added the ring-work castle which excavation has shown to have been situated directly to the west of the cathedral.[91] In 1164, however, there were inhabitants, who fled on the approach of Somerled, and so some kind of settlement. There may have been two settlements: one was probably close to the cathedral in order to serve the cathedral, its shrine and its clergy, and the other down the hill and by the River Clyde. Glasgow was given formal status as a burgh by King William (1175 x 1178) with a market every Thursday, though this may simply have formalized an existing arrangement. This, the first recorded formal grant of a market to a burgh, may have been a reward for Jocelin's part in defending the independence of the Scottish Church.[92] It fits into a pattern of grants to the bishop in the later 1170s: Bedlay, given in compensation for depredations committed by the king and his officials during the vacancy in the see, tofts in Montrose and Dumfries, and a family of neyfs.[93] It seems that the new burgh was to be laid out much farther down the hill, but above the flood level of the Clyde, with its center at Glasgow Cross, since even by 1773 there was little beyond ribbon development along High Street between the cross and the cathedral, and virtually none north of the

---

89. *Chron. Melr.*, 48. Professor Duncan has attempted to reconstruct the details of this disagreement: Duncan, "Roger of Howden and Scotland," in Crawford, *Church, Chronicle and Learning*, 136–38.

90. References to the burgh, unless otherwise stated, are from Shead,"Glasgow: an ecclesiastical burgh," in Lynch, *The Scottish Medieval Town*, 16–32.

91. Unfortunately this excavation remains unpublished, but is noted in *Medieval Archaeology* 35 (1989), 236. See, however, Yeoman, *Medieval Scotland*, 94.

92. Duncan, "St. Kentigern," 10.

93. *RRS*, ii, no. 192, 210, 216, 217; there is a similar pattern about the time of the granting of the fair, with the grants of tofts in Forfar and Stirling: *RRS*, ii, nos. 283, 325. Neyfs *(nativi)* were serfs who could be granted out as if property.

cathedral. Such a site had the advantages of access to the ford (the date of construction of the first bridge is unknown), to the river, and to a route along its north bank. There is no evidence as to the incentives offered to those who came to settle in the new burgh, nor as to how it was laid out. It may, however, be assumed that regular plots were laid out and that newcomers either constructed their own dwellings and, where appropriate, workshops, or were perhaps offered the incentive of free building materials. The only glimpse of this is a reference in one of Bishop Jocelin's charters to "that toft which Ranulf of Haddington built in the first building of the burgh"; this has led to the suggestion that Ranulf "contributed experience gained in Haddington to the layout . . . of the burgh."[94] All that can be said of that is that Haddington had certainly been a burgh since the reign of David.[95] The king's grant of a fair between 1189 and 1195 added further not only to Glasgow's status, but also to the revenue from booths and tolls which came to the bishop as lord of the fair. The fair was to be held, not about the feast day of the local saint (January 13), but from the octaves of Saints Peter and Paul (June 29). This was not solely a matter of weather: the first day of the fair fell on July 6, the day chosen for the dedication of the cathedral in 1197. The date was perhaps chosen to associate the fair with the commemoration of the dedication and perhaps with an intended feast of the translation of St. Kentigern.[96] The dedication may have prompted the commissioning of new music.[97] The granting of a fair was an unusual concession by the king, perhaps the first example of the grant of a fair by charter, though it may not be the earliest fair in practice.

Having apparently abandoned interest in Waltheof, Jocelin as bishop of Glasgow was anxious to promote interest in St. Kentigern and to procure formal canonization of him. One step in this direction was to commission Jocelin of Furness to write a new Life of Kentigern.[98] Another reason for the new life may have been the need after 1159 to have papal approval for recognition of sanctity. Jocelin of Furness admitted in his preface that he had found no evidence of posthumous miracles and in the text was reduced to relying on generalizations; the only specific

---

94. Gibb, *Glasgow*, 14.

95. Pryde, *The Burghs of Scotland*, 5.

96. Duncan, "St. Kentigern," 20.

97. Preece, *Our Awin Scottis Use*, 221. Perhaps this commission was linked to the creation of the office of precentor.

98. Printed in Forbes, *Lives of St. Ninian and St. Kentigern*, 27–119.

example, a thief who died after stealing a Glasgow cow, borders on the risible. It has been suggested that the dedication of Jocelin's cathedral had been intended to coincide with the translation of Kentigern's relics, but that, papal permission lacking, the bishop was forced to confine himself to the dedication. The next year that July 6 fell on a Sunday (the appropriate day for both a dedication and a translation) would be 1203, and perhaps Jocelin feared that he would not live to see it. If the purpose of the Life was to secure papal recognition of Kentigern's sanctity, it was not a success.[99]

The relics of Kentigern recorded in the fifteenth-century inventory of the cathedral's treasures[100] have been ascribed to Jocelin's interest in the saint. Their juxtaposition with matching relics of St. Thomas Becket (their combs and portions of their shifts) could also be attributed to Jocelin.[101] There was, in any case, some connection between Glasgow and Canterbury in the twelfth century, exemplified by a pontifical from Canterbury adapted for use in Glasgow.[102] Interest in Canterbury presumably sprang from the murder of Becket, the most horrifying event of Jocelin's lifetime. Jocelin was the first witness of King William's foundation charter of the abbey of Arbroath, dedicated to St. Thomas, and may have believed that associating the martyr with Kentigern through common relics would enhance Kentigern's claims to papal recognition.[103] Shortly after his election Jocelin attempted to improve the resources of the cathedral by decreeing that the books and vestments of canons who died intestate should pass to the cathedral;[104] otherwise they might have passed to the king.[105]

It would not be surprising if enlargement and re-decoration of the cathedral were part of Jocelin's plan. There are, however, some difficulties about the chronology and extent of change. Why did the Melrose chronicler choose 1181 to record that "Bishop Jocelin enlarged the episcopal

---

99. Duncan, "St. Kentigern," 16, 17, 20.

100. See Dowden, "Inventory of ornaments."

101. Duncan, "St. Kentigern," 11-12.

102. Illustrated in Fawcett, *Medieval Art*, Plates XXIIIA and XXIIIB. The MS is described by Brueckman, J., "The Medieval English Coronation Order," in Sandquist, *Essays in Medieval History*, 106; I owe this reference to Professor Duncan. See also Preece, *Our Awin Scottis Use*, 219.

103. Duncan, "St. Kentigern," 11-12.

104. Shead, *Scottish Episcopal Acta* [hereafter SEA], i, no. 85.

105. Robertson, *Concilia Scotiae*, i, c and n. l.

see, and gloriously glorified the church of St. Kentigern?"[106] It cannot refer to the end of the building campaign, for the dedication, duly noted in the chronicle, did not take place until 1197.[107] The wording of this second entry is quite different, stating that he had constructed the cathedral anew. Between these two dates there had apparently been a serious fire, referred to in a royal charter of 1189 x 1195 as having happened "in hiis diebus nostris" and therefore presumably recently;[108] the fire cannot be dated more closely. It seems possible that two different actions were involved: enlargement of the cathedral dedicated in 1136 and, after the fire, rebuilding. It may be that Walter Bower's source hit the nail on the head when it said that Jocelin "both by new building and re-building enhanced the church of St. Kentigern."[109] Jocelin had evidently regarded the cathedral which he inherited as too small,[110] and the fire seems to have provided the opportunity to build something more fitting to house the shrine of St. Kentigern. Jocelin acted with vigor, consulting the clergy of the diocese, presumably in a diocesan synod, and setting up a fraternity *(fraternitas)* to gather funds for the re-building.[111] A royal charter is the only specific evidence for the fraternity, but there is perhaps other, if somewhat oblique evidence, of its existence in grants by King William, and perhaps the king himself was a member, "even if a remote and inactive one" in a fraternity which contained both clerics and lay people. The word *fraternitas* as a description of such a society was very rare at this date and if its inspiration was a society of lay people at Canterbury, it is further evidence of a link between Glasgow and Canterbury.[112]

Little of Jocelin's cathedral survives: for some time the only known remains consisted of a vaulting shaft *in situ* in the south-west corner of the lower church, a painted Romanesque voussoir, the detached rectangular plinth of a wall-shaft with spurs in two of its angles and a base molding, and a capital in Corinthianesque style.[113] However, excavations in 1992–93 added other architectural fragments.[114] Large numbers of

106. *Chron. Melr.*, 43.
107. *Chron. Melr.*, 49.
108. *RRS*, ii, no. 316.
109. Watt, *Scotichronicon*, iv, 341.
110. *Letter*, 311.
111. *RRS*, ii, no. 316.
112. Duncan, "St. Kentigern," 12–13.
113. Radford and Stones, "The remains of the cathedral of Bishop Jocelin," 221–23.
114. See Driscoll, *Excavations at Glasgow Cathedral*.

worked stones were found: thirty-six were carved pieces of considerable architectural interest,[115] and eighteen bore painted decoration.[116] Construction began at the east end, which must have been what was dedicated in 1197, for the nave walls, though well-built as far as they went, were incomplete and there was no west front.[117] The shaft in situ was evidently attached to the east wall of a transept, and seems to have been part of a cruciform enlargement of the east end to provide a sizable area round the tomb of Kentigern,[118] no doubt to allow for the movement of pilgrims. The east end was two-storied.[119] So, too, is the east end of the cathedral at Lund, where Jocelin's consecrator, Eskil, was archbishop.[120] One can only speculate as to whether this is more than coincidence. The painted fragments exhibit work of "scintillating quality"[121] stylistically comparable to work in northern England. They come from the lower church and may belong to a cycle of paintings on the life of Kentigern.[122] The quality of the painting and of the masonry suggests that if Jocelin's cathedral had been finished it would have been a major Romanesque church. The fact that Jocelin's immediate successor, Hugh of Roxburgh, died before consecration, that William Malveisin was translated to St. Andrews after only two years, and that Floris of Holland remained bishop-elect for five years and was never consecrated, may suggest a hiatus in interest in the building work, and explain why in the thirteenth century Jocelin's work was completely superseded.

JOCELIN AS BISHOP

By the time of Jocelin's election, a dean and cathedral chapter had come into being, the first undoubted reference being March 7, 1161.[123] By 1164

115. Driscoll, "Highlights of the excavations in Glasgow Cathedral in 1992–93" [hereafter Driscoll, "Highlights"], in Fawcett, *Medieval Art*, 31.

116. Park, D. "Late twelfth-century polychromy from Glasgow Cathedral," in Fawcett, *Medieval Art*.

117. Driscoll, "Highlights," 30.

118. Fawcett, *Medieval Art*, 2.

119. Fawcett, *Medieval Art*, 2.

120. I am grateful to Dr. Driscoll for drawing my attention to this and for lending me the guidebook to Lund Cathedral.

121. Park, "Polychromy," 35.

122. Park, "Polychromy," 35, 36, 37, 39.

123. *Glas. Reg.*, i, no. 23 = *Scot. Pont.*, no. 73, but for the date see Barrow, 73, n. 50,

there were seven prebends,[124] providing for six canons and the dean, who perhaps already held the church of Cadzow.[125] Jocelin who, as bishop, had the patronage of the prebends,[126] added only one, the church of Camwath, created as a prebend between 1180 and 1186.[127] The number of canons revealed by a document of 1181 x 1185/6[128] is open to dispute: six or seven?[129] The problem hinges on whether "Helia Philippo" represents one person or two, for there is no point between the names (although one appears in the printed version) as there is between others; moreover, the charter is an original and so Philippo cannot be a scribal error for some form of Partick.[130] It was possible, however, for two names not to be separated in this way: e.g., in one instance William and Walter, two of the bishop's clerks.[131] Philip was not a common name among clerics of this period, and Philip the clerk (otherwise unspecified) witnessed two acts of Bishop Jocelin which can be dated 1179 x 1196.[132] If Carnwath were already a prebend by the date of Melrose no. 43, there were prebends for the dean and seven canons. No dean is named: Dean Salomon did not appear in Jocelin's *acta*, and Herbert was not yet dean. The archdeacon had no prebend in the twelfth century, and special arrangements were made for him as late as 1231, pending the church of Peebles becoming vacant.[133] There is, therefore, room for a canon called Philip, but the question remains open.

Jocelin's contribution to the development of the chapter, a single prebend, thus seems meager. However, it is possible that, parallel to his rebuilding of the cathedral, he was responsible for creating more dignities in the chapter: by 1196 the treasurership had been created.[134] It is possible that the office of precentor was also created at this time. The only

---

of the present volume.

124. Cowan, "The Organization of Secular Cathedral Chapters," in Kirk, *The Medieval Church in Scotland*, 84.

125. Cf. *Fasti*, 152.

126. *Glas. Reg.*, i, no. 32.

127. *Glas. Reg.*, i, nos. 52 and 53.

128. *SEA*, i, no. 93.

129. Duncan, "Roger of Howden," 152 n. 14.

130. Helia de Perthec occurs in *SEA*, i, no. 90.

131. *Melr. Lib.*, i, no. 30.

132. *SEA*, i, no. 99.

133. *Fasti*, 217.

134. *Fasti*, 208.

reference to the first known precentor, Simon, can be dated only 1179 x 1221.[135] However, on stylistic grounds the document is more likely to be of the late twelfth rather than the early thirteenth century: e.g., the use of *justicia* rather than *justiciarius*.[136] Before the end of the century the chapter had acquired its own seal.[137] Jocelin's clergy, canons, clerks and chaplains, seem to have been a close-knit group. The one outsider was Richard, monk and bishop's chaplain. He was perhaps a monk of Melrose who accompanied Jocelin to Glasgow. The only references to him can be dated 1175 x 1178 and 1175 x 1195;[138] both therefore could belong to the very beginning of the episcopate, and thereafter the bishop's chaplains were secular clerks. If the personnel seem rather limited in numbers, with much internal promotion, it may be that Jocelin as a monk, had no wide circle of secular clerics to draw on. Given the difficulties which might arise from the appointment of a monk to be bishop in a cathedral with a secular chapter,[139] Jocelin's early concession (1175 x 1178) that canons might bequeath their prebends for a year[140] looks like a gesture of goodwill. William, who frequently attested Jocelin's charters, appears as bishop's clerk and steward and also as canon and steward.[141] It was not unusual for canons to be members of the episcopal household;[142] their employment was financially useful since they had prebends from which to draw revenue.[143] One of the two canons named Helia had been a clerk to bishops Herbert and Ingram[144] and initially to Jocelin also.[145] The other Helia had been a canon in the time of Bishop Herbert.[146] Ingram the canon had been chaplain to Bishop Ingram,[147] Walter the clerk had been

135. *Fasti*, 199.
136. I owe this suggestion to Professor Duncan.
137. Illustrated in Fawcett, *Medieval Art*, Plate IVC.
138. *SEA*, i, no. 85, 96.
139. Crosby, *Bishop and Chapter*, 33–34.
140. *SEA*, i, no. 85.
141. *Melr. Lib.*, i, nos. 131, 129.
142. Crosby, *Bishop and Chapter*, 45.
143. Cheney, *English Bishops' Chanceries*, 9.
144. *SEA*, i, no. 73; *Archaeological and Historical Collections relating to Ayrshire and Galloway*, iv (1884) 55.
145. *Liber Cartarum Sancte Crucis* [hereafter *Holy. Lib.*], no. 53.
146. *Glas. Reg.*, i, no. 16.
147. *Holy. Lib.*, no. 52.

chaplain to Bishop Herbert,[148] and Nicholas the clerk had served Bishop Herbert in the same capacity.[149] Although only one title from the bishop's household—*dapifer* or *senescallus*—is known from this period, Jocelin employed two at the same time, William and Alexander.[150] It is quite clear that, contrary to the general trend of the time,[151] Jocelin was not interested in employing graduates: the sole exception, Mr. John de Roxburgh, who ended his career as the first known treasurer of the cathedral, was already a canon when Jocelin was elected.[152] On the basis of the witness lists of his charters, Jocelin worked closely with Archdeacon Simon, appointed by Bishop Ingram, and his own appointee, Dean Herbert.

Jocelin sought papal support in dealing with diocesan problems: securing the payment of teinds for the upkeep of parish churches (the south-west of the diocese, especially Galloway, seems to have been a difficult area in this respect);[153] avoiding long vacancies in parish churches, whether appropriated or in secular patronage; securing recognition of the right to have disputes over patronage heard in the bishop's court; setting a time-limit on appeals; forbidding ecclesiastics to burden their benefices with loans; preventing intrusion into churches with an existing incumbent; securing the payment of synodalia; and gaining support for the removal of hereditary priests,[154] which struck also at clerical marriage.[155] A bull of 1186 claimed that, because of the scarcity of churches in much of the diocese, children frequently died without baptism and adults without confession and the *viaticum*: "many people" wanted episcopal permission to build and consecrate churches and hallow cemeteries.[156] At first sight this appears to be a serious criticism of Jocelin as diocesan. However, it seems likely that the information came from Jocelin himself and was to prepare for church building in the diocese, for the bull authorized him to use ecclesiastical censure to compel cooperation from

---

148. *SEA*, i, nos. 73, 75; *Kel. Lib.*, ii, no. 415.
149. *SEA*, i, no. 73.
150. *Melr. Lib.*, ii, no. 571.
151. Cheney, *English Bishops' Chanceries*, 10.
152. *Glas. Reg.*, i, no. 16; for his career see Watt, *A Biographical Dictionary*, 473-74.
153. *Scot. Pont.*, nos. 88, 89; *RRS*, ii, no. 374.
154. *Scot. Pont.*, nos. 88, 89, 105, 138, 108, 134, 109, 132, 133, 139.
155. Barrow, "Hereford bishops and married clergy," 7.
156. *Scot. Pont.*, no. 140.

anyone who resisted such developments. Armed with this, Jocelin could presumably overcome the opposition of landholders.

The absence of a comprehensive list of parish churches until Bagimond's Roll in the later thirteenth century[157] makes it difficult to be sure if there was a substantial program of church building or parish reorganization under Jocelin. The church of St. Andrew at Peebles was dedicated by him in 1195,[158] but it is not certain that the building was new. Perhaps the chapel dedicated to St. Thomas in Glasgow might be included, given the interest in Becket, but the first certain reference to it is not until 1320.[159] There was certainly a new oratory dedicated to St. Thomas which was granted to the church of Maxwell.[160] Symington ceased to be a chapel of Wiston and had become a parish church by 1195.[161] In the later 1170s the chapel of Longnewton was separated from St Boswell's.[162] In 1193/4 an attempt was made (successful later if not at the time) to erect the chapel of Hutton Magna into a parish church.[163] As bishop, Jocelin would have had to give permission for such changes, but what initiatives he took are unknown. In two cases Jocelin was involved in the settlement of disputes over churches. Roger of Valognes acknowledged that patronage of the church of East Kilbride had belonged to the church and bishop of Glasgow (presumably exercised jointly by bishop and chapter) since the time of Bishop John.[164] Pursuing a matter which had arisen in Bishop Ingram's time, Jocelin secured from Robert Bruce two churches and the patronage of three more; this seems to have been a dispute of some seriousness, since part of the settlement was that Bruce and his successors were to do homage to Jocelin and his successors for the sake of peace.[165] Jocelin's episcopate provides the first abundant evidence for the existence of deans of Christianity in the diocese of Glasgow. Only one is certainly known before 1175; thereafter there are references to nine deaneries.[166] There is a greater number of surviving episcopal *acta* after

157. On Bagimond see Watt, "Bagimond di Vezza and his 'Roll.'"
158. *Chron. Melr.*, 49.
159. *Glas. Reg.*, i, no. 267.
160. *SEA*, i, no. 96.
161. *SEA*, i, nos. 105, 90.
162. *Liber S. Marie de Dryburgh* [hereafter *Dryb. Lib.*], nos. 57, 62.
163. *SEA*, i, no. 52; cf. *Glas. Reg.*, i, no. 114.
164. *SEA*, i, no. 107.
165. *SEA*, i, no. 108.
166. *Fasti*, 229-39.

1175 (twenty-eight of Jocelin's acta survive as opposed to twelve for his three predecessors); nonetheless it is hard to believe that that explains the larger number of deaneries. Jocelin's episcopate also produced the first evidence for an Official[167] to assist the bishop in diocesan business and in the administration of that "diocesan law" referred to by the pope.[168] Thus 1175 seems to mark the beginning of a more structured administration of the diocese.

Jocelin was the Scottish prelate most frequently appointed as a papal judge-delegate, even if evidence survives for his acting only on four occasions. Three of these cases involved Kelso Abbey, which suggests that Kelso may have asked for his appointment.[169] In another case he acted as the ordinary with the judges-delegate.[170] Another case throws light on procedure in what must have been the archdeacon's court. The land at issue had had its bounds perambulated by a group which included Archdeacon Simon, who judged the dispute and administered the oath to keep the agreement, but the settlement was made in the bishop's presence.[171]

Of the forty surviving non-royal acts to which Jocelin was a witness, more than half were benefactions to his old monastery, Melrose. Those whose charters he witnessed were mainly magnates and barons or men associated with them: Duncan, earl of Carrick and his knight, Roger of Scaleborc;[172] the Avenel family;[173] the Moreville family;[174] Alan, son of Walter, the Steward[175] and his man Richard le Walais;[176] the de Quincy

---

167. *Fasti*, 240. Although Richard de Hassendean is not specifically described as bishop's official, it seems too early a date for him to have been archdeacon's official: Ollivant, *The Court of the Official*, 22.

168. *Scot. Pont.*, no. 139.

169. Ferguson, *Medieval Papal Representatives in Scotland*, 22.

170. *Glas. Reg.*, i, no. 81.

171. *SEA*, i, no. 103.

172. *Melr. Lib.*, i, nos. 29–34.

173. *Melr. Lib.*, i, nos. 39–41.

174. *Melr. Lib.*, i, nos. 94, 95, 106, 108; Atkinson, *Coucher Book of Furness Abbey*, ii, 334–37.

175. *Melr. Lib.*, i, nos. 70, 97; *Pais. Reg.* 11–12.

176. *Melr. Lib.*, i, no. 69.

family;[177] the Bruce family;[178] and Earl David, the king's brother.[179] The reason for witnessing a charter by Patrick de Rydale was that Jocelin and his successors were to act as guarantors of the grant.[180] The bishop was called upon to witness few acts of ecclesiastics: two of these, acts of successive abbots of Kelso, freed the first abbots of Arbroath and Lindores from subjection to their old monastery, Kelso.[181] Others were a general confirmation by Roger, bishop of St. Andrews, of Arbroath Abbey's churches in his diocese,[182] and the confirmation by the dean and chapter of Glasgow of the settlement of the dispute between king and bishop over the church of Hassendean.[183] Jocelin also witnessed the settlement of a number of disputes: between the abbeys of Jedburgh and Dryburgh over the churches of Newton and St Boswell's; between the canons of St. Andrews and the nuns of Haddington over rights in Haddington parish church; between Kelso Abbey and Hervey the marshal over the church of Keith; and between the bishop of St. Andrews and the abbot of Arbroath over cain and conveth from the abbey's churches.[184]

The absence of place-dates makes it difficult to explain the circumstances in which Jocelin was called on to act as witness, but some of these occasions arose when he was at court. Then the witnesses might include the king: for example, on the occasion of Earl David's foundation charter for Lindores Abbey, when the first abbots of Lindores and Arbroath were freed from subjection to Kelso, or when Bishop Roger issued his confirmation of Arbroath Abbey's churches. Other witness lists, with a mixture of ecclesiastical and lay magnates, also suggest the court: for example, Robert Bruce's grant of the church of Haltwhistle to Arbroath Abbey was witnessed by another bishop, two earls and Philip de Valognes. The charter of Alan, son of Walter the Steward, quitclaiming Blainslie to Melrose Abbey was witnessed by another bishop, the king's brother, two more

177. *Registrum S. Marie de Neubotle* [hereafter *Newb. Reg.*], nos. 64, 65.

178. *Melr. Lib.*, i, no. 169; *Liber S. Thomae de Aberbrothoc* [hereafter *Arb. Lib.*], i, no. 37; *Kel. Lib.* i, no. 275.

179. *Chartulary of the Abbey of Lindores* [hereafter *Lind. Cart.*], no. ii.

180. *Melr. Lib.*, i, no. 166*; the gaps in the text can be made good from ii, no. 571.

181. *Arb. Lib.*, i, no. 3; *Lind. Cart.*, App. I.

182. *SEA*, i, no. 238.

183. *Melr. Lib.*, i, no. 122.

184. *Dryb. Lib.*, no. 62; *Liber Cartarum Prioratus Sancti Andree*, 334; *Kel. Lib.*, i, no. 95; *Arb. Lib.*, i, no. 148. Cain was payment to a lord to signify his lordship. Conveth was a hospitality rent to the king from lands which were or had been royal estates.

earls, the Constable and two abbots. Other lists suggest large clerical gatherings: for example, a list which also included the abbots of Dunfermline, Kinloss, and Coupar, and the archdeacon of Lothian;[185] however, at this date there was no machinery for assembling a provincial synod other than by a legate or other formal emissary on the pope's behalf.[186] Simple local business within the diocese probably explains why the other witnesses to a grant of land in Hownam were the archdeacon of Glasgow and the dean of Roxburgh.[187]

At first sight, Jocelin appeared to be a generous benefactor to monasteries, not all in his own diocese, but his ostensible grants were confirmations, almost without exception. Paisley Abbey was most favored, since there is documentary evidence relating to nine churches.[188] Eight of these apparent grants were, however, confirmations, and the ninth, Dalziel, may have been too.[189] It is not clear why Paisley, a Cluniac house, should have been so favored, but the convent had moved from Renfrew to Paisley as recently as c. 1169 and in one charter Jocelin confirms a grant "because of the poverty of the church of Paisley."[190] It was, in addition, the monastery closest geographically to Glasgow itself. Jocelin's undoubted gifts are thus reduced to two tofts in Glasgow and the church of Hassendean.[191]

CONCLUSION

On March 4, 1199, the day after Ash Wednesday, Jocelin arrived at his old abbey of Melrose. That night he was struck by illness, apparently a heart attack, and died on March 17.[192] On March 29 he was buried in the monks' choir on the north side of the church[193] in a tomb which he

185. *Melr. Lib.*, i, no. 69.

186. Watt, *Medieval Church Councils*, 31.

187. *Meir. Lib.*, i, no. 69.

188. Pollok, Mearns, Craigie, Kilbarchan, Kirkoswald, Dalziel, Cathcart, Rutherglen, and Carmunnock: *SEA*, i, nos. 99, 100. 101, 102; *Registrum Monasterii de Passelet*, 428.

189. Cowan, *The Parishes of Medieval Scotland*, throughout.

190. *SEA*. i, no. 101.

191. *SEA*. i, nos. 97, 93, 94.

192. *Letter,* 311–12; the date of death is corroborated by *Chron. Melr.*, 50, and by Howden (in *AMW*, 313–34).

193. *AMW*, 314.

had had prepared some years before.[194] No trace of this now remains, destroyed either by enemy action in 1322 or 1385, or in the rebuilding which followed.[195] Much of Jocelin's public career was recorded by two chroniclers who had connections with him, the writer of the Melrose Chronicle and Roger of Howden, author of two chronicles, who became a canon of Glasgow late in Jocelin's episcopate.[196] It may be for that reason that he is the only notable, lay or ecclesiastical, named in certain events, such as escorting Queen Ermengarde to Scotland after her wedding. However, record evidence, including royal acta and papal bulls, corroborates his importance. It has been suggested that it was his personality, and perhaps even his policy, which prevented St. Andrews from becoming an archbishopric.[197] He was certainly close to the king, blessing the king's wedding and baptizing King William's son and heir, Alexander; he was not simply an envoy and courtier. Despite disputes with Robert Bruce, the Steward, Richard de Moreville and Roger Valognes, he was nonetheless called on to witness charters by three of them and by other men of similar standing. He was the founder of a burgh with a great, if unforeseen, future, and the builder of what, even in its unfinished state, must have been one of the most impressive cathedrals in Scotland. He upheld the rights of his see and reorganized its administration; he served the pope as judge-delegate and in the matter of the dispute over St. Andrews; yet he remained a Cistercian at heart, keeping in touch with his old monastery and arranging to be buried there. He was the outstanding Scottish bishop of the later twelfth century.

---

194. *Letter*, 312.

195. Richardson, *Melrose Abbey*, 5. I am grateful to Professor Richard Fawcett for information about excavations at Melrose Abbey since it was taken into state care in 1919; none of these excavations found any trace of Jocelin's tomb.

196. Duncan, "Roger of Howden."

197. *Scot. Pont.*, no. 10 (personality); Broun, "Welsh Identity" (policy).

7

Glasgow Cathedral and its Clergy in the Middle Ages

Ian B. Cowan

In this chapter, Professor Ian Cowan reviews what is known about the canons of Glasgow Cathedral in the fifteenth century. The evidence suggests that they were more concerned about adding to their "plurality of benefices" than performing their duties.

Over the years architectural and historical investigation has revealed more and more about the fabric, altars, and ecclesiastical furnishings of Glasgow's ancient cathedral. Less attention has been paid, however, to the men who served in it, and while a full analysis of such a topic would be a very lengthy process indeed, it is possible by taking one particular point in time to make some slight contribution to the fuller account which one day may emerge.[1]

As it is certain that the cathedral chapter consisted of twenty-three prebends in 1401, the turn of the fifteenth century provides an appropriate point at which to examine the composition of the chapter which then

---

1. This chapter is based on a lecture originally delivered to the Society of Friends and printed in the Annual Report for 1976. The printed version did not include references and Norman F. Shead has kindly provided the footnotes which cover the majority of sources consulted.

consisted of the dean, chanter, chancellor, treasurer, the archdeacons of Glasgow and Teviotdale, the sub-dean and sixteen simple prebends[2]— Ancrum, Ashkirk, Ayr, Barlanark, Cardross, Carstairs, Durisdeer, Eddlestone, Erskine, Glasgow Primo and Secundo, Govan, Moffat, Old Roxburgh, Renfrew, and Stobo.[3]

Who were the men who held these canonries? Significantly, they did not include the bishop as the bishop of Glasgow was not a canon in his own cathedral. This may have been a handicap and in 1487 Bishop Blackadder made a determined effort to remedy this when he petitioned the pope to the effect that if he, and any future bishop of Glasgow, were a canon of that church and held the prebend of Barlanark the canons would benefit by the presence of the bishop at capitular acts.[4] In order that the canons would not suffer a diminution of their number by the creation of an episcopal prebend, the bishop offered to erect his mensal church[5] of Dryfesdale into a prebend for the support of the canonry at that time dependent upon the revenues of Barlanark. The benefits foreseen by the bishop were not so obvious to the chapter, however, and the bishop was forced to resign all rights in the prebend.[6]

Were the disadvantages faced by the bishop so overwhelming? The bishop had many hidden advantages, not least of which was his power of patronage which allowed him to present canons to a majority of the cathedral prebends. It is significant, however, that the nine prebends founded after 1401 were all in lay patronage and a change in the patronage structure may have been a factor in forcing Blackadder to seek a seat in the chapter. In the late fourteenth century, however, such problems were still in the future as a study of two episcopates at the end of the fourteenth century reveals. Thus, Walter de Wardlaw, bishop from 1367 until 1387 utilized his position, which was further enhanced by the conferment of a cardinal's hat in 1383, to ensure that various members of his family were launched on successful and presumably lucrative ecclesiastical career.[7] His brother William was chanter of the cathedral by 1378 and

2. Prebend: the stipend assigned by a cathedral or collegiate church to a canon or member of the chapter.

3. *Registrum Episcopatus Glasguensis* [hereafter *Glas. Reg.*], ii, no. 320.

4. i.e. acts passed by the chapter.

5. A term used to denote a church or benefice whose revenues were appropriated to the bishopric (literally for the maintenance of the bishop's table).

6. Bliss, *Calendar of Entries in the Papal Registers*, xiv, 172–74.

7. Watt, *Biographical Dictionary*, 564–75.

held it until his death in 1387 when Henry de Wardlaw, a nephew of the Cardinal, who as a student had obtained the prebend of Old Roxburgh on September 22, 1379, and was then provided to the chantership which he obtained despite the death of the cardinal shortly before his provision. Yet another nephew, Alexander, held the prebend of Eddlestone until his death shortly before September 22, 1388, while another member of the family, Walter, held the prebend of Carstairs in 1378. Walter's patronage, however, was not restricted to relations, and at least two of his household chaplains, John de Merton[8] presented to Barlanark in June 1388 and John de Vaux[9] who was already a canon in 1388 and eventually succeeded to the prebend of Old Roxburgh on the promotion of Henry de Wardlaw to the bishopric of St. Andrews in 1403, obtained prebends through his favor.

Such a grouping constituted an episcopal center of power which only one other group—those appointed by royal favor—could rival. Thus, during Wardlaw's episcopate, royal influence was exerted on behalf of Thomas Stewart[10] who, at the petition of his natural father Robert II, succeeded his brother James[11] to the prebend of Stobo on November 10, 1380, while in 1387 Hugh Raa,[12] who then obtained the sub-deanery, is described as a kinsman of John, Earl of Carrick, the future Robert III. Others who owed their prebends to royal intervention include a royal clerk, David de Strevelyn,[13] who held an undesignated prebend in 1381 and Duncan Petyt,[14] the king's former secretary who obtained the prebend of Ayr in 1386. As Wardlaw himself enjoyed royal favor, an identity of interest between these two groups may be considered a foregone conclusion and to this end little friction was likely in a chapter in which royal and episcopal interests coincided. It is clear that this is how Wardlaw intended it should be and in 1383 Thomas Ewar[15] complained, apparently ineffectively, that although he had been presented to the prebend

---

8. Burns, *Papal Letters to Scotland of Clement VII* [hereafter *CSSR Clement VII*], 126.

9. *CSSR Clement VII*, 138–39.

10. *CSSR Clement VII*, 41.

11. *CSSR Clement VII*, 38, 41.

12. *CSSR Clement VII*, 77, 136.

13. *CSSR Clement VII*, 63.

14. *CSSR Clement VII*, 116.

15. *CSSR Clement VII*, 98.

of Moffat by the rightful patron, Walter "against all justice" refused to admit him.

The death of Cardinal Walter in 1387 marked the end of the family supremacy and although his nephew secured the chantership and eventually became bishop of St. Andrews in 1403, he was less successful in Glasgow, failing in his ambition to exchange his chantership for the archdeaconry of Glasgow, a cause which he pursued from May 1398 until his elevation to St. Andrews, but in which he was thwarted by Symon de Mandeville, nephew of Wardlaw's successor as bishop of Glasgow. The new bishop was Mathew de Glendinning who held the see from 1387 until May 1408.

The influence of the bishop is again to the fore and at least three nephews obtained preferment in the cathedral. Of these, Symon de Mandeville, student of law at Orleans, already held the prebend of Durisdeer on August 22, 1395 when he was provided to the prebend of Glasgow Primo.[16] In practice he does not appear to have secured possession, but before August 10, 1403 he had obtained greater preferment having acquired possession, probably in mid-1399, of the archdeaconry of Glasgow while still a student of decreets at Avignon—a canonry and prebend of Dunkeld, provision to the church of Magna Cavers in January 1404 and further provision to single canonries in the churches of Aberdeen and St. Andrews on August 27, 1408. Whether the death of his uncle, three months before, would have halted a career, which by this date was equally founded in his curial ability as an auditor of appeals, must unfortunately remain unanswered as Mandeville did not long survive his uncle, being dead before November 11, 1409.[17]

The careers of two of Mathew's other nephews do, however, provide an answer to that question. They prospered while their uncle lived, but their fortunes suffered a marked decline after his death. Of the two, Robert de Moffet,[18] who began his ecclesiastical career as vicar of Peebles, was provided to a canonry of Glasgow with expectation of a prebend on October 13, 1403. An attempt to gain the prebend of Ancrum to which he was provided in 1405 proved unsuccessful, but he had obtained the prebend of Durisdeer before December 24, 1407. During the same period, William de Glendinning, another of the bishop's nephews, while

16. McGurk, *Papal Letters to Scotland of Benedict XIII*, [hereafter *CSSR Benedict XIII*], 84, 106.

17. *CSSR Benedict XIII*, 43-4, 116, 184-5, 211.

18. *CSSR Benedict XIII*, 111-12, 167-68; Watt, *Biographical Dictionary*, 398-99.

still a student of civil law at Orleans, and about twenty-four years of age, is found in possession of the prebend of Renfrew on April 2, 1405. After his uncle's death, his career took a downward turn. His attempt to follow his cousin Symon de Mandeville as archdeacon of Glasgow failed despite papal provision on November 11, 1409, and he eventually resigned his rights in the archdeaconry in January 1413 in an attempt to obtain the sub-deanery.

Nevertheless, the effects of his struggle for the archdeaconry continued for some time after his resignation as legal action he had initiated against the possessor of the archdeaconry, John Forrester, took its course and provided an example of the practical consequences within the cathedral of such a dispute. In an effort to excommunicate the bishop, dean and chapter who had refused to admit him to the archdeaconry, John de Barry, who had been chosen by Glendinning as his sub-executor, proceeded to publish the letters of excommunication by affixing them to the nave of the Church of Glasgow. For his pains, Barry was thereupon thrown into the bishop's prison, while a Thomas Curant, a familiar of the bishop of Glasgow, took down the letters of excommunication from the nave. Glendinning's appeal against this action was ineffective, as was his attempt to gain the sub-deaconry of Glasgow which he resigned without possession on September 25, 1414 when he obtained, in exchange, provision to the prebend of Moffat. As a canon he had at least been restored to the position which he had held before his uncle's death. Throughout this period he appears to have been an absentee, receiving on January 12, 1416 an indult to continue his studies at university until he obtained a doctorate, and while he subsequently added a canonry of Tours to the canonry of Aberdeen and parsonage of Glencairn, which he held with his canonry of Glasgow by this date, no further preferment at Glasgow came his way.[19] The subsequent career of Robert de Moffet[20] provides a close parallel as attempts to gain the provostry of the collegiate church of Bothwell appears to have been unsuccessful and he too by February 3, 1411 had to rest content with an indult allowing him to collect the full fruits of his canonry and prebend of Durisdeer while studying letters at a university. If the Glendinning interest continued to prevail after their uncle's death, it did so in only a modest manner and at Glasgow itself the

---

19. *CSSR Benedict XIII*, 133–34, 211–14, 268–69, 299–300, 338.
20. *CSSR Benedict XIII*, 198–99, 231.

new bishop, William de Lawder, whose brother Alexander[21] was a canon before April 1415, was already building up his own coterie of friends and relations.

An analysis of the chapter in the time of Mathew de Glendinning reveals that of the twenty-three canonries in the cathedral chapter, three had been appropriated before his death to members of his own family. All three holders, however, appear to have been permanent absentees—two as university students and the other as a curial official. If the bishop sought support at chapter meetings, he must have sought it elsewhere. Royal nominees could have supplied such support and such candidates were in evidence. Thomas Stewart, natural son of Robert II continued to hold the prebend of Stobo along with the archdeaconry of St. Andrews. Hugh Raa, kinsman of Robert III, continued to hold the sub-deaconry until his death in 1405 when he was succeeded by John Stewart[22] who already held a prebend within the cathedral and like his predecessor was related to the royal family. Of the simple prebends, Barlanark was held in 1395 by another illegitimate son of Robert II, Alexander Stewart[23] who was succeeded in this prebend by Walter Stewart,[24] another natural son, before October 1414.

Royal servants were equally to the fore. John de Hawick,[25] chaplain to David, Duke of Rothesay, first obtained the prebend of Carstairs, then exchanged it for Renfrew and subsequently in 1398 was provided to the precentorship, although possession was not gained until Henry de Wardlau demitted office in 1403. The prebend of Ayr continued to be held by Duncan Petyt, senior,[26] who had been a royal secretary, until his death in 1399 when he was succeeded in the prebend by Duncan Patyt, junior,[27] also a royal nominee. Yet another royal servant, Richard de Cornell[28] who had been chaplain to the queen in 1385, a member of the household of David, earl of Carrick, and later still an envoy to the curia for Robert,

21. *CSSR Benedict XIII*, 314.
22. *CSSR Benedict XIII*, 131–32.
23. *CSSR Benedict XIII*, 42–43.
24. *CSSR Benedict XIII*, 304–5.
25. *CSSR Clement VII*, 152; *CSSR Benedict XIII*, 85–86, 133–34, 121; Watt, *Biographical Dictionary*, 260-2.
26. *CSSR Benedict XIII*, 388–89.
27. *CSSR Benedict XIII*, 390.
28. *CSSR Clement VII*, 97; *CSSR Benedict XIII*, 114, 178–79, 181; Watt, *Biographical Dictionary*, 12–13.

duke of Albany, was provided to a canonry of Glasgow with expectation of a prebend on October 21, 1403 by virtue of which he obtained the prebend of Erskine and the attached sacristanship of the cathedral shortly before Bishop Mathew's death in 1408.

Like the bishop's nephews, some of these men were absentees, and it is clear that at any given time, few of the canons were present at the cathedral, even at chapter meetings. Such gatherings must have been small, and their actions all the more easily controlled. The statutes of the cathedral confirm this state of affairs. As early as 1266 it is recorded that "certain of the canons of the cathedral of Glasgow are pleased to bear the name . . . but they entirely neglect to perform the duties of their office."[29] In the early fifteenth century, the same state of affairs still prevailed and statutes drawn up during the episcopate of Bishop John Cameron (1426–46) reveal the nature of the problem.[30] The dean, precentor, chancellor, treasurer, and sub-dean were bound to reside for at least six months each, while the other canons were to be in residence for a period of three months, although this need not be continuous. The imposition of financial sanctions had little effect, and in 1455 the abbot of Paisley reported that "few or none" of the canons made residence in person. Yet a select number of canons may have found it financially rewarding to remain in residence and at least two of the canons—John Wishart and John de Vaux[31]—were active in cathedral circles during the episcopate of Mathew de Glendinning. Wishart was canon of Govan and de Vaux, holder of an undefined prebend before 1388, then obtained provision to the prebend of Old Roxburgh, which he eventually acquired on the demission of the holder Henry de Wardlaw in 1403. Both these canons frequently acted as papal mandatories, between 1395 and 1403 in the case of de Vaux, and 1395 and 1409 in the case of Wishart. The dignitaries and a few working canons appear to have thus constituted the core of the chapter resident at any time, and in these circumstances, the bishop must have derived an administrative advantage in which failure to hold a personal canonry and prebend may have mattered little.

For the canons themselves, it was clearly the status, or possibly the emolument, which was the prime consideration in acquiring a prebend. It was as much this desire as any wish to augment divine service which

---

29. *Glas. Reg.*, i, no. 212*
30. *Glas. Reg.*, ii, no. 342.
31. Watt, *Biographical Dictionary*, 560–1, 584–85.

led to the creation of nine additional prebends during the course of the fifteenth century. Nevertheless, insofar as substitutes, or vicars choral, had to be provided for most of these canons, the net result was an increase in the total personnel present at services within the cathedral. Of the thirty-two canons who eventually constituted the chapter, all but two were bound to pay vicars choral, while the two excepted prebends—Durisdeer and Cumnock—had to maintain six choir boys and a sacristan respectively.[32] Such payments did pose difficulties, however, and the niggardly stipend paid at Glasgow to the vicars of the choir who were leaving for more remunerative posts elsewhere, led in 1480 to the doubling of their stipend.[33] Separate residences were also supplied for these vicars who from the episcopate of Andrew de Durisdeer constituted a college in their own right and thereafter held property in common.[34]

These men, rather than the canons, were at the very heart of cathedral life, both spiritually and socially. But who were they? A study of their opposite numbers at Dunkeld reveals in their ranks, advocates, notaries, and consistorial clerks. All are praised for their musical ability, one is "steady in the chant," another is "highly trained in the theory of music as well as in the art of singing," while others are described as having been accustomed from their youth to take their part in service and rule the choir. Such details are unfortunately absent at Glasgow and the vicars choral remain shadowy figures. Not so the canons, who as we have seen emerge as a well-born elite, related either to the bishop, the king or some other notable family who might hold the patronage of their prebend. Most, without exception, were university educated, and well suited to their office, if they cared to exercise it. But with the exception of some of the dignitaries and a few working canons most were more concerned with adding to their plurality of benefices. Their career, wherever it lay, seldom involved them in their duties as canons of the cathedral and it is perhaps ironic that while their names and offices have come down to us through the ages, the clergy who gave life and vitality to this great cathedral before the Reformation must remain unhonored and unsung.

32. *Glas. Reg.*, ii, no. 342.
33. *Glas. Reg.*, ii, no. 426.
34. *Glas. Reg.*, ii, no. 391.

8

The Blacader Choir Screen and the Crossing Area in Glasgow Cathedral

David McRoberts

The nave and choir of the cathedral are separated by an ornate stone pulpitum or screen. There are altar platforms in front of it and the presence of the arms and initials of Archbishop Blacader[1] have led to the belief that the screen was constructed in his time. Monsignor David McRoberts challenges this assumption, and speculates on the appearance of the crossing area in medieval times.[2]

ONE OF MY VERY earliest recollections of the High Kirk of Glasgow was, as a small boy, overhearing a guide telling a party of visitors that the Rood Screen had been built by Archbishop Blacader. I remember the incident distinctly, not because a Rood Screen meant much to me at that age but because the surname "Blacader" was new to me and it did sound rather sinister.

---

1. There are various alternatives spellings of this name. David McRoberts uses "Blacader" here whereas John Durkan (chapter 9) uses "Blackadder." Throughout this book the form of spelling chosen by each of the contributors has been retained.

2. This chapter is based on two articles which appeared in the Annual Reports of the Society of Friends for 1965 and 1967.

In subsequent years I have often found the same assertion made both in speech and in print but, with the passage of years, not only has the surname of Blacader lost its sinister ring but also the assertion that that archbishop erected the Rood Screen, or Choir Screen, has grown less and less convincing. We must always remember that Archbishop Blacader came at the very end of what seems to have been a full century of work devoted to the rearrangement of the entire chancel area of the cathedral. The fifteenth century was a time of great increase in the personnel of the cathedral foundation: one only needs to look at the number of new altars and chaplainries which came into existence during that time. As far back as 1420, Bishop Lauder was proposing to remove the shrine of St. Mungo from the eastern bay of the chancel and, after some delay, it was actually removed to a new location at the Altar of the Tomb in the Lower Church. This was done to allow the choir to be enlarged to make space for the greatly expanded ceremonial life of the cathedral. The work continued through several episcopates and, as part of the scheme, a new Choir Screen was erected between the two eastern piers of the crossing. The earlier wooden Rood Screen, which stood between the western piers of the crossing, may, in consequence, have been removed or remodeled or it may even have been left intact in its place; we seem to have no information about it.

Because his coat of arms adorns the altar-platforms which stand in front of the Choir Screen, it has generally been assumed that Archbishop Blacader erected the entire structure between the two piers; though it is well to remember that his coat of arms does not appear anywhere on the actual screen. Apart from these sculptured coats of arms, the only surviving document, which refers to Blacader's work at this place, is the charter, recorded in the Cathedral Register, instituting three chaplainries; two in the cathedral, at the altars of the Name of Jesus and of Our Lady of Pity, and one at the chapel of St. Mungo at Culross. Now, the entering of this charter in the Cathedral Register appears to have been carelessly done: the Jesus Altar is described as being north of the door of the church, a statement which has led antiquarians, notably Archbishop Eyre, to locate this altar in the nave to the north of the great west door. This version of the charter also commits Blacader to the improbable course of "constructing and repairing" this Holy Name Altar. We are fortunate in having an accurate copy of Blacader's charter, entered in the Register of the Great Seal. This clears up the problems and states that the two altars, of the Name of Jesus and of Our Lady of Pity, stood in front of the screen on either side of the entrance to the choir, the Jesus Altar standing to the north of the entrance and the other altar to the south. The important point is that, in this charter, Blacader claims to have built only the southern altar, that of Our Lady of Pity—"per ipsum edificatum": the northern altar was already apparently in existence and he claims only that it was repaired, or remodeled, by him—"per ipsum reparatum." This charter clearly suggests that the Choir Screen, with its northern altar already built, was in existence when Blacader succeeded to the See of Glasgow.

When work was resumed under the new bishop, some change of plan was made (possibly involving a new stair to the lower Church): the northern altar-platform, with its altar of the Name of Jesus, would be remodeled to fit into the new scheme and an entirely new southern altar provided and dedicated to Our Lady of Pity. This would mean that the Choir Screen was erected, not by Robert Blacader, but by Bishop John Laing or even by some earlier bishop.

There is another point which has never been discussed, as far as I know, and which may prove a useful clue. In the four compartments, on either side of the entrance, the Choir Screen originally had eight statues, standing on corbels. The statues have gone and the corbels have been chiseled away. When was this done? I suggest that this is not an instance of iconoclastic vandalism (because the other sculptures on the screen are intact) but that this has been done at the end of the medieval period and done for a very definite purpose. The two altars in front of the Choir Screen would have the normal late-medieval type of altar-piece—wooden panels, painted with representations of the Holy Name and of Our Lady of Pity, each framed in gilded tabernacle work. The statues and corbels were presumably removed to allow these altarpieces to stand flat against the arcaded front of the screen.

For what it is worth, I outline my own idea of the history of the cathedral Choir Screen for more competent people to discuss. It seems to me that the great difference in style, spirit and craftsmanship between the carved work on the parapet of the screen and the somewhat debased sculptures of the altar-platforms, constructed in the Blacader period, demands a very considerable lapse of time between the execution of the two pieces of work. From this, one might argue that the actual screen must be much earlier than Blacader's time, possibly as early as the episcopate of William Turnbull (1447–54) or even John Cameron (1426–46). When first built, the screen was not intended to have altars in front of it and it was decorated (like a simpler variant of the magnificent screen in York

Minster) with figures of saints or kings, standing on corbels in each arched panel. As convenient locations for new altars gradually grew scarcer in the cathedral in the fifteenth century, a new altar, that of the Name of Jesus, was eventually erected against the Choir Screen, to the north of the doorway. Then came Blacader, with a plan for reorganizing the whole area in front of the screen: he reconstructed the recently founded Jesus Altar (perhaps to make it fit in with a new approach to the Lower Church and, of course, he adorned its platform with his own coat of arms): he built a corresponding altar on the south side of the door, dedicated to Our Lady of Pity, and at some point in all this work of reconstruction, the original statues, which adorned the front of the Choir Screen, were removed and their corbels were chiseled away to allow the altarpieces of the new altars to be fixed securely against the arcaded wall. This seems to be the sequence of events which best fits the available evidence.

However, no matter what the experts may decide, we will probably all go on calling the Choir Screen by Archbishop Blacader's name.

From time to time the nineteenth-century stone balustrades, which stand in the north and south transepts of Glasgow Cathedral, come in for a measure of criticism. These balustrades date from the restoration of the cathedral which was carried out in 1854–56; they are heavy and out of proportion to the architectural details around them and no doubt the appearance of the whole area would benefit by their removal. Few architects, however, are prepared to say what should take their place. An interesting contribution to any such discussion would be to establish what the crossing area of the cathedral looked like in the Middle Ages. For this purpose I have prepared a sketch of what I think the area looked like at the end of the medieval period. This reconstruction is conjectural but it is by no means purely fanciful and in the notes which follow I will attempt to justify the various details of the picture.

This 1967 drawing by David McRoberts illustrates the probable appearance of the crossing area in the early sixteenth century. The Rood Loft bridged the space between the two western piers and seems to have been supported on either side on short screens. The altars of the Holy Name and of Our Lady of Pity were built on platforms against the Choir Screen. The organ, standing on the Choir Screen, would face east but the back of its case and the doors would be painted with some devotional imagery which was popular at the period.

When the crossing area of the cathedral was completed internally, some time in the thirteenth century, the access to the Lower Church, which housed the tomb of the patron saint, was planned with noble simplicity. On either side of the entrance to the choir, north and south, flights of steps, the whole width of the transepts, led down to entrance porches of three open arches and the roof of these porches formed the floor space of the transepts. These entrances to the Lower Church probably did not remain long in their original state. At some unknown, but early, date the western arch of both the north and south porches was covered over to provide flights of steps ascending from the central floor space up to the higher floor levels in the two transepts. Dr. John Honeyman, writing in the early years of the twentieth century, could not see any reason why these flights of steps should have been introduced. A clue to the circumstances which brought them into being is, however, provided by the drawing of the crossing area made by James Collie in 1833, before the evidence was destroyed by the erection of the present balustrades.

The flights of steps are shown clearly in Collie's drawing but, in place of the balustrades, they are contained within a section of wall, which is carried forward at the level of the transept floor and, in the south transept, this wall still retains on its upper course the remnants of the mullions of a screen which appears to have enclosed the stairs and then turned east, on the line of the modern balustrades, to meet the Choir Screen. These sections of screen work are of considerable interest because, occupying this position, they could only have formed part of the substructure of the medieval Rood Loft about which we are so ill-informed. The Rood Screen, with its entrance gates in the nave and aisles, would run the whole width of the church on the line of the western piers of the crossing. Above this screen was the Rood Loft (its access stair is still to be seen in the northeast corner of the north aisle of the nave). This Rood Loft had to be broad enough at the center to accommodate the Holy Cross Altar which stood in front of the Great Rood. To achieve sufficient space the Rood Loft apparently stretched back into the crossing area, bridging the central space in a broad arch which rested on the two short screens to north and south. The passages formed between these short screens and the western piers were contrived as access stairs which conveniently linked the central area with the transepts and obviated any need to go out and in through the doors of the Rood Screen.

Some time in the early fifteenth century, the original (and probably wooden) Choir Screen was replaced by the stone screen which still exists. Originally this screen did not have altars in front of it but its panels were adorned by statues standing on carved corbels. The central area in the Middle Ages was thus entirely surrounded by screens of wood or stone: the Choir Screen cut it off from the chancel: the Rood Screen cut it off from the nave: and the lateral screens cut it off from the transepts. These screens, with their extensions, formed an important part of the security arrangements which every large medieval church tried to maintain. The lateral screens at Glasgow were probably solid and, like the Rood Screen, probably incorporated the presses and cupboards in which vestments, altar vessels and ornaments were stored. The screens, in effect, made the central area and the transepts into three passages, linking up the nave and its aisles with the eastern section of the church. These are the three transes or passageways mentioned by Bishop Andrew Muirhead in the instructions he issued for the cathedral sacristan in the year 1459, where he speaks of "omnia ornamenta ecclesie que sunt infra illam clausuram seu ingressum ad chorum per tres transitus Anglice et vulgariter nuncupatis le Gemma duris"— all the church ornaments which are kept within that enclosure or entrance to the choir through the three transes which in everyday English we call "the Gemma Doors."[3]

Some time, possibly in the episcopate of Bishop John Laing (1473–82), the altar of the Holy Name of Jesus was erected in front of the Choir Screen to the north of the entrance. Later, Bishop Robert Blacader erected the corresponding altar on the south side, dedicated to Our Lady of Pity. The construction of these altars is extremely unusual. Two "pedestals" were built in front of the Choir Screen on the stairs to the Lower Church. A bridge was thrown from these "pedestals" to the floor-level of the transepts, thus forming two platforms, which would be surrounded by a railing in stone, wood or metal, and which would be entered from doors in the lateral screens. The altars were erected on these platforms and the statues and corbels of the Choir Screen were removed to allow the painted altarpieces to be fixed to the wall of the screen. These platforms must have blocked up the eastern arches of the two entrance porches leading to the Lower Church. The two "pedestals" still survive and, in the nineteenth-century restoration, they were given heavy freestone cornices to make them look like altars but the springer corbels of the arch, which linked the south "pedestal" with the pavement of the transept, still remain to show the original design and, in James Collie's drawing of the south transept, this connecting bridge is shown as still existing in 1833.

The general aspect of the area under the central tower as it probably appeared in the early sixteenth century is reconstructed in the accompanying sketch. Standing between the western piers, with one's back

---

3. The editor is grateful to Dr. Simon Taylor and Professor Richard Fawcett for help in elucidating the phrase *Gemma duris*. Dr. Taylor suggests substituting J for G (which would be the same sound) to give *Jamma*. That would indicate something in three sections, perhaps a three-sectioned door. Professor Fawcett points out that the rood screen must have extended across the nave and both aisles, presumably with doors in both the nave and the two aisles. On the basis of this advice it might be suggested that the *Gemma duris* were the three doors in the rood screen, which might fit with the three *transes* (passageways) in the text.

to the Rood Screen, the arch carrying the Rood Loft would be directly overhead. On either side would be the screens which supported the arch of the Rood Loft and which enclosed the stairs to the north and south transepts. On either side of the entrance to the choir two small platforms, entered from gates in the lateral screens, contained the fifteenth-century altars of the Holy Name and of Our Lady of Pity. These would be adorned with typical altarpieces of the period and an acquaintance with late medieval artistic traditions makes it easy to reconstruct their imagery. The great organ of the cathedral would stand on the Choir Screen. It would face towards the chancel but, since it occupied such an important position, the back of it would be highly decorated and probably, like the organ in King's College, Aberdeen, it would display a picture of the Madonna and Child. I have suggested a picture of "Sancta Maria in sole," which was a popular devotional image in Scotland in the late Middle Ages and which appears in other northern churches in this position. On either side, the thirteenth-century flights of steps lead down through the remaining central arches of the entrance porches to the Lower Church and the tomb of St. Mungo. The painted and carved work on the screens over these entrances to the Lower Church would very likely depict something of the life and miracles of the patron saint to enkindle a proper sense of veneration in those who approached his tomb. Among the flagstones of the floor would be the brasses and carved tombstones which marked the graves of prominent men and women of the past.

This central area of Glasgow Cathedral was quite remarkable for the rather bewildering and dramatic variations of floor level it displayed. Like the rest of the cathedral, it would be resplendent with gilding and vivid with color and, as we reconstruct in imagination the splendid vistas to be seen on every side through screens and doors, we can appreciate the pride which the medieval citizens of Glasgow had in the mother church of the city.

9

Archbishop Robert Blackadder's Will

John Durkan

Robert Blackadder (d. 1508) was the first archbishop of Glasgow.[1] After studying at St. Andrews and Paris he became abbot of Melrose and was bishop-elect of Aberdeen when translated to Glasgow. He played an important role in the government of James IV who supported the creation of an archbishopric by the Pope in 1492. One reason behind this decision was the alleged danger of having ecclesiastical power vested in only one archbishop, but Blackadder's fulfillment of his ambition led to a bitter rivalry with the archbishop of St. Andrews. As was common in this period, diplomacy was also part of the Archbishop's role. He made trips to Rome, France and Spain and, in 1505, was involved in negotiating the marriage between King James IV and Margaret, eldest daughter of Henry VII of England. Blackadder died while on a pilgrimage to Jerusalem in 1508. His will was drawn up in Venice before leaving for the Holy Land and in this chapter John Durkan discusses his various benefactions.

---

1. Biographical details can be found in the online *Oxford Dictionary of National Biography* https://doi.org/10.1093/ref:odnb/2505

Seal of Robert Blackadder (1500) from Robert Renwick's "Glasgow Memorials."

IN THE LATE 1950S, working in Italian archives, Rosamond J. Mitchell[2] chanced upon a notarial copy of the will of Robert Blackadder, archbishop of Glasgow, made in Venice before his ill-fated departure for the Holy Land in the summer of 1508. She reported her findings, with a transcript of the copy in the *Bolletino dell' Istituto di Storia della Società e dello Stato Veneziano*, i (1959), 169–178. As her find seems to have been overlooked, it seems worth drawing attention to it here, and linking any information in it with other scattered facts liable to throw light on the history of Glasgow Cathedral.

Blackadder left Scotland sometime in February 1507–8, probably calling at Orleans and spending Easter in Rome before visiting the doge in Venice on May 16 and asking his advice on how best to travel on to Jerusalem.[3] Among those present were the Cattaveri who looked after the pilgrimage arrangements, and during the last fortnight in May the archbishop agreed with the owner-captain, Bernardo di Marconi, to charter a small ship to carry himself and thirty-five retainers to Jaffa. Both this vessel and the regular pilgrim galley left and returned to Venice on the same day. Blackadder stayed over for the ceremony of the wedding with the

---

2. Rosamond J. Mitchell (1902–63) was an English historian and author of various books, mostly on the medieval period.

3. *Innes Review* 20, 92–94.

sea, lodging meantime at the Cà Frizier in the Cannaregio and remaining certainly till as late June 13, the date of his will.

This will is registered among the Venetian testaments under the rubric "Robertus Blavater" by the notary, Cristoforo Bortolo.[4] The original probably returned to Scotland, so that we must rely on this registered copy by an Italian scribe quite unfamiliar with Scottish proper names.

The preamble states that the doge, Leonardo Loredan, was approached in council by Roland Blackadder, subdean of Glasgow, and John Shearer, archdeacon of Ross, the archbishop's executors. This was on November 20. They explained that Blackadder drew up his will in Venice on June 13 according to Scottish custom, that it was deposited with the Florentine bankers, the Nerli, and that he afterwards proceeded towards the holy sepulchre on the way towards which he died: that is, therefore, probably not at Jerusalem as a near-contemporary chronicler says.[5] On the request of the two executors, the doge agreed to have the will copied verbatim by his chancery, three witnesses having previously confirmed that it was authentic and in the archbishop's own hand.

Blackadder leaves his "wretched little soul" to God, Mary and all saints, and his "wretched body" to be buried, if he dies in Scotland, in the church of St. Kentigern and before the choir in the presence of the image of Jesus on the cross at his head. On his right would be the altar of the name of Jesus; on his left, the altar of the Virgin Mary of Pity, and at his feet, the image of the Blessed Virgin Mary of Consolation. After all debts have been paid, he wishes first to leave £100 Scots for trigentals of masses to be celebrated immediately on his death, and likewise £100 to the poor to pray for him. To the Friars Minor of Glasgow he leaves 40 merks and to those in Ayr £20 "to preach the word of God in the diocese" (in which there had been some Lollard troubles) and similarly to the Glasgow Blackfriars £10 and to those in Ayr five merks.

He leaves towards the building in the college of Glasgow of a church in honor of the names of Jesus and Mary a sum of £60 out of the debts owed him by Mr James Merchamstron (probably for Merchamstoun) as is clear in his account book which the archbishop's chamberlain keeps with other books in his small study. He orders 300 merks to be spent on that part of the crossing begun by him and not yet finished.

4. Archivio di Stato di Venezia, Sezione Notarile, Testamenti, Busta 1229, Protocollo 1, *n.* 145, *cc.* 121 verso–122 verso.

5. *Registrum Episcopatus Aberdonensis*, ii, 248: "qui Hierosolimis peregre profectus ibidem ultimum clausit diem."

He also leaves all his goods in his Glasgow and Edinburgh houses, along with his scarlet cope, to his successor. All his other robes he wishes to be sold and the money accruing from this sale given to the poor.

There follow some other donations to different chapels: 200 merks to complete the perpetual feu for the chaplain and repair of the church of "Bentamel," as he thinks the king will permit the purchase of the necessary lands; £10 to the repair of the chapel of our Lady of Edrom and the same to that of the church of St. Kentigern near Culross; likewise also to the chapels of our Lady of "Estnesbet" (East Nisbet) and of "Gervualtu" (Garvald possibly).

Other personal bequests follow, first of all to his household:100 French gold crowns to John Heriot plus his expenses for returning to Scotland and likewise twenty to Forton, "quocho" (Colquhoun?), Forman and "Gloriat" (Stirling of Glorat probably).[6] Forty are to go to Charles Blackadder, ten to Alexander Barber, five to "Bronster," twenty to Adam Blackadder, forty to Baldred his brother-german[7] and to his sister Elizabeth, ten to John Hamilton's wife and to David Lindsay's, twenty to Euphemia Hunter, because she was pleasing at all times to all and to those other relatives whose names do not come to mind according to their need and his executors' discretion. The rest of his goods in gold and silver are to be sold for giving to the poor or for masses.

The goods which Jeronimo de Frescobaldis has of his are to be held on bond between the rector of Glasgow and Heriot at Orleans. There is a deposit with Alessandro Nerli at Venice including robes: Master Hugh "Gerulan" holds the bond and the "memorials." His chamberlain is aware of his money and goods in Scotland, but, if he were to die before returning there, he wishes to be buried in any church before the images of Jesus crucified and his mother, Mary.

Finally he appoints as executors Roland Blackadder, subdean; Robert Blackadder, rector of Glasgow; John Scherar, archdeacon of Ross; Sir Andrew Marchell, rector of "Lyus" (probably Lyne), his chamberlain or any three, or two, or one of them. The king himself is declared superior of his testament. The will is endorsed with a reminder to the king of his long services and the great consideration he has always shown him. The witnesses are the doge, two councillors, and the notary.

---

6. A William Gloret is recorded in *Liber Protocollorum M. Cuthberti Simonii*, 470. [Hereafter *Prot. Bk. Simon*].

7. That is, a full brother as opposed to a half-brother or step-brother.

One would like to know more about the twenty-seven dead among the Scots pilgrims, and exactly when news of the disaster became available in Venice: certainly it was in the hands of the secretary of Domenico Grimani, cardinal of St. Mark, by October 23, 1508, having been brought to Rome post-haste by Sir Thomas Halkerston, royal proctor.[8] The Glasgow chapter was aware of it by November, although the Marconi galley did not return to Venice till November 14. Presumably therefore Roland Blackadder and Shearer were in the party. Thomas Fortoun is probably the man referred to in the will, as he seems to be making arrangements to leave Glasgow for abroad on February 13 as also George Akinhead, vicar of Dalziel (not in the will).[9] The wife of John Hamilton referred to is presumably Margaret Hynd.[10] John Heriot returned, but possibly not Alexander Barbour.[11] The David Lindsay mentioned is the Glasgow bailie, Lindsay of Dunrod.[12] Hugh Greenlaw was commissary of Nith, Desnes and Annandale.[13] "Bronster" is either Alexander or Sir Andrew Browster.[14] The latter took the curate of Glasgow's place in the lower church before high mass on October 5, 1494, at the second proclamation of the banns of marriage for Patrick Blackadder of Tulliallan and Elizabeth Edmundston,[15] the parishioners being gathered in "a copious multitude." He was preceded at the first proclamation the previous Sunday by Mr John Scott, curate, making the announcement to the parishioners "before the altar of St. John the apostle and evangelist in the lower church of Glasgow." On the third occasion on October 12, Scott, described then as "vicar curate," made the announcement and Robert Blackadder, canon of Aberdeen, as procurator for the couple, took instruments before the notary, John de Thornton, in the presence of several Glasgow burgesses. This interesting document shows the correctness of my surmise that this was the parish altar, and Scott was perhaps vicar pensioner *in rure*.[16]

8. *Letters of James IV*, no. 222.
9. *Prot. Bk. Simon*, 264–65.
10. *Prot. Bk. Simon*, 40.
11. *Prot. Bk. Simon*, 435, 246.
12. *Prot. Bk. Simon*, 37.
13. *Prot. Bk. Simon*, 280. *Fasti*, 247.
14. *Prot. Bk. Simon*, 495, 192.
15. Beveridge, *Culross and Tulliallan*, ii. 320, says Tulliallan came to the Blackadders through inter-marriage with Edmondstones.
16. National Records of Scotland [hereafter NRS], GD1/393/1; Scott was vicar pensioner of Glasgow, *Prot. Bk. Simon*, 138; cf. Also my remarks in *Innes Review* 21,

Forman may be the John Forman who is one of the archbishop's retainers who had a royal remission for the murder of a Rutherford at Jedburgh.[17] Robert Blackadder, rector of Glasgow, and James Heriot, vicar of Dumfries, were both at the university of Orleans as law students in 1507.[18]

It is clear from Blackadder's description that his proposed tomb was to be in the center of the transept with his head to the rood screen behind him (and that therefore by this date the rood screen was the present stone screen): this does not eliminate a possible earlier screen which may have stood further west, as the ogee-headed doorway at the north end suggests. To his right (and on the north) was to be the Jesus altar, to his left (and south) the Lady of Pity altar; and, hanging in mid-nave between the great west pillars of the central tower and at his feet, the image, or painting of our Lady of Consolation: that is, moved to the center and into the light from the adjoining altar of St, John Baptist, where originally it was perhaps intended to stand.[19] This would place the site of the latter altar at the south-western pillar of the tower, with St. Cuthbert and St. Kentigern to follow at the second and third bays further west. That the St. Kentigern altar was at this third pillar from the present screen is confirmed by the site of the Stewarts of Minto tomb "still to be seen in the choir of the cathedral upon the left of the main entrance."[20]

McUre tells us something about the area where the proposed Blackadder tomb was to be, which is worth noting, as he wrote before two disasters that struck the central tower, one in 1739 and another in 1756. After 1739 the vault supporting the tower had to be renewed with exchequer assistance by James Cross, it would seem at great cost; and again by his former apprentice, Mungo Naismith, in 1756, so much so that it was feared it would have to be taken down but for his expertise.[21] Perhaps

---

51, 59.

17. Hood, *Rutherfords of that Ilk*, lxxvii–lxxviii, and supplementary notes (after 56).

18. *Miscellany of the Scottish History Society*, ii, 47–114.

19. *Registrum Episcopatus Glasguensis*, ii. 519; *Innes Review* 21, 50.

20. This "main entrance," now blocked up, was in the second bay of the nave (Denholm uses "choir" for the east end of the nave as do many writers of the time): Denholm, *History of Glasgow*, 282; *Innes Review* 21, 66.

21. James Cleland, *Annals of Glasgow*, i, 33; *Extracts from Glasgow Records*, vi, 20–1, 27, 49, 483; compare also v, 406. Two soldiers in the nave were killed by falling stonework: Gordon, *Glasghu Facies*, i, 421.

therefore the apparent inaccuracies of Slezer's drawing of 1678 (where the central tower looks different from, for example, the representation in Robert Paul's print) are less glaring than they seem. McUre, writing in 1736, uses "nave" for "choir" and "choir" for the east end of the nave (though his usage is not consistent, perhaps because sometimes he is borrowing from other sources).[22] He states that Blackadder founded several altarages

> "in the Choir (=east end of nave) and caused place his Arms above them, in the Roof of the lower Area . . . without either Mytre or Crosier; and above it, in large capital Letters, *Robertus Archiepiscopus* (the vaulting above before the steeple flooring was renewed). He raised the Ascents of each side of the church by steps, from the Nave (=present choir) to the Floor, of fine Work, with Effigies, as I take it, of the Apostles, neatly graved; and in the Descent, on both Sides, you will see the Archbishop's Arms, in several Places at large, with his Mytre and other *Pontificalia*, with the Initials of his Name."

Some of this work was obviously destroyed in the restoration work after the two hurricanes. My conjecture is that the site of the proposed tomb was taken up by the later St. Thomas Martyr altar (to which, I believe, was added, by the same founder, the chaplainry of St. Anne), described as "next to the choir" (*iuxta chorum*).[23]

There is no further evidence that the university chapel proposed by the archbishop ever took form. There were arms of the Blackadders of Tulliallan on the university principal's house as late as the nineteenth century, but these would represent the addition of property belonging to the chaplainry founded by them at St. Mungo's tomb.[24] Nor is there evidence that the completion of the second story of the Blackadder aisle was ever attempted. McUre says of it, "I apprehend he has intended to have made it a Wing, to enlarge the Cross towards the South, to answer the Ruins of some Appartments for the Priests that are towards the North."[25] In the seventeenth century this aisle was called the Fergus aisle, and it is worth

---

22. *View of the City of Glasgow*, 26–27; cf. his use of "choir" on 213. McUre patently thought the site of the medieval high altar was that of the post-Reformation pulpit (in his day in mid-choir to the south), as he refers to royal arms to the left of it as on the *south* (83).

23. *Innes Review* 21, 60.

24. Sir Michael Connal, *Diary*, 151, 268.

25. *View*, 27.

noting that at Aberdeen from which Blackadder had come as bishop to Glasgow, there was kept a relic of "Saint" Fergus.[26] But apart from the "ile of car Fergus" carving, there seems no reason to postulate any motive on the archbishop's part except a two-story shrine to St. Mungo, enshrining his relics, it may be over the site of the Fergus tomb. The "appartments" in the northern part of this cross are represented now by a small boiler house: they probably constituted a medieval treasury with sacristy above, as others have suggested. This was known in the nineteenth century as the "dripping aisle" as, due to its roofless state, water oozed from it into the main church. Earlier names are perhaps more indicative, as it would seem there was no external door to the lower part. In 1807, the problem of the rainwater is noted when it is called "the droping isle."[27] In 1749 somebody is seen coming through the churchyard "at the end of the Dreeping isle."[28] There was for a time a door in the south end of Blackadder's aisle, but this was created for funeral purposes in 1649 when it became a burial place for ministers.[29] It can be seen on old prints.

To return to the will. The church at "Bentamel" suggests Bentmill, lands near Melrose.[30] If we, however, reverse the name, we get Welbent, where we know Blackadder made a foundation. It is probably the chaplain of Welbent who is found interloping in the glebe at Carstairs by Alexander Panter, vicar, in 1504/5: if so, he denied that the Glasgow diocesan authorities were competent judges.[31] Blackadder was forced to fall back on the petty customs from the waulk mill at Partick on the Kelvin for its maintenance, and, of course, this could be the Welbent-mill.[32] The chaplain of Welbent in 1566 was David Gibson.[33] There is reason to think that Blackadder did not get the king's consent to the purchase of additional revenues, as in 1512 Alexander Panter had to buy endowments in Glasgow, in the High Street and Fishergate.[34] Its name is left blank in a grant to James Hamilton of Liberton after Carstairs barony's annexation

26. On 1464/5 and 1496/7 his silver relic is mentioned: *Aberdeen Registrum*, ii, 143, 167.
27. *Extracts from Glasgow Records*, ix, 566.
28. NRS, CH2/173/4 (Barony minutes), 315.
29. *Glasgow Records*, ii, 157.
30. *Melrose Regality Records*, i, 153, 155.
31. *Prot. Bk. Simon*, 75–76.
32. *Glasgow Registrum*, ii, 519; occupied by Donald Lyon in 1517: *Rental Book*, 75.
33. Renwick, *Protocols of Glasgow*, v, 1535.
34. *Prot. Bk. Simon*, 457–59.

to the crown.³⁵ But it reappears in 1606 as Ladiewelbent in a procuratory of resignation by Hamilton of Avondale in favor of James Lockhart of Lee.³⁶ The executors of Blackadder by 1511 were able to announce the terms after three weeks' notice on the south doors of the cathedral. They were the same persons named in the will, but the archbishop's successor, James Beaton, protested that its terms should not be prejudicial to him.³⁷

The chapel of St. Mary of Edrom is better attested. The Blackadders originally came from this neighborhood and Edrom is on the Whiteadder water at no great distance from Blackadder: it had at one time been a popular shrine. At first attached to Durham, its parsonage revenues were held by Coldingham.³⁸ In a foundation of January 12, 1499/1500, Archbishop Blackadder mentions the chaplainry in the aisle newly built by him within the parish church of "aderhame" in honor of our Lady and St. John Baptist, with presentation to the laird of Blackadder and collation to the archbishop of St. Andrews.³⁹ The chapel with a Marian dedication at East Nisbet was a pendicle of Edrom and also attached to Coldingham.⁴⁰ It too is near the Blackadder domain. It is not the Nisbet in Jedburgh parish, although the archbishop's arms adorn the north transept of Jedburgh abbey.

The chapel of St. Mary of "Gervualtu" causes greater problems. It is unlikely to be Garvald near Haddington, though the archbishop's chapel at Edrom was maintained from revenues in the Lipirgate and elsewhere in that town. It seems equally unlikely to be the parish church of Garvald (or Garrell) in Nithsdale which Blackadder tried to donate to Glasgow university in 1506.⁴¹ The rector of Garvald then was Patrick Coventry who with Adam Colquhoun was involved in an action against Failfurd monastery in 1509 to be judged by Archbishop Beaton's commissaries: I suspect this action concerned Garvald. However this may be, the

35. *Acts Parl. Scot.,* iii, 622, cited in *Origines Parochiales,* i, 124.
36. NRS, GD1/59/38.
37. *Prot. Bk. Simon,* 426–28.
38. Cowan, *Parishes of Medieval Scotland,* 60.

39. National Library of Scotland, Advocates MS 9A.1.9, 198/206. Gordon, in his *Vade Mecum* (201) writes: "An aisle of the Parish Church of Edrom, Berwickshire, formed the burial place of the family of Blacader. It bears this inscription: 'Founded by Robert Blacader, Archbishop of Glasgow, in the year 1499.' On the S.E. corner: 'Repaired by S. John Horne, of Blackader, in 1696.'"

40. Cowan, *Parishes,* 60.
41. *Prot. Bk. Simon,* 132.

Trinitarians of Fail undoubtedly acquired Garvald and held it till the Reformation.[42]

There is another possibility, however. The reading may be Gareaucht or something similar. There was an image of our Lady of "le Garroch" in the cathedral in medieval times.[43] If this is the local Garroch on the Kelvin, in early times often called "the Garroch,"[44] it might point to a shrine maintained like that at Welbent. If not, it could be a statue recalling the well-known shrine of our Lady of the Garioch near Balquhain, Aberdeenshire, perhaps donated by Walter Leslie of Balquhain, university principal in Glasgow 1483–85, who founded a service of Sts. Mungo and Thenew at the church of St. Nicholas, Aberdeen.[45] It is worth noting that the name survived in 1743. In that year on April 23, it was stated in the Barony records that a great part of the collection for the lower church was lost because there were no collectors at that door "that enters into that part of the Church called the Garrioch Spence" and members who last time collected at the great door of the church were henceforward to collect at the Garrioch Spence door and go between the said door and the pulpit door.[46] (The great door to the lower church is on the south and the pulpit stood within sight of it. There was a north door facing that and the Garrioch Spence door may have been the small one near the medieval treasury). At St. Machar's, Aberdeen, the northern appendage or "tuffal" had a north door and inside this was an altar of St. Ninian at which in 1454 the bishop founded a chaplainry of Westhall[47]: but there is no sign of a north door in the earliest Glasgow prints of the "dreeping aisle."[48] In any event, there is no need to equate this shrine with that of Blackadder's proposed gift, which on the balance of evidence must be assigned to Garvald in Nithsdale.

Blackadder's will[49] is a firm basis from which to revise our story of Glasgow Cathedral, though it does not answer all our questions. It shows

42. *Prot. Bk. Simon*, 324–25: called "monasterium de Furd"; Cowan, *Parishes*, 72.

43. *Glasgow Protocols*, ii, 112.

44. *Rental Book*, 95, 105, 109, 127.

45. *Cartularium Ecclesiae Sancti Nicholai*, ii, 341; *Munimenta Universitatis Glasguensis*, ii, 89, 97, 230–51.

46. CH2/173/4, 90. In the rental (1511) of "Gareauch" deanery, teinds include "Glasgow major" and "Glasgow minor": *Aberdeen Registrum*, i, 357.

47. *Aberdeen Registrum*, i, 268.

48. Illustrated in *Innes Review* 21, facing 148.

49. The complete Latin text of the will can be found at the end of the original article

him having not a merely local interest, however, but to have an eye on the wider national scene. In the age of James IV, the answer to whatever challenge was presented by the Lollards, was a new cult of national shrines, the memory of which almost disappeared completely in the religious revolution which lay only a few decades away.

---

in *Innes Review* 20 (1972) 138–48.

10

The Tombs of St. Kentigern and Bishop Wishart in the Lower Church

E. L. G. STONES

In the late 1960s Professor Lionel Stones published a number of short articles on various aspects of the architecture and furnishings of Glasgow Cathedral. This chapter consists of two of these which deal with the tombs in the lower church, believed to be those of St. Kentigern (St. Mungo) and Robert Wishart (1271–c.1316), bishop of Glasgow during the Scottish Wars of Independence and a supporter of William Wallace and Robert Bruce. Wishart was so committed to the cause that he used timber given to him by King Edward I for repairs to the cathedral's bell-tower to make siege engines against the English troops.

ST. KENTIGERN[1]

VISITORS TO THE LOWER church are familiar with the square stone platform near to its western end, over which rises a canopy of stone arches. The arrangement is most unusual, and possibly unique. It must have been

---

1. Source: Stones, "Notes on Glasgow Cathedral," *Innes Review*, 18 (1967) 88–98 (slightly condensed).

meant to give special dignity to whatever lay in that position, but nothing is now left to show what that thing was. The notice placed there at present says that it was the tomb of St. Mungo, meaning, presumably, the place where the body actually lay in the Middle Ages. Now a great thirteenth-century church (this part of the cathedral appears to have been built in the time of Bishop Bondington, 1233–58) did not usually place the body of its saint, if it possessed one, down in a crypt or undercroft. The normal position was on a high stone pedestal behind the high altar. Structures of this kind, now deprived, of course, of the saint's body, may still be seen in England at St. Albans abbey (dating from the early fourteenth century),[2] at the cathedrals of Ely (1252), Chester (c.1310), and Oxford (1289), and at a few other places. At Westminster even the body of Edward the Confessor still survives as well, though since the Reformation it has been removed to a position in the base of the pedestal above which it was originally placed in 1269.[3] Occasionally the pedestal was situated elsewhere than behind the high altar, but it was always high (in order that the shrine on top of it could be seen from a distance) and, except at Glasgow, there seems never to have been any suggestion that it was put down below the level of the main floor of the church.

The Tomb of St. Mungo in the lower church. Photo: Glen Collie.

2. *Guide to St. Albans Cathedral*, frontispiece. This is the shrine of St. Alban himself; but the abbey has also the pedestal of the shrine of St. Amphibalus. This is illustrated in Cook, *Portrait of St. Albans Cathedral*, plate 47.

3. O'Neilly and Tanner, "The Shrine of St. Edward the Confessor," 129–54; Perkins, *Westminster Abbey*, 105, 115.

If we assume that Bishop Bondington and his architect dealt with the body of St. Kentigern in the way that they would see adopted elsewhere at the time, they would leave a space in the upper church behind the high altar, and place there an arcaded stone pedestal, like those mentioned above as surviving now in England, standing probably well above head-height, and with its long axis running east and west. On top of it would rest the richly decorated coffin or shrine, often called the feretory, containing the remains of the saint. The reredos of the high altar would be low enough[4] to permit worshipers in the western part of the church to see the feretory rising above. So it was in Westminster Abbey where, to quote a contemporary chronicler, King Henry III in 1269 so translated the relics of Edward the Confessor "that they were no more like a light hidden under a bushel, but raised high, as on a candlestick, to offer an ample spiritual light to men as they came and went."[5] There are many drawings in medieval manuscripts which show the original appearance of the raised shrines.[6]

It will be useful to consider what can be learned from some thirteenth-century documents. When Edward I visited Glasgow in 1301 he made offerings in the cathedral which are recorded in the accounts of his wardrobe. Cosmo Innes printed one of these passages in his edition of the *Registrum* of Glasgow. It is as follows:

> Vicesimo die Augusti [1301] in oblationibus regis ad feretrum Sancti Kentegerni in ecclesia cathedrali Glasguensi: vij.s.[i.e. 7 shillings].
>
> xxj. die Augusti in oblationibus regis in ecclesia predicta ad magnum altare, vij.s.et ad feretrum sancti Kentegerni, vij.s.
>
> xxj. die Septembris in oblationibus regis ad feretrum sancti Kentigerni in ecclesia cathedrali Glasguensi: vijs.[7]

Cosmo Innes did not, however, print another extremely important passage on the same folio of the manuscript. Fortunately it was later

---

4. In the later Middle Ages the view was often obscured by a higher reredos, as a Westminster Abbey (see Perkins, *Westminster Abbey*, 66–67).

5. Chronicle of Thomas Wykes in *Annales Monastici*, iv, 226.

6. The appearance of the precious coffin which lay on top of the pedestal can best be appreciated from surviving examples in Germany, for example at Aachen, Cologne, and Marburg.

7. Innes, *Glasgow Registrum*, 621.

printed by Joseph Bain, but its existence seems hardly to have been noticed by Glasgow antiquaries. It is as follows:

> xxiiij° die Septembris [1301] in oblationibus regis ad magnum altare in ecclesia Glasguensi, vij.s.,et ad tumbam Sancti Kentegerni in volta ejusdem ecclesie, vij.s.[8]

Obviously these passages taken together suggest that there were two places in the cathedral where veneration was offered to Kentigern: (a) the feretory and (b) the tomb "in the vault," that is the lower church. These documents in themselves are not absolute proof, because unfortunately Edward did not leave offerings at both "feretory" and "tomb" on the same day; it is, therefore, just possible that (a) and (b) are different names for the same place. Search for further evidence from royal offerings at Glasgow has not been fruitful. Edward I was in Glasgow only in August and September, 1301[9] and there seem to be no other allusions in the English wardrobe accounts of that period.[10] But we are helped by evidence from Edward's offerings in other great churches. The account-book of the controller of Edward's wardrobe for 1299–1300 has been in print since 1787, and the thirty pages devoted to the king's alms-giving, as he traveled round the country, are a mine of information about the local cult of saints. At York Minster Edward gave 7/– [seven shillings] at the feretory of St. William, and also "ad tumbam ubi idem sanctus primo sepeliebatur."[11] At Beverley there is no mention of a feretory, but 7/– was given "ad tumbam ubi sanctus Johannes de Beverlaco primo sepeliebatur."[12] These records at once remind us of the circumstances at a still more famous church, the cathedral of Canterbury. After the murder of St. Thomas in 1170, his body was temporarily laid to rest in the crypt. In 1220 it was translated to the celebrated shrine in the upper church, which rested on a stone pedestal of the usual type. The empty tomb in the crypt continued, however, to be a center of the cult, and luckily it is depicted for us in several of the stained glass windows in the present cathedral of Canterbury.

---

8. *Cal. Docs. Scot.*, iv, 449.

9. Gough, *Itinerary of Edward I*, index.

10. Nor, apparently, are gifts to the shrine mentioned in the Scottish Exchequer Rolls, or Lord High Treasurer's Accounts, in such a way as to provide any clue.

11. *Liber Quotidianus*, 39.

12. *Liber Quotidianus*, 25 and cf. 37.

The relationships between shrines in various parts of Britain are not very well known, but it seems probable that the cult of an empty tomb at so famous a church at Canterbury would be a powerful stimulus to imitation elsewhere, and this probably explains the cases which we have noted at York and Beverley, where translations took place late in the thirteenth century.[13] At Glasgow the analogy was emphasized by the re-planning under Bondington, within twenty years of the translation of St. Thomas, to provide a spacious lower church like that of Canterbury. The Canterbury arrangement of a feretory above and an empty tomb below must have been well known in Glasgow, and it is very reasonable to suppose that it was imitated there.

It is interesting to speculate on the possible form of the "tomb" in the lower church at Glasgow. Canterbury had a long, low, structure, with oval apertures in the sides through which pilgrims could insert their hands. On top were placed candles, a money-box with a slit for coins, and coils of wax left as offerings. All of these objects do not always appear in the various windows at Canterbury, which sometimes show only some of them, and sometimes, indeed, nothing but the bare top itself. One point to bear in mind is that these empty tombs seem, as a rule, not only to have been the containers in which the relics lay before translation, but also to have commemorated the precise spot where the former burial had been. It is not architecturally impossible to suppose that the present stone canopy marks the place where the relics of St. Kentigern rested in Jocelin's church, dedicated in 1197. If the relics had originally been deposited, in what we may call the Celtic church of Glasgow, in a carved sarcophagus, like that which survives at Govan, or the much finer one at St. Andrews,[14] it is conceivable that it remained in the lower church, in its position of 1197, when the actual relics were moved upstairs into the sanctuary of Bondington's church. It must be emphasized that this is only a guess, and that other possibilities exist. At York Minster we know that the site of the original burial of St. William, at the west end of the nave,

---

13. At York St. William was translated from the nave to a feretory behind the high altar in 1284 (Harrison, *York Minster*, 200-201). For Beverley, see Leach, *Memorials of Beverley Minster*, 299-301 (contract for feretory dated 1292, with full details of construction).

14. For the Govan and St. Andrews sarcophagi, see Allen, *Early Christian Monuments of Scotland*, iii, plates 93, 72. The original burial of St. Kentigern is described by Jocelin as "under a stone on the right-hand side of the altar." (Forbes, *Lives of St. Ninian and St. Kentigern*, 218. One wonders if Jocelin was describing the position in his own day).

was covered with a fairly elaborate superstructure, large enough to seem big even when set in so great a building.[15]

Whatever there was at Glasgow must have been made in proportion to the canopy. We can also be sure that lights hung above, and around it, from the bosses above, and near to, the canopy.[16] A window at Canterbury seems to indicate that there was an arched canopy above the empty tomb of St. Thomas, with a light in the center of it, so that the parallel with Glasgow is certainly very close. We may add that it would certainly be vain to excavate beneath the platform of the tomb area, in the hope of finding the original tomb or the relics there, though this suggestion has sometimes been made.[17]

The Evidence from the Chapter Seal of Glasgow

We give here a few observations on the designs which appear on the contemporary chapter seal because they may be relevant to the study of both tomb and feretory as they were in the same century.

The oldest impression which is known to have survived from the matrices of this particular seal is found on a charter now in H. M. Register House.[18] Since this charter bears also the seal of Bishop Robert Wishart, it must have been issued between his election in 1271, and his imprisonment by Edward I in 1306. In 1903 P. Macgregor Chalmers suggested that the designers of this chapter seal intended to depict on it the feretory of St. Kentigern. In the light of what has been said above, his suggestion is well worth reconsideration now.

There is nothing inherently improbable in Chalmers's view. There is a very convincing example, which he does not quote among his parallels, on the thirteenth-century chapter seal of Dunkeld. The obverse of that seal[19] shows a casket with a sloping roof, and its sides decorated with arcading. In the center there is a gabled projection like the transept

---

15. Clutton-Brock, *Cathedral Church of York*, 126–27.

16. The stumps of iron hooks survive in the bosses, and the documents in the *Registrum* several times refer to the lights around the tomb.

17. Chalmers, "The Shrines of St. Margaret and St. Kentigern," 319, note: "the space within [the] four columns was excavated a few years ago. No trace of a tomb was found."

18. *Melrose Charters* (GD 55) no.327. The text is printed in *Liber de Melros*, i, 288–91.

19. Reproduced in Birch, *History of Scottish Seals*, ii, no. 73

of a church, but, as if in order to prevent misapprehension, the casket is provided with four feet, showing that a shrine, and not a church, is intended. To make the identification even more certain, there stands behind the casket a crozier whose form is that of a "bachul reliquary," i.e., a crozier *(baculus)* enclosed in a reliquary. The casket stands on three arches, below which are three adoring human figures. At the sides are adoring angels; and above is a structure which may vaguely represent the cathedral of Dunkeld, as it were enclosing the two relics. The intention of the whole design must have been to show the relics of St. Columba as the central feature of the church, and the proudest possession of the Dean and Chapter.

The two sides of the thirteenth-century Chapter Seal of Glasgow.
Drawings by Gregor Smith, RSW.

The Glasgow seal, therefore, may be examined with some reasonable hope that it, too, illustrated some features of the contemporary arrangements for the relics of the local saint.[20] It will be seen that the obverse depicts a structure with sloping roof and arcaded sides, a central tower and spire, and gabled ends surmounted by crosses. The structure rests on an arcade of three arches. In the central arch stands an altar with a chalice on it, and a hand is placed above, pointing downwards to the chalice. In the two side arches stand figures of robed clergy in the attitude of prayer. The reverse is unfortunately less well preserved. The central feature is a half length figure of a bishop, set on a table or platform which is supported by three arches. On either side of the episcopal figure is a curious object looking like a spire, surmounted by a cross. These "spires" look hollow inside, and may, therefore, be some kind of tripods resting on the table. In front of the table kneel three figures, engaged in prayer.

Chalmers made no attempt to identify the reverse with any of the features of Glasgow Cathedral, but he thought that the structure on the obverse was the shrine of St. Kentigern. One must confess that this identification is less convincing than that of the Dunkeld shrine, though one cannot rule it out altogether. The Glasgow structure is not standing on feet, like that of Dunkeld; it has a tower and spire, features which are certainly not common (if known at all) in shrines of this period. Moreover the Glasgow structure lacks the rich decoration of the Dunkeld casket. The latter could not possibly be a church, whereas the most natural interpretation of the Glasgow picture is that it does represent a church. We must bear in mind that it is perfectly normal for church buildings to be used as designs on seals.[21] With some regret, therefore, we must probably dismiss Chalmers's suggestion.

We are left, however, with the mysterious reverse of the Glasgow seal, with its bishop and its "spires." For the latter we can at the moment offer no convincing interpretation, though we may remember the curious variety of objects to be seen on the empty tomb of St. Thomas. The bust of the bishop may well be a head-reliquary, containing relics of St. Kentigern. Such reliquaries are well-known. There is a famous one of Charlemagne at Aachen, and we have evidence that they were used in

---

20. A very clear drawing of the seal is printed in Renwick and Lindsay, *History of Glasgow*, i, plate opp. p. 130.

21. For example, St. Andrews Cathedral (Birch, *History of Scottish Seals*, no. 66). This has two towers.

medieval Scotland.[22] Now if the actual body of the saint was kept in the upper church at Glasgow, in a feretory of the normal thirteenth-century type, it is quite possible that a head-reliquary stood in the lower church. Can it be supposed that the table shown on the reverse, with arches below it, represents the empty tomb of Glasgow, and that, like the empty tomb of Canterbury, it had various objects standing on top of it, one being the head-reliquary? This is mere conjecture, but one may hope that it is not unhelpful, as showing the kind of question which still needs to be asked about the internal arrangements in Glasgow Cathedral in the Middle Ages.

A word must be said, in conclusion, on the three kneeling figures shown on the reverse. They appear to be wearing flat caps which overhang the head at back and front. Whether these really show on the seal itself is perhaps debatable but if flat caps are intended, they recall the "pilgrims' caps" which are familiar from the pictures of medieval pilgrims to Compostella. The presence of pilgrims on the seal would not only be very welcome early evidence of pilgrimages to St. Kentigern's relics in Glasgow. It would also suggest that the side of the seal on which they appear may indeed represent one of the centers of the cult in the cathedral, and very possibly the "tomb" in the lower church.

The Evidence from the Architectural Fragments in the Lower Church[23]

In a corner of the lower church of Glasgow Cathedral stand some stones, worked as small scale architectural details such as characterize internal features like screens, tombs and shrines.

The stones include three which together form twin trefoil arch heads and a right jambstone of identical height, having shafts and molded caps, now much damaged. The corresponding left jambstone is missing. Below these four, but not originally contiguous to them, are two jamb stones and one mullion stone, all eleven inches high. The architectural style of the fragments is suggestive of a late thirteenth-century date.

---

22. Mackinlay, *Ancient Church Dedications*, 76.

23. The notes on the architectural fragments were written by George Hay of the Office of Public Works and appeared as an addendum to the article by Professor Stones in *Innes Review* 18 (1967) 95–98. Hay's notes are reproduced here with the omission of some passages of detailed description.

In a paper to the Royal Philosophical Society of Glasgow in 1905 MacGregor Chalmers produced a conjectural reconstruction of the structure to which these stones belonged, in the form of an unusual screen which he called a tomb. This he sited under the north arcade of the lower church in the second bay from the east, setting it eccentrically to the arcade center line.

The main difficulty in devising a conjectural restoration of the original feature derives from the fact that what survives can represent no more than a fractional part of the whole composition. The paucity of the fragments could possibly be accounted for by the dispersal of the original structure, and the reuse of some of the stones in a secondary erection, such as a screen partition between certain of the piers, the last a possible reason for the colored rear faces. The fragments still to hand, along with others now missing, would be consistent with an arcaded shrine of unknown dimensions bearing a feretory above it such as has been described by Professor Stones in the preceding note. Accepting as plausible such a notion, then the present symmetrical structure will be seen to represent either an end or a side of such a shrine. If the former, then the side may reasonably be conjectured as of three bays and result in a structure some ten feet long by eight feet wide. If on the other hand, the side, like the St. Amphibalus shrine at St. Albans, was two bays wide and the end of one bay, we have a structure about eight feet long by six feet wide.

The question of site for such a shrine immediately arises. It is at once apparent that a structure of neither of the dimensions suggested could stand within the arcaded tomb space in the lower church, which measures nine feet square, from center to center of the pillars. From what is known of the use of the cathedral church, and the disposition of its altar sites and liturgical fittings, there remains only one possible position, namely in the eastmost bay of the choir behind the high altar. Entrance to this space could be gained from the pilgrim ambulatory formed by the north, south and east choir aisles. Such an arrangement would be in accordance with normal medieval practice, and occurs at St. Albans, Canterbury and Lincoln, as well as the other examples cited by Professor Stones.

It may be that a full and final solution of this matter will never be found, but it is suggested that the foregoing notes are at least a logical development of the evidences known to us.

BISHOP WISHART[24]

Glasgow can identify only five of her bishops as certainly buried in the cathedral, and for three of these the information about the whereabouts in the cathedral is very vague. The impression has perhaps therefore grown that Glasgow bishops were less anxious to be buried in their own cathedral than other bishops were; and this impression has possibly been strengthened by the undoubted fact that the three who were most concerned with the fabric, John, Jocelin, and William de Bondington, were all buried in one or another of the Border abbeys. We propose to consider here, first, what is known of the general practice of episcopal burial in Scotland; then we shall try to establish the facts for Glasgow in particular, and finally devote some attention to the actual remains at Glasgow, and especially to the effigy supposed to be that of Bishop Robert Wishart.

The general position in Scotland can be studied by taking from Dowden's *Bishops of Scotland* (1912) the facts given about burials. Dowden lists about 316 Scottish bishops down to 1560 whose appointments actually became effective. Of these we know the burial places of only about sixty-seven. Of these sixty-seven, only thirty-six seem to have been buried in their own cathedral; that is slightly more than half the number of whom anything is known. The remaining thirty-one are divided as follows: in monasteries other than their own cathedral, eighteen; abroad on journey, or in exile, seven; in parish churches and chapels, four; in colleges of their own foundation, two. Thus, if these sixty-seven are in any way typical of the whole, we might expect only about half of the 316 to have been buried in their own cathedrals.

It is in the light of the above facts that we should consider the position at Glasgow.

The five bishops said to be buried in the cathedral are as follows: Robert Wishart (died c. 1316), buried "Betwixt the altars of St. Peter and St. Andrew,"[25] i.e., in the lower church, at the east end, between the two chapels; John Lindsay (died 1335), buried "Nigh to altar of Blessed Virgin," i.e., in the lower church[26]; Andrew Durisdeer alias Muirhead (died

---

24. Source: Stones, E. L. G. "The Burials of Medieval Scottish Bishops, with particular reference to the bishops of Glasgow." *Innes Review* 20 (1969) 37–46. (Slightly condensed).

25. Spotswood, *History of Church and State*, 114.

26. Spotswood, 114.

1473), buried "In the choir"[27]; John Laing (died 1483), buried "In the lower church"[28]; Gavin Dunbar (died 1547), "In the chancel."[29]

It will be noticed that only two of the above references (those concerning Laing and Dunbar) go back to the time before the Reformation. We have to use what materials are available, and to hope that writers in the seventeenth and eighteenth centuries were recording genuine traditions which are now lost. We have quoted Spotswood from the edition of 1677, but he died in 1639, and as one who graduated at Glasgow in 1581 he certainly had the opportunity of being well informed about the cathedral within twenty years of the Reformation.[30]

Another nine bishops of Glasgow are known to have been buried elsewhere.[31] Thus, fourteen bishops out of the total of twenty-five who held office between Bishop John (1118–47) and the Reformation can be accounted for. If we guess that the remaining eleven followed the division suggested by our previous figures as typical of the general Scottish practice, so that about half of them were buried away from their cathedral, it means that only about six burials in the cathedral are unrecorded, and that the total number of burials in the cathedral would be about eleven. This is very nearly the actual recorded total at York. If our rough estimates by analogy, therefore, are not wholly unreasonable, Glasgow bishops need have been no less inclined to be buried at home than their contemporaries elsewhere. When we are picturing the cathedral at the close of the Middle Ages, of course, we have to reckon not only with eleven or so episcopal tombs, but also with a number of tombs of cathedral clergy, such as still survive at Hereford Cathedral, together with some tombs of prominent layfolk.

This collection of tombs must, at the end of the Middle Ages, have formed a splendid series of monuments, possibly including some brasses, a type of monument which has now almost entirely vanished in Scotland.

27. Nisbet, *System of Heraldry*, ii, 260.

28. Allusion to "the lair of Bishop Layng" in deed of 1539 printed in Renwick, *Protocols*, iv, 119.

29. Provision in his will for a tomb, presumably in the cathedral, since he left funds to Dean and Chapter for it (*Crosraguel Charters*, i, 110, 112). Said to be in chancel in Crawfurd, *Lives of Officers of Crown and State*, 77.

30. Biographical details can be found in the online *Oxford Dictionary of National Biography*, https://doi.org/10.1093/ref:odnb/26167.

31. Details of these are given in Stones, "The Burials of Medieval Scottish Bishops," 39–40.

Of all this artistic wealth, there now survives in the upper church nothing whatever.

An effigy at the east end of the lower church is commonly regarded as that of Robert Wishart. It may be in its original position now, though it has certainly been removed from it during the nineteenth century, and later replaced. That Wishart was buried in the cathedral we may take as virtually proved by the evidence of Spotswood, and the position given by Spotswood between the altars of St. Peter and St. Andrew, is definable from independent sources[32] as being between two eastern chapels of the crypt where there is now the effigy traditionally called that of Wishart. But there is a twofold difficulty arising from the present condition of the remains at this point. It may be stated thus: (i) Was there ever a burial at all beneath the site of the present effigy? (ii) Even if there was, is the effigy now in its original position? We must now consider these two points in turn.

(i) The question of burial beneath the effigy is one that required some archaeological exploration, and in November 1965 the nature of the wall between the chapels was investigated by the Ministry of Public Building and Works. When the pointing was removed from the wall on each side it became apparent that the whole wall down to the level of the bench-tables on each side was a crude rebuilding of the nineteenth century, with straight joints at either end, where the wall met the piers. There were even packing-pieces of brick and slate mingled with the stonework. But below the level of the bench-tables a cavity had been formed, by placing slabs of stone transversely from side to side, and on the floor of that cavity there rested a number of the longer bones of a human skeleton. It was impossible to explore this chamber fully without risk to the stability of the whole structure above, and so, when photographs had been taken, the investigation was ended and the stonework was replaced. Some thought was given to the possibility of dating the bones by scientific tests, but the advice given by specialists on the chances of obtaining a reliable result under these conditions was not encouraging enough to justify the attempt at this juncture.

The disturbance of the remains since medieval times had obviously been so great that it was very hard to tell for certain where the medieval burial had been, if it had been there at all. The thickness of the wall above the bench table is about three feet two inches, and the width between the

---

32. Eyre-Todd, *The Book of Glasgow Cathedral*, 319.

piers about six feet three inches. This allows but little space for inserting a full-sized coffin, if allowance is made for the thickness of the stone, and it seems more likely that a cavity further down would have been used. But the origin of the bones now there must be doubtful, in view of the extensive use of the lower church for burials in modern times, and especially of the need to transfer bones, from time to time, from the main floor area to more remote hiding places, in order to make room for further burials.[33]

(ii) So much, therefore, for the burial. It remains to consider the effigy. It is made from a piece of local sandstone,[34] and consists of a figure of a bishop in full pontificals. The head is missing. Until recently it was thought that there was an animal at the foot[35] but when photographic lights were played on the effigy in November 1965 it was observed that the "animal" was really the remains of two kneeling human figures, and that there were in fact four such figures, two at the feet and two on opposite sides of the head. Such attendant figures are relatively common from the thirteenth century onwards.[36]

A very strange feature of the effigy is that it is rather too long for the space between the piers in which it at present stands. Were it not for the fact that the feet are now missing, the effigy could not be inserted in

---

33. A coat of arms appears faintly on the wall above the arch surmounting the effigy; this is doubtless evidence of post-medieval use of the neighborhood for burials.

34. The stone was examined by Dr. Brian Bluck of the Department of Geology in Glasgow University. His report contains the following passage: "The stone bears a strong resemblance to the local building stones quarried at Bishopbriggs and Giffnock. I found no criteria enabling me to say that the stone is definitely local. But I have not found any other British sandstone which better matches the characteristics of the effigy samples than do those of local origin." (December 2, 1965).

35. So MacGibbon and Ross, *Ecclesiastical Architecture of Scotland*, ii, 178: "The lion at the feet has had to be cut away." This mistake was much easier in the darkness which prevailed in the lower church before the recent removal of the stained glass.

36. For examples additional to that of plate xvi, see. e.g. Hell, *Great Pilgrimage of the Middle Ages* (1966), plate 113 (tomb of St. Dominic at Santo Domingo de la Calzada, thirteenth century); tomb of Bishop Walter de la Wyle in Salisbury Cathedral (c.1271), illustrated in Gardner, *English Medieval Sculpture* (1951), fig. 299; tomb of Bishop Bronescombe in Exeter Cathedral (c. 1280), Gardner, fig. 317; and for later examples, the tomb of Philip the Bold (c. 1404) at Dijon, illustrated in J. Bonnerot, *Bourgogne* (Les Albums des Guides Bleus, 1955), color plate IV; and the tomb of Bishop Elphinstone (ob.1514) at Aberdeen, described in 1542 as having "at the head two angels carrying two candlesticks and at the feet two *mercenarii* (bedesmen, or chaplains) carrying an epitaph inscribed in brass." (F. C. Eeles, *King's College Chapel*, Aberdeen (1950), p. 10). The tomb of Abbot Mackinnon (c. 1500) at Iona Cathedral seems also to have remains of angels at the head.

the space at all, and the two "angels" (calling them such for convenience, without committing ourselves) at the foot-end are most uncomfortably crowded against the shafting of the piers. How are we to explain this? One possibility is that the effigy was made to order at some distance from Glasgow, and that the measurements were wrong. There is perhaps a parallel case at Ely Cathedral, where the tomb and canopy of Bishop Hotham (died 1337) do not fit each other, and may have been made in different places. But we have seen that the Glasgow effigy is probably of local stone, and so was probably sculptured locally. The arch under which it is placed is not part of the original arrangement of the east end of the crypt. The wall between the two chapels was at first pierced by a double arch, like those between the chapels on either side. Only when the tomb was planned did the double arch give place to a single one. There is, therefore, very little doubt that a burial was intended here, but we cannot know whether the plan was made, and the arch opened up, at the same time that the effigy was procured, or whether the latter was delayed, with the possibility of some error occurring. On the whole, one would expect the arch and the effigy to be prepared at the same time, and with due regard to fitting.

Another possibility is that the effigy which we have is not that intended for, and originally mounted on, the present site. After all, there would be plenty of bishops' effigies in the cathedral for which there was no further use after 1560, and this may be a stray which has found its way, since then, to a site which is just too small for it. Unfortunately it is not easy to trace the history of the present effigy. The earliest reference to it at present known seems to date from 1790. In the journal of bishop John Geddes (1735–99)[37] we read of the bishop visiting the cathedral on St. Mungo's day 1790, and noticing in the lower church "the *tasken* [effigy] of a bishop, under which they say St. Mungo is buried." Unluckily Bishop John does not say exactly where the effigy was in 1790.

The next evidence seems to be in James Collie's drawings of the cathedral,[38] published in 1835, one of which shows what it calls "Joceline's tomb." The plate depicts what is undoubtedly the present effigy, in its present position, and makes very clear both the excessive length of the effigy for its place under the arch, and the looseness of its attachment to the wall beneath. The straight joint at the east side is also very obvious.

37. Anderson, "Ambula Coram Deo," 55.
38. Collie, *Plans, elevations, sections*.

Next we meet the effigy in a new position, on the platform under the canopy where traditionally lay the tomb of St. Mungo, or, as we prefer to think, the empty tomb. It is shown there in a picture published in 1854,[39] and a pamphlet published in the same year by the architect John Honeyman says that this removal took place "at the time of the restoration of the cathedral," which is explained elsewhere in the pamphlet to mean "twenty years ago," i.e., in or about 1834.[40] It would seem, then, that the effigy was moved very soon after Collie made his drawing, and presumably the move was due to the belief that the effigy was that of St. Mungo, and should lie under the canopy where he was supposed to be buried.

We do not know when the effigy was taken back to its present position, though we may guess that the cause was the pamphlet of 1854, in which Honeyman argued very persuasively that the effigy, and the tomb at the east end, were both those of Wishart.[41] No doubt the crude rebuilding of the wall, to which we have referred above, also took place when the move was made. It is fairly clear by now that we have to choose between two theories. Either the effigy was made for its present position and made too large; which is certainly not impossible. Or it was made for some other place in the cathedral, and is thus a relatively modern intrusion, like the effigy of Bishop Robert Colquhoun (1475–c.1496) now in Luss parish church, but presumably not in its original position there. If the second view is the truth then we shall never know who is depicted. It is fair to say that the character of the effigy is quite consistent with its belonging to the period of Wishart's death. We are still left with the question of where the body of Wishart was buried. Archaeology does not help us to say how his remains were disposed in the wall under the arch, but whatever we think about the effigy, we cannot have much doubt that the predecessor of the present wall in some manner enclosed his remains. For what it is worth, the evidence, given in the Appendix below, that about 1804 a ring and crozier were found at this spot by a London collector, or by McLellan, may be taken to confirm this view.

---

39. *Munimenta Alme Universitatis Glasguensis,* iv, illustration on p. xvi.
40. Honeyman, *The Age of Glasgow Cathedral,* 4, 3.
41. Honeyman, *The Age of Glasgow Cathedral,* 18.

APPENDIX

It would have unduly interrupted the above argument to refer to the vague reports which exist about exploration of the possible sites of tombs in the cathedral before 1965. But the student may find it useful to have a note on them here, though they help only at one point in the problem of Wishart's burial.

(i) A coffin in the choir, believed then to be that of archbishop Dunbar, was exposed in 1804, and "ransacked" by a youth named Archibald McLellan.[42] A coffin, then believed to be the same one, was uncovered in 1856. It lay between two pillars, south of the original High Altar, and was two feet below the floor of the choir, in the cavities of the vault above the lower church.

One may be surprised at the boldness of excavating in these cavities, for this vault at its thinnest points is only a couple of feet thick. One might expect burials in the choir to have been made only in tomb chests standing on the floor. However, we have the recently discovered burials at Whithorn as parallels to this practice of burial in the vault.[43]

On the occasion of the discovery of 1804[44] it seems that an episcopal ring was removed from the tomb. In 1856 the skeleton was for some reason removed and deposited "in a hole dug at the foot of the steps" inside the western door of the nave.[45] Presumably it is still there. A cast of the skull, and samples of the vestments, are said to have been deposited in the National Museum in 1856.

(ii) Part of a crozier, exhibited at the Glasgow Exhibition of 1888, was alleged to have been found, along with an episcopal ring, by "William Bullock, the London naturalist and collector." The place of discovery was thought, in 1888, to have been the tomb now called that of Wishart, in the crypt, and the date to have been about 1804.[46] The present whereabouts of the crozier and ring are not known.

(iii) Some confusion is added to these reports by the existence of an alternative tradition, according to which the body found in 1856

---

42. Gordon, *Vade Mecum*, 207. The youth McLellan later became the author of *Essay on the Cathedral Church of Glasgow* (1833).

43. A photograph illustrating the cavities in the Glasgow vaults, which were revealed in 1916, may be seen in the *Antiquaries Journal*, 44 (1964), pl. lxii.

44. Gordon, *Vade Mecum*, 207.

45. Gordon, *Vade Mecum*, 208.

46. *Scottish National Memorials*. Glasgow: 1890, 215.

was thought then to be that of Bishop Cameron, who died in 1446, at Glasgow. The same source states that the coffin raided by McLellan was "in one of the low dividing walls in the crypt under the lady chapel" (i.e., not in the choir at all) and that he removed the skull and a crozier, as well as a ring.[47] This statement was written in 1856,[48] and on the whole it is better attested than (ii), since the writer gives the impression that he had personally known McLellan in later life, when he had put aside the habits of his youth and become a Glasgow magistrate, and was devoting a good deal of time to the restoration of the cathedral.

(iv) It should also be mentioned here that in the years before 1914 the architect P. Macgregor Chalmers "with Government sanction" probed below the present paving, in various places, looking for the foundations of "the Norman cathedral,"[49] and in the crypt for recesses in which burials had taken place. He found one such in the sleeper wall, to the full extent of the western arch north of the Lady Chapel,[50] but there is no record of his work in the files of the Ministry of Public Building and Works, and his personal papers have now disappeared. His work should, however, remind us that the present paving is of early nineteenth century date, and that it has certainly hidden some earlier features, such as this cavity. Future excavation, therefore, may reveal the positions, at least, of some former burials, and conceivably some fragments of actual tombs and effigies.

47. Pagan, *History of Cathedral and See of Glasgow*, 101.
48. Pagan, *History*, 97.
49. Chalmers, *Cathedral Church*, 14.
50. Chalmers, *Cathedral Church*, 54 and Chalmers, "A Thirteenth Century Tomb in Glasgow Cathedral," 184–89. The article mentioned also describes an excavation on the site of the empty tomb of St. Kentigern (186); and it shows that the conjectured site of an eastern apse, belonging to the Cathedral of Bishop Jocelin was explored, with no result (186).

11

"Their Own Parish Kirk"
Jurisdictional Jealousy and Sacramental Spaces Across the Reformation Divide

DANIEL MACLEOD

> 1560, the year of the Reformation Parliament in Scotland, is often taken to represent the "central fulcrum" of the country's religious history. Before that date, Scotland was Catholic; after that date, Scotland was Protestant. The true picture, however, is more complex. Dr. Daniel MacLeod's research on church life in Glasgow during the sixteenth century has shown how considerable links remained between the Reformed practices of the later decades of the century and their medieval Catholic roots.[1] In this chapter, he argues that "Glasgow Cathedral stood, and stands, as a testament to this continuity."

THE REFORMATION ERA IS often characterized by what it reveals about division. The theological and social disruptions as well as horrific rhetoric and violence they inspired demonstrate the implications changing religious ideas have on how societies think, pray, or organize themselves. As

---

1. See MacLeod, *Servants to St. Mungo*.

so many scholars have demonstrated, the Reformation inspired communities to take Christianity in new directions, to renew their commitments to God in a changing world, and to assert a new place for themselves at the heart of Christianity.[2] And since these changes emerged from conversations Christians had with the societies in which Christianity operated, they also changed these societies, taking them in directions that Luther, Calvin, Knox, and others could not have imagined. The nature of the divisions was thus unanticipated and longstanding, reaching beyond the purely theological and into the social, political, and cultural. These wide-ranging effects of Reformation divisions have been documented by historians for some time, and they have been refined and nuanced over the last number of generations. These fascinating divisions can, however, distract the gaze from the bedrock of commonality shared by Christians in the early modern world, a point that has begun to be remedied by a number of historians.[3] The more modern historiography of the Reformation in Scotland and elsewhere has proven this point out, as historians have revealed Christian communities in a long-term give and take with one another as they forged new communities in the decades after the Reformation Parliament.[4] Glasgow Cathedral stood, and stands, as a testament to this continuity. It looked down over a changing Christian reality in the sixteenth and seventeenth centuries and its walls housed people and events central in telling the Reformation story in the town. This chapter will examine how the cathedral served as a crucial character in the story of the Reformation in Glasgow. Its status as the town's pre-eminent sacred space was used by Catholics and Protestants alike to stake their claim to authority, history, and sacramental authenticity in the period. In this way, the cathedral served as a critical space for defining the terms of the Reformation in Glasgow, as Glaswegians sorted out their religious lives in the building that housed the remains of its founder.

As the final resting place of St. Mungo, the cathedral was, of course, the pre-eminent holy place in the town in the period both before and after the Reformation. An inventory of the pre-Reformation relics at the site attests to this importance, and includes pieces of Jesus's manger and a vial of the Virgin Mary's milk. It also contained the bones of St. Mungo and other holy people, as well as Mungo's comb and a number of other

2. An excellent general history of the Reformation is Eire, *Reformations*.
3. For England, see Duffy, *Stripping of the Altars*, and Walsham, *Church Papists*.
4. Todd, *Culture of Protestantism*; Graham, *Uses of Reform*. On Glasgow, see MacLeod, "Servants to St. Mungo."

sacred items.[5] People from Glasgow and beyond traditionally traveled to the cathedral to make use of the healing power of these holy objects, which included utilizing pieces of a cross made by St. Mungo as a cure for madness.[6] Thus even though those tasked with the project of making Glasgow a Protestant town would have frowned on the miraculous uses of the cathedral and its contents, for townspeople it had long been associated with holiness, and had served as a conduit through which they could request intercession, cures, or any number of requests that encounters with these objects might inspire. More than twenty years after the Reformation Parliament, when Mungo Wilson stood as a cautioner in the kirk session in 1583, he surely knew that the bones of the man he was named for were only down the street, and that the holiness of these bones was a fact that generations of Christians thought significant.[7]

The prominence of the cathedral as a holy place thus led to its role as a contested Christian space throughout most of the sixteenth and early seventeenth centuries, and its use can teach us a great deal about the changing religious realities of the town. In the pre-Reformation context, the building was the stage for the major status-dispute among the most prominent churchmen of sixteenth century Scotland. At dispute was an exemption granted to the Archbishop of Glasgow to free him in perpetuity from the authority of other churchmen in Scotland. The particulars of Glasgow's exemption lay in the late-fifteenth century. It began in 1472 with the elevation of St. Andrews from a bishopric to an archbishopric. This had troubled Robert Blacader, then bishop of Glasgow, who appealed to Pope Innocent VIII who then delivered "remedy" for the well-liked Blacader in 1488, granting the exemption to Glasgow, taking the see "under the protection of St. Peter and the apostolic see and the pope, and exempt[ing] them from all jurisdiction, etc., of the said archbishop [of St. Andrews]."[8] This was a process that Leslie MacFarlane described accurately as "taking away with his left hand what he had just given with his right"[9] and the endurance of the friction was almost guaranteed by an Act of Parliament in January 1488 which elevated Glasgow

5. Dowden, "The Inventory of Ornaments", 280–329. 298–305.

6. Cowan, *Death, Life and Religious Change*, 61–62.

7. Glasgow Kirk Session Records, NRS, CH2/550/1, 23. A good discussion of relics and holy intercession can be found in Cowan, *Death, Life and Religious Change*, 52–81; on local religion, see Laven, "Encountering the Counter-Reformation", 709–10.

8. Twemlow, "Vatican Regesta 732: 1488."

9. MacFarlane, "Primacy of the Scottish Church", 117.

to an Archbishopric "with such privileges as accords with the law and just like the archbishopric of York".[10] The prospect of a second archbishopric, especially one "just like York", must have worried some in the Scottish Church considering the historic tensions between Canterbury and York in England, but a papal bull on January 9, 1492 confirmed the change nonetheless.[11] Blacader would become Glasgow's first archbishop and the bishops of Dunkeld, Dunblane, Galloway, and Argyle his suffragans, essentially dividing the Scottish Church equally between the two archbishoprics and muddying the waters of ecclesiastical authority.[12]

It is interesting to note that the exemption's nature allowed for a malleability of these privileges across contexts. Barbara Rosenwein described exemptions as "chameleons" and "flexible instruments of political and social life."[13] Glasgow churchmen's use of the exemption certainly proves this out. One bishop could use it to protect against the encroachments of another, or it could be used by local laymen to assert their autonomy. The exemption could be overlooked or enhanced based on the personalities involved or the requirements of circumstance. Attitudes toward it could also be altered based on changes to individual opinions or personal conditions, as they certainly were when James Beaton was transferred from Glasgow to St. Andrews in 1523 and almost immediately requested that Glasgow's exemption be dissolved after years of pushing for its extension.[14] An exemption, then, is interesting because it both required a clarification of membership and provided a portal through which religious communities could express themselves.

The changing nature of Glasgow's exemption thus resulted in a variety of flare-ups, the most famous of which was the so-called "fracas at Glasgow" occasioned by a June 1545 cathedral meeting of Gavin Dunbar, Archbishop of Glasgow and Cardinal David Beaton. The controversy involved the cardinal bearing his cross in the presence of Dunbar, a point that threatened the archbishop's exemption from the authority of Beaton. The most detailed narrative of the event comes from Knox. He begins:

> But while they remain together, the one in the town, the other in the Castle, question rises for bearing of their crosses. The

---

10. *Records of the Parliaments of Scotland to 1707*, 1489/1/4.
11. *Charters and Other of Glasgow*, i, Part 1, 9.
12. Scott, *Fasti Ecclesiae*, 187.
13. Rosenwein, *Negotiating Space*, 4–5.
14. Renwick, *History of Glasgow*, i, 329.

Cardinal alleged, by reason of his Cardinalship, and that he was *Legatus Natus*, and Primate within Scotland, in the kingdom of Antichrist, that he should have the pre-eminence, and that his cross should not only go before, but that also it only should be borne wheresoever he was . . . the foresaid Archbishop, lacked no reasons, as he thought, for maintenance of his glory: he was an Archbishop in his own diocese, and in his own Cathedral seat and Church, and therefore ought to give place to no man; the power of the Cardinal was but begged from Rome, and appertained but to his own person, and not to his bishopric; for it might be that his successor should not be Cardinal. But his (own) dignity was annexed with his office and did appertain to all that should ever be Bishops of Glasgow.[15]

In terms of our understanding of this event, the description is valuable because of its near flawless communication of the issues at stake in the exemption dispute. The details are correct, and Knox provides a valuable description of the claims of both men. He correctly identifies that Beaton had a claim to the *Legatus Natus* title by way of his cardinal's hat, and that Dunbar's claim was also legitimate, as the exemption had been granted *ex officio* and therefore had permanence beyond the life of the cardinal.[16] That this material was likely relayed to Knox by a third party is also significant, as the detailed understanding of the intricacies of the exemption controversy demonstrate a high level of understanding. That those not directly involved in the controversy would know the details and report them accurately signifies the importance of the exemption for townspeople as well.

With typical energy, Knox goes on to relay the physical altercation that took place among the two churchmen's attendants. As the men tried to make their way through the choir door, they began jockeying for the position of their crosses until the disagreement arose, which "from glowming [scowling] they come to shouldering; from shouldering, they go to buffets, and from dry blows, by neffs and neffeling [fisticuffs]." The attendants then argued over "which of the crosses was finest metal, which staff was strongest, and which bearer could best defend his master's pre-eminence" until "no little fray" broke out between the two groups, resulting in crowns and crosses being cracked and attendants being thrown to

15. Knox, *History*, 73.

16. It is true, however, that Dunbar had been nominated unsuccessfully for a cardinalship by both James V and Ferdinand and Isabella. See Robertson, *Concilia Scotiae*, cxxiii–cxiv.

the ground. Knox opined that it was a shame that very few of the men wore beards; otherwise, they could have pulled on them as well! Towards the end of his description Knox writes that Dunbar said to the cardinal that "he (Dunbar) was a bishop when the other was but Beaton."[17]

That these senior clergymen and their attendants would actually come to blows in Glasgow Cathedral speaks to the exasperation of those involved in the exemption dispute. Knox's chiding aside, it is important to note the gravity of the situation. Pre-Reformation Catholicism was a panoply of symbolic movements, gestures, and parades and the positioning of the crosses mattered a great deal to medieval clergymen and those witnessing these processions. In his interesting study of Constance and Augsburg, Jeffery Tyler writes that bishops "served and ruled through ritual" and were "tethered" to their cities by these ceremonies through which "they continued to lay claim to cathedral compound and civic spaces."[18] For all intents and purposes, a dispute over the public raising of episcopal crosses at the pre-eminent Christian space in the town was a singular opportunity for Scottish bishops to put the strength of the exemption to the test, which is why the attendants protected these rights so fiercely. One study of seventeenth-century English cathedral chapters shows that competition among chapters for prominence in public ritual was of equal or more importance to royal approval of local authority, and there is little doubt that these later contests for authority were inherited from their pre-Reformation predecessors.[19] In fact, in the English context, the dueling archbishoprics of York and Canterbury, upon which the Glasgow-St. Andrews relationship was modeled, had similar disputes regarding primacy and the bearing of the bishops' crosses in the fourteenth century. This dispute was solved by Innocent VI in 1352 when he decided that neither bishop should lead in processions in the other's diocese and that both crosses should be carried abreast of one another.[20] Again, the papal intervention exemplifies the complex relationship between ritual and power.

Although Alec Ryrie has noted the shock emerging from the fight in Glasgow, perceived violations of clerical jurisdiction were a chronic problem in medieval Europe, and the infighting among monks, mendicants,

---

17. Knox's description of the event can be found in its entirety in Knox, *History*, 72–74.

18. Tyler, *Lord of the Sacred City*, 108.

19. Estabrook, "Ritual, Space, and Authority," 597.

20. *Concilia Scotiae*, cxxxi–cxxxii.

secular clergy, and bishops, physical and otherwise, provided significant material used by Protestant Reformers in their early criticism of the Catholic clergy.[21] Disputes over the Archbishop of York's late-thirteenth century visitation to Durham in violation of a monastery's rights resulted in a popular uprising of men from the town who chased the archbishop from the pulpit and cut off the ear of his horse.[22] Protests against bishops and their infringement on the liberties of local communities can also be found in other medieval towns, as groups expressed protectiveness of local control.[23]

In particular it is interesting to consider Dunbar's role. The meteoric rise of David Beaton to the position of cardinal and primate of Scotland had come at the expense of Dunbar and as a consequence of changing Scottish policy after the death of Dunbar's most loyal advocate, James V. The early stages of this "pro-French" policy under the influence of Mary de Guise deprived Dunbar of his chancellorship at the end of 1543. Margaret Sanderson accurately describes the "frustration and pent-up personal animosity" embodied in the "Bishop when the other was but Beaton" remark attributed to Dunbar by Knox.[24] Dunbar surely felt that he had been pushing against a "Beaton wall" for as long as he was in leadership positions in the Scottish Church where three members of that family held prominent positions in the hierarchy. The event at Glasgow may have demonstrated that Dunbar and his followers reaching their limit.

It is also plausible, as Sanderson has suggested, that the attendants who represented the interests of Dunbar and Beaton "took matters into their own hands" in engaging in the fight.[25] This action demonstrates the shared interests of those beyond the individual bishops in maintaining the exemption. Lay defense of the exemption can also be seen in a letter circa August 1535 in which the Earl of Lennox asked his brother John, Lord D'Aubigny, to advance the cause of Dunbar's exemption in Rome. Lennox wrote to his brother, "we are both servants to Saint Mungo and bound to defend the interests of that Kirk."[26] A dearth of sources

21. Ryrie, *Origins of the Scottish Reformation*, 23; MacCulloch, *Reformation*, 33; Mullan, *Episcopacy in Scotland*, 10.

22. Cohn, *Popular Protest*.

23. Cohn, *Popular Protest*, 251–62; Burns, "Popes, Bishops and the Polity," 534–56.

24. Sanderson, *Cardinal of Scotland*, 117.

25. Sanderson, *Cardinal of Scotland* 116.

26. Marwick, *Abstracts of Charters*, 15.

prevents us from knowing the full extent of lay advocacy on behalf of the exemption, but Lennox's letter proves that there is no doubting its existence, which is sensible considering the mingling of Church interests in the economic, social, and political life of the town. There is also little doubt that Dunbar's petition to have the exemption made *ex officio* can be seen as his defense of the long-term interests of the archbishopric and the Christian community in the town, especially as it was expressed in its holiest place.

That lay people in Glasgow seemed to value sustaining the exemption adds another layer of interest to the already complicated 1545 fracas. Sanderson has noted that "to be archbishop of St. Andrews was to rule a kingdom within a kingdom."[27] If we consider the archbishopric of Glasgow in this light, Dunbar ruled a kingdom within a kingdom within a kingdom, where nearly all of the jurisdictions were under question and subject to change and negotiation. In Glasgow, Dunbar and Beaton were clearly acting out a very personal dispute that had been carried through two Beatons' ecclesiastical careers, and the fight at Glasgow was far from the "sudden discord" described by Lesley.[28] The dispute was the culmination of tensions reaching back into the fifteenth century, but the exemption had come to mean many things to many different groups all of which came to a head in 1545. The exemption represented the rights of the local Glasgow community against individual bishops intruding on its authority.[29] It also signified the wider interests of the suffragan bishoprics of both St. Andrews and Glasgow, along with the regional and geographical differences one might identify. It clearly embodied the interests of the papacy in Scotland, along with the complicated domestic and international political instability brought on by the death of James V, the Rough Wooing, and the English Reformation more generally. Of course, it is important to mention that all of this was also taking place within the context of a burgeoning Scottish Protestantism. These were problems of religion, and of culture, and of politics at local, national, and international levels. All of these relationships were represented in the cathedral's hosting the processions of the bishops, which were in line with a vibrant tradition of

---

27. Sanderson, *Cardinal of Scotland*, 96.
28. Lesley, *Historie*, 178.
29. MacLeod, "Servants to St. Mungo," 49–51; 84.

ritualized procession in the medieval Church, whether associated with the saints, the guilds, *Corpus Christi* or other religious celebrations.[30]

Tyler's study of the German bishops offers an interesting contrast with the Glasgow dispute. Tyler's work concentrates on the relationship between the civic and religious leaderships in the contest for public space in the cathedral city. In the case of mid-fifteenth century Constance, its bishop engaged in negotiation with the city council as to how his public entry into the city would take place and the route of his travel. According to Tyler, success was achieved when both the civil and religious authorities cooperated, allowing each other to express aspects of their own identities in the processions.[31] In Constance, both the civic and religious interests were served by negotiating an appropriate amount of recognition for both parties, a task made easier by at least some difference in the mandates of civic and religious leaderships. Tyler notes that "the ultimate prize in this clever game was not victory . . . [but a] grateful stalemate that would undergird civic and episcopal cohabitation."[32] In Constance, the struggle was for basic inclusion and recognition of civic authority in opposition to or cooperation with the religious authority. In Glasgow, however, both groups sought recognition of the same thing—the identical spiritual supremacy—rendering negotiation more difficult. It was also clear that this authority was best expressed in a specific place, the cathedral, where all could see and be seen. The competition for supremacy was enhanced by its location. As noted, Knox writes that Dunbar claimed authority because he was "in his own cathedral seat and church, and therefore ought to give place to no man."[33] Here we see the ultimate use of the cathedral as a wedge to determine supremacy, as its walls enhanced sacred authority, which ultimately led to the intractability of the positions of both sides.

Like the cathedral, intractability survived the Reformation in Glasgow. And like their Catholic predecessors, newly-Protestant Scots used the cathedral as a stage to enhance the seriousness of their concerns. These concerns were in some ways different than those of the pre-Reformation period, but they shared a common thread in terms of

30. On *Corpus Christi*, see Rubin, *Corpus Christi*. On craft and guild associations with Catholicism, see Lynch, *Edinburgh and the Reformation*, 30–31 and Fitch, *Search for Salvation*, 100–103.

31. Tyler, *Lord of the Sacred City*, 131–39.

32. Tyler, *Lord of the Sacred City*, 136.

33. Knox, *History*, 73.

their relationship with status, sacredness, and authority. The disputes of the post-Reformation kirk were also expressed more frequently by laypeople, which was a key difference in the Protestant regime, but one we saw expressed to some degree in discussion of Glasgow's exemption as well. One particular dispute provides an interesting exemplar of the central importance of the cathedral in the lives of Glasgow's Christians, and the lengths Glasgow's townspeople would go to protect their access to the building and the holiness it housed.

The dispute began with the presbytery establishing "a flock of their own" for the Barony parish in Glasgow in 1596, which essentially contained the land "without the burgh" or the rural areas surrounding the town.[34] It was decided that the minister would be Alexander Rowat, who had been the third minister in Glasgow for a time, but was now being given charge of this new parish that would worship in the Blackfriars Kirk. As was custom, Rowat was instructed to preach before the parish in order for them to assess his "life and doctrine." When only one member of the parish attended, the presbytery passed an act insisting that the parishioners attend or else "they shall receive no benefit of the Kirk, which are the sacraments of baptism and the holy supper of the lord Jesus and the celebration of marriage."[35] When the parishioners continued in their absence, the presbytery threatened to deny the "benefits" again.[36]

At issue was the desire of many of the parishioners "without the town" to remain a part of the cathedral parish and receive the sacraments in the cathedral rather than the less distinguished Blackfriars. Many of these "Barony men" protested their requirement to listen to the preaching "as a congregation separated from the inhabitants of Glasgow" and were likely troubled additionally by the social isolation they foresaw, especially considering they had been long time parishioners at High Kirk.[37] John Cooper, the undisputed champion of intractability among the ministry in Glasgow, disagreed and passed an act against all who refused, insisting that they should be denied the sacraments if they did not attend the preaching.[38] Cooper went even further ordaining "the parishioners

---

34. Glasgow Presbytery Records CH2/171/32A, 79.
35. Glasgow Presbytery Records 83–84.
36. Glasgow Presbytery Records 102–3.
37. Glasgow Presbytery Records, 103.
38. Cooper was the subject of much criticism throughout his tenure and on several occasions charged parishioners with slandering him. In 1594, Cooper brought Walter and William Bowie before the presbytery for blaming him for their wife and mother's

of Glasgow without the town be a particular and special congregation by themselves, separated and divided from the town of Glasgow" and instructing the ministers from the surrounding parishes to deny these people the sacraments unless they hear the word from Rowat.[39]

The Barony men were not defeated easily, and they persevered by securing an act from the March 1596 General Assembly ordering Cooper and the Glasgow ministry to provide the "benefits of the Kirk." The ministers continued to refuse, noting that the sacraments were easily available to these men as it stood, and that they already had a minister who was "daily ready to minister to them the sacraments." The Barony men protested this act as well, noting that they preferred to receive the sacraments in the "Cathedral of Glasgow as their own parish Kirk, according to their old accustomed use . . . since the time of reformation."[40] Just as we saw with the Catholic Earl of Lennox's appeal to the historical relationship between a people and its church in the 1530s, so too do these Protestant Christians note the close relationship between community, church, and Christianity.

As it did in the pre-Reformation Church, the disagreement over jurisdiction, authority, and access to holiness ended in an act of violence in the cathedral. On March 20, 1596, as John Cooper was preaching prior to celebrating baptisms, Arthur Colquhoun expressed his displeasure:

> And there having his sword in his hand, [Colquhoun] leaping over the women and crying up in a fury to the said Mr John being in pulpit what is this that the said Mr. John will not baptize their bairns (the bairn the said Arthur had not being his). And that the said Arthur said he was a Barony man as the said Mr John was a minister, and that he would have their bairns baptized or else there should none be baptized the said day. And that he said the pulpit was theirs and that he will have them baptized in the choir or else he should make the house do.[41]

---

death. Glasgow Presbytery Records, 212-19, 229. In 1599, two men were brought before the burgh court for posting a piece of writing containing "blasphemous, vile and menacing words" against Cooper on the minister's gate at night. They were fined and made to promise not to repeat their crime. *Glasgow Burgh Records*, 200-201; the most famous case might have been his behavior in the case of Margaret Aitken, the so-called "Great Witch of Balweary" and his subsequent disputes with Marion Walker. Discussion can be found in MacLeod "Servants to St. Mungo," 195-202.

39. Glasgow Presbytery Records, 103-4.
40. Glasgow Presbytery Records, 109-11.
41. Glasgow Presbytery Records, 114-15.

Needless to say, Colquhoun's accosting of John Cooper upset the church authority who called him before the session for his actions. Colquhoun appealed his charges to the presbytery at Dumbarton in order to get a more just trial, but the records for that presbytery do not exist for this period so we do not know for certain what happened to Colquhoun.[42] More important than the outcomes for Colquhoun, however, is the similarity in how both Catholic and Protestant Scotland utilized the sacred space of the cathedral to mark their territory. In an ironic twist, the holiness of the space likely contributed to the occurrence of violence. Whether disputing primacy in the Church or access to the sacrament, Christians across the Reformation divide recognized the cathedral as the stage where disputes could *really* be settled, and they refused compromise in pursuit of their objectives.

It is also important here to consider how Colquhoun's case exemplifies the integral role the sacraments played in the operation of the post-Reformation kirk. The cathedral's status as the central meeting place for Glasgow's Christians before and after the Reformation was to some degree predicated on its hosting sacramental celebrations. With all of the centrality of the word, it is the sacraments that are described as "the benefits of the kirk" by the ministry of the town. It was the sacraments that were the primary tool with which the presbytery attempted to leverage parishioners into conformity with its mandate. In threatening to refuse them, the presbytery withheld the supernatural experiences of the divine as well as the religious and community memberships sacraments provide. These were significant threats from the presbytery, but in its view these threats were necessary to maintain control over a system that could be flexible at times, but which was ultimately pursuing a particular vision of the kirk that necessitated good order and, according to the *Confession of Faith*, "right administration" of the sacraments.

Those who doubt the degree to which early modern people understood the sacraments or the various happenings at church in the sixteenth century need look no further than Arthur Colquhoun's case. Colquhoun and his neighbors were upset at Glasgow kirk's expansion, which seemed to be happening at the expense of the prestige of their community and threatened the longstanding Christian relationship they

---

42. In June 1597, a man named Wilkeyne "who dwells with Arthur Colquhoun" was called before the presbytery, but there is no proof that this was in an attempt to contact Colquhoun or whether it was regarding another matter. Glasgow Presbytery Records, 145.

had with the cathedral. The "Barony men" felt that they had been shortchanged in the new scheme, and wished, like many modern people do, to practice their faith in the community and congregation they knew best. In order to express his frustrations, Colquhoun targeted what he believed to be the heart of the kirk—the sacraments. He verbally and physically abused the minister and he used the event of the sacrament to transform the cathedral into a place of protest. He insisted that a "Barony baby" receive baptism, and threatened the entire community by indicating that no baptisms would be performed if these barony children were ineligible. Further to this, by indicating that "the pulpit was theirs" he insulted the minister and demoted the power of the clergy—just as Knox and many others had done in the pre-Reformation kirk. Finally, and most interestingly, Colquhoun threatened to subvert the entire order of the Reformed kirk by asserting the power of the parishioners to take sacramental matters into their own hands. In threatening to have babies baptized in private and at home he clearly knew that he was striking at a key element of Reformed theology that Calvin had envisioned, making baptism "a child's entrance not only into the Church, but into society more generally."[43] Colquhoun was explicitly threatening to resuscitate the Catholic theology of baptism in Glasgow. Just as the kirk had used the sacraments to leverage its cause against parishioners, so too did the parishioners use the sacraments against the kirk. If Protestants were in search of a "priesthood of all believers" they certainly found it in Glasgow.

Colquhoun's case provides an interesting comparison with aspects of C. Scott Dixon's study of the German principality of Brandenberg Ansbach-Kulmbach.[44] As the region endured tensions during the first generation of reform, its ministry sometimes came under attack by parishioners. In one case, where the focus of the dispute was financial provision for the clergy, rural parishioners centred their criticism on their minister's inabilities in preaching, claiming "the principal act of the clergyman ... was abused in his hands."[45] Dixon argues that these criticisms represented a strategy of resistance for parishioners who used their knowledge of the key duties of the ministry to leverage a case, "irrespective of the real issue under dispute."[46] He goes on to note that popular and specific knowl-

---

43. Spierling, *Infant Baptism*, 54.
44. Dixon, "Rural Resistance," 99–100.
45. Dixon, "Rural Resistance," 100.
46. Dixon, "Rural Resistance," 100.

edge of the ministry's duties was, "in a backhanded way, testimony to the impact of the Reformation" which had communicated to parishioners these new roles and responsibilities. Yet, Colquhoun's hijacking of a baptism in the cathedral shows that some in Glasgow continued to consider the administration of the sacraments among the primary duties of the clergy. Although Colquhoun commented on the minister's duties to preach, John Cooper's major fault was undermining the provision of the sacrament in the place Colquhoun and his community were accustomed to accessing the sacred. Colquhoun's response indicates beyond doubt that popular devotion to the sacraments in Glasgow was intertwined with devotion to the cathedral.

Historians of the early years of the Scottish Reformation have established that the word, the sacraments, and kirk discipline were engaged in a complicated dance during this period.[47] Leaders of the these changing Christian communities established new rules for worship and Christian life and engaged in a long-term process of assessment and fine-tuning. There is little doubt that the presence of Glasgow Cathedral added another dancer to the mix in the town. As we have seen, while it stood as a symbol of the Christian community's history, people also derived status from its prominence. In this way, the cathedral was a central and contested character in the narrative of the Reformation in Glasgow. It endured change alongside the devoted Christians it housed, and in understanding its role we are better equipped to understand the period.

A final Reformation-era dispute at the cathedral might best represent how the space was continually contested by Glasgow's Christians. The 1578 attempted demolition described by John Spottiswoode in his *History of the Church in Scotland* indicates again how the disputes it housed are helpful in understanding the period more fully. According to Spottiswoode, Andrew Melville, then principal of Glasgow University, and other churchmen convinced the town's magistrates "to demolish the Cathedral" in the spring of the year and use the materials to construct a number of smaller churches.[48] Among the reasons provided for this were the overly large size of the building that made it difficult to hear the sermons, the Reformers' desire for removal of "the idolatrous monument" and the tendency of "superstitious people to do their devotion at

---

47. Dawson, *Scotland Re-Formed*, 1488–1587, 216–39.
48. Spottiswoode, *History of the Church*, ii, 258–59.

that place."⁴⁹ As the group sounded a drum calling the workers to begin the demolition, members of the local craft guilds supposedly intervened to protect the building insisting that "he who cast down the first stone should be buried under it" and forcing the demolition to stop before it began. The Reformers then took their cause to the thirteen-year-old James VI, who sided with the crafts insisting that "too many Churches had been destroyed" as a result of the religious change.⁵⁰

This story has survived in the lore of Glasgow's crafts and of the cathedral itself, and for a time tourists were welcomed to the cathedral by a large mural depicting the event. In spite of its prominence, however, it is difficult to fully assess the veracity of both the events and motivations ascribed to those cited as protecting the cathedral. First, the only existing account is from Spottiswoode, who was not only antagonistic to Melville's vision of Christianity, but also a critic of the wanton destruction of churches in the period.⁵¹ Second, even if we grant that the craft guilds protected the cathedral, it remains difficult to accurately assess their motivations. As a place of work, the prominence and size of the cathedral would certainly render it a point of pride for a number of crafts whose brethren had devoted countless hours to its construction and maintenance.

There are clear reasons to believe that the crafts could have had some religious motivations for protecting the cathedral. Michael Lynch has shown the key role that craft guilds played in maintaining Catholicism in Edinburgh, and there is no doubting the longstanding connection of the guilds with the Catholicism.⁵² Throughout their history, the crafts made significant financial contributions to the cathedral for masses and altars. They had been forced to abandon these in favor of donations to the poor in the post-Reformation period, which may have garnered a level of resentment for the new establishment.⁵³ In particular, the Webster craft in Glasgow had made significant contributions to an altar at the cathedral honoring St. Serf, who was essentially the step-father of St. Mungo and a highly influential figure in Glasgow's patron's life. These devotions

---

49. Spottiswoode, *History of the Church*, ii, 259.

50. Spottiswoode, *History of the Church*, ii, 259.

51. David McRoberts notes that Spottiswoode was "in a position to know the facts," but still calls the event "curiously circumstantial." McRoberts "Material Destruction," 441.

52. Lynch, *Edinburgh and the Reformation*, 30–31.

53. *Charters and Documents*, 534–38.

may have motivated both the desire to remove the "superstitious" visits referenced by Spottiswoode as well as the intervention on the part of the Websters to preserve the cathedral.[54] The involvement of the Glasgow crafts in further discussions in 1582–83 to maintain the cathedral also speaks to their devotion to the building, although these were less identifiably spiritual.[55] However limited the evidence for the crafts' role in protecting the cathedral, it is relatively easy to see at least the shadows of religious conservatism in their behavior, further emphasizing its place at the spiritual center of the town's Christian life. It also serves as important reminder of the fulsome integration of the cathedral and Christianity into the economic, social, and political lives of early-modern townspeople. Their Christianity was not something they pursued as a kind of pastime. It was connected to their friendships, their families, their work, their geography, and their history; and the relationships among all of these helps underscore the true scale of the change sought in the Scottish Reformation.

The mixture of history and lore we see in the story of the 1578 attempted destruction of Glasgow Cathedral is illustrative of the larger story of the cathedral in the Reformation-era in the town. Like so many important buildings, people, or ideas in the history of Christianity, the cathedral was subjected to use, re-use, and misuse, as it became entangled with the communities that made up this fascinating period Scottish history. Its ever-presence and its housing of the sacred rendered it more than a building, of course. It was also an important symbol within the community and its symbolic power was leveraged to cement authority and mark difference, which meant it frequently staged disputes central to role-definition and power. The nature of these disputes changed with the change of religion, and as a result the cathedral housed important questions about clerical authority, sacramental authenticity, and the relationships between Christianity and a variety of aspects of people's lives. It was thus a site of continuity and change and in this way endures as a symbol of the entirety of the Reformation-era.

---

54. Renwick, *History of Glasgow*, i, 352.
55. *Glasgow Burgh Records*, i, 100–102.

12

Archbishop Spottiswoode and the See of Glasgow

James Kirk

In the judgment of Dr. Thomas McCrie, historian and minister of the Original Secession Church and later Moderator of the Free Church, Archbishop John Spottiswoode (1565-1639) was "a shrewd and crafty politician . . . engaged in all the jesuitical plots of the government for overthrowing Presbytery."[1] Spottiswoode followed Scottish reformers like John Knox and Andrew Melville in rejecting the claims of the Papacy yet at the same time he upheld the notion of bishops as heirs to the apostles. Seen as a "pliant instrument" for King James VI to use in modeling the Scottish church along his own lines, Spottiswoode was appointed to the archbishopric of Glasgow in 1603. In this chapter, Professor James Kirk argues that "Spottiswoode and his royal master set off along the road that was ultimately to lead to the Covenanting revolution of the 1640s and the repudiation of episcopacy by the Glasgow Assembly of 1638."

---

1. McCrie, *The Story of the Scottish Church*, 107.

Archbishop John Spottiswoode, from an etching by Wenceslaus Hollar.
Image courtesy of National Galleries of Scotland.

IN DIFFERENT PERIODS OF history, differing significance was apt to be attached to the name and office of bishop. The contrast between the duties exercised by New Testament bishops or presbyters (synonymous terms, that is, for the men who watched over the government of a Christian congregation) and the work and wealth of medieval prelates (including some bishops of Glasgow Cathedral), with all the prestige, power, and patronage in secular and ecclesiastical affairs which such an office automatically conferred, is readily demonstrable and could scarcely have been more marked. Such disparity between early example and later practice also makes intelligible the antipathy exhibited at the Reformation by those who criticized the existing episcopate—the existing body of bishops; and this, in turn, invited a reassessment of the episcopal office itself. In Scotland, this reappraisal was carried so far that the name of bishop was not immediately retained but allowed to lapse by the reformed kirk during the 1560s. The new church, in short, had no use for the old bishops unless they reformed themselves by jettisoning much of their medieval past and by becoming preaching pastors, an implicit recognition that there was no higher office in the church than that of the ministry of the Word and sacraments.

If the precise sense attached to the word "bishop" had thus undergone radical alteration during 1500 years of history, it was still possible for different men even within one church in the same country to adopt divergent attitudes in their understanding of the correct significance to be attached to this word "bishop." Two such churchmen, holding incompatible ideas on episcopacy, were John Spottiswoode (1565–1639), archbishop of Glasgow (and later of St. Andrews) in the reign of King James VI, and the principal of Glasgow University, where Spottiswoode studied, Andrew Melville (1545–1622), whose forthright views on the invalidity of diocesan episcopacy were such as to earn him the not inappropriate title of "episcoporum exactor," the "flinger-out" of bishops. As a student, John Spottiswoode might have sat at Melville's feet and dutifully listened to what the principal of the college and theology professor (the two offices which Melville occupied) had to say; but, as sometimes happens, Spottiswoode grew up to reject his former teacher's theorizings on this subject at least, in much the same way as James VI himself had proceeded to denounce the political ideology which his tutor, George Buchanan, a few years earlier had attempted to instil in the young king during his formative years.

Yet in few cases have a teacher's views been so decisively discarded as Melville's objections to the episcopal office by John Spottiswoode. In just two decades after graduating from Glasgow in 1581, Spottiswoode found himself advanced by King James to the archbishopric of Glasgow in 1603, and his younger brother, James, who entered Glasgow University in 1579 (the year preceding Melville's move to St. Andrews University) and who graduated in 1583, was later rewarded by King James with the Irish bishopric of Clogher for his faithful service to the crown and Church of England in which he ministered, though he declined Charles I's offer of further preferment as an Irish archbishop. Both brothers, therefore, profited through their service to the crown, and both were buried in Westminster Abbey, a fitting tribute to their unstinted work in advancing the claims of episcopacy as the appropriate system for administering the church under the supreme governorship of the crown itself.

In his steadfast advocacy of episcopacy Spottiswoode repudiated the ambitious claims of popes to be the sole inheritors of the apostles' work by arguing, instead, that all bishops were the apostles' successors. This, in itself, did not commit the archbishop to any precise theory of the apostolic succession operating through bishops. It is true, he revered the antiquity of the episcopal office in the Christian church; and consistent with such a standpoint, in his *History of the Church of Scotland*, completed in the 1630s, he sought to demonstrate the early succession of bishops in Scotland. He therefore took issue with the claims of John Major and George Buchanan, which the archbishop considered were very ill-informed, that the Scots initially had been "instructed in the Christian faith by priests and monks, without any bishop" and that the early church in the land we know as Scotland had been "governed by monks without bishops with less pride and outward pomp but greater simplicity and holiness." Indeed, many of the early bishops, free from the corrupting influence of the later papacy, were expressly commended by Spottiswoode for their piety and learning. He therefore sought to portray these early bishops stripped of the legends invented by what he called "idle and ignorant monks." Admittedly, Kentigern, whom he described as "commonly called St. Mungo," is virtually shorn of his sainthood, but he is nonetheless depicted as the founder of a "stately church" in Glasgow and "worthy to have been made a subject of truth to posterity, not of fables and fictions as the legends of the monks have made him." Yet, it is noticeable that Spottiswoode nowhere attempted to identify himself as a successor to Kentigern in the see of Glasgow.

Nor is this surprising. After all, at the Reformation the reformers had explicitly rejected any notion of a personal succession as the mechanism for conferring the characteristics of a valid ministry. Instead, what counted was a succession of apostolic doctrine, the wholesome faith transmitted since the days of the apostles. In this way, John Knox could claim "we are able to show the succession of our Kirk directly and lawfully to have flowed from the Apostles." Although the archiepiscopal seal of Glasgow, even after the Reformation, continued to depict a mitered figure in episcopal vestments, presumably a representation of Kentigern, enthroned and flanked by several crosses with crozier before him (which might suggest some sort of continuity with the past with all its evident appeal to the conservatism of the lawyers and others involved in the transactions which the seal authenticated), Spottiswoode himself preferred to use a simpler seal, devoid of episcopal emblems, portraying simply a shield, with three trees, a boar's head and salmon with ring, and the legend "S Iohannis Archiepiscopi Glasgvensis." Again, in common with the other Scottish bishops, he wore neither miter nor other elaborate episcopal garb, and refused to dress like an English bishop at King James's funeral in 1625. For Spottiswoode, too, what he called a "lineal succession of pastors" counted for very little; what really mattered was recognition that, regardless of origin, the churches which professed the faith of the apostles and were free from the blemishes and errors of later ages were truly apostolic churches. "We are not a new Church," Spottiswoode affirmed on the kirk's behalf, "but one truly apostolical, that we can derive the doctrine we profess from the apostles of our Lord and from their next successors."

In this, at least, the archbishop was at one with John Knox, whose death in 1572 occurred when Spottiswoode was merely a boy of seven years of age, possessing little personal recollection of the reformer's work—though of his stormy career he had ample record by the time he came to prepare his History. Yet, if profession of a common faith, articulated in the various confessions, was a subject which united archbishop and reformer, there were other issues on which Spottiswoode showed a readiness to depart from earlier Reformation standards and practices.

For a start, Spottiswoode was the first Protestant archbishop in Scotland to receive consecration in 1610 at the hands of three English bishops, at the king's behest, in London. For James, the issue was a simple one. In the king's eyes, the standing of the Scottish bishops, whom he had so painstakingly restored, was anomalous and defective. After all, at the outset, they owed their precarious position to the king's prerogative power. The bishops whom James had appointed in the 1600s were, at best, nominal bishops. Their appointments were then largely titular: those ministers, like Spottiswoode, advanced to bishoprics were initially assigned no ecclesiastical power other than the privilege of voting as bishops in parliament. That apart, they had no episcopal functions to perform. These were the men known as the king's "parliamentary bishops." But the way was now open for James to advance his bishops to positions of real power and influence. Thus, in 1606, parliament provided the bishops with the prospect of sufficient endowment by recovering lands and rents lost to the crown by the Act of Annexation in 1587; then, by 1607, James proceeded to assign his bishops an ecclesiastical role by placing them as permanent moderators of synods. Two years later, the bishops' old consistorial jurisdiction was restored; and, by 1610, two Courts of High Commission, one for the province of Glasgow and the other for St. Andrews, had been created to deal with disciplinary cases, especially the subversive speeches of ministers who, by declaring their preference for the former presbyterian system, were seen to threaten the stability of the new regime which James had constructed. In that year, too, a carefully-managed General Assembly at Glasgow, over which Spottiswoode presided, was induced to accept the powers of bishops in excommunication, absolution and in the supervision of ministers including admissions and depositions; and the substance of its findings received ratification from parliament in 1612. Diocesan episcopacy had been revived.

To place the final seal of approval on his new order in the church, James decided to have Spottiswoode and two other Scottish bishops consecrated in England. Why the king should have required Spottiswoode and his colleagues to submit to such a ceremony in England is less readily determined. It cannot have simply been, as it is sometimes claimed, that until this step was taken the Scottish bishops altogether lacked "spiritual authorization." This is merely to take the king's explanation at its face value. Besides, it ignores the fact that the Glasgow assembly of 1610, which preceded the bishops' visit to London for consecration, had already accorded the bishops the necessary ecclesiastical authority for their work. Yet, as James had learned from painful experience, what an assembly might grant at one point, another assembly as readily could withhold at a later date. As it was, the king was increasingly attracted to English forms of procedure and worship. He was also unwilling to have the powers of his bishops made dependent on the approval of a General Assembly whose powers he had striven to curb in the expectation that he might ultimately succeed in suppressing it completely. Indeed, it took all the skill and tact of Spottiswoode's moderating influence to persuade the king to summon an assembly at all and to proceed by securing a measure of consent instead of resorting to confrontation. All in all, to James's agile mind, the bestowal of episcopal consecration had the decided merit of demonstrating the respectability and legitimacy of his bishops in Scotland, as well as ensuring an antidote to the continued supremacy of the General Assembly.

Even here, however, Spottiswoode and his two companions, the bishops of Brechin and Galloway, were reluctant to participate in a ceremony of consecration to which their own church had long attached no spiritual significance whatsoever (and whose vestigial survival as terminology in the disposition of titles to bishoprics was designed merely to satisfy the legal procedures devised by the lawyers). In essence, James's persuasive argument was that he had summoned the bishops south for consecration in recognition that no king alone had power to make men bishops, nor could they themselves assume that function, given the dearth of surviving bishops in Scotland to consecrate the newcomers. Even although, as ministers, they lacked episcopal ordination, a practice customary in England but not in Scotland, there was no serious suggestion made, despite one English bishop's misgivings, that Spottiswoode and his colleagues should first receive ordination as presbyters, in English fashion, as a prerequisite to their consecration as bishops. Nor did the king permit the two English archbishops to play any part in the ceremony, thereby allaying Scottish fears of a possible revival of the ancient claims of York and Canterbury to jurisdiction over the Scottish church. If all this looked like mere window-dressing, it was nonetheless symptomatic of James's deeper determination to remodel the church in a direction of his own choosing; and in Spottiswoode he found a pliant instrument to effect his innovations in the church.

Even on so minor an issue as the practice of confirming children, for example, which caused far less protest than the king's insistence in 1618 that worshipers kneel at communion, and which had hitherto met with neither recognition nor approval by the kirk, Spottiswoode was ready to advance the king's will and, with it, the power of bishops. Susceptible as he was to English influence, and deferential to the sustained assault by King James to win greater uniformity between the two national churches by imposing his "Five Articles of Perth" in 1618, Spottiswoode characteristically defended confirmation as "one of the most ancient customs of the Christian Church," since, so the archbishop claimed, "it is clear by all antiquity that the power of confirming appertained ever to bishops." King James might have exclaimed "no bishop, no king," but his archbishop appreciated that the obverse dictum—"no king, no bishops"—was no less true. Only the king's exceptional determination had made bishops a reality in Scotland; and Spottiswoode proved himself the king's most faithful of servants.

This episode, however, was by no means an isolated instance in which Spottiswoode sided with the ploys of the king rather than with received practice in the church. As archbishop, Spottiswoode shared King James's distrust of presbyteries, the district courts of the church, whose power rivaled those of proper bishops. He therefore hoped to reduce the scope of presbyteries for independent action so that, as he told the king in 1610, ultimately they would become "a bare name, which for the present may please, but in a little time shall vanish." Yet this dream was beyond his grasp, and so he had to settle instead for controlling presbyteries through the appointment from 1606 onwards of selected ministers on whom he could rely to manage presbyteries as constant or permanent moderators. In later life, Spottiswoode also voiced his misgivings on the nature of the eldership, a characteristic feature of the presbyterian system, by denouncing ruling elders as "a mere human device," detrimental to both church and state. Here, too, he remained faithful to the claims of his royal master who in 1610, perhaps mindful of the remarks of an earlier archbishop in 1583, had instructed the kirk that "laic elders have neither warrant in the word, nor example of the primitive church." Equally, Spottiswoode disapproved of the presbyterian doctrine of a parity or equality in jurisdiction among ministers. The appearance of bishops, even of the notional variety, plainly infringed this doctrine of parity, which he contemptuously dismissed as "the breeder of confusion." In a well-ordered church, claimed Spottiswoode, "I am verily persuaded that the government episcopal is the only right and apostolic form."

How far such views were compatible with the continued existence of the General Assembly, as the church's governing body, it might be hard to say. Certainly, Spottiswoode was far more cautious than his royal master, who had little time for assemblies, intent as they seemed to be on thwarting royal policies. More realistically, Spottiswoode persuaded James to work through assemblies; but by 1618, having lost his patience, James had decided to summon no more assemblies; even the decision to call an assembly that year was against the king's better judgment; and in a letter which Spottiswoode read twice to the assembled gathering, King James disclosed that he had been "fully resolved never in our time to have called any more assemblies." Perhaps despairingly, Spottiswoode acquiesced in James's policy of holding assemblies infrequently as the prelude to their disappearance. Above all, he implicitly believed James was entitled so to behave: the prince had the right, he maintained, to order the church's external government as he saw fit, and it was therefore the duty of subjects to render him obedience in all matters not inconsistent with God's Word. Accordingly, he readily acknowledged the king's supreme governorship of the church, a sensitive issue on which the General Assembly had successfully withheld its express approval. In doing so, he helped enforce royal claims that "bishops must rule the ministers and the king rule both" to the extent that he was latterly able to quip that "the king is pope now, and so shall be." In all of this, the archbishop was a thorough-going Erastian.

Whether or not the ideas which he came to formulate in the course of his career were initially so clearly defined as this, it is nonetheless plain that any defense of his new office inevitably brought him into conflict with the presbyterian party. Even his appointment as a nominal or parliamentary bishop in 1603, which he combined with his parish ministry at Mid Calder, caused difficulties in the synod of Lothian where in 1604, as a member of Linlithgow presbytery, Spottiswoode was accused of seeking to subvert the established discipline in the kirk and was reminded of his subordination to the assembly. Spottiswoode, it seems, was no stranger to the synod's rebukes: he had earlier been reproved for playing football on a Sunday; and he gave great offense to some, as titular archbishop, by riding out of Haddington on the Sabbath while the people were dutifully resorting to church to hear the sermon. Admittedly, he was heading south to see the king in London; taking with him a letter from the synod of Lothian; but the impression one forms is that Spottiswoode was no Sabbatarian of the more rigid variety.

At what stage he was first drawn to support episcopacy is not easy to determine. If his education at Glasgow under the Melville regime had done little in a positive sense to enhance his perception of bishops, there is still the possibility that family background and upbringing may have left an indelible impression, especially so as his father had been minister since the Reformation of the same parish of Mid Calder to which the son succeeded. In his History, the archbishop claimed that his father had held that "the doctrine we profess is good but the old polity was undoubtedly the better," a remark interpreted as an indication of his father's preference for episcopal rule.[2]

Yet, it is assuredly hard to reconcile this claim made by the archbishop in later life with the reality, first, of his father's participation in preparing the Book of Discipline in 1560, which intended to scrap the old system; secondly, of his father's willingness to undertake work (in addition to his parish duties) as superintendent of Lothian, an office introduced by the reformers to replace the old order; and thirdly, of his father's readiness, at his election as superintendent, to eschew lordship and dominion and accept correction and admonition. All in all, the disparity between the father's deeds and the son's description rather suggests that the archbishop in old age had lost touch with the substance of his father's work.

---

2. The reported remark bears a curious resemblance to the advice, preserved by Spottiswoode, of John Hamilton, the Catholic archbishop of St. Andrews, to John Knox in 1560, that "he should do wisely to retain the old policy which had been the work of many ages." (Spottiswoode, *History*, i, 372).

If accurately recorded, Spottiswoode's own entry to the ministry, as assistant to his father in 1583, two years after graduating, occurred at a time when the presbyterians were in power; but, soon afterwards, a reaction set in when a new government, in 1584, declared its hostility to presbyterianism by discharging presbyteries from meeting and by handing over power to bishops instead. The industrious Robert Wodrow, writing in the eighteenth century, thought he had uncovered evidence of Spottiswoode's opposition to bishops, at this point, in a document signed by thirty or so ministers, including one John Spottiswoode, from the synod of Merse, in 1586, denouncing episcopacy. But Wodrow's identification was inaccurate and rests on an unfortunate coincidence. Although Spottiswoode's family came from the Merse, the John Spottiswoode who signed the document opposing bishops was another individual of the same name who was already serving as a minister at Longformacus and Mordington when Spottiswoode, the future archbishop, was still a student at Glasgow."[3]

Whatever Spottiswoode's own thoughts were on the replacement in 1584 of presbyteries by bishops, the experiment did not endure; and after 1586 an essentially presbyterian system soon resumed. At that point, too, Spottiswoode, who seems to have opposed any accommodation with Archbishop Adamson, was selected by the assembly in 1586 as a suitable agent to be entrusted with the task of re-establishing Linlithgow presbytery, and the presbytery and synod, in turn, sent him as a commissioner to the assembly in 1590 and 1593, the years of presbyterian ascendancy. Indeed, his standing with his fellow ministers was such that they elected him moderator of the synod of Lothian in October 1594. Either his distaste for the salient features of presbyterianism still lay with the future or he was remarkably expert in disguising his feelings. In 1597 he lent his support to the stricter presbyterians by approving a reply which Robert Bruce, minister in Edinburgh, had prepared to refute the king's charge that a riot in the capital, in December 1596, had been instigated by the ministers. Again, in 1599, he was sufficiently forthright to warn the ministers of his synod to guard against any "loss of the liberty of Christ's kingdom," but he was also prepared in 1600 to countenance ecclesiastical representation in parliament, which, of course, helped prepare the way for King James to have his bishops.

---

3. He was later minister at Nenthorn, and was presented to the vicarage of that parish in May 1599.

Perhaps the moderating influence of his father-in-law, David Lindsay, minister at South Leith and soon to be advanced to the bishopric of Ross in 1600, may have counted for something here. Spottiswoode's marriage, at any rate, had taken place by 1599. In 1600, he figured as one of the influential commissioners of assembly, who advised the king between assemblies, and through whom, susceptible as they were to the king's powers of persuasion, James preferred to work in molding opinion within the kirk. Spottiswoode's ministry at Mid Calder was interrupted, however, when he agreed in 1601 to act as chaplain to the Duke of Lennox (with whose house his family had long-standing links) on the duke's appointment as an ambassador in France, where Spottiswoode's curiosity appears to have got the better of him to the extent that he witnessed—or so it was said—the celebration of mass in Paris.

The Lennox connection has a particular significance, for not only had the duke a financial interest in the lands and rents of the archbishopric of Glasgow, but he was feu superior of the regality of Glasgow, with right of nominating the provost and bailies of the burgh. These rights, however, were temporarily set aside in 1598 when the last Catholic archbishop of Glasgow, James Beaton, long-resident in France since 1560 and ambassador to James VI, was restored by the king to the revenues of the archbishopric till his death in 1603, when Lennox recovered possession. Yet, despite these setbacks for Lennox, it was not for nothing that the town council held a banquet for the duke in 1601 to celebrate his appointment as an ambassador, and thoughtfully provided him with an escort of forty men to accompany him to Edinburgh, and a surgeon for his journey to France where he was greeted by Archbishop Beaton in Paris as he journeyed to the court of Henry IV.

Nor need it be doubted that Lennox was appropriately placed to commend his own chaplain, Spottiswoode, as a candidate for archbishop when James decided to make a fresh appointment. Besides, Spottiswoode himself was so well-known to James VI that, in 1603, he accompanied James south to England. With the benefit of having a bishop as his father-in-law, a noble duke as patron, and the ear of the king as well, it is stating the obvious to say that Spottiswoode was well-placed for promotion. For Spottiswoode, as for James, that journey to England in 1603 proved decisive. At Burleigh House came news of the death in Paris of James Beaton, the pre-Reformation archbishop of Glasgow, whom James had restored as titular archbishop in 1598. Accordingly, James selected Spottiswoode to fill the vacancy in 1603.

Spottiswoode's position as titular archbishop of Glasgow, with a seat in parliament, and yet still an ordinary member of Linlithgow presbytery and parish minister, was, to say the least, anomalous and unsatisfactory. Yet, in heightened form, this apparent paradox merely underlined the tensions between what was expected of a minister and a bishop. Different people had often widely differing perceptions and expectations.

In Glasgow, the town council and burgh looked for "benevolence" and goodwill from their archbishop, who, as lord of the regality of Glasgow, exercised a temporal jurisdiction over the lands and people of his regality. He had wide-ranging judicial powers which were delegated to his bailie to discharge; and, besides his right to present ministers of his choice to churches in his gift, he had the power and patronage at his disposal to nominate the provost and bailies of the council, though at times the king himself might intervene in a bid to secure his own man as provost.[4] It was not for nothing, then, that Spottiswoode found himself addressed customarily as "my lord of Glasgow." He wielded enviable authority—spiritual, social, and political.

To underpin his prestige and power, the archbishop had, of course, his castle or palace, which, like the cathedral, was designed on a scale to overawe lesser men. This was a focal point where local ecclesiastical and other business was concluded, and patronage distributed to the archbishop's clients and friends. Traditionally, the archbishop had several smaller castles or houses, such as Daldowie, Haggs, Lochwood, and Partick, most of which were leased to lairds; Lochwood itself, a mere six miles from the cathedral, had fallen into disrepair and had passed into the possession of the Boyds of Badinheath, and Partick was long ruinous; there was even a property in Edinburgh, described as ruinous in 1592. Daldowie, however, is known to have been occupied by Spottiswoode in 1609; and he also acquired accommodation in Edinburgh where he conducted much of his business as a servant of the crown.[5] These residences were still a reminder of the archbishop's extensive, if somewhat diminished, powers, and a reflection of the incomes derived from the surrounding lands.

4. For details of earlier disputes between archbishop and burgh over the election of magistrates, see National Records of Scotland [NRS], RH11/32/1, Charters, depositions of witnesses and productions relative to the claim of the archbishops to appoint the provost and bailies of the city of Glasgow, 1543–57. In 1611 the burgh was formally erected into a royal burgh.

5. Much of the archbishop's surviving correspondence is dated from Edinburgh. Two letters were dated from Glasgow and one from Moffat.

Some property was located as far away as the baronies of Carstairs in Lanarkshire, Ancrum, Lilliesleaf, and Ashkirk, all then in Roxburghshire, and Stobo and Eddleston in Peeblesshire.

The archbishop's assistance and protection were therefore sought by lesser men. To the tenants on his estates, what counted was good lordship. Bishops were reputedly less exacting landlords than some of their temporal counterparts who prized their rights of heritable tenure. As here-today, gone-tomorrow administrators, bishops may have had less incentive to conserve their patrimony and to resist the temptation to dilapidate in favor of family, kin, and servants. But, as members of the reformed ministry, they were also conscious of their obligations to act as generous landlords by setting an example in caring for tenants and for "the poor labourers of the ground," and by avoiding all suspicion of rackrenting or other forms of exploitation, which, as preachers, they condemned in others. Some failed to measure up to such exacting standards; others were prodigal in their grants of lands and pensions.

Spottiswoode himself saw the need to preserve a balance between his obligation to dispense patronage at a variety of levels and the need to conserve resources (especially so in a period when episcopal incomes had drastically fallen as a consequence of the inroads of the laity and the pressures of inflation). In some of his earliest enactments the archbishop granted numerous feu charters to sitting tenants, who were thereby raised to the status of owner-occupiers. Many of them were small, independent men, of modest means, whose relative poverty was recognized in 1606 when parliament exempted certain feuars in the barony of Glasgow from paying their customary composition fee on receipt of their charters. Then again, valued and trusted officials in his own household like the Englishman, Robert Blunt, were rewarded for their service with grants of land.

To the nobility and gentry, the archbishopric, as a source of wealth, offered a variety of potential rewards, in the form of leases, feus and pensions which the archbishop might be induced to grant. Apart from the financial attractions, the promotion of a kinsman or servitor as archbishop might assist a magnate to consolidate and extend his political influence in the region. But there were also rewards of office which the archbishop had at his disposal—the officials necessary for administering his scattered baronies. The offices of bailie and chamberlain, for example, enabled families to increase their hold over particular areas. The post of bailie, in particular, enabling as it did the holder to exercise lordship over lesser men, was especially prized by nobles and lairds alike. Thus, in 1606,

Spottiswoode recognized the Earl of Roxburghe as his bailie and justiciar within the baronies of Ancrum, Lilliesleaf and Ashkirk. Again, in 1607, he affirmed the rights of the Elphinstones of Blythswood as heritable bailies and justiciars of the barony of Blythswood, near Glasgow. Competition for the post of bailie of the regality of Glasgow itself was particularly fierce. Over the decades, a succession of magnates—the Earls of Lennox and Arran, Lord Boyd, the Stewarts of Minto and Blantyre—had all aspired to so coveted an office. On Spottiswoode's accession, the Duke of Lennox was in command as bailie, having retrieved his family's earlier dominance in the area.

Yet there were potential disadvantages, too. The return to the bishops of sufficient property in 1606 meant that less was available for distribution elsewhere in landed society. Besides, the social status of bishops, as local and national figures, was such that their actions were apt to acquire a political significance which nobles might readily resent. This was all too apparent in 1606, when the archbishops and bishops, dressed in silk and velvet, rode to parliament, it was observed, in great pomp and splendor between the earls and lords, a display which one bishop found so distasteful in ministers of religion that he proceeded on foot instead. At the close of parliament, when the bishops were denied the precedence they claimed was theirs as members of the first estate, the nobles felt it necessary to take a stand, fearing, it was said, that the bishops had been "set up to cast them down." Spottiswoode himself seems to have developed a taste for riding in style, and so, at his request, the town council in Glasgow provided him with ten men to ride to parliament in 1609. This apart, other danger signals were there to be read. Thus, in 1609, despite steadfast opposition from the lawyers, Spottiswoode urged the king to appoint a churchman as president of the College of Justice, even although the office had been held by laymen since 1584. Besides, the creation of two courts of High Commission in 1610 alarmed those who resented ecclesiastics being "invested with such power." Episcopal pretensions were beginning to stir and to assume an overtly political character, which some found objectionable.

For the king, however, the presence of an archbishop like Spottiswoode, vigilant in supervising an ordered ministry not only in the archdiocese itself but throughout the whole western province (including the sees of Galloway, Argyll, and the Isles), proved an irresistible attraction. In the king's eyes, it made for good government. Besides, as the archbishop was the king's hand-picked man for the job, it offered the crown direct influence and control over the church. It even provided a measure of social cohesion and control by reinforcing respect for the traditional values of an ordered, hierarchical society in church and commonwealth alike. Spottiswoode thus found that he had an almost bewildering and endless variety of roles to fulfill. In temporal and ecclesiastical affairs, he—or his deputies—had the task of punishing transgressors and of instilling a healthy respect for his and the king's laws. After all, apart from his lordship of Glasgow, Spottiswoode was expected to act as a lord of parliament, a member of the privy council, an extraordinary lord of session, a principal member of the Court of High Commission for Glasgow, a commissioner, and then president, of the Exchequer, a judge in consistorial matters, a commissioner of the peace, chancellor of Glasgow University, with a voice in the election of the principal and teaching staff, and a trusted royal counsellor whose advice ranged from episcopal appointments to James's cherished notion of a union of the kingdoms.

Nor was it easy for the reformed ministry to reconcile the disparate nature of Spottiswoode's work with any pattern of apostolic ministry. If anything, it looked like a reversion to many of the features associated with medieval prelacy which the reformers had condemned in 1560. For many ministers, and for others in secular society too, attempts at reducing the power and wealth of lordly prelates by replacing them with salaried, preaching supervisors—superintendents, commissioners or visitors—had a powerful and sustained appeal. Assailed, as they were, from above and below, the bishops found their position all too precarious; and, on finding his "burdens insupportable," Spottiswoode as early as 1609 considered resigning his archbishopric, hoping "the world should see that ambition did not set me on work, but a desire to serve your Majesty in a good work that hath many enemies."

In the church, what counted was effective oversight. Court bishops, immersed in affairs of state, were only too liable to end up as absentee bishops, neglectful of their spiritual duties; and Spottiswoode had many calls on his time. He was often absent in Edinburgh or London; most of his surviving correspondence is dated from Edinburgh, where he regularly attended meetings of the privy council; and by 1621 he recounted how he had made no fewer than forty-one expensive journeys to court in London. He almost seemed more at home outside his diocese than in it. This largely arose not from his own making but from all the tasks the king placed upon him. Although technically the archbishop of St. Andrews, as primate, was senior to Spottiswoode in Glasgow, James had long preferred to work through Spottiswoode as his right-hand man in the church. More than any other churchman, Spottiswoode had prepared the way for the return of episcopal government, enabling James to declare: "bishops must rule the ministers, and the king must rule both."

When resident in Glasgow, Spottiswoode acted as constant moderator of the presbytery; he was expected to preside over his diocesan synod twice yearly, to conduct diocesan visitations at least every three years and provincial visitations every seven years; he was the agency for ordinations, confirmations and for presentations to benefices; and his approval was necessary for excommunication and absolution.[6] Although the relevant ecclesiastical records are largely lost, incidental glimpses are afforded of the archbishop's work in his diocese. Admittedly, the start to his work was so inauspicious that, in 1607, Glasgow presbytery had ordered the archbishop to compear[7] before the synod to answer charges of non-residence and negligence. The presbytery's powers were still sufficiently strong in 1608 to enable it to appoint the archbishop as one of its four commissioners to attend the general assembly at Linlithgow, and again, in 1609, to order the archbishop with two other members to conduct a presbyterial visitation of the cathedral.

Although exceedingly few traces of the archbishop's work are to be found in the presbytery records, a working relationship was established between archbishop and presbytery, though by 1610 the tables had been turned: it was then the task of the presbytery to consult the archbishop on a wide range of matters, from stipends and vacant charges to the seemingly timeless problem of squabbles in congregations. Within the archdiocese as a whole, Spottiswoode is known from other sources to have

---

6. The MS Register of Presentations to Benefices by the Crown sheds some light on the archbishop's role in examining candidates and in granting collation to benefices. During the 1600s presentations by the crown to benefices in the archdiocese were normally directed to the presbytery alone or, alternatively, to the commissioner alone, or, in other cases, to the presbytery or commissioner as the specified agents for supervising admissions. By July 1609, however, a presentation by the crown was directed to the archbishop or presbytery; some subsequent presentations continued to specify the presbytery or commissioner as the recognized agency for examination and collation; but by April 1610 royal presentations were invariably directed to the archbishop as the recognized authority. As a consequence, between 1610 and 1615, Spottiswoode had to supervise admissions to the benefices of Peebles, Kirkpatrick-Durham, Hownam, Hassendean, Kelso and Maxwellheuch, Bowden, Morebattle and Mow, Dryfesdale, Staplegorton, Southwick and Colvend, Dalgarnoch and Closeburn, Inntertig, Oxnam, Lessudden, Kirkpatrick-Irongray, Lanark, Maybole, and Ayr and Alloway.

7. To make a formal appearance before a court (a term from Scots law).

presided over a synod at Peebles, and another at Irvine, in 1611, when he was then engrossed with the case of the nonconformist minister of Ayr, George Dunbar, who was imprisoned in Dumbarton castle for praying publicly for the banished ministers, and whose parish the archbishop considered filling with an Englishman. Again, his attention to detail is apparent at a synod in Glasgow in 1612, when Spottiswoode approved a series of rules and procedures to be observed in disciplinary cases by every kirk session and presbytery in the area.

Also in his thoughts was the case of the outspoken presbyterian minister of Kilsyth, William Livingston, whose behavior had infuriated the king but on whose behalf the archbishop had nonetheless interceded with the king. This was the man who had earlier preached at Glasgow in 1605 to the effect that "it is a sin to call a bishop lord bishop and he may as well be called a moderator as lord bishop," which drew from the presbytery the mild rebuke that his expression was uncharitable, but he nonetheless refused to retract.

The problem of presbyterian nonconformity was a serious one, which confronted the archbishop from the outset of his rule. In 1607 he encountered "in the beginning great opposition" from ministers to his appointment as constant moderator of the synod of Clydesdale; and it took the presence at the synod of the Earl of Abercorn, as the king's commissioner, for royal policy finally to prevail. Even then, the ministers of Dumbarton and Drymen walked out of the synod rather than acknowledge the archbishop as moderator. As best he could, Spottiswoode sought to resolve the difficulties which beset him with a display of firmness rather than undue severity.

He was familiar enough, however, with James VI's tactics to outwit and browbeat the presbyterians into submission. After all, he had taken part in the conference at Hampton Court in 1606 which the king had arranged to interrogate eight presbyterian ministers, including the Melvilles, who had disobeyed royal wishes in 1605 by holding a general assembly at Aberdeen in defiance of the king. As a consequence, they, and others, were punished with imprisonment and banishment. In Spottiswoode's own diocese, the minister of Ayr, John Welsh, was summoned before the privy council for having attended the Aberdeen assembly, and in the archbishop's presence was sentenced to imprisonment, and was later banished to France. The sentence was undeniably severe and even Spottiswoode's father-in-law, the bishop of Ross, spoke out in council against the treatment of the banished ministers, which he considered was harsher than that accorded to Jesuits or murderers. Even so, further prosecutions followed and, within the archdiocese of Glasgow, the ministers of Craigie, Loudoun, Beith, and Hawick found themselves summoned before the privy council for approving the proceedings of the Aberdeen assembly.

If royal policy was plainly to intimidate the opposition, the archbishop's role was rather to conciliate. Yet James Melville, warded in Newcastle, saw Spottiswoode's tactics in another light and, at first, declined even to meet his former pupil "because he had left the right course and followed the world." Undeterred, the archbishop continued to seek reconciliation, urging the ministers to submit and receive the king's clemency. He even held out hope that their leader, Andrew Melville, languishing in the Tower of London, might be released "to teach in Glasgow, if he pleased." But, intercede though he did on the ministers' behalf, Spottiswoode soon discovered that James was in no mood for leniency.

Thereafter, his work on the High Commission for Glasgow, created in 1610 by the king's prerogative power, helped cast the archbishop in the role of judge and inquisitor. Despite the absence of the records of these courts, some four dozen recalcitrant ministers are known to have been summoned before the High Commission by the time of James's death in 1625. Certainly, within the archdiocese of Glasgow, between 1620 and 1622, the ministers of Ayr, Lanark, Ochiltree, Dailly, and Irvine were all deposed from their ministry by the united Court of High Commission, over which Spottiswoode then presided as archbishop of St. Andrews. Yet earlier, as archbishop of Glasgow, Spottiswoode had shown himself prepared to act as mediator between the king and recalcitrant ministers. It is perhaps a measure of his success that, in 1611, the king agreed to free four offending presbyterian ministers imprisoned in Glasgow; then, in 1612, the archbishop secured the release from prison of the outspoken William Livingston, who the king agreed should become minister at Lanark, and, by 1613, he was ready to allow the imprisoned ministers of his diocese to attend meetings of synod and presbytery, provided the ministers acknowledged their obedience to .the king.

Other issues attracting Spottiswoode's attention were the routine tasks of improving ministers' stipends, raising funds for the university and effecting repairs to his cathedral and palace, in which was to be found "a silk bed" and even a "chamber within the dungeon of the castle of Glasgow hung with tapestry," once the property of the Countess of Lennox (and possibly of the crown) which the archbishop had acquired. By

1614, however, the question of Catholic recusancy had come to the fore in a synod at Glasgow which led both archbishop and synod to petition the king for urgent action in suppressing recusancy.

This was the prelude to the sensational trial for treason of the Jesuit, John Ogilvie, in whose arrest, examination, and trial Spottiswoode played a leading part. The trial, in Glasgow, took place not in the ecclesiastical courts nor even in the court of justiciary but before a special commission established by the king; and it was for treason in affirming papal supremacy and declining King James's authority that Ogilvie was tortured (by depriving him of sleep), then tried and convicted by a jury and executed in 1615, amid heightened feelings in the aftermath of the Gunpowder plot, ten years earlier, and the attempted assassination of the king and his English parliament. The moderation and restraint which characterized Spottiswoode's archiepiscopal rule in Glasgow could not be extended to those who repudiated the king's authority.

In all, Spottiswoode by 1614 believed that he had "sure information" of twenty-seven Jesuits at work in Scotland; and in prosecuting recusants, the secular and ecclesiastical courts had each their part to play. In Ayr, the presbytery sought the archbishop's assistance in dealing with a priest, Gilbert Kennedy, and his associates; and the archbishop himself instructed Paisley presbytery to secure a confession of faith from individuals suspected of unsound religion. In Glasgow, the presbytery showed vigilance in pursuing Ogilvie's associates: one culprit, who denied he knew Ogilvie was a Jesuit and thought him a soldier, was ready to testify to his own religious orthodoxy by observing that he had satisfied the Archbishop of Canterbury of his rectitude by embracing the religion professed in England and, for good measure, affirmed that his wife had taken communion in Glasgow "out of my lord of Glasgow's own hands." Another offender who offered to make amends to the presbytery for entertaining Ogilvie was referred to the archbishop and was subsequently convicted (with another burgess) in the justiciar's court held in Glasgow by Spottiswoode and three others, only to obtain from the crown a remission for life for his crime. As privy councillor, high commissioner, justiciar, and archbishop, Spottiswoode saw it as his duty to suppress Catholicism whenever detected.

Outside his diocese, Spottiswoode earlier had confronted the problem of Catholic recusancy from his seat on the council where he had prosecuted several Jesuits, denounced the Marquess of Huntly and the Earls of Errol and Sutherland for popery, approved enactments for suppressing recusancy and accepted that a priest under interrogation might be subject "to the torture of the boots." Besides, during a visitation of the Borders, commissioned by the king in 1609 for repairing churches and appointing ministers, the archbishop had arrested one priest and, after breaking into the residence of the last Catholic abbot of Sweetheart, Gilbert Brown, had publicly burned most of the "popish trash" uncovered, for which he won the king's approval. As a reward, he received from the crown a gift of some of the abbot's confiscated books, and five years later he found himself the recipient of the more lucrative prize of the abbacy of Kilwinning, which a grateful king had conferred on him for life in August 1614. Nor was this all. In 1612, the archbishop's younger son, Robert, had won from King James the abbacy of Sweetheart itself;[8] and in 1613 his elder son, John, gained from the crown the attractive gift, for life, of the abbacy of Holyrood, a fitting reminder of the need (as some of his Protestant predecessors had discovered) for the archbishop, as a married man, to secure appropriate provision for his own immediate family.

For his unstinted service to the crown Spottiswoode was elevated by the king in 1615 to the archbishopric of St. Andrews. His work in Glasgow had amply prepared him for his role as primate. Yet it was with reluctance that he left Glasgow. In the years ahead, Spottiswoode and his royal master set off along the road that was ultimately to lead to the Covenanting revolution of the 1640s and the repudiation of episcopacy by the Glasgow Assembly of 1638. They need not have continued to tread that path to the bitter end. Indeed, there were signs that James knew when to retreat. Yet he bequeathed a bitter legacy to his hapless successor, Charles I. Under his new royal master, Spottiswoode found himself advanced to the chancellorship of the kingdom.[9] Although king and archbishop appeared to be winning all the battles, their victory was a singularly pyrrhic one, and ultimately they lost the war. Lamenting how "all that we have been doing these thirty years past is thrown down at once," Spottiswoode retreated to England and, in his absence, was deposed from his archbishopric and excommunicated by the Covenanting general assembly, which met in Glasgow Cathedral during November and December 1638.

---

8. Calderwood and Gordon both record that Archbishop Spottiswoode himself was the recipient of Sweetheart (or New Abbey) in 1612; but the Register of Presentations to Benefices discloses that it was his son, Robert, who received a gift of the abbacy from the crown in 1612.

9. January 14, 1635. He relinquished the office in 1638.

Even in death, the archbishop's wishes were not respected. In his testament, drawn up in 1639, he asked to be buried "without all manner of pomp," beside his wife in the country church at Dairsie in Fife which he had painstakingly restored. Instead, he was buried in Westminster Abbey, amid great ceremony, and attended by many mourners and torchbearers, including nobles from both England and Scotland who were then at court. In a way, this epitomizes Spottiswoode's whole career and the contradictions which made him a reformed minister yet a lord bishop, a leader of souls yet a servant of the crown. In that contradiction may be detected the kernel of his ultimate failure.

PRINCIPAL SOURCES

Cameron, *The First Book of Discipline.*
Kirk, *The Second Book of Discipline.*
Durkan, *The University of Glasgow.*
Innes, *Munimenta Alme Universitatis Glasguensis,* 4 vols.
Shead, *Fasti.*
Maidment, (ed.) *Spottiswoode Miscellany.*
Napier, Spottiswoode's *History of the Church of Scotland.*
Laing, *The Works of John Knox.*
Stevenson, *Scottish Heraldic Seals.*
Thomson, *Acts of the Parliaments of Scotland.*
National Records of Scotland, Edinburgh: Register of Presentations to Benefices; Justiciary Court Records; Books of Adjournal (Old Series).
Thomson, *The Booke of the Universall Kirk of Scotland.*
Calderwood, *The History of the Kirk of Scotland.*
Laing, *Original Letters.*
Burton, *Register of the Privy Council of Scotland.*
Donaldson, *Scotland: James V–James VII.*
Livingstone, *Register of the Privy Seal of Scotland.*
Scott, *Fasti Ecclesiae Scoticanae.*
Kirk, *The Records of the Synod of Lothian and Tweeddale.*
Thomson, *Register of the Great Seal of Scotland.*
Marwick, *Extracts from the Records of the Burgh of Glasgow.*
Marwick, *Charters and other Documents relating to the City of Glasgow.*
Glasgow City Archives: Glasgow Presbytery Records.
Pitcairn, *Ancient Criminal Trials in Scotland.*
Row, *History of the Kirk of Scotland.*
Peterkin, *Records of the Kirk of Scotland.*

13

The Glasgow Assembly of 1638[1]

ROGER A. MASON

When King Charles I imposed a new prayer book on the Scottish church, the result was, in John Buchan's words, "to fire the heather and to unite all Scotland against him."[2] This led to the famous scene in the Greyfriars Kirkyard in Edinburgh in 1638 when, in an outburst of religious and patriotic fervor, nobles, ministers and burgesses put their signatures to the National Covenant, some vowing in their own blood "to recover the purity and liberty of the Gospel." The General Assembly held in Glasgow in November then overthrew the episcopal system, rejected the recent innovations in worship and reasserted the place of lay elders in the courts of the church.[3] Professor Roger Mason examines how this Assembly had far-reaching—and unintended—consequences.

LATE IN 1638 THE small but increasingly prosperous burgh of Glasgow witnessed one of the most momentous occasions in seventeenth-century Scottish history. For four weeks, between November 21 and December 20, a large and motley crowd of notables packed into the nave of the

---

1. This chapter is a revised and expanded version of a lecture delivered to the Society of Friends of Glasgow Cathedral in January 1987.

2. Buchan, *The Kirk in Scotland*, 38.

3. Henderson, *The Church of Scotland*, 66–69.

town's ancient cathedral and, after due deliberation, passed a series of measures which in effect amounted to a declaration of war against their lawful sovereign, King Charles I. Ostensibly an ecclesiastical gathering—the first General Assembly of the Church of Scotland to have met for twenty years—the Glasgow Assembly was in reality a gathering of those disaffected Scots—lay as well as clerical—whose opposition to the king's religious and political policies had led them earlier in the same year to subscribe the National Covenant. Among the members of the Glasgow Assembly few can have doubted that their deliberate defiance of the royal will—in particular their decision to abolish and abjure episcopacy—would lead to war against their king. But even the most prescient of the covenanters could hardly have foreseen that they were embarking on a course of action which would initiate a decade of civil strife—in Ireland and England as well as in Scotland—and lead ultimately to the abolition of the monarchy itself. Only with hindsight does it become clear that in 1638 Glasgow Cathedral was the scene of a decisive moment—a critical turning-point—in the history of Charles I's unhappy relations with all three of his troubled kingdoms.

Although no previous occasion can quite match it in importance, 1638 was not in fact the first time that Glasgow had played host to a General Assembly of the kirk. Two contrasting but equally notable Assemblies had been held there in the past. The first such meeting, in April 1581, had seen the ratification of both the Second Book of Discipline—Andrew Melville's and supporters' visionary blueprint for a presbyterian Scotland—and the Negative or King's Confession—a rather less elevated attack on all things popish which was, significantly enough, to lie at the heart of the National Covenant of 1638. Just as important, though in complete contrast, it was another Assembly sitting in Glasgow in June 1610 which saw James VI & I finally realize his dream of taming the radical presbyterians within the kirk through the full restoration of diocesan episcopacy in Scotland. It was a victory long looked for, sorely won, but soon to be reversed in the reign of his son and successor. As will be seen, had Charles I not sought to tamper with the ecclesiastical settlement hammered out by his father, the Glasgow Assembly of 1638 might never have met and the shade of Andrew Melville might never have returned to haunt him. As it was, the king's religious innovations provided the ideal focus for his Scottish subjects' profound distaste for the policies of their thoroughly Anglicized monarch, while the Glasgow Assembly was to prove the ideal forum for the expression of their seething resentment and discontent.

Some sense of the excitement and apprehension stirred up by the Assembly is conveyed in the pages of Robert Baillie's incomparably informative *Letters and Journals*.[4] Baillie is one of those people whom it is hard to imagine being anything other than perpetually middle-aged. He was, however, only in his mid-thirties when the Assembly took place. Then minister of Kilwinning in Ayrshire, he was already betraying signs of that blend of censoriousness and pomposity which well suited him to his future career as a professor of divinity and which impart to his writings a uniquely comic flavor of which he himself was blissfully unaware. Here, for example, is his description of Glasgow in the heady days preceding the Assembly:

> The town did expect and provide for huge multitudes of people and put on their houses and beds excessive prices; but the diligence of the Magistrates, and the vacancy of many rooms, did quickly moderate that excess. We were glad to see such order and large provision above all men's expectation; for this that town got much both thanks and credit; it can lodge easily at once, both Council, Parliament, Session and General Assembly, whenever it shall be required.[5]

Not untouched by local patriotism, Baillie evidently thought that Glasgow could rival the capital city in its provision of conference facilities. This, however, was probably not an opinion shared by Archibald Johnston of Wariston, the anguished young advocate who, as a fanatical adherent of the presbyterian cause, was to play a key role as clerk of the Assembly. Himself an Edinburgh man, Wariston lamented to God in his diary that, on arriving in Glasgow for the Assembly, he had had to waste a day's hard labor trudging "from house to house seeking lodgings."[6] He succeeded eventually in finding shared accommodation for himself and two other prominent presbyterian figures. One of these was Alexander Henderson, minister of Leuchars in Fife, who was to be the Assembly's moderator and

---

4. Laing, *The Letters and Journals of Robert Baillie*, i, 118–76. Baillie's account of the Glasgow Assembly is given in a long letter to his cousin, William Spang, minister of the Scots kirk at Campvere, written up from notes some six months after the events he describes. Quotations from Baillie and other contemporary sources are rendered in modern English.

5. Laing, *Letters and Journals*, 121

6. Paul, *The Diary of Sir Archibald Johnston of Wariston*, 400–401.

who, until his death in 1646, was to remain the covenanting movement's most astute and formidable religious leader. The other was the now aging David Calderwood, an esteemed veteran whose knowledge of the early history of presbyterianism in Scotland was to prove as invaluable to the radicals in the Assembly as it is to the historians of today.

While they agree on little else, both Baillie and Wariston do testify to the fact that in November 1638 Glasgow was bursting at the seams as people converged from all over Scotland to attend the Assembly. In a long passage overflowing with humorous touches and worth quoting at length, Baillie also testifies to the problem of fitting everyone into the cathedral for the Assembly's opening session.[7] With some indignation he describes how

> On Wednesday, the 21st of November, with much ado could we throng into our places, an evil which troubled us much the first fourteen days of our sitting. The Magistrates, with their town guard, the noblemen, with the assistance of the gentry, whiles the [King's] Commissioner in person, could not get us entry to our rooms, use what force, what policy they could, without such delay of time and thrumbling through as did grieve and offend us.

He then goes on, with growing puzzlement and plaintiveness, to consider what might lie behind the unseemly conduct of his fellow countrymen:

> Whether this evil be common to all nations, at all public confluences, or it be proper to the rudeness of our nation alone, or whether in these late times, the love and admiration of this new reformation, have at all public meetings stirred up a greater than ordinary zeal in the multitude to be present for hearing and seeing, or what is the special cause of this irremediable evil, I do not know; only I know my special offence for it, and wishes it remedied above any evil that ever I knew in the service of God among us.

"As yet," Baillie adds sourly, "no appearance of redress." He then concludes in terms that contrive to be at once grudgingly ecumenical —at least in things indifferent—and endearingly homely:

> It is here alone where, I think, we might learn from Canterbury, yea, from the Pope, from the Turks or pagans, modesty and

---

7. Laing, *Letters and Journals*, 123–24.

> manners; at least their deep reverence in the house they call God's ceases not till it have led them to the adoration of the timber and stones of the place. We are here so far the other way, that our rascals, without shame, in great numbers, make such din and clamour in the house of the true God, that if they minded to use the like behaviour in my chamber, I could not be content till they were down the stair.

In his evident respect for the fabric as well as the function of the building, Baillie must surely rank as one of the early friends of Glasgow Cathedral.

Before leaving Baillie's account of the Assembly, it is worth quoting one further passage in which he provides a uniquely detailed description of how this vast throng of people actually arranged themselves within the cathedral. At the east end of the nave, he writes, sat the King's Commissioner, the Marquis of Hamilton, "in his chair of state," and "at his feet and on both sides" sat the chief members of the privy council. In addition,

> at a long table in the floor [sat] our noblemen and barons, elders of parishes, commissioners from presbyteries ... Few barons in Scotland of note, but were either voters or assessors; from every burgh, the chief burgess; ... from all sixty-three presbyteries three commissioners, except a very few; from all the four universities also; sitting on good commodious rooms, rising up five or six degrees, going about the low long table. A little table was set in the midst, foreanent the Commissioner, for the Moderator and Clerk. At the end a high room prepared chiefly for young noblemen ..., with huge numbers of people, ladies, and some gentlewomen, in the vaults above.[8]

Quite clearly, this was no ordinary meeting of the General Assembly of the Church of Scotland. To be sure, no Assembly had been held since 1618 and there was some doubt—to which reference will be made later—as to who was entitled to attend. But the Assembly of 1638, packed with noblemen, lairds and burgesses as well as ministers, looks for all the world like a meeting of the three estates, a parliament representative of all the most powerful sections of Scottish society and dominated—as such a gathering would be—by the landed elite.

There is no room for doubt that this situation was deliberately engineered. As will become clear, the elections to the Assembly were rigged not only to ensure that it was dominated by signatories of the National

---

8. Laing, *Letters and Journals*, 124.

Covenant, but equally to ensure that the covenanters were themselves dominated by the lay leaders of Scottish society, the lairds and magnates. The appearance of social strength, respectability and unanimity was a matter of the first importance to the covenanters, for in reality their movement was never a wholly united, homogeneous organization. It was an alliance, a coalition of disparate interests, a marriage of convenience between principally a cadre of presbyterian ministers and a group of disillusioned magnates. In time, of course, these interests were to diverge, and ultimately the magnates were to fall victim to the ministers' radical vision of a godly society which was wholly at odds with their own conservative longings—idealized and distorted by nostalgia—for a past aristocratic order. In 1638, however, the brittleness of the covenanter coalition was not yet apparent. As the Assembly approached, ministers and magnates were conscious only of the imperative need to maintain a united front in their opposition to the king. Besides, whatever their more deep-seated differences, superficially they did at least have one thing in common: a marked dislike of the episcopal bench and a mounting desire to limit—if not wholly to eliminate—its power and influence in the land.

The role of bishops in both church and state had been a matter of dispute in Scotland ever since the Reformation of 1560. There is no need here to rehearse the history of the long drawn out conflict between the proponents of episcopacy and their presbyterian opponents. Suffice it to say that, long before his death in 1625, James VI had won a resounding victory over the Melvillians and established an Erastian church in which royally appointed bishops played a dominant role in ecclesiastical administration. Critically, however, they were also employed as officers of state. While this caused few problems under the comparatively restrained and judicious governance of James VI, his son showed neither restraint nor good judgment. Unlike his father, Charles I was heavily influenced by the so-called Canterburian party within the Church of England led by the increasingly powerful Bishop (later Archbishop) William Laud. Drawn both by their Arminian theology—much less rigidly austere than orthodox Calvinism—and by their desire to adopt much more ceremonial liturgical practices, the king allowed Laud and his fellow Canterburians to assume a position of pre-eminent influence in both church and state. Generally speaking, the Scottish bishops—concerned to preserve the independence of the *Ecclesia Scoticana*—were much less Canterburian in their outlook than their English counterparts. Yet in Scotland too Charles I came to rely heavily on the episcopate in civil as well as in ecclesiastical administration. By the early 1630s bishops were sitting regularly and in increasing numbers on the privy council and—at least in the eyes of their enemies—were threatening to monopolize the ear of the king. The worst fears of the anti-episcopal lobby were apparently confirmed when in 1635 Charles elevated John Spottiswoode, archbishop of St. Andrews, to the chancellorship. Not since before the Reformation, since the heyday of Cardinal David Beaton, had a cleric held this, the highest office of state.

King Charles I (1640-49) as depicted by the Dutch portrait painter Daniël Mijtens. Image: Metropolitan Museum of Art/Creative Commons Public Domain.

Under the circumstances it is perhaps not surprising that by 1638 the episcopate had become both the focus and symbol of all that was thought to be wrong with Charles I's government of Scotland. It was through the bench of bishops—or so it was perceived by his subjects—that the king was seeking to rule the country. As a result, when his policies proved unpalatable—as many of them did—it was the bishops who bore the brunt of the criticism. Opposition to the bishops provided an ideal rallying point for the diverse, often contradictory, social, political and religious interests which stood—seemingly united—behind the National Covenant. But in many respects, as was suggested above, that unity was much more apparent than real. A closer look is required therefore at what lay behind the alliance of ministers and magnates which spearheaded the covenanting movement and at the motives which prompted their animosity towards episcopacy.

As regards the ministers, it hardly needs saying that the committed presbyterians among them were by definition anti-episcopal. There was no place for bishops in the pure Melvillian scheme of church government. Still less was there room, given the presbyterians' belief in the complete separation of church and state, for the highly politicized episcopate created by Charles I. Doubtless to a man, the presbyterians would have echoed Wariston's sonorous condemnation of episcopacy as "that great-grandmother of all our corruptions, novations, usurpations, diseases and troubles."[9] In 1638, however, presbyterians as committed as Wariston certainly was to "the utter overthrow and ruin of episcopacy" were in a distinct minority. For the most part, the Scottish clergy had conformed to the hybrid system of ecclesiastical government established by James VI. While James had ensured the reimposition of episcopacy, he had not sought to abolish the lower church courts—the kirk sessions and presbyteries—but had merely given the bishops a controlling interest in their operation. However grudgingly, the majority of ministers accepted this arrangement and it gradually became apparent to all but a few diehards that bishop and presbytery could coexist and even work in harmony. By the 1630s, just as there were few survivors—David Calderwood aside—who could recall first hand the epic battles between James VI and the Melvillians, so there were few new recruits prepared to follow in the footsteps of their embattled predecessors. The river of pure Melvillianism had been reduced to a trickle.

It had not, however, completely dried up. There did remain in Scotland a small but significant body of able, intelligent and energetic ministers whose commitment to presbyterianism remained unshaken by the success of James VI's experiment and was only reinforced by Charles I's promotion of Canterburian episcopacy. It was these men—led in the first instance by Alexander Henderson and David Dickson—who were the real architects of the Covenanting Revolution. A militant but well-organized minority, they were able in the later 1630s to exploit the growing

---

9. Paul, *Diary*, 347

discontent with Charles I's government and to radicalize the opposition as it developed, pushing the moderate clerical majority to ever more extreme solutions. They were in the short term astonishingly successful.

To be successful, however, this militant minority had to find some purchase among their less radical colleagues. In this respect, Charles I played straight into their hands, providing leverage in abundance, not just through his attitude to the bishops—though that was clearly not unimportant—but also through his attempts to alter the liturgy—the established rituals of public worship—in the reformed kirk. Such liturgical changes had in fact first been mooted by James VI who, in the interests of uniformity of worship throughout his British realms, had sought to bring Scottish practice into line with that of England. In 1618, for example, through the Five Articles of Perth, he had attempted to introduce kneeling at Holy Communion, the observance of Holy Days, private baptism and communion, and confirmation. Immensely proud of their own well-established forms of worship and deeply suspicious of the Anglicizing policies of the king, the Scots were appalled by these attempts to corrupt what they saw as the pristine purity of the kirk. Nevertheless, the king was able to force his proposals through a well-managed General Assembly at Perth in 1618 and, with greater difficulty, through a rather less well-managed parliament in 1621. But the extent of the opposition to the Five Articles warned him off trying to enforce them with any rigor and they were widely disregarded. King James apparently learned his lesson and did not pursue further his ultimate aim of rewriting the Scottish liturgy in conformity with that of England. His son, however, failed to take note of—or chose to ignore—his father's experience and by the time of his ill-fated visit to Scotland in 1633 it was well known that he intended introducing extensive liturgical reforms based on the practice of the English Canterburians.

Despite the distinctly audible rumblings of discontent, Charles I pressed ahead with his policy. The outcome was the publication in January 1636 of a Code of Canons which not only incorporated the Five Articles of Perth, but also intimated that a revised liturgy was in preparation and was shortly to be published. The new Prayer Book —"Laud's Liturgy"—finally appeared the following year. Its actual contents are of much less significance than the fact that, long before it was published, it was widely rumored in Scotland to be not so much Canterburian as overtly Catholic in both substance and inspiration. Such fears were fanned by the manner in which it was prepared and introduced. Drawn up with minimal consultation and approved by neither General Assembly nor parliament, the Prayer Book was imposed on Scotland by virtue of the royal prerogative alone. The king's arbitrary handling of a highly-charged issue had presented the militant presbyterian minority with a perfect opportunity to further their aims. They made the most of it. The Edinburgh riots which greeted the first use of the Prayer Book in July 1637—what Wariston dubbed with heavy irony "the fair, plausible and peaceable welcome the service book received in Scotland"[10]—were hardly spontaneous. On the contrary, they were large scale demonstrations orchestrated by men—Henderson and Dickson to the fore—who were not afraid to manipulate and exploit the prejudices of the mob.

The nature of these prejudices is nowhere better illustrated than in the writings of another young presbyterian zealot, Samuel Rutherford. In 1636, Rutherford was exiled from his parish of Anwoth in Kirkcudbrightshire for his persistent radicalism and packed off to Aberdeen in the fond but futile hope that contact with the conservative divines of the north-east would promote his theological re-education. Unable to preach and bereft of genuine companionship, the intensely pious Rutherford maintained a wide-ranging correspondence in which he poured out— often in vividly sensual detail—the unrequited yearnings of his tortured soul for spiritual transcendence. Yet for all his mystical piety—virtually unique in the annals of Scottish Protestantism—Rutherford could also be both extremely practical and bitterly partisan. Among his correspondents, significantly enough, were not only Henderson and Dickson, but also prominent lay covenanters such as Lords Balmerino and Loudoun. If this is additional testimony to the close-knit nature of the group which directed the protests of 1637, the letters—particularly those to his own former parishioners—also indicate the nature of the popular prejudices which they sought to exploit. For example, writing to Anwoth just ten days before the Prayer Book was introduced, Rutherford warned his flock in no uncertain terms of the terrible fate at God's hands which awaited those who "turned from the good old way to the dog's vomit again." That the "dog's vomit" consisted, among other things, of the Five Articles, the Canons and the Prayer Book is evident from what follows:

> I counsel you to beware of the new and strange leaven of men's inventions, beside and against the word of God, contrary to the oath of the kirk, now coming among you. I instructed you of the

---

10. Paul, *Diary,* 347

superstition and idolatry in kneeling in the instant of the Lord's Supper, and of crossing in baptism, and of men's days without any warrant of Christ our perfect Lawgiver. Countenance not the surplice, the attire of the mass-priest, the garment of Baal's priest. The abominable bowing to altars of wood is coming upon you: Hate and keep yourselves from idols. Forbear in any case to hear the reading of the new service book, full of gross heresies, popish and superstitious errors, without any warrant of Christ, tending to the overthrow of preaching. You owe no obedience to the bastard canons; they are unlawful, blasphemous and superstitious. All the ceremonies that lie in Antichrist's foul womb, the wares of that great mother of fornications, the kirk of Rome, are to be refused.[11]

Rutherford was nothing if not colorful in his letter writing. But rhetoric of this kind echoed up and down the land in the latter half of 1637. Drawing on a long-standing, now almost pathological fear of Roman Catholicism and reflecting on the allegedly singular purity of the reformed Scottish kirk, it proved powerfully effective as a means of mobilizing popular opposition to the king's religious innovations.

At the same time, moreover, it could be used to blacken still further the name of episcopacy. For indeed the bishops, albeit reluctantly led by Spottiswoode, had helped to draw up the new liturgy and did comply, whatever their misgivings, with the king's instructions for its introduction in July 1637. As a result the presbyterians were not only able to portray the Prayer Book as crypto-Catholic at best, but also to find the bishops guilty by association of pro-papal leanings. In the eyes of the zealots, the bishops were quite simply agents of the Antichristian church of Rome who, having no warrant in Scripture, had no place in a truly reformed kirk. Ultimately, or so the radicals believed, the bishops had not simply to be removed, but their office had to be formally and finally abjured. It was, however, some time before they dared openly canvass the abjuration of episcopacy in this way. The radicals were well aware that many of their more moderate clerical colleagues, while sharing their suspicions about the Romanizing tendencies of the Canterburians, were less than convinced that the episcopal office itself had no Scriptural warrant. There were many, like Robert Baillie, who hankered after the good old days of James VI and who would have settled simply for limitations being placed on the nature and extent of the bishops' powers. In consequence,

---

11. Bonar, *The Letters of Samuel Rutherford*, 440.

the radicals were obliged to proceed more cautiously, more subtly and with more regard to ecclesiastical and constitutional precedent than their violent invective might at first lead one to suspect.

The most telling example of this is of course the National Covenant itself. Drafted by Henderson and Wariston towards the end of February 1638, the most noteworthy feature of the National Covenant—aside from its dullness—is its conservatism. Essentially a list of statutes favorable to the reformed kirk, it ventures no overt criticism of the king and no overt mention of episcopacy. It was a document made deliberately vague so as to appeal to a spectrum of opinion which was as diverse and contradictory as it was wide. In the fevered atmosphere created by the virtual collapse of the crown's authority, it proved remarkably successful. First signed in Greyfriars' Churchyard in Edinburgh on February 28, copies were rapidly circulated around the country and attracted near unanimous support in almost every corner of the realm except the north-east. The majority of signatories evidently believed that they were protesting merely against the unconstitutional manner in which the Canons and the Prayer Book had been introduced. As was later revealed, however, its authors believed that the National Covenant contained proof positive that episcopacy too was unlawful. For incorporated within the National Covenant was the Negative Confession of 1581, a document consisting largely of a detailed abjuration of those many aspects of popery which were thought abhorrent and detestable— including, crucially, the papacy's "worldly monarchy and wicked hierarchy." Apparently unbeknown to many of the National Covenant's signatories, this was a phrase which the presbyterians had no hesitation in construing as a reference to and condemnation of episcopacy. In effect, if such an interpretation were deemed correct, a great many Scots—not least the moderate clergy—had been duped into signing a document with which they did not necessarily or wholeheartedly agree. Whether or not this masterly piece of deception can be attributed to Wariston's forensic skills, there is no doubt that written into the fine print of the National Covenant was a crucial clause which the radicals could—and did—invoke to their considerable advantage.

As yet, however, it was still not clear to the militants that clerical opinion could be so manipulated—or so intimidated—as to ensure the removal of episcopacy root and branch. At this stage, in the early months of 1638, it was more politic to focus public attention on the outrage which the imposition of the Prayer Book and the Canons was generally seen to represent. Yet in private the presbyterians were already uncovering a quite gratifying level of support for their attitude to episcopacy. This emanated, however, not so much from the clergy as from the laity. Among laymen, and especially among the nobility, resentment at the political heights to which the bishops had been elevated ran deep. One leading lay covenanter, John Leslie, sixth Earl of Rothes, began his personal memoir of the events of 1637–38 with a sweeping attack on the bishops, who, he believed—"having encroached so by degrees"—were responsible for loosing a "flood of illegal violence to overflow the truth of religion and liberties of the subject."[12] Rothes, together with two other prominent noblemen, James Elphinstone, Lord Balmerino, and John Campbell, Lord Loudoun, sat on the small committee which revised and finally approved Wariston's draft of the National Covenant. All three had a history of opposition to Charles I's regime; all three had suffered real or imagined slights at the hands of the episcopate; and all three were intent—at the very least—on stripping the bishops of the secular powers which they had recently acquired. It is not hard to imagine such men being more than susceptible to the arguments of Wariston for the wholesale extirpation of the episcopal bench. But the same in fact applies to the nobility as a whole for, whether or not they were committed presbyterians, the landed elite had sound political reasons for being hostile to Charles I's government in general and his bishops in particular.

The Scottish aristocracy had a great deal to grumble about in the late 1630s. For over a century, rising prices and falling rent-rolls had been eroding their incomes and, in the view of some historians, threatening the very fabric of the economic order on which were founded both their social status and their political power. If this is so—and the argument perhaps deserves more credit than it is sometimes accorded—the policies of Charles I served only to deepen an existing crisis. His celebrated Act of Revocation, for example, hurriedly issued in the first year of his reign, was viewed by many noblemen as a quite unprecedented and wholly unconstitutional assault on their landed wealth, their jurisdictional rights over their tenants and hence on their traditional authority in the localities. The details of the Revocation are not of immediate concern, but it is significant that, from the very outset of his reign, the king found himself at loggerheads with the Scottish ruling elite. The nobility, already made uneasy by their fluctuating economic fortunes, were made to feel decidedly uncomfortable by royal policies which appeared to undermine

---

12. Rothes, *A Relation . . . of the Affairs of the Kirk*, 1.

the basis of their privileged and hitherto unchallenged position in local society. Thus aroused, the climate of suspicion was never fully dispelled.

To make matters worse, it was not just in the localities that the nobility felt threatened, but also at the center of power. The problem here stemmed originally from the Union of the Crowns of 1603 and the removal of the royal court to London. The union dramatically altered the traditionally close and informal relationship between the Scottish crown and the Scottish aristocracy, distancing the latter from the decision making processes and depriving them of an effective political voice. While James VI was on the throne, the full significance of this was to some extent obscured by his vast experience of Scottish problems and his long familiarity with most of the leading Scottish politicians. Charles I, born in Dunfermline but long since thoroughly Anglicized, could boast neither of these advantages. Nor, characteristically, when he came to the throne did he make any attempt to compensate for the lack of them by continuing to rely on the privy councillors who had for twenty years mediated with such skill between James VI and his Scottish subjects. On the contrary, Charles at once set about dismantling the conciliar system which had served his father so well, ridding himself of councillors who were likely to prove obstructive and replacing them by political nonentities whose major—or sole—qualification for office was a willingness to do the king's bidding. The consensual approach to Scottish government, founded on the mediating role of a privy council trusted by both king and aristocracy, was swiftly jeopardized. At the same time, the extent to which the union had diminished the nobility's influence over the crown—rendering them, in effect, politically impotent—was exposed as never before.

This was brought sharply home to the Scots in 1633 when Charles I paid his promised but long-postponed visit to Scotland for his coronation. The whole affair was a disaster and a ruinously expensive one into the bargain. Not only had the king taken an insultingly long time to embark on his pilgrimage north, but his stay was insultingly short—little more than a month—and he was clearly delighted to see the back of his native realm at the earliest opportunity. More significantly in political terms, however, the visit made plain what little store Charles set by the advice of—or even consultation with—the Scottish landed elite. For some years, between 1628 and 1633, Charles had been protected from the folly of his own ignorance and the fury of the Scottish aristocracy by placing some reliance on the advice of William Graham, Earl of Menteith. Menteith was both sufficiently sensitive to Scottish issues and sufficiently trusted by the king to mitigate the full effects of royal policy in Scotland. In 1633, however, on the eve of the king's visit, Menteith fell from power, and there was no one to take his place as an unofficial adviser on Scottish matters and to prevent the king riding roughshod over the interests and prejudices of his Scottish subjects. The consequences hardly augured well for the future. When, for example, parliament met briefly to consider, among other things, certain religious innovations, the king did his utmost to gag discussion and ostentatiously sat and took note of those with the temerity to vote against his proposals. Moreover, when the discontented tried to approach the king by way of a written supplication, he not only refused to receive their petition, but had Balmerino arrested, tried and convicted of treason for being in possession of a copy of it.

Although Balmerino was subsequently pardoned, actions such as these were hardly calculated to endear Charles I to the Scottish nobility. Indeed, in political terms, it was sheer lunacy. Even as staunch a royalist as the poet William Drummond of Hawthornden was galvanized into action by the king's outrageous treatment of Balmerino. Drummond had little sympathy with Balmerino's religious views, but on the eve of his trial in July 1635 the poet composed an *Apologetical Letter* in which he upheld Balmerino's right to petition the monarch and subjected the king's government to some trenchant criticism. He even went so far as to furnish Charles I with the quite astonishing piece of advice that he should read George Buchanan's *De jure regni apud Scotos* "for his own private and the public good."[13] To find Wariston perusing the radical political tracts of Buchanan and other advocates of tyrannicide occasions very little surprise. To find the loyal and conservative Drummond actually recommending them to the king is both a telling indictment of Charles I's government of Scotland and eloquent testimony to the mounting anxiety of the landed elite.

Of course Drummond's real point was by no means radical. He was concerned simply, as he put it, that "the voice of the people should not be kept from the ears of a prince." He therefore went on to implore the king to listen to those— primarily the nobility—who in all sincerity were interested in "amending disorders and bettering the form of his government."[14] In this respect, the poet was in fact doing no more than to articulate the deep-rooted prejudices of the landed elite as a whole. It was

13. Ruddiman and Sage, *The Works of William Drummond*, 134.
14. Ruddiman and Sage, *Works*, 133.

a commonplace of contemporary political thought that the nobility were duty-bound by birth and breeding to advise the monarch, while the monarch was in turn obliged to seek out that advice and to consult with his born counsellors, the leading men of the kingdom. Where Drummond betrayed his essential conservatism was in his belief that such consultation—however highly to be commended—was nevertheless undertaken entirely at the discretion of what he described as a "loving prince." The king, insisted Drummond, was not accountable to the nobility for any of his actions and the nobility had no right—under any circumstances—to disobey or to resist his will. Charles I was accountable to God and God alone.

What lay behind this heavy emphasis on the duty of unstinting obedience to the crown was an acute fear that political dissent would culminate in civil war and civil war in social anarchy. In another pamphlet, written in the fateful year of 1638 and aptly entitled *Irene*, Drummond reiterated his belief that absolute obedience was fundamental to the preservation of the political order and argued that the resistance then clearly being contemplated by the covenanting leadership could only lead to the dissolution of the state and the disintegration of society.[15] Such fears as these—ultimately, after all, to be vindicated—were undoubtedly shared by many among the landed elite. In all probability they also preyed uneasily on the consciences of the covenanting leadership. Certainly, these men were not social or political revolutionaries, far less—as their opponents sometimes charged—republicans. It was no part of their intention to overthrow monarchical government. They were intent rather on restoring it to the form in which—in their own estimation—it had functioned in the past. If anyone was a revolutionary, it was a monarch who, in ignoring the advice of his born counsellors, was flouting age-old conventions and traditions of government. The covenanting nobility were seeking only to recreate an ideal political order in which crown and aristocracy together governed the realm.

Yet the problem remained unresolved as to how this was to be achieved without defying the authority of their anointed but stubbornly uncooperative sovereign, Charles I. So long as the king refused to recognize or participate in the aristocracy's idealizing nostalgia for a past political order, treasonable resistance appeared the only alternative to meek acquiescence in the face of an arbitrary royal will. It is at this

---

15. Ruddiman and Sage, *Works*, 163–73.

point, however, that the bishops emerged—conveniently enough—from the shadows to rescue the landed elite from the awful consequences of confronting their conservative consciences head-on. For could it not be argued that the king himself bore no responsibility for the ill-judged policies being pursued in Scotland? Was it not rather his evil and upstart counsellors—the bishops—who were to blame? Not only then was Charles innocent, but the nobility could not themselves be accused of disobeying and resisting him. On the contrary, they were defying the bishops for the sake of the king. What appeared to be acts of resistance to Charles I were in reality displays of loyalty to him. Such a scenario will be instantly recognizable to anyone familiar with the rebellions of the medieval aristocracy in Scotland and elsewhere. The cry of evil counsel and the lynching of allegedly evil counsellors was a common enough way of protesting against royal policy without incurring a charge of treason through challenging directly the sovereign himself. It was a fiction not only of surpassing convenience, but one which had seriously distorted the Scottish nobility's reading of their own feudal past.

The point is well illustrated in the principal historical work—the *Annales of Scotland*—of Sir James Balfour of Denmilne. Balfour was a distinguished antiquary with an interest in history in general and heraldry in particular who rose in the 1630s to a position of some prominence as Lord Lyon King of Arms, the senior heraldic office in Scotland. In this capacity he officiated at the coronation of Charles I in 1633. Subsequently, however, he became disillusioned with the administration he was appointed to serve and spent much of his time in semi-retirement compiling an invaluable work chronicling Scotland's history from the reign of Malcolm Canmore in the eleventh century down to that of Charles I in his own day. While the *Annales* are primarily a monument to seventeenth-century antiquarian scholarship, they also bear witness to the nostalgic conservatism of a landed gentleman who firmly believed that in the past the key to the good governance of the realm had lain in the traditionally close relationship between the crown and the aristocracy. In the present, however, in the dark days of the 1630s, this relationship—and with it the welfare of the kingdom—was under threat, not so much from the Union of the Crowns nor even from the defects of the king himself, but from the evil machinations of the ambitious, upstart counsellors—"these unhappy bishops"—who had come to dominate Charles I's privy council.[16]

---

16. For the Annales, see Haig, *The Historical Works of Sir James Balfour*, i and ii.

In the perspective of history, Balfour had little difficulty in finding the bishops responsible for the myriad problems which afflicted Scotland in the 1630s. "They were evil counsellors," he wrote, "but worse musicians: for they tempered their strings to such a pitch of ambition and superstitious foolery, that before ever they yielded any sound, they burst all in pieces."[17] As far as Balfour was concerned, the bishops were the precise contemporary equivalent of the self-seeking upstarts—the "mushrooms" as he liked to call them—who had troubled Scottish monarchs in the past. With more relish than accuracy, for example, he described how in 1482 the Scottish nobility had saved King James III from the corrupting influence of his low-born favorites by having them summarily hanged at Lauder Bridge. The king, opined Balfour, "had addicted himself totally to the counsel of Thomas Cochrane, William Rodger and James Hommill, mushrooms sprung up out of the dregs of the commons, whom he had raised to overtop his nobility, misgovern the country, and foster him in his lusts, riots and wicked courses." James III was well rid of such sycophantic parasites. A much more appealing model of kingship was provided by his son and successor, James IV, who, according to Balfour's approving analysis, made "choice of a select number of the nobility and gentry to be of his privy council and did solemnly promise to do nothing in the government without their counsel and advice."[18] Here in a nutshell was the landed elite's ideal version of their feudal past and it was one with clear implications for the role of bishops in Charles I's government. In Balfour's view, the bishops were simply upstarts—mushrooms—intent on advancing themselves "to overrule both church and state contrary to the laws of God and this nation." They had usurped the functions of the nobility, monopolized the ear of the king, and were imposing policies on Scotland which were bound to alienate the people from their prince. It was the bishops who were to blame for the debacle of the 1633 parliament; the bishops who had engineered the trial of the innocent Balmerino; the bishops who were responsible for the Canons and the Prayer Book; and the bishops who were driving covenanted Scots—reluctantly—into armed rebellion.[19]

Admittedly, this is merely the testimony of one man. Yet as Scotland's senior herald Balfour perhaps does have some claim to speak for

17. Haig, *Historical Works,* ii, 140.
18. Haig, *Historical Works,* i, 205-6, 217-18.
19. Haig, *Historical Works,* ii, 262, 200, 216, 223.

the landed, arms-bearing, elite. In any case, it seems not unreasonable to suggest that Balfour's vision of Scotland's past—not least his understanding of the traditional relationship between the crown and the aristocracy—was widely shared by the embattled political community of the later 1630s. Likewise, it seems not unreasonable to suggest that, in the same way as Balfour, the lay leaders of Scottish society found it both convenient and consoling to sidestep a direct confrontation with Charles I by heaping their grievances on the heads of his unfortunate bishops. The bishops were an ideal scapegoat for both the inadequacies of the king's government and—just as important—the inhibitions of their own conservative consciences. Thus the basis of the unlikely alliance between the radical presbyterians and the conservative nobility becomes more understandable. They were indeed, though for very different reasons, at one in their detestation of episcopacy. At the same time, moreover, in the light of this, the Glasgow Assembly emerges as an occasion of critical significance. For not only did it witness the final abjuration of episcopacy, but thereby it also—paradoxically enough—exposed the underlying brittleness of the covenanting coalition.

It is therefore appropriate, by way of conclusion, to return to the Glasgow Assembly itself. It was suggested earlier that the elections to the Assembly were deliberately rigged by the covenanting leadership. What lay behind this blatant gerrymandering was the imperative need to engineer the attendance with voting rights of sufficient laymen to ensure that, together with the rump of committed presbyterian clerics, they could successfully challenge and overthrow the authority of the bishops. By the late summer of 1638 it was no longer possible to fudge the strongly anti-episcopal interpretation which the militant presbyterians had from the outset placed on the Negative Confession and hence on the National Covenant. Yet it was by no means clear that their more moderate colleagues could be persuaded to go beyond placing "cautions" or "limitations" on the exercise of episcopal power. The covenanting leadership was thus faced with the prospect of an Assembly dominated by a clerical majority, with deep misgivings about their "hidden" agenda of abolishing and abjuring episcopacy. The moderates had therefore to be outvoted and/or intimidated and the best way to achieve this was to pack the Assembly with sympathetic laymen of substantial social importance.

This was accomplished partly by resurrecting and reinterpreting the role of "ruling elders" in the hierarchy of ecclesiastical courts established under the presbyterian system. The mechanics of the elections and the manner in which they were manipulated are of bewildering complexity and need not be examined in detail. What is important is that the covenanting leadership was able to ensure that powerful local landowners were elected to sit alongside the ministers as representatives—commissioners—of each of Scotland's sixty-three presbyteries. This may not have produced the desired numerical majority, but the election of seventeen peers, nine knights and twenty-five lairds—not to mention forty-seven burgh commissioners—did ensure a substantial lay presence whose influence was far out of proportion to its numbers. In addition, and here the covenanters fell back on blatant intimidation, they instructed that any nobleman who had signed the National Covenant might attend the Assembly; that four to six gentlemen from each presbytery were to accompany their commissioners as what they euphemistically termed "assessors"; that each burgh commissioner was also to be attended by up to six lay assessors; and that—just to make sure that no sympathetic layman of substance need feel excluded—gentlemen not chosen as commissioners or assessors might attend in any case of their own volition. This was surely loading the dice with a vengeance. While none of these latter groups had voting rights, their very presence in such numbers would prove sufficient to overawe all but the most independently-minded of the moderate clergy.

Small wonder, then, that Glasgow Cathedral was thronged to bursting point in November 1638; small wonder too that the bishops themselves did not dare to attend the Assembly; and small wonder that their supporters among the moderate clergy—with the sole exception of the querulous but conscientious Baillie—were terrorized into complete acquiescence in the dissolution of the episcopal order. In fact, the proceedings of the Assembly went better than even the most optimistic of the covenanting leadership could have hoped. The King's Commissioner, the Marquis of Hamilton, never really stood a chance of controlling it. He was outmanoeuvred at virtually every turn by the astuteness of Henderson, the resourcefulness of Wariston and, perhaps above all, by the fact that both he and his opponents knew well enough that whatever concessions he made in the king's name, Charles I would never stand by them. On November 28, a week after the proceedings had begun, Hamilton abandoned the Assembly to its own devices, the dignity of his retreat marred only by the fact that the door of the cathedral was locked and the key temporarily mislaid. Under the circumstances, a certain sympathy must be felt for the Commissioner when he complained piteously to the king that "next [to] Hell I hate this place."[20]

With Hamilton gone, the Assembly got down to the real business in hand. The commissioners worked extremely hard: as Baillie put it, with evident satisfaction, it was resolved "to have but one session in the day, to sit from 10 or 11 [in the morning], to 4 or 5 [in the evening], so we were all relieved of the expense of a dinner."[21] After much debate—richer and doubtless hungrier—the Assembly passed a long and historic series of measures which rejected the liturgical reforms recently introduced by the king, overturned the established ecclesiastical system and, in so doing, created a constitutional crisis which would be resolved only by recourse to arms. On December 6, the Canons and the Prayer Book were annulled; on December 8, episcopacy was abjured and removed; on 10 December, the Five Articles were condemned; on December 13, the bishops were individually deposed and excommunicated; on December 19, clerics were forbidden to hold civil office; and on December 20, annual General Assemblies were reinstituted. Within two weeks, the Glasgow Assembly had done its work. The Covenanting Revolution was well underway.

Yet as the commissioners dispersed and the euphoria over their triumphantly successful handling of the Assembly died down, the leaders of the covenanting movement may well have paused to consider some more sobering reflections. The seemingly united front presented by the Assembly was after all the product of terror tactics rather than a spontaneously achieved consensus. Moreover, and perhaps more seriously still, in destroying the episcopate the Assembly had also destroyed the basis of the alliance between the ministers and magnates. With the bishops gone, the landed elite could no longer indulge in the luxury of using them as scapegoats for the evils of the king's government. Many, perhaps most, would have known all along that the "evil counsellors argument" was no more than a smokescreen, a device which shielded them from having to confront directly either the king or their own consciences. In the course of the Assembly, however, the smoke gave way to fire and illuminated for all to see the true nature of the problem. And the problem was of course King Charles I himself. A king whose commitment to his religion was as profound as that of any presbyterian, but a king whose comprehension of the art of politics was as non-existent as his understanding

---

20. Quoted in Stevenson, *The Scottish Revolution*, 122.
21. Laing, *Letters and Journals*, 128.

of his Scottish subjects. Temperamentally incapable of compromise and conciliation, Charles I viewed political grievances as personal insults and a king's promises as instantly and infinitely frangible. His attitude is well conveyed by his justly infamous instructions to Hamilton, during the protracted negotiations preceding the Glasgow Assembly: "flatter them with what hopes you please," he told his Commissioner, "until I be ready to suppress them."[22]

Despite this, however, the Scottish landed elite clung hopelessly to the belief that Charles I would one day fulfill their antiquated expectations of kingship and govern Scotland in the way they imagined it had been governed in the past. They opposed him, defied him, went to war with him, but all the time protesting their fundamental loyalty to him. Like Drummond of Hawthornden, the rebel nobility knew only too well that they, the king and the social and political order they collectively represented must ultimately stand or fall together. Gradually, however, in the years after 1638, they lost control of those radical elements in the covenanting movement whose ideas were fundamentally at variance with their own. The presbyterian radicals wanted to reshape society in their image of godliness. The conservative nobility wanted to recreate it in their image of an idealized feudal past. The two were wholly contradictory. Moreover, unfortunately for the nobility, so long as Charles I refused to lend substance to their idealizing nostalgia, the cycle of violence and revolution escalated and the presbyterians grew ever more powerful. Perhaps Balfour, however, may be permitted the last word, for in a passage in his *Annales*, written in the late 1640s, he captured quite succinctly not only the self-deluding loyalism of the landed elite, but also their mounting fear in the face of the overweening ambition of the presbyterian zealots:

> It is to be remembered, the chiefest bellows that has blown this terrible fire, were first the unhappy bishops of both kingdoms; and now the preachers and ministers . . . who in lieu of obedience and conformity to government, and compliance with the necessities of so good and religious a King, did teach and obtrude to the people . . . nothing more than Christ's cause, religion, liberty and privilege of the subject, whereby they have not only embittered the affection of the vassal but in effect quite poisoned them against their native sovereign and prince.[23]

22. Quoted in Donaldson, *Scotland: James V–James VII*, 317.
23. Balfour, *Historical Works*, iii, 426.

A NOTE ON FURTHER READING

Although the interpretation of events offered here is entirely the author's responsibility, he is enormously indebted to a number of historians who have dealt with the period at more length and in more detail than is possible within the confines of a single lecture. The best introduction to the political and religious issues covered here is volume 3 of the Edinburgh History of Scotland: Gordon Donaldson, *Scotland: James V–James VII*. Maurice Lee Jr., *The Road to Revolution: Scotland Under Charles I, 1625-1637*, is a lucid and very readable account of how relations between the king and his Scottish subjects deteriorated so rapidly, while David Stevenson, *The Scottish Revolution 1637-44: The Triumph of the Covenanters*, carries the story forward into the revolutionary era and contains an excellent chapter on the Glasgow Assembly itself. As its subtitle implies, Walter Makey, *The Church of the Covenant 1637-51: Revolution and Social Change in Scotland*, approaches the covenanting period from a social and economic perspective and provides many valuable insights into the changes in the nature of Scottish society which lay behind the events of 1637 and their aftermath. Of more specialist interest, Gordon Donaldson, *The Making of the Scottish Prayer Book of 1637*, and David Mullan, *Episcopacy in Scotland: The History of an Idea 1560-1638*, will both repay detailed study.

14

The Western Towers of Glasgow Cathedral

JAMES H. MACAULAY

Until the 1840s the western facade of Glasgow Cathedral featured two towers of different heights. Some at the time thought these "obscured and deformed" the appearance of the front and they were demolished. However, Dr. James Macaulay, architectural historian and Chairman of the Society of Friends, regrets the loss of the towers. In this chapter he traces their history and examines the process that led to their demise.

An engraving from "Old England: A Pictorial Museum of Royal, Ecclesiastical, Baronial, Municipal and Popular Antiquities" (London: Charles Knight & Co., 1845) showing the western towers of Glasgow Cathedral.

SCOTLAND'S TWO GREATEST ARCHITECTURAL losses in the nineteenth century both occurred in Glasgow.[1] They were the destruction of the Old College in the High Street and, a generation earlier in the eighteen forties, the removal of the western towers of the cathedral which hitherto had survived intact from the Middle Ages. The loss of the towers was particularly regrettable because of their antiquity and because, too, they enlivened the west front of the cathedral while adding interest to what became Infirmary Square in the later eighteenth century.

Of the greater medieval ecclesiastical buildings in Scotland only the cathedrals of Elgin, Aberdeen and Glasgow (out of twelve cathedrals) and the abbeys of Arbroath, Dunfermline, Holyrood and Kilwinning had pairs of western towers. At Elgin, Aberdeen, and Arbroath the towers were a symmetrical pair, enclosed within the main building lines.

---

1. The author is indebted to Dr. Ronald Cant, to Dr. John Durkan and to Professor Richard Fawcett for reading the typescript of this article whilst it was in preparation and for much helpful comment; and to Mr. Philip McWilliams for allowing excerpts to be quoted from his thesis on Paisley Abbey. Some of this article first appeared as "The Demolition of the Western Towers of Glasgow Cathedral," in *The Architecture of Scottish Cities* (ed. Deborah Mays) in 1997.

That was intended, too, at Paisley Abbey, as can be seen in the internal structural arrangements in the most westerly bays of the nave aisles. At Holyrood the towers were identical and were integral components of a west front which was designed as a unified composition as at Elgin and Aberdeen. Most unusually, however, the Holyrood towers extended beyond the north and south aisles and projected from the west front so that the processional doorway appeared to be recessed.[2] There was a similar disposition of towers at Glasgow Cathedral; but they were dissimilar in area and in height although both were aligned on the nave arcades. A lateral continuation of the west façade also happens in some measure at the cathedrals of Brechin and Dunkeld, each of which has a projecting tower at the north-west corner.

If one compares the ground plans in Banister Fletcher's rollcall of the major "English cathedrals" it will be noted that four Welsh cathedrals are included as well as Christ Church in Dublin, with Glasgow as the sole Scottish choice.[3] Of the thirty-one selected examples in the British Isles only about half have western towers. These are integrated within a balanced and unified west front which is a feature, too, of the cathedrals without western towers. The sole exception is Glasgow, not only in the asymmetry of the west front but in the frontal and lateral projection of the towers. In these respects why was the west front of Glasgow so different?

Was it because the towers are the incomplete remnants of an ambitious building program which was abandoned, as occurred at Paisley Abbey? Such a supposition is dependent on the date ascribed to the towers.[4] Were they part, as has been suggested,[5] of the building of the nave in the early thirteenth century which was halted and not resumed until the end of the century? Or were they begun then with the grant of timber by the laird of Luss in 1277 for the *campanile et thesauria*, with the former being intended as the north-west tower?[6] Are they of the late fifteenth century?[7] Or is it to be accepted, as was put forward some few years ago, that unfinished and of late date, they were not very good towers."[8]

2. McAleer, "A Unique Facade in Great Britain," 263–75.

3. Fletcher, *A History of Architecture*, 410–13.

4. Talbot ("An Excavation at the Site of the N.W. Tower . . .") came to no conclusion about the date of the tower.

5. Radford, *Glasgow Cathedral*, 23.

6. Waddell, "The Western Towers of Glasgow Cathedral," 62.

7. Coltart, *Scottish Church Architecture*, 156.

8. Cruden, *Scottish Medieval Churches*, 155.

Then again the asymmetry of the towers may indicate different building dates. But which dates? Certainly, when additions to the cathedral were required they would of necessity have had to be placed at the west end, since structural problems, and hence the in-gathering of the transepts, may have shown that the terrain to the east was too difficult for building because of the crossfalls and the soft, boggy ground conditions. But why should new buildings be required? The answer must have been the need for additional accommodation, of which the cathedral has always been chronically short. It is cause for reflection that the cathedral, the mother church of the most extensive diocese in Scotland, had little administrative space or storage for the furnishings of the numerous chapels.

By the close of the fourteenth century much of the cathedral as seen today was in place, with a completed choir and nave and above the crossing a timber and lead covered steeple, which may have housed the belfry—an example of which remains at the church of St. John in Perth. The Glasgow steeple, having been struck by lightning prior to 1406, was replaced by the present stone tower by Bishop William Lauder (1408–25), whose arms adorn the parapet, and was finished with the stone spire by Bishop John Cameron (1426–46). The same lightning strike and subsequent fire seems, too, to have damaged severely the vestry, the north choir aisle and the chapter-house.[9] The latter was repaired and embellished with his armorial insignia by Bishop Lauder and subsequently, according to the heraldic evidence, heightened by Bishop Cameron and finished by his successor, Bishop Turnbull.

With the loss of much of the original central tower, and its subsequent rebuilding over many decades, a new bell tower may have been required as a matter of urgency. If that was how the north-west tower came to be, then haste could explain a plain appearance. If it was supplied by Bishop Lauder, then the argument for an early fifteenth-century date[10] can be supported by reference to Aberdeen, Brechin, Dunkeld, and Dunblane, all of which were finished with additional towers (with the exception of Dunblane which was heightened) in the same century.

Apart from old views and one set of ground plans there are two literary sources relating to the towers. John Honeyman, the late

---

9. Durkan, "The Great Fire at Glasgow Cathedral," 89–92.

10. In the late seventeenth century Robert Mylne, a writer in Edinburgh, set down that Bishop Lauder "built ye lower stiple at ye west of ye cathedral." Edinburgh University Library, Dc.4.32, Rental of Assumptions, 166. Durkan, "Notes on Glasgow Cathedral," 73.

nineteenth-century Glasgow architect who devoted much time and study to the cathedral, recorded, "I was told by one who examined it at the time, that the jambs of the west window of the north aisle, which was covered by the tower, were found when exposed to be quite fresh. There was no chase cut for glazing, and evidently the window had never been used before the erection of the tower."[11] More significant, perhaps, is an item (which does not seem to have been noted by scholars) provided by Archibald McLellan. Writing when the north-west tower was still in place he observed that "the original corner buttresses of the nave are discoverable from the joints of the masonry, where they have been overlaid by the walls of the tower."[12]

At Glasgow the north-west tower was thirty-three feet square overall, compared to the thirty-five feet square of the south-west tower and the forty feet square of the chapter-house, with two single lights on its west and south sides at ground level, above which it was windowless except for a pair of cusped lights on each face of the final stage which overtopped the nave ridge. These lights were similar to the cusped panels on the pulpitum. The north-west tower was finished with an oversailing parapet and a stumpy leaded spire which corresponded with the towers at Brechin, Dunkeld, and Dunblane.

Little is known about the interiors of the Glasgow towers. The plans by Collie in 1835 indicate that the ground floor chamber of the north-west tower was vaulted and "at the four angles from whence spring the ribs of this vaulting," according to McLellan, "are corbells carved into the semblance of ludicrous human figures."[13] Three of these, which are unlike any other capitals in the cathedral, survive, matching the style of the figurative carving on the fifteenth-century pulpitum.[14] The center of the vault had a circular opening to allow for the raising of materials to the windowless upper floors fitted no doubt with wooden staging with ladders giving access to the bell chamber. The north-west tower was the consistory house[15] as well as the belfry, thus fulfilling the same dual functions

11. MacGeorge, *Old Glasgow*, 104.
12. McLellan, *Essay*, 36.
13. McLellan, 62.
14. Richardson, *The Mediaeval Stone Carver*, 58, attributes the carvings from the north-west tower and those on the pulpitum to John Morrow.
15. According to McUre, Bishop Cameron "established the Commissariat Courts of Glasgow, Hamilton and Campsie, to be held thrice a week . . . in the Consistorial House, upon the West end of the High Church." Gordon, *Glasghu Facies*, 64.

as the towers at Brechin and Dunkeld; such multi-story, multi-purpose structures were not uncommon even for the larger churches such as St. Giles' in Edinburgh.[16] Indeed, at Glasgow there was the double-storied treasury and sacristy abutting the north-west aisle of the choir.[17]

Although the tower at Brechin seems to have been begun in the thirteenth century, to judge from stylistic evidence, the upper part must belong to the late fourteenth century.[18] There is a ground floor vault, which is carried at the angles on stiffleaf capitals, with a central opening as at Glasgow. At Dunkeld the vaulted ground floor has wall ribs between which there are painted biblical judgment scenes. On the north wall is the Judgment of Solomon from the Old Testament and on the west wall is depicted the Woman Taken in Adultery from the New Testament. The other scenes are now fragmentary. Is it coincidence that the Dunkeld tower, begun in 1469, and the unusual double storied chapter-house were provided by Bishop Thomas Lauder, a nephew of Bishop William Lauder of Glasgow?[19] There is, too, the detached campanile of Cambuskenneth Abbey. Of mid-thirteenth century date, it has a vaulted ground floor. The existence of a number of related thirteenth-century towers, the observations of Honeyman and McLellan and recent excavation of the site,[20] all point to a late thirteenth-century date for the commencement of Glasgow's north-west tower. Thereafter work was abandoned until the fifteenth century, an argument that can be sustained by the height of the buttresses which would indicate a single story structure.

The best illustration of the south-west tower at Glasgow is by W. L. Leitch "who later migrated to London and became drawing master to Queen Victoria's family."[21] It shows[22] in 1836 a plain rectangular structure reaching as high as the wallhead of the nave. Buttresses on the west and

16. Hay, "The Late Medieval Development of the High Kirk of St. Giles', Edinburgh," 251.

17. McRoberts, "Notes on Glasgow Cathedral," 40–42.

18. Progress on the tower at Brechin extended over a lengthy period. The vicar of Lethnot "had also given a cart and horse to lead the stones to the building of the belfry of the Church of Brechin, in the time of Bishop Patrick," who held office between 1354 and 1384. MacGibbon and Ross, *The Ecclesiastical Architecture of Scotland*, 204, 212–13; McAleer, 7, note 7; Fawcett, "The Blackadder Aisle," 281.

19. Root, *Dunkeld Cathedral*, 7, 17.

20. McBrien, "An Interim Report on Excavations at the West Front of Glasgow Cathedral," 6,7.

21. Blackie, *Blackie and Son*, 21.

22. MacGeorge, *Old Glasgow*, frontispiece.

south faces correspond in height with the roof of the south aisle. The tower was repaired with a crow-stepped cap-house in the early seventeenth century. The ground and first floors were illuminated by square-headed windows set within pairs of lancets. As the fenestration was similar to that in the upper tier of the chapter-house, it may be that the south-west tower was begun by Bishop Cameron or by his successor.[23] Was it a temporary structure while the chapter-house was undergoing repair? Certainly, the lack of external articulation might indicate haste in its construction. In McLellan's time, when "the commissary of Glasgow still holds its courts,"[24] the ground floor of the south-west tower was "fitted up with benches, and on the western wall is some paneled wood work, in the central compartment of which is painted the royal arms, with the initials of Charles the Second. These fittings are all in a state of decay."[25]

Both towers were entered from the nave aisles. But how? Bearing in mind Honeyman's remark, was it by a doorway with a window above? McLellan says that the vault of the north-west tower was a third of the height of the tower[26] which would correspond with the height of the aisle vault. Given that the only daylight was from four narrow lights set low one could surmise that the entrances from the aisles were high arched openings, to judge from Collie's plans, whereas with doorways molded jambs appear on the approach side only.[27]

After the Reformation the town council undertook repairs to the cathedral even although the building was not its property. Thus, as early as 1574 the council "have and (sic) respect and consideratio unto the greit dekaye and ruyne that the hie kirk of Glasgow is cum to throuch taking awaye of the leid, sclait, and wther grayth thairof in thir trublus tyme bygane, sua that sick ane greit monument will alluterlie fall doun and dekey without it be remedit" agreed to pay "for helping to repair the said kirk and haldyng it wattirfast." Later, there are references to the western towers. In 1624, "The provest, baillies, and counsall ordanis that

---

23. A date prior to the end of the fifteenth century is confirmed by a recent archaeological excavation of the foundations of the south-west tower (see McBrien, note 20 above).

24. Wade, *The History of Glasgow*, 43.

25. McLellan, *Essay*, 63.

26. McLellan, *Essay*, 62.

27. The stonework on the inner faces of the west wall of the north and south aisles seems to indicate that once there were large apertures. Waddell, "The Western Towers," 60.

the laich steple (or north-west tower) of the Heich Kirk be theikit with leid." Four years later there is the mention of money being "debursed for poynting the tua stipllis of the Metropolitan Kirk." Earlier in that same year "the proveist, bailyeis, and counsell has condescendit and aggreit that James Colquhoun, wricht, and John Boyid, masoun, build and repair the dekayet pairtis of the Librarie hous (the south-west tower) of the Hie Kirk, putt the ruiff thairon, geist and loft the samyn, and theik the samyn with leid, and do all things necessar thairto for 3100 merk."[28] By such means the cathedral survived the continuing religious upheavals of the seventeenth century.

If one discounts the burgh records it may be that the first recorded mention of the western towers was by an English traveler, Sir William Burrell, in 1758, whose remarks were not flattering. "The Church itself is a Stately Edifice, of large Extent and excellent Workmanship, but seems never to have been entirely finished, for, at the Entrance into most Cathedrals there are 2 Towers, here only 1 appears Compleat another has been begun but small progress was made on it . . ." He then remarks on the internal divisions of the cathedral. "This Building . . . is miserably spoil'd, I might say defaced within, by the Stupid Contrivance of the People of Glasgow, who have divided it into 2 Churches, and fitted both of them with Pews. . . . They have likewise very ingeniously walled up the grand Entrance."[29]

Pejorative remarks about the appearance of the western towers multiplied once the remains of the bishop's castle were cleared away to make way for Robert Adam's Royal Infirmary in the early 1790s. Until then the towers were integral parts of a varied architectural and topographical ensemble. The cathedral was approached from the south-west, with both vista and route prescribed by the castle to the north with its southern limits marked by the defensive tower at the south-west angle, then by the precinct wall (such as survives still at St. Andrews) with the view closed by the cathedral's towers giving presence and dignity to the west front. In that scene much of the contrast, the play of forms, the changing scale was lost with the disappearance of the castle. Thereafter the cathedral was isolated and more exposed, for, lacking an architectural foreground, it was brought into more prominence. Early nineteenth-century depictions show the infirmary to the north, the cathedral to the east and to

28. MacGeorge, *Old Glasgow*, 102–4; Gordon, *Glasghu Facies*, 148; Durkan, "Notes on Glasgow Cathedral," 76.

29. Burrell, "A Tour, 1758."

the south the Barony Church (whose. congregation had worshiped in the cathedral's crypt, which on their departure then became a place of sepulture). Given the disposition of public buildings around the cathedral and the laying out of a paved square it was perhaps inevitable that interested attention should focus on the cathedral. Questions about its use, condition and appearance came to be asked by the antiquarians, prompted in part perhaps by the contemporary building programs on the truncated remains of Paisley Abbey and at St. Giles' Cathedral in Edinburgh. At the former, where the roof of the nave (the only part of the medieval abbey then in congregational use) needed repairs in 1825, the heritors and others were becoming aware of the antiquarian worth of the abbey, whereas a generation earlier there had been a desire to pull down the surviving parts and use the stones to build a parish church.[30]

More important, in view of subsequent attitudes in Glasgow, may have been the remodeling, externally as well as internally, of St. Giles' Cathedral by William Burn between 1829 and 1833. Once the surrounding Krames had been demolished the exterior of St. Giles', according to William Chambers, "had a very ragged appearance," which was remedied by Burn's demolition of side chapels, the erasure of idiosyncratic excrescences and the imposition of a fictitious symmetry over the fabric now clad with polished ashlar.[31]

Indeed, it cannot be coincidence that in 1833 there appeared an *Essay on the Cathedral Church of Glasgow*, published at his own expense by Archibald McLellan, one of the city's richest merchants, a noted art connoisseur and a member of the town council. McLellan provides valuable information about recent changes to the fabric of the cathedral, such as the unblocking of the west window in 1812; although in 1833 the west doorway and the south porch were still blocked, so that the entrance to the cathedral was by a doorway in the eastern portion of the nave.[32] That led into a no-man's land between the two congregations with one occupying the western arm of the nave and the other the choir, a physical separation still to be seen in the church of St. Nicholas in Aberdeen.

The aim of the *Essay* was to promote the improvement of the cathedral, especially in the nave where "the grandeur of its appearance, however, is completely destroyed by a partition wall of rough masonry

---

30. See McWilliams, "Paisley Abbey."
31. Hay, "Late Medieval Development," 246.
32. McLellan, *Essay*, 47, 50.

... and the necessity of the removal of which it is one of the principal objects of this essay to illustrate." As for the western towers, however, "Little time need be consumed in describing these portions of the structure" since to McLellan they were "ungainly forms . . . they have not even the merit of antiquity."[33] That most damning statement in an age of antiquarianism seems to have been accepted without debate by subsequent commentators. With the unquestioning optimism of his age and, possibly, with the radical overhaul of St. Giles' in mind, McLellan saw "no limit to the extent of our operations in improving the Cathedral. We may live to see two magnificent transepts, in fulfillment of Bishop Blackadder's original design, completed—the unsightly buildings which deform the western front removed, and their places supplied by such an elevation as the grand western front at York."[34] Thus were the seeds sown for the destruction of the western towers.

A drawing of the existing western front of Glasgow Cathedral from the "Plans and Elevations" published in 1836. The caption reads: "Western elevation shewing the recent erections which obscure & deform it; together with the Columns of the Great Doorway, half buried in the soil."

33. McLellan, *Essay*, 62.
34. McLellan, *Essay*, 90.

In the Prefatory Notice to his *Essay* McLellan deponed that it had originally been a lecture delivered "to the members of the Glasgow Dilettanti Society" several of whom had suggested its publication. In doing that McLellan took the opportunity to call for "a more complete and detailed history of the See of Glasgow." Such "an extended work" might be accompanied "by an architectural description of the edifice illustrated by external and internal views, with accurate ground plans and sections of the principal parts" on the model "of Dodsworth's Salisbury or Britton's English Cathedrals."[35] Or, he might have added, of Paisley Abbey and the publication by James Russell, a local architect, of the first measured survey of both the exterior and the interior with accompanying notes "in an effort," he wrote, "to counter balance the lack of published material on Scottish ecclesiological architecture when compared with that available in England."[36]

McLellan's plea did not fall on deaf ears, for almost immediately the suggested task was undertaken by James Collie, an architect practicing in the 1820s in Aberdeen (which he subsequently quitted[37] doubtless because of the monopoly of architectural commissions held by the local men, John Smith and Archibald Simpson). Collie went to Glasgow and in 1835 published *Plans, Elevations, Sections, Details and Views of the Cathedral of Glasgow*, which was the first measured survey of the cathedral. The plates included elevations of the western towers as well as their ground plans which, being the only recorded ones, have been utilized by every historian since. It is the plan of the north-west tower which shows the ribbed vault; the south-west tower has its stair-case, while both plans show the entrances from the nave aisles. Collie followed McLellan in supposing Bishop Bondington "to have erected the north-western tower and the consistory house," of which "there is nothing worthy of remark."[38] In delineating the cathedral Collie also harked back to McLellan's unillustrated *Essay* with its list of suggested improvements. Thus, Collie not only shows the nave uncluttered by internal partitions but he provides pictorial evidence as to now vanished roofs and the evident cracking of the structural framework in the west wall of the north transept.

35. McLellan, *Essay*, vii.
36. See note 29.
37. Colvin, *Biographical Dictionary*, 230.
38. Collie, *Plans, Elevations*, 1,4.

As a result of awakened interest in the cathedral, proposals for its repair and for additions were published in 1836 by a local committee, motivated by McLellan,[39] whereupon several interconnected and contending issues appeared over the roles of the Lords of the Treasury, as the owners of the cathedral, of the Edinburgh architects George Meikle Kemp and James Gillespie Graham and of McLellan himself.

The main thrust of the argument as put forward by Kemp was that the cathedral, as it stood, was incomplete for "it wanted transepts ... nor was its western front at all suited to the grand and impressive character of the rest of the structure."[40] Having accepted that the building was not in good repair, with the north transept, for instance, "fully two feet off the perpendicular," the Lords of the Treasury had asked Robert Reid as head of the office of works in Scotland to make a survey and cost the necessary repairs, with the proviso that any improvements "they leave to the good taste and right feeling of the community" for whom additions had been drawn up "by a professional Gentleman of great eminence and experience in Gothic architecture."[41] That was Gillespie Graham. It is at this point that the controversy begins, since the prospectus for the beautification of the cathedral had included drawings by Kemp (but without acknowledging the artist) alongside the "Western Front by James Gillespie Graham Esquire; as approved by the Right Honourable the Lords of the Treasury."

Kemp had been collecting material for an aborted work on Scottish Cathedrals and Antiquities on the lines of those published by John Britton in England. He decided to supplement his studies of Glasgow Cathedral with a perspective showing "the probable plan of the original architect for the completion of the building" with supporting drawings and with costs obtained from an Edinburgh surveyor. Eventually, there was a wooden model, "about 12 feet long, by 6 feet broad, and the central spire rises about 8 feet from the ground," which Kemp opined "may last a thousand years." As its construction took more than two years it was not until 1839 that it could be dispatched to Glasgow for public viewing. The cost was to have been borne by McLellan, but at the halfway mark his advice to Kemp was not to continue "for Mr. Graham had got up a design,

---

39. In a letter Kemp mentions McLellan's "claim to priority in originating the idea of restoring Glasgow Cathedral." Quoted by Bonnar, *Biographical Sketch of George Meikle Kemp*, 76.

40. Bonnar, *Biographical Sketch*, 67.

41. Collie, *Plans and Elevations*, 5, 6.

and that it was useless for us to contend with him, because he had the ear of the Lords of the Treasury."

Like others before, Kemp considered that the transepts "bear evident marks of an unfinished condition; while the great western front appears to considerable disadvantage from its want of detailed finishing." For him the north-west tower was "clumsy" and its companion "a building of a peculiar and unseemly character." Kemp wished to extend the nave to the line of new symmetrical towers to be only slightly lower than Bishop Cameron's spire. Kemp's proposals were criticized for the "diminutive central pinnacles on the western towers" and because his south transept only partially covered Blackadder's Aisle. As Kemp wrote to McLellan, "You have corrected the one error; the plans of Mr. Gillespie Graham correct the other."[42]

G. M. Kemp's proposed western towers from the "Plans and Elevations" published in 1836.

42. Bonnar, *Biographical Sketch*, chapter 3. Kemp's correspondence, a fragment of the model of Glasgow Cathedral (a choir window head), and James Collie's presentation copy of his book to Kemp are in the Writers' Museum, Lady Stair's House, Edinburgh.

Why were Kemp's proposals jettisoned? McLellan was ready to blame the Lords of the Treasury who since 1836 had been discussing with Gillespie Graham a scheme to restore the remains of Holyrood Abbey as the meeting place of the general assembly of the Church of Scotland.[43] If Glasgow Cathedral was to receive embellishments there would be no objection provided they were in keeping stylistically and by a government-appointed architect.[44] However, when the Glasgow town council appointed Gillespie Graham that was accepted.[45]

The true reason why Kemp lost out was because, despite his superior knowledge of medieval Gothic, he had built nothing of any import, whereas Gillespie Graham had not only some fifteen Gothic revival churches to his name but had worked on the medieval churches of Linlithgow, Stirling, and Perth as well as Dunblane Cathedral. Yet how did the connection between Gillespie Graham and McLellan come about? Probably through the surveyor William Kyle, who had worked for many years with the architect and had contributed a section to McLellan's *Essay*.

Early in 1837 the Glasgow Dean of Guild court, of which McLellan was a member, ordered the north transept to be shored "to prevent danger to the lieges."[46] Some months later, "As the Designs for our Cathedral are now finished," Gillespie Graham was instructed to forward them to the Treasury. "I have no doubt," wrote Baillie Henry Paul, "that we shall be able to raise in Glasgow a subscription that may be sufficient to build the West Front and Spires and therefore I do hope that the Treasury will proceed this summer to build the Transepts."[47] Gillespie Graham did as requested, and appended a note saying that the north transept should be dismantled and rebuilt "which will not probably exceed £7,000." He also enclosed a report on the "Lithographic Plans." Referring indirectly to Kemp's proposals he advised that "the contemplated additions are, in my humble opinion, somewhat at variance with that decided simplicity of outline which characterizes the Venerable Minster of St. Mungo." He rested his case for the acceptance of his own designs on an analogy with Lichfield Cathedral with its triple spires, the central one similar to that at

43. Macaulay, "The Architectural Collaboration Between J. Gillespie Graham and A. W. Pugin," 410–11

44. Copy of Treasury Minute. 1 Nov. 1836. SRO, W/1/188/Pt/I and hereafter.

45. R. Reid Office of Works, Exchequer Buildings, Edinburgh to H. H. Seward, Office of Woods. January 3, 1837.

46. Gillespie Graham to Seward. Edinburgh, August 9, 1837.

47. Henry Paul to Gillespie Graham. Glasgow, May 30, 1837.

Glasgow, "and warrants on high authority the restoration of the others . . ." Unlike Lichfield and other cathedrals, however, Glasgow "is well seen from many parts of the surrounding country, and with its group of three spires, could not but have a peculiarly picturesque and magnificent effect." To demonstrate the affinity between all three towers, "as a perspective view alone is very inadequate for such a purpose," he enclosed new drawings of the west and south elevations and a plan showing the south transept extending laterally beyond Blackadder's Aisle.[48]

What Gillespie Graham did not say, and what was not known until recently, was that the three new drawings had been prepared by the twenty-four-year-old A. W. Pugin[49] who had just been converted to Catholicism. What would the brethren of the kirk have said if they had known! Since 1829 Pugin had been paid by Gillespie Graham to supply drawings for schemes as diverse as the new castle at Murthly, Perthshire, and St. Margaret's convent in Edinburgh, the first in Scotland since the Reformation. Pugin was no doubt the "high authority" who made the comparison between the cathedrals of Glasgow and Lichfield. The Glasgow drawings intended for publication are probably those referred to by Pugin in his diary early in 1836[50] and would have been based on Collie's survey, a copy of which Pugin possessed.[51] A further diary entry by Pugin in May 1837 records: "Finish(?) churches for Mr. G. 6 drawings" which were later priced as "3 drawings . . . of Glasgow £10:10:0" and "3 ditto altered £15:15:0."[52] Three of these survive—a plan with expanded transepts and before and after south elevations—and show evidence of Pugin's hand in lettering, in the impressionistic rendering of window tracery and in the vigor of the architectural presentation.[53] These conform to the published west elevation which was more elegant than Kemp's four layered composition. In his rival's scheme the aisled transepts and the acute west gable set between thin towers, which read as high bases for the spires,

48. Henry Paul to Gillespie Graham. Glasgow, May 30, 1837.

49. For an analysis of the working relationship between Graham and Pugin see Macaulay, "Architectural Collaboration," 406–22.

50. The relevant Pugin diary is in the Victoria and Albert Museum, MS. 86 MM. 55 and 56. See also Wedgwood, *A. W. N. Pugin and the Pugin Family,* for transcriptions of Pugin's diaries.

51. Sale Catalogues of Libraries of Emblem Persons, vol. 4, Architects (introduction by David J. Watkin), London, 1972, 254.

52. V and A, MS. 61 ii. 49.

53. Ministry of Works MSS., Glasgow Cathedral.

imitate Lichfield—although the slenderness and details of the spires seem to correspond to a foreign source, namely the church of St. Elizabeth at Marburg in Germany.

Approval came from the Treasury "both as regards the harmony of style preserved in the proposed restoration and the general beauty of the designs."[54] While it was accepted that a new west front, costing £10,296 over two years according to Gillespie Graham,[55] was Glasgow's burden, the Treasury still would not meet the cost of extending the transepts, accepting liability for the repair of the existing fabric only.[56]

Early in 1840 Edward Blore, the surveyor of Westminster Abbey and a well-known, if uninspired, authority on medieval architecture, was ordered "to proceed to Glasgow and make a careful survey of the Cathedral in that City..." While accepting that the north transept was indeed unstable he saw no need for its enlargement, doubting "whether the Tower derives any effective support from the Transept." Blore included the western towers in his report but, despite his knowledge of Scottish medieval architecture, could see little merit in them. The upper portion of the north-west tower had fractured because of decayed timbers and the weight of the lead spire, and his recommendation was that it should be rebuilt; its fellow he condemned as dilapidated, unsightly and of no use "and the inside a scene of great neglect and desolation." By removing that tower the west front could be restored to its original design "so far as it has been damaged, or disfigured, by the addition of this excrescence.."[57] In June the Treasury yielded sufficiently to promise £10,000 towards the cost of Gillespie Graham's scheme provided the balance was guaranteed by the town council,[58] which had opened a subscription the year before with £1,000.[59]

Four years later, and with little progress on the cathedral, two papers summarized the situation. In the first it was calculated that £29,563:15:11 would pay for a new west front and new transepts. Against that the local committee had failed, having raised £5,000 only, which was half the

54. Ministry of Works, Glasgow Cathedral, 1. "Copy of a Treasury Minute, 29 Septr., 1837."
55. Lord Provost of Glasgow to the Treasury, n.d.
56. Copy of a Treasury Minute. 4 Feb., 1840.
57. Blore, "Report on the State of Glasgow Cathedral, 29 March, 1840."
58. Copy of a Treasury Minute. June 10, 1840.
59. "Extract from a letter of the Lord Provost of Glasgow to A.Y. Spearman, Esq. Dated 1st March, 1839."

sum required. The recommendation, therefore, was for the government to rebuild the north transept in its existing form for £3,105.[60] Blore had further reported that "as regards the designs furnished by Mr. Gillespie Graham . . . I think them extremely objectionable inasmuch as they would be utterly destructive of the unity and simplicity of the original design" and "completely at variance with its spirit and proportions." By now he had changed his mind about the north-west tower, which he wanted replaced with "one of better and more ornamental design"[61]—which for him meant a Scottish corona of pinnacles.[62] Blore's scheme of repairs was fully sanctioned, which meant the early disappearance of the south-west tower. *The Builder* in an account in 1847 of the repairs underway in the cathedral merely said, "The south-east corner . . . where formerly stood the Consistory Court, has also been completely rebuilt."[63] Within a year its companion had been felled,[64] although not without a signed protest from "twenty gentlemen ten of whom are architects" that the cathedral would be diminished by the subtraction of a feature as old as any part of the building, a plea which was not supported by Archibald McLellan "of which there was none had a more thorough knowledge." His stance provoked "Groans from the Auld Bell Tower of the Hie Kirk . . . but I ken I'm at least sax hunder; and this is admitted even by that crouse child that's sair on me in the bonnie beuk he wrote on the Hie Kirk—I mean him that mak's coaches."[65]

Thus perished Glasgow's unique assemblage of towers. A sorry tale, perhaps best summarized by a later commentator: ". . . what followed all the enthusiasm of the (Local) Committee? A change of architects, and the utter disappearance of the feature it was their main object to preserve."[66]

60. W. Nixon. Office of Works, Edinburgh to the Commissioners of Woods. February 3, 1844.

61. E. Blore to the Office of Woods. March 19, 1844.

62. Victoria and Albert Museum, drawings collection.

63. *The Builder*, vol. V (1847), 187.

64. Eyre-Todd, *The Book of Glasgow Cathedral*, 286. In a text published fifty years after the demolition of the north-west tower it is stated that a stone, bearing the arms of Bishop Wardlaw, was found on the floor. His arms also appear on the western vault of the north aisle. (Fairbairn, *Relics of Ancient Architecture*).

65. *Scotch Reformers' Gazette*, August 19 and 26, September 2 and 16, 1848. The protest was got up by Charles Hutcheson who sketched the partially demolished north-west tower. NLS, MS. 2773, f. 8. Information from Dr J. Durkan.

66. Billings and Burton, *The Baronial and Ecclesiastical Antiquities*, vol. 3, 9.

15

The Makers of the "Munich Glass"
The Munich Royal Glass Painting Works

Elgin Vaassen

Between 1859 and 1864 the windows in the "Upper Church" of Glasgow Cathedral were reglazed by the Royal Stained Glass Factory of Munich. There was opposition at the time to the contract being given to a German firm and over the following century tastes changed and atmospheric conditions caused the windows to deteriorate. As a result, in the mid-twentieth century practically all of this glazing was replaced, as explained in Part One of this book. In recent decades, however, the value of the Munich windows has been re-assessed and, as Richard Fawcett says, we are beginning to appreciate what we have lost.[1] In this chapter, originally delivered as a lecture to the Society of Friends, Dr. Elgin Vaassen, an expert in the history of the Munich Glass Factory, offers a reappraisal of the mid-nineteenth-century windows.

---

1. Fawcett, *Glasgow's Great Glass Experiment*, 12.

"The Dream and the Promise": a restored Munich glass panel, on display in an illuminated case in the lower church, depicting Jacob's dream at Bethel as recounted in Genesis 28. Photo: Glen Collie.

In the 1860s the Königliche Glasmalereianstalt—the Royal Bavarian Stained Glass Establishment—made the glass for most of the windows in Glasgow Cathedral. I find myself in the rôle of "defense counsel" for something that, with the exception of two windows in the transept clerestory and the small coats of arms in the clear glass windows of the nave, is no longer visible.

In opposition are all the voices that have condemned the Munich glass, in consequence of an attitude to these windows that has its origin either in ignorance or, worse, in jealousy. This attitude, together with evidence that the windows had been decaying, led to their removal some decades ago.[2] I am faced, too, with the undeniable fact that sketches, full-sized cartoons, photographs, and such of the glass itself as still exists,

---

2. They are now stored in racks in the triforium; three panels are on display in the lower church.

all show that, for the most part, the windows made for Glasgow Cathedral really did not represent the highest standards of the Glasmalereianstalt.

But my aim is not to retrieve at all costs the honor of the Munich artists—that is the last thing they need—but rather to clear the way for viewing objectively both the Glasmalereianstalt and glass-painting of the nineteenth century in general.

Both on the Continent and in Britain the manufacture of stained and painted glass on a monumental scale had ceased about the middle of the seventeenth century. In the United Kingdom, however, in contrast to the Continent, the tradition was later re-established, after an interval of war and Puritan excesses. But in the initial stage of the revival, due to a shortage, if not indeed a total lack, of colored pot metal glass, it was the formerly common technique of painting *on* glass with enamel colors that was mainly practiced.[3]

From about 1770 a new interest in the Middle Ages, and particularly in the Gothic era, led to the renewal of interest in colored pot metal glass. Such glass was needed to mend the many-colored church windows which had again come to be held in high regard, and the emerging band of "restorers" wanted it to supply missing parts in the panels.

All over the Continent, from about 1800, there began a widespread rediscovery of the lost art of glass painting, and a revival of the manufacture of colored pot metal glass. The people concerned were all either transparent hollow glass painters or porcelain painters,[4] followers of a new craft which had sprung up in the early eighteenth century, continuing, however, to use the colors favored by the earlier glass painters. These colors now again came into the service of painters on glass.

Depending on whether their interests were in the Nazarene movement or in the study of the Middle Ages, they found their ideals and models either in the early Renaissance period or in late medieval times. So in Munich artists took up glass painting at the point, where it had reached its most sophisticated, brilliant stage in the sixteenth century. Artists then had painted *on* glass with enamel colors, for this period had seen a decline in the use of pot metal glass and increasing practice in

---

3. That the windows at New College, Oxford, made by Thomas Jervais in 1785, are still, two hundred years later, called an "exceptional monstrosity" (by Cowen in *A Guide to Stained Glass in Britain*) is typical of a still-existing subliminal identification with nineteenth-century thought.

4. Their closely related palette of colors was easily made suitable for painting on glass.

the use of paint. From this rediscovery of the art originated a mixture of style, embracing Raphaelesque and late medieval German-Flemish figure composition and "old German" ornament (say of the period 1480–90). And just as in the early eighteenth century the colors of the glass painters had "migrated" to serve the new material, porcelain, so they now came back to the service of glass. Although glass painting and the production of pot metal glass had more or less ceased to be practiced for about 150 years, the glass works could still refer to a rich tradition in writing.[5]

In 1818, in accordance with the wishes of Crown Prince Ludwig (later to become King Ludwig I of Bavaria), Michael Sigmund Frank from Nuremberg was appointed glass painter of the Royal Bavarian Porcelain Manufactory in Munich. Frank had been trained as a porcelain painter, and had also done painting on hollow glass. He had had little opportunity of using colored pot metal glass, especially flashed glass. King Ludwig, keen to encourage the use of old as well as new techniques in art, made Frank try manufacturing pot metal glass at the state glass-works at Benediktbeuern, a monastery south of Munich. In 1824 Frank started his experiments—completely out of the blue, for he had never before seen a glass works from the inside. His results, not surprisingly, were poor; and in 1832 he was replaced by Max Emanuel Ainmiller, who, working with exact recipes, soon had full control over the métier.

In 1827 King Ludwig ordered the first window on a monumental scale for Ratisbon Cathedral; the date of this commission is usually accepted as marking the foundation of the Royal Bavarian Stained Glass Establishment—the Königliche Glasmalereianstalt. This window—it was destroyed during the war—was said to be too transparent. For the next window which the king ordered, paint and enamel colors were made deeper in tone. At the same time the glaziers and artists at the Glasmalereianstalt tried, by frosting the reverse of the panels, to intensify the coloring. It was believed that with ground glass one could catch the effect of the corroded surface of medieval glass; and most people were convinced that with the technique achieved in these windows they had already surpassed the Middle Ages.[6]

---

5. For example, one of the various editions of the *Arte Vetraria*, first published in Florence in 1612, compiled by Antonio Neri. Up to 1817 a number of German, Latin, Italian, French, and English versions were published.

6. We may laugh at their idea, yet there is no reason for doing so. Only he who has ever tried to copy a single piece of glass from this early period can assess the high artistic and technical level the assistants of the young Glasmalereianstalt had achieved

In 1831 the Glasmalereianstalt made another window for Ratisbon Cathedral. The cartoon was criticized as being too much like a painting, because of its landscape background, and for lacking the ornamental character thought to be necessary for a stained glass window. Consequently, in transferring the cartoon on to glass, the very element which for us today is the most charming and exciting in the older window was eliminated. It had become the accepted opinion that for a Gothic cathedral the old style of art must be adhered to, instead of—as was believed to be the case in England—following the principles of oil painting.

The man who made possible the rise of the Glasmalereianstalt to its European rank was the painter Ainmiller. He was born in Munich in 1807, studied architecture and ornamental design at the Academy of Fine Arts, and in 1822 entered the Royal Porcelain Manufactory as an apprentice. In 1828 he transferred to its new department of glass painting, soon becoming foreman there, and in 1837 technical inspector. It was his task to oversee glass painters and glaziers, to control the teaching of apprentices, to supervise the production of paint and enamel colors, the pot metal glass and the firing. For orders from the king it was his duty to design ornaments and architectural settings. Soon he was thought to be nearly irreplaceable. In 1851 he took over whole establishment as a private enterprise. Soon after his death in 1870 the Glasmalereianstalt was closed down.

In the late 1830s the king ordered nineteen large windows for the newly-built Neo-Gothic Maria-Hilf church in Munich. These windows were destroyed during the war, but fortunately some slides were taken just before the devastation, and give at least some impression of what these windows looked like: much as in late medieval altar-pieces, scenes were enshrined within an architectural framework, above which grisaille panels filled the remaining space.

In 1841 came the first order from abroad—windows for Christ Church in Kilndown, Kent. In these windows a white layer was added to the reverse side; this was yet another way of intensifying color and preventing sunbeams from destroying the effect, while at the same time trying to imitate the special surface effect of medieval glass.[7] This white layer is omitted where jewels are shown.

---

within a few years.

7. A coat of white gypsum that covers the reverse side completely.

Between 1844 and 1848 the Glasmalereianstalt was busy with a gift which the king of Bavaria had promised to Cologne Cathedral: five windows for the south aisle, each fourteen meters high. The overall slightly mosaic impression of these windows, and the manifold, though very delicate, use of transparent and enamel colors, later came under harsh criticism when German Neo-Gothicism gathered strength.

The Glasmalereianstalt did not make "picture" windows only. For several churches that were to get an alfresco decoration its artists designed ornamental windows—for instance, for the chapel of the saltworks at Reichenhall in southern Bavaria, for the Royal Chapel of All Saints in Munich, and for the Russian Orthodox chapel at Wiesbaden, among others.

The windows for the Maria-Hilf church in Munich and those for Cologne Cathedral had made the Glasmalereianstalt world-famous, and it remained the foremost establishment for many parts of Germany, Austria and Switzerland, despite its extremely high prices. But, then, nowhere else had there been a king as employer; nowhere else had a glassworks cooperated with artists from as highly-renowned an Academy as Munich's then was; and nowhere else had there been such an efficient and expert head as Ainmiller.

The 1850s brought orders for Peterhouse in Cambridge. Here the glass painting of the Nativity is a mixture of late medieval panel paintings: the arched ruins are taken from Dürer's so-called Paumgartner altar-piece, and so are the two shepherds in the background; the figure of Joseph resembles that of Rogier van der Weyden's Columba altar-piece; and Mary, kneeling before the Child, is nearly the same figure as in Memling's "Seven joys of Mary" picture. All these belong to the Alte Pinakothek in Munich, and (apart from the Dürer) were bought by King Ludwig I. In the panel "St. Peter healing the Lame" the modern illumination of the house in the background can be noticed—it has gas-light: the very thing in the early 1850s! The *Ecclesiologist* magazine reported of these windows in 1855 that they showed a uniform tone, achieved by a general coat of frosting on the back of the glass.

I consider the memorial windows for Joseph Görres in Cologne Cathedral, made in 1855, to be, in general, one of the best pieces of art in the glass painting of the time. In them the delicate treatment of heads that originated in porcelain painting was combined in a most balanced way with the newly fashionable idea of a mosaic-like tapestry showing the "true nature" of glass painting. The architectural design, with its canopies, etc., is based on a mid-fourteenth century window in the south aisle of Ratisbon Cathedral, "improved" for nineteenth-century eyes that could not bear deficiency in design, perspective and naturalism.[8]

In that same year the Duke of Northumberland ordered a window for a church in Alnwick. It was made to a design and cartoon by William Dyce, in which the canopy work was based on Italian Gothic and full recognition was given to the English love for clear glass. But in his attitude to figure composition and naturalistic treatment Dyce, in this window, was far from satisfying any parochial Neo-Gothic taste.

At the end of the 1850s the gigantic order for St. Mungo's Cathedral was given to Ainmiller and his artists, and kept the establishment busy for about ten years. But before any detailed examination of the Glasgow commission is undertaken, it will be as well to appreciate something of the method of working at the Glasmalereianstalt, so as to understand how its products differed from most British glass, and how arguments arose during the execution of the contract.

The art of glass-painting is unique in one respect, thanks to its very material: glass. All other forms of art are dependent upon light falling on the surface; in glass-painting it is light shining *through* the material which gives form and substance to the image. And, it might be added, glass, as an artificial mineral substance, is a unique material.

In the first decades of the nineteenth century pot metal glass was at the glass-painters' disposal in only a few colors. They had to paint on the glass they had: blown window glass—for that is what it was—in blue, violet, yellow, green and "white" (i.e. clear glass). It was not until the late 1820s that, for most glass-works, the technical problem of producing ruby-red flashed glass was overcome.

In the beginning, therefore, the cut glass used for a window came in a rather fierce range of colors. For outlines undiluted paint, opaque and black, was used. Then came the so-called half-tones: shades and layers that are half-opaque and translucent, according to the way they are used, as a greyish, brownish or greenish shading.

Of course the cutting of the glass, and with it the way the leadlines were handled, helped in the first instance to separate the different colors. But it served the formal linear design only in so far as it did not injure the forms of outlines wished for. The latter were achieved by an inner contour, following a "natural" design—i.e. done with a brush, and not with stiff

---

8. See Vaassen and van Treeck, *Görresfenster*.

lead. Moreover, artists mastered the technique of achieving an extremely large amount of color gradation among the light and the dark individual glass pieces; they were not seeking, like the later pure Neo-Gothicists, to achieve flatness and a graphic, linear design, as in early Gothic painting. Instead they cared in general for spacious depth and picturesque quality, for modeled three-dimensional figures and rounded-off full colors.

This contrasted with the structure of a classical Gothic window, where all main outlines are given by the leadlines; cut pieces of glass are small; most individual pieces of colored glass have a medium translucent intensity and vivid luminosity; the inner contours are painted with black paint; so-called smear-shading, a homogeneous gray in different gradations, is applied in a flat manner; and beyond that there are few more elaborate details. On the reverse side of the glass in such windows, to support the modeling, back-painting is applied in thin layers of half-tones, thin opaque coatings, to refract light. In consequence, the glass is left clear in a few spots only.

Today, most of these layers and half-tones have disappeared, due to corrosion; and this is one reason why nobody can tell exactly what a medieval window really looked like. The general effect, however, was of a linear, flat structure—a kind of "tapestry" to fill the holes in the walls of the building.

Such a medieval method was unthinkable for glass-painters adhering to Nazarene paintings and thoughts. They had to shade in a naturalistic way, in order to get a picturesque representation, and to a certain degree they transferred to glass the technique of oil-painting.[9] Instead of smear-shading, a finished technique of scratching out was used, and a shading which more and more led to a brilliant hatching.

From about 1835, when the glass-works could produce a rich range of colors, the procedure of painting on glass with enamel and transparent colors became simpler, but even so the more graphic (i.e. more mosaic-like) structuring of a glass-painting was mainly limited to non-figural parts. Eventually, a decidedly professional division of labor began. Already, at the stage of drawing the sketch, different "hands" made architectural and ornamental forms and figure compositions or coats of arms. Three distinguishable methods of painting, for ornaments, garments, and heads, resulted from this; and at the same time a hierarchy of glass

---

9. In the work of the Glasmalereianstalt, painting on glass has a complicated, up to sevenfold, structure, rich in details; and several of the layers have been applied without intermediate firing—a method that displays considerable skill.

painters was established, which was to be valid until the second world war. In the middle of the century—partly due to an increasing influence of English theories—the way was paved for the adoption of the "classical" language of architecture and ornament belonging to the thirteenth and fourteenth centuries. Yet, even so, figures remained three-dimensional, naturalistic. A good example of this is the above-mentioned Görres window in Cologne Cathedral.

Whereas the Neo-Gothicists on both sides of the Channel tried merely to *imitate*, and by so doing produced retrospective art, the people of the Glasmalereianstalt created glass paintings that did what every old glass painting (and, in fact, every other branch of art) had done: mirror the actual and current way of painting with oil on canvas.

In England, too, a new style was created by the firm of Clayton and Bell, and followed, later on, by Morris and his company. But their aims were different from those of the Munich artists; and, so, too, had been their starting point.

As for the history of the Glasgow windows,[10] I shall not bother you by enumerating the complete documentary material—hundreds of letters which were exchanged between Glasgow and Munich, between Charles Heath Wilson, the architect who had to organize the huge task, and Ainmiller. Some points, however, I want to mention, that are relevant for understanding why the glass paintings were made in this particular manner.

The scheme for the re-glazing had been known about in Munich since the summer of 1855. In February 1856 Wilson wrote his first letter to Munich, announcing the intention officially and asking for an estimate of the price for painted glass of the finest quality. "We wish to introduce," he said, "Scripture subjects, finely drawn and composed, in the spirit of the thirteenth century; but we wish to avoid the rude drawing. We wish the drawing to be *perfect*."[11]

---

10. There exist a number of publications contemporary with the installation of the windows; but they are mainly descriptive: Wilson, *Descriptive catalogue of painted glass Windows in Glasgow Cathedral*, 1866; Annan, *The painted windows of Glasgow Cathedral*, 1867; Eyre-Todd, *The Book of Glasgow Cathedral*, 1898, and others. A more detailed history of the windows can be found in Fawcett, *Glasgow's Great Glass Experiment*, 2003.

11. Subjects to be depicted were: scenes from the Old Testament in the nave; the teaching of Our Lord in the Chancel; the Apostles in the Lady Chapel. Below each scene were to be placed the arms of the donor.

In September 1856, at the second meeting of the committee set up to coordinate the ideas of subscribers and officials, Wilson summed up his experience so far: "If we compare our glass painters with those of the Continent we find them inferior as designers, but, generally speaking, superior in their method of execution. They have a truer sense of the real nature and properties of glass painting than the German artists who have so high a reputation. What is wanted is a peculiarly qualified artist to take charge of the designs, and a harmonious plan for the whole enterprise."

The advice to go abroad to Belgium, France or Germany for new glass paintings had come from Charles Winston, the famous lawyer, who did so much research on medieval glass, and whose notes are still worth studying. He wrote to Wilson in March 1857: "If you dabble with English glass painters, you will get into a sad scrape." So letters inviting offers were sent to Dresden, Munich, Brussels, and Tours.

The decision to go to Munich brought about a storm of jealous criticism that was to last for more than twenty years. As one historian has put it, "An entire generation of artists felt that they had been robbed of their birthright."[12] The main critics were a number of architects, among them James Salmon, and also the glass painter Ballantine from Edinburgh. In 1857 Salmon, commenting on the committee's official note, wrote " . . . and is it from Munich that we are to bring architects to tell how much light our cathedral requires?" And the *Scotsman* in 1857 feared that the Munich people "will have numberless designs for all kinds of subjects . . . they will just cut down or stretch out . . . all the old material they have on hand; so that the Glasgow people will, after all, only get the leavings and second-hand property of the German School." Using cartoons more than once was, by the way, common practice in Gothic times.

According to Wilson, an "archaeological" party requiring exact imitation and a "progressive" party demanding art opposed each other in the country. Wilson and Winston belonged to the latter. Wilson wanted "a nineteenth-century design fit for nineteenth-century glass, but at the same time harmonious with a thirteenth- to fourteenth-century building." And since it was said that Munich glass and its method of enamel painting destroyed the lucidity of the glass, and that the windows looked like painted blinds, Winston, through Wilson, stressed "that the method of painting be that of the old glass: pot metal, clear on the lights like sparkling gems, and no enamel but brown in the shadows", and that it would

---

12. Donnelly, *Glasgow Stained Glass*, 6.

be better "to have art without transparency than transparency without art." The demand for "gems" sounds rather arbitrary if one recalls the corrosion crusts on the reverse of medieval glass.

Sample windows were made, and in March 1858 a window for the crypt arrived from Munich and was set up for comparison with other windows. In the same year Wilson sent to Ainmiller specimens of glass imitative of medieval glass, made under Winston's direction. Henceforth he and everybody praised that glass euphorically as vastly superior in color and texture.[13] There are, in fact, few people who can tell the old from the new "antique glass", as we call it today, even from a short distance. But although the Glasgow customers were convinced that the new "antique glass" was vastly superior to the pellucid glass used hitherto, they did not insist on its use.

Wilson also sent detailed descriptions, giving precise instructions as to how a scene was to be depicted: that figures were to wear Raphaelesque garments; what expression faces ought to have—no Teutonic features! — and so forth. For example: in the description for the parable of the talents it was laid down that the judge should be enthroned, with two angels standing behind him; one of whom should be represented with the palm, looking towards the faithful servant, the other looking towards the idle servant with a sad expression.

But would *you*—without a note at the bottom of the window, quoting chapter and verse of the New Testament—be able to tell which scene you were looking at? And in the parable of the "Sower" Wilson wanted the figure of the Sower to appear three times, one for each light of the window. Can you imagine an interesting design for that? At the same time, Wilson assured Ainmiller that he was entirely free to select from the Testaments the subjects he would think most suitable, and that Wilson's notes were not meant "as fettering the artists." However, of every sketch that was sent over for a new window, and which had to be approved by the Ministry of Works in London, Wilson made traced copies. Later, when the glass arrived, it was carefully and painstakingly compared with the tracing to make sure that no item had been omitted.

The Committee tried, in vain, to have Ainmiller come to Glasgow to study the architecture of the cathedral in order to make ornaments and

---

13. Harrison is the only one who, up till now, has stated that "most of the aesthetically satisfying windows produced before about 1855 achieved their success without the aid of the new glass"—which is absolutely correct. Harrison, *Victorian Stained Glass*, 23.

architectural settings that matched the style of the building. In letter after letter it was stressed that the ornament must be in complete harmony with the architecture, "figures perfectly well drawn, still, however, with that dignity and simplicity observable in the best period of glass painting"—which for Wilson and the Committee was represented by the style of the sixteenth century.

In October 1864 the first part of the task was finished, and Wilson wrote to Munich: "I thank you all gratefully and respectfully for your uniform courtesy and consideration and patience with me." If you knew his letters you would understand why he mentioned patience! Some years later Wilson had to report that in some of the glass paintings beards that had been painted over with blue enamel had come off. He added: "Our enemies will write volumes about it if they discover it."

A letter published in *The Builder* in 1865 affords evidence that Ainmiller generally stuck to the rule: "no enamel but brown in the shadows." The writer of this letter had gone with a friend to Glasgow Cathedral to see the windows. The friend said, "How lovely", and he answered "it is indeed"—but he was thinking of the loves of two sparrows he observed on a neighboring building "through the medium of one of the Apostles, clothes and all."

Long before this, the "enemies" had started to criticize the Munich glass. When the *Ecclesiologist*, the magazine of the influential Cambridge Movement, reviewed Ballantine's book *A treatise on painted glass*, published in 1845, it said that he had "clearly got on the right scent; e.g., he condemns the Munich School for not confining their subject by the monials."[14] To quote Ballantine (though I could as well take any other book, for all had the same drift), " . . . painted glass is, no doubt, a species of mosaic, and the artist must depend entirely on continuity and firmness of outline."[15] His own window, still in the crypt, contradicts this statement completely. Compared with the leadlines of the first window from Munich to be installed (in 1858), Ballantine's panel shows all the mistakes of which he accused his competitors.[16]

Elsewhere in the same book Ballantine commented: "In Bavaria . . . the glass artists . . . have lost sight of the leading principles of their art.

14. Monial: a mullion or strut separating the glass panels in a window.

15. Ballantine, *A Treatise on Painted Glass*, 19.

16. Wilson, in a letter of March 1860 to Sir William Stirling Maxwell, wrote that Ballantine's windows in most parts had been painted with enamel colors on white glass, and that the faces at first had been done with varnish colors.

They have carried their designs entirely across and from top to bottom of the window without regard to the interference of mullions or tracery. Like the French manufacturers of pictorial paper hangings, such designers seem to make their cartoons without any reference to the sight or shape of the windows for which they are intended, and they cut them into stripes to suit the various compartments for which chance may destine them. It surely is not pleasant to see a beautiful arm dissevered by a stone mullion, suggesting the disagreeable idea of amputation."[17] The sketches made of every window before production of the cartoons prove the nonsense of Ballantine's assertion. Of course there are parts of figures, such as folds, or arms, that are cut by a mullion; but this treatment is neither new—it is already to be found in fourteenth-century glass—nor is it limited to German windows as can be seen, for instance, in the famous Hedgeland window in Norwich Cathedral, made in 1854—which, by the way, was made of the new antique glass!

"The Risen Christ": a restored Munich glass panel from the South Transept, now on display in an illuminated case in the lower church. Photo: Glen Collie.

17. Ballantine, *Treatise*, 21.

In periodicals like *The Builder* and the *Ecclesiologist* all these ideas about what a window must or must not look like were constantly reiterated. The "Credo" ran like this:

> Glass must be like a tapestry that has been removed from the wall to a window.[18]
> Medallions only, or one single figure per light, are allowed.
> No pictorial treatment.
> No landscape in the background.
> No enamel color, apart from black and silver stain.
> Colors must be deep, "mystical," sparkling like gems.

What astonishes most is that, though the British were said to dislike the Munich glass, they ordered it for several other prominent buildings, such as St. Paul's Cathedral in London and Parliament Hall in Edinburgh. There are other churches, too, in Scotland, such as Irvine and Dalry, where glass from Munich was installed. At the time when the transept windows for Glasgow were being made—one of them, the angel, is on display in the crypt at the moment—Dr Robertson from Irvine commissioned windows for his church, and, as his biographer tells us, had a good deal of trouble to get what he thought suitable: "He had a dread of there being put into the design the conventional fat angel . . . that appeared to have been fed on German sausages."[19] He was, however, satisfied with the end result.

The Dalry windows were installed after Ainmiller's death. Those from the chancel—the figures only, for all the rest is new—give an idea of what the figures in the great east window of Glasgow Cathedral (after the design by Johann von Schraudolph) looked like. And the west window in Dalry, showing the figures of Aaron, Moses and Samuel, can be compared with Glasgow's north transept window by Heinrich Maria von Hess.

The glass painter William Warrington published in 1848 a history of stained glass in which the plates show "medieval" windows in various styles, all made by Warrington himself. He wrote to *The Builder* to voice objections to the work of the Glasmalereianstalt in Glasgow. Clients of his, he wrote, had been to Munich, had visited the Glasmalereianstalt, and had asked for a design for a Norman triplet. "After much searching

---

18. The trouble with tapestries is that hardly anyone could have maintained that he had seen one that could be dated before 1400, because even in the nineteenth century there were only three or four still in existence.

19. Guthrie, *Robertson of Irvine*, 183.

... a colored print was produced as the very best thing they could recommend, stating that it was faithful to the original, and that they could not do better than to adopt it." As chance would have it, his clients recognized it as a window that Warrington had made for them. So is it really the Glasmalereianstalt that should be blamed? Or is it Warrington himself, who pretended to reproduce genuine medieval art?

I cite also a third letter to *The Builder*, written in 1865 which says that the only color placed upon glass should be the black lines to designate outlines: "this is the English and true manner." The writer was annoyed by the "cold" Munich coloring, especially with the "cold dazzling blue." He praised the old blues in Venetian paintings, adding, "and surely these are good colors, which all have a tone of green in them." In fact, the Venetian blue, and the blue in almost every medieval panel painting, has a greenish tone because its oil adhesives, or the varnish used, have turned yellow! The Gérentes, the French glass painters, who were held in high regard, used the same cold blue, but since they copied faithfully nobody ever found fault with *their* windows.

The insistence by the Neo-Gothicists and the glass-painters' guild that only black paint and yellow stain should be allowed is a purely arbitrary claim, because painting with black paint is nothing but a *special form* of enamel painting on glass, whose ingredients, of course, were the easiest to get—at every coppersmith's or blacksmith's forge.[20]

From the moment, round about 1300, when glass painters discovered how to use silver oxide as yellow stain, they had a modest palette of colors for painting at their disposal. By adding black paint or yellow stain in different shades to the various colors of pot metal glass, a considerably differentiated range of colors can be achieved within a single panel. From about 1320 black paint was used not only for drawing outlines and main folds, but as a *color*, for the whole surface. Precisely here, during what nineteenth-century opinion regarded as the golden age of glass painting, took place the radical change to a painting *on* glass—even if it was still with black paint only.

The early Gothic contrasting blue/red color scheme was later superseded by the refined coloring of Burgundian book illumination. Under that influence (where the great name is Jean Pucelle) and under the

---

20. It may be recalled that painting with enamel colors is much older than monochrome painting with black paint. The former was the technique regularly used in Roman times for decorating hollow glass. Enamel colors were used during the Middle Ages as well, but for earthenware only.

influence of Giotto, architectural canopies suddenly became little chapels for figures or scenes—"dolls' houses," as Erwin Panofsky called them.[21] The "architectural window" was created, and soon became more and more three-dimensional. Its architectural setting, and the sketch plans produced by masons engaged in building cathedrals, resemble each other closely.

Martin Harrison wrote (and he is only one in a long line who have expressed, *mutatis mutandis*, the same view) that before Pugin, "stained glass artists were beginning to recognize a fundamental property of the medium [i.e. glass]—that it is, by its very nature, two-dimensional."[22] By the same right that claims a two-dimensional structure for windows, tapestries and wall-painting, one could argue that all oil-paintings and frescoes must be two-dimensional, because canvas and walls are as flat as glass.

From about 1320, when the "architectural" window began to appear, medallions were no longer confined to one light: they grew larger and spread over several lights. So did scenes. Examples are to be found in the very centers of glass-painting, Strasbourg, Cologne, and Königsfelden in Switzerland.

Unlike earlier renaissances, the Gothic Revival in general did not produce a new style, for all attempts—including the painted glass of the Munich school—were stopped, more or less, by Neo-Gothic theorists. *They* wanted nothing but imitation, the more meticulous the better, and they believed themselves capable of building and painting in the same way as men of the Gothic period. But, simply because a Neo-Gothic building or window is new, it needs must differ from its model, which has grown older in the course of time and bears the signs of age: in the case of a window, corrosion, a dense surface, discoloration, bulges, pitting, additional leading, and loss of paint, among others.

The *Ecclesiologist* in its first volume affirmed that "it is no sign of weakness to be content to copy acknowledged perfection: it is, rather, a presumption to expect to rival it in any other way." This typical nineteenth-century phenomenon, a belief in the early vigor, maturity, and subsequent decline of an art form, has been called a "biological fallacy."[23] Together with a tendency to dogmatism and a growing intolerance of

---

21. Panofsky, *Early Netherlandish painting*, 30.
22. Harrison, *Victorian Stained Glass*, 15.
23. Scott, *The Architecture of Humanism*, 165–85.

any disagreement, the search for correctness became a dominant feature; and, to a considerable degree, writing on stained glass is still under the influence of these principles. For the Ecclesiological Society the final authority was to be "conformity with ancient usage," or, more precisely, the Society's concept of ancient usage. The architect Sir Gilbert Scott in later years recalled that "the Society's law was so imperious that anyone who dared to deviate from it . . . well knew what he must suffer."

To sum up: to Munich glass was attributed everything that was considered unsuitable for glass-painting: pellucid, flimsy glass; enamel painting; use of perspective; three-dimensional figures; naturalistic design and landscape in the background; disregard of mullions (i.e. spreading scenes over several lights). All this is found in French and British glass as well; but, whereas it is hardly ever criticized there, the whole catalog of sins is still invoked today when describing German nineteenth-century glass in general. Writers of our generation, when considering the re-glazing of Glasgow Cathedral with Munich glass, have always spoken of it in terms of a disaster—though most of them were far too young ever to have seen the glass *in situ*.

I think it is unfair to operate a double standard: what is sauce for the goose ought to be sauce for the gander too. In this sense I ask you to return your verdict: *in dubio, pro reo*.[24]

---

24. "[When] in doubt, for the accused": in other words, if there is any doubt about guilt, the court and jury should side with the accused person.

16

"Reverent and Cultured Ritual"
Worship in Glasgow Cathedral, 1865–1915

Andrew G. Ralston

The renewed interest in the architectural worth of Glasgow Cathedral during the Victorian period was followed by the adoption of a more elaborate and liturgical style of worship under George Stewart Burns (minister between 1865 and 1895) and Pearson McAdam Muir (minister between 1896 and 1915). This chapter considers the nature of their ministries and the relationships between the liturgical, architectural, and aesthetic changes of the era.

AT THE DEDICATION SERVICE for new stained glass windows in the Blacader Chapel of Glasgow Cathedral in January 1961, Dr. Nevile Davidson reminded the congregation of the purpose of the building. "How sad would it be," he reflected, "if we were ever tempted to think of this ancient church as a splendid historic monument rather than a House of God."[1] The functioning of the cathedral as a "House of God" before and after the Reformation has been thoroughly investigated by historians, but coverage of later centuries has tended to focus more on the "monumental"

1. *Glasgow Cathedral Chronicle*, February 1961, 4

side of the building. As a result, there remains much to discover about how the cathedral continued to fulfill its primary role as a place of worship in which "prayer is wont to be made."

The comparative lack of research into the eighteenth and nineteenth centuries may to some extent be related to the fact that the cathedral ceased to be the seat of a bishop under the presbyterian system of church government and was divided into three churches in which separate congregations—the Inner High Kirk, the Outer High Kirk and the Barony—worshiped, a situation which lasted until 1835. As Professor E. L. G. Stones once pointed out, one problem facing any historian investigating that era was that "much of what would have to be said of the building between 1560 and 1840 would deal with things which are no longer there."[2] From the 1840s onwards, the city of Glasgow became more conscious of the value of its architectural heritage and extensive work was undertaken to restore the cathedral to its original layout, while the installation of new furnishings and glazing dramatically changed the appearance of the interior.

The process of restoration and beautification in the nineteenth century has been well-documented.[3] But how did this impact on what went on inside the cathedral Sunday by Sunday? At the same time as the amenities of the building were being improved, there was a growing reaction within the established Church of Scotland against the austerity of traditional Scottish presbyterian worship with its lengthy sermons, verbose extempore prayers and precentor-led psalm-singing, in favor of a more liturgical style of worship. In 1865 the Church Service Society was formed to encourage this trend and provide suitable printed resources.[4] A building as magnificent as Glasgow Cathedral was the ideal setting for the more elaborate and dignified services envisaged and it was therefore fortuitous that 1865 also happened to be the year when one of the Church Service Society's early members, Rev. (later Rev. Dr.) George Stewart Burns, took over as minister, a post he held for thirty-one years. He was followed by Rev. Dr. Pearson McAdam Muir, minister from 1896 until 1915, who not only shared his predecessor's tastes in worship but took a

---

2. Society of Friends Annual Report, 1970, 9.

3. See, for example, the essays in Fawcett, *Glasgow's Great Glass Experiment*.

4. For a detailed history of the development of styles of worship in Scottish churches from the time of the 1843 Disruption to the present day, see Spinks, *Scottish Presbyterian Worship*.

more active part in the national church and in the Church Service Society of which he served as secretary.

Thus, over a period of half a century Glasgow Cathedral witnessed considerable liturgical, architectural and aesthetic change. This chapter seeks to show how these developments were inter-related and to evaluate the significance of the ministries of Burns and McAdam Muir through an examination of their backgrounds and personal qualities, style of preaching and ecclesiological views.

"A BROAD AND CATHOLIC MIND":[5]
THE MINISTRY OF GEORGE STEWART BURNS

While attending the General Assembly in May 1863 Rev. Dr. John Robertson (1824–65), minister of Glasgow Cathedral at the time, displayed the first signs of the serious heart condition which led to his premature death less than two years later at the age of forty-one. Robertson had only been in the charge for seven years but during that time he had gained a reputation as a powerful preacher and had tentatively expressed himself in favor of certain steps towards a more dignified style of worship. He approved of the use of organ accompaniment to praise "in such congregations as may wish it";[6] he saw benefits in the "partial adoption" of a liturgy involving perhaps one or two read prayers—though "it would be a great loss . . . were the liberty of free prayer to be withdrawn"[7] and thought "there could easily be some arrangement which would admit of both."[8] Robertson lived just long enough to witness the restoration of the cathedral building and the installation of new stained glass and, although too frail to attend the official presentation of the windows in October 1864, he wrote a letter to the committee in charge of the project in which he outlined the principle which underpinned many of the aesthetic and liturgical changes at Glasgow Cathedral over the next century:

> Believing that every form of true and noble cultivation is closely connected with every other, I am sure that a relish for the beauty of art is not without a favorable influence as regards appreciation of the beauty of holiness, and that everything which tends

---

5. *Montrose, Arbroath and Brechin Review,* December 21, 1888.
6. Robertson, *Pastoral Counsels,* 202.
7. Robertson, *Pastoral Counsels,* 204.
8. Robertson, *Pastoral Counsels,* 207.

to refinement of feeling may be so used, under God's blessing, and to aid us in rendering to Him ever higher and higher forms of that only acceptable worship which must proceed from the Spirit, and be offered in truth.[9]

In these ways, Robertson prepared the ground for a successor who might wish to develop such ideas further.

Rev. Dr. George Stewart Burns, 1830-96

The choice of that successor was in the gift of the Crown, as the system of patronage in the established Church of Scotland—the issue which had split the denomination at the Disruption of 1843 when a third of the ministers and members of the Established Church left to form the Free Church—had still not been abolished.[10] However, this was something of a formality as the applicant selected by the congregation was appointed, the choice again falling on a fairly young candidate, Rev. George Stewart Burns of Montrose. As was often the case at that time, he was a son of the manse, brought up in Auchtergaven, Perthshire where his father, Rev. John Burns, was minister. After an education at Perth Grammar School (where, he said, Latin was "flogged into" him) and St. Andrew's

---

9. Quoted in Henderson, *Dr. McAdam Muir's Ministry*, 194.
10. Patronage in the Church of Scotland was eventually abolished in 1875.

University, his rise had been a rapid one. At thirty-five years of age he had already held four charges—Chapelside in Dundee, Newton-on-Ayr, Houston and the first collegiate charge of Montrose—which might suggest to some that his ambition took precedence over his commitment to his flock. Reporting on his appointment to the cathedral, the *Glasgow Herald* saw things rather differently:

> The very fact that his call on this occasion is the fourth within the short period of about eight years of his ministry . . . bears ample testimony to his popularity and acceptability as a minister and that we have got "the right man in the right place."[11]

Other comments about Burns at various stages of his career suggest that the *Herald* was not alone in assuming that popularity was a sign of a good minister. His rapid translation from Houston to Montrose was seen as inevitable as "to a large extent he was hiding his light under a bushel; his sphere of labor was too contracted for his ability and active habits of mind."[12] Similarly, he had been called to Montrose as he was "a very popular preacher"[13] and he even impressed his clerical colleagues, for as well as preaching to the congregation on Sunday he had been required to deliver a trial sermon before the Presbytery of Brechin on the Monday morning—"a very able and impressive discourse" which "abounded in ready and graceful illustrations."[14] So keen were the people of Montrose to have him as their minister that the formal document of call contained 2,000 signatures and stretched to thirty feet in length.

At Montrose Burns lost no time in starting up a series of Sunday evening lectures for which the church was filled long before the stated hour. Effectively a form of public entertainment in an era before radio, cinema, and television, such lectures took place in many churches and it is hard not to see them as a kind of popularity contest between rival local ministers. The first lecture of the series, "the World's Debt to Christianity," turned out to be anything but a dry theological discourse. Those expecting a Calvinistic denunciation of sin were instead told that "[the] form of Christianity which makes the world a waste and life a burden, and denounces everything as sinful, which is simply human, surely must

---

11. *Glasgow Herald*, June 23, 1865.

12. Rev. Mr. Robertson of Greenock as reported by the *Montrose Standard*, February 22, 1868.

13. *Montrose Standard*, October 3, 1862.

14. *Montrose Standard*, December 26, 1862.

be wrong."[15] The theme of the lecture appears to have been that we have Christianity to thank, not just for the hope of heaven, but for the joys of earthly life. There was no instance on record, claimed the speaker, of Christ ever refusing an invitation to dinner; the Savior spoke warmly of family relationships and the pleasures of social life, gracing with his presence the "festal table" at the marriage of Cana. What exactly the pleasures of hunting had to do with "the World's Debt to Christianity" was less apparent, but here Burns's imagination took flight:

> When the horn winds those merry notes—short, loud, decisive—which some so well know and so deeply love; when the anxious pack fills the wood with music—to some, the sweetest of sounds; when the "view hulloo" rends the air and the mettled horse puts itself to speed, and skims over springy lea and sedgy brook, and ugly bar, without whip or spur, he would not be man whose pulse beat calmly and whose spirit caught no enthusiasm from the scene.[16]

The minister practiced what he preached. For his summer holidays he used to rent a house at Phesdo on the Fasque estate near Fettercairn, Aberdeenshire, where he enjoyed hunting and riding, for he was "a capital shot, and an expert angler." He was a keen golfer, too, having learned the game while a student at St. Andrews. His friend R. Herbert Story, sometime Moderator of the General Assembly and Principal of Glasgow University, remembers that the first time he met young Burns at a service of induction in Greenock he was, like David the Psalmist, "ruddy and pleasant to look upon, and (unusual at an ecclesiastical function) wearing riding boots."[17] The parallel between Burns and Mark Robarts, the vicar in Trollope's novel *Framley Parsonage* "who followed the hounds," is obvious.

---

15. *Montrose Standard*, November 20, 1863. It is interesting to compare Burns's worldly outlook with the more austere approach of his Free Church counterpart. In February 1863 Rev. William Nixon of St. John's Free Church, Montrose delivered a lecture to young women on the subject of "Dress". He said: "That style of dress which in a measure exposed nakedness—and it was to be deplored that this was so much adopted by the women of the present age—not only implied a wantonness in the wearer but it was the cause of exciting a corresponding wantonness in others." The journalist noted that "the church was not entirely filled on the occasion." (*Montrose Standard*, February 20, 1863).

16. *Montrose Standard*, November 20, 1863.

17. Henderson, *Dr. Burns's Ministry*, 6.

Having gained "golden opinions"[18] in two years and four months at Montrose, Burns was already thinking of a still more prestigious appointment and his move to the Glasgow was no doubt assisted by his friendship with Professor John Caird, his predecessor at his earlier charge in Houston and another future Principal of Glasgow University, who happened to be on the cathedral's selection committee. At the induction service on June 23, 1865 Caird delivered an address of monumental length on "the qualities of the ministry today." He was scathing about many of his clerical colleagues:

> success depends in most cases on the capacity to get up one or two showy sermons. It will happen that a man with a few superficial graces, a man whose whole stock-in-trade is composed of fluency, self-sufficiency, good looks, sound lungs and a sort of vulgar histrionic power, will carry the day against solid learning and modest power.[19]

It would be unkind to suggest that Caird's description is an unintentionally ironic picture of the new incumbent at the cathedral, but it could hardly be claimed that Burns was a theologian of any distinction. According to the satirical Glasgow magazine *The Bailie*, "he delights in the use of eloquent phrases. So that a sentence has a good ring, he seldom stops to inquire whether its words really mean a great deal—whether the sense is equal to the sound."[20] Unlike his predecessor or his successor, he did not publish any book of a devotional or theological nature. He did contribute a chapter to a book entitled *The Faiths of the World* (1882) which consists of transcripts of lectures delivered by various speakers in both Glasgow and St. Giles' Cathedrals during the winter of 1881–82. Burns's topic was "Teutonic and Scandinavian Religion" and his effort makes for uninspiring reading, being largely lifted from reference books and offering nothing in the way of comparative analysis or evaluation.[21]

Just five years after Burns's death, the cathedral session clerk John Henderson lamented: "Dr. Burns's Sermons. Where are they? It is very much to be regretted that . . . he had no desire to have them printed."[22] Henderson nevertheless managed to find one or two which he reprints

---

18. *Glasgow Herald*, June 27, 1896.
19. *Glasgow Herald*, June 23, 1865.
20. *The Bailie*, October 28, 1874.
21. *The Faiths of the World*, 1882.
22. Henderson, *Dr. Burns's Ministry*, 88.

in his book *Dr. Burns's Ministry and Labours in the High Church Parish, 1865–1896* and from these, it seems, Burns adhered to orthodox Reformed doctrine. The following communion address gives a flavor of his preaching:

> There may be some who come to the Communion Table unprepared; there may be some who will take their seats conscious of sin and unconscious of having yet obtained pardon; there may be some who know Christ only through His teaching, and have seen His divine power only as pointed out in His Word, but have never made a trial of Him as the Savior of their soul; to such I say, "Do not go away, you are in your proper place if you will only recognize the privilege that is placed within your reach." An opportunity is given to you of turning to Christ. The symbols of His dying agony are in your hands. He will be as near to you at the Communion Table as He was to the thief on the Cross, and if you will only say to Him in profound penitence and humble faith, "Lord, remember me in Thy kingdom, that kingdom which through sore anguish Thou hast won for me, and such as me," you will hear His sweet voice saying to you, "This day shalt thou be with Me in paradise."[23]

In spite of the evangelical tone of such appeals, Burns was essentially a "broad" churchman. "I shall be glad to work alongside of men of every sect and denomination," he said at his induction in June 1865, and he always stuck to his view that "Christianity is not a grim and gloomy system . . . but a glad and grateful faith, whose grand object is to make men happy in this world, and happy in the world to come."[24] That did not endear him to his stricter Free Church colleagues. In 1874 the *Free Church Monthly Record* attacked the cathedral minister for saying in a public address that "Believe me, vital life in Christ, hard earnest work for Christ, are far better than any, even the most orthodox, beliefs," thereby appearing to stress the importance of personal experience and good works over dogma.[25]

More than one commentator points out that Burns did not play an active role in ecclesiastical politics and disliked controversy of any kind.[26]

---

23. Henderson, *Dr. Burns's Ministry*, 81.
24. *Montrose Standard*, February 20, 1863.
25. Quoted in Smith, *Obedience and Prophetic Protest*, 276.
26. *Aberdeen Press and Journal*, January 27, 1896.

He seems to trouble himself very little about Church politics; the questions that rouse the ardent spirits in the Presbytery to eloquence or anger have a very slight interest for him; he allows Assemblies to come and Assemblies to go, while he keeps on the even tenor of his way.[27]

One of the few occasions on which he raised his head above the parapet occurred soon after he came to Glasgow, during the "Sabbath Controversy" of 1866. Norman Macleod (1812–72) of the Barony Church had taken what was deemed to be too liberal a stand on the matter of running trains on a Sunday. With the hyperbole beloved by churchmen of these times, MacLeod was accused of trying to "set up a Lord's Day on his own authority" and his stance condemned as "a betrayal of the Son of Man with a kiss."[28] Burns announced that he would explain his own views in a sermon, guaranteeing a packed church on Sunday, January 21. In a lengthy address, printed in full in the *Glasgow Herald* the next day, he said that in his humble opinion the Sunday question had been made "a great deal too much of." The Old Testament Decalogue had been "abrogated" by the New Testament, he believed, and he drew a series of contrasts between Judaism and Christianity: "Judaism deals with the outward—Christianity with the inward; Judaism rejoices in law—Christianity in liberty; Judaism looks to the act—Christianity to the motive which prompted it." Somewhat illogically, Burns accused "our stern sabbatarians" at one and the same time of "flaunting the veriest rags of Popery" and holding to a narrow view of the Sabbath derived from the English Puritans and not from the Scottish reformers. Had not John Knox himself traveled and written letters on a Sunday? Burns's position on the Sabbath was simple: "The Lord's Day demands cessation from labor. What its rest should be, let every man be fully persuaded in his own mind." He ended his sermon by saying that "I have taken little part in the discussion and with me it has now closed."[29]

It was far from closed as far as his opponents were concerned. Rev. George Macaulay, minister of Stockwell Free Church, published a 120 page pamphlet entitled *The Lord's Law and Day: A Review of Dr.*

27. *The Bailie*, October 28, 1874.
28. Macaulay, *The Lord's Law and Day*, 4.
29. *Glasgow Herald*, January 2, 1866. In spite of the vehemence of opinions expressed at the time, the dispute over the Sunday Question did not permanently affect Norman Macleod's standing: three years later he was unanimously chosen as Moderator of the General Assembly.

Macleod's speech, with criticisms of a sermon preached in the cathedral by Rev. G. S. Burns attacking the cathedral minister's "ill-considered and ignorant harangue" which was "full of heresies and abounding in false and railing accusations against godly men."[30] The dispute was still simmering two months later when Burns felt he had to make a statement to Glasgow presbytery claiming he had been misrepresented. He "emphatically declared . . . his adherence to the Confession of Faith" and added that "so far from attacking the Divine authority of the Lord's Day, his sole object was to show that the Sabbath rested upon a thorough basis of Divine authority."[31] This appears to have drawn a line under the matter and Burns kept well away from such ecclesiastical disputes thereafter.

However, something that Burns did support was the movement for liturgical reform. He made use of the Church Service Society's *Euchologion* or Book of Common Prayer, first published in 1867 and intended, not as a prescribed liturgy, but as "a kind of treasury of prayers on which the ordinary minister might draw."[32] Allied to this was the trend towards installing organs in churches to replace the traditional Scottish practice of unaccompanied psalm singing. Burns was keen for the cathedral to lead the way and in 1872 he tried, unsuccessfully, to interest the Glasgow public in raising the necessary funds. That same year he married Frances Stewart Grant, the wealthy widow of George Grant whose Mile End cotton mill employed some 1200 people. Perhaps as a result of persuasion by her new husband, Mrs Burns decided to fund the installation of an organ in memory of her late daughter and "no time was lost by Messrs. Willis, London, in erecting the most handsome instrument that money and skill could procure."[33] The cost amounted to £3840. The cathedral was crowded on Easter Sunday 1879 to hear the organ for the first time at the skillful hands of the new organist, Dr. A. L. Peace, and its mighty sound enhanced "the gorgeous scene of joy and congratulation" when Queen Victoria was present at a service to mark the Golden Jubilee of her reign in 1887.

As a gesture of thanks to Mrs Burns for her gift, the kirk session commissioned the popular portrait painter Robert Herdman (1829–88)[34]

---

30. Macaulay, *The Lord's Law and Day*, 55.
31. *Montrose Standard*, March 30, 1866.
32. Cheyne, *The Transforming of the Kirk*, 95.
33. Henderson, *Dr. Burns's Ministry*, 35.
34. The painting is stored at the Glasgow Museum Resource Centre.

to paint a picture of her husband and at a ceremony to hand this over in May 1881 Burns gave a significant speech which reveals much about his views on worship. Some thirty years ago, he said, there would have been great opposition to the installation of an organ. He paints an amusing picture of services of the old style:

> The psalm or paraphrase, sung to the leadership of a precentor, sometimes not much of a musician nor remarkable for the beauty of his voice, and losing half a note at every verse, then the long opening prayer, often of more than half an hour . . . and dealing with most of the leading events in human history from the Fall to the Judgment, to which it might have been supposed that reference was unnecessary to the Deity, then the sermon, made up in divisions and sub-divisions . . . incomplete if in the course of its evolutions it had not brought upon the field most of the chief doctrines of the Confession of Faith—then the concluding prayer, almost as long as the opening—then another psalm, then the benediction—that I can remember as the ordinary Presbyterian church service; and I have no hesitation in saying that it led to the withdrawal from the Church of many men of taste and culture and high religious sentiment.

All this he contrasted with what he considered to be the great improvement that had taken place since. It was not that something new had been introduced, but rather something very old: a style of worship as it was before "it had been disfigured and debased by English Puritanism." Previously, he maintained, a liturgy was used and "I trust that the time is not far distant when throughout the whole Church it will be in use again . . . and should it be so we shall have the satisfaction that in the Cathedral of Glasgow there was a partially liturgical service when in few Scotch churches besides."[35] It was also in Burns's time that communion in the cathedral began to be celebrated on a monthly basis, another measure favored by the Church Service Society which wished to place greater emphasis on the sacrament.

Plenty of presbyterians viewed these developments with horror as being the first steps on the road back to Roman Catholicism. The leading Free Churchman Dr. James Begg (1808–83) said he "could point to a good many men connected with the Established Church who would not object to having a mitre on their brow."[36] The most vocal resistance came from

---

35. *Glasgow Herald,* May 21, 1881.
36. *The Scotsman,* November 19, 1881.

the maverick Rev. Jacob Primmer (1841–1914) who considered even the title "Reverend" to have Popish connotations and referred to himself as "Pastor" instead. In addition to being minister of Townhill Church, Dunfermline, Primmer traveled throughout Scotland holding rallies or "conventicles" at which he denounced ritualism in the Established Church. What he called "The Secret Romanising Church Service Society" was his favorite target and his use of sarcasm could be devastatingly effective. In response to the idea that a man cannot pray to God properly without a prayer book, he inquired, "what would Jonah have done in the belly of the whale?" And if Jonah had complained that he could not praise God without instrumental accompaniment, the whale may well have replied that it had enough to swallow without gulping down a harmonium!

Primmer naturally had something to say about developments at Glasgow Cathedral. In his eyes the brass eagle lectern decorated with onyx and agate stones installed there in 1890[37] was idolatrous and when a miscreant broke a stained glass window and vandalized the offending object with a coal hammer, Primmer could hardly contain his *schadenfreude*. He told a meeting in Irvine that the Town Council of Glasgow considered the act of "throwing down an image of one of the fowls of the air" to be worse than murder, for they had offered £100 for evidence against the perpetrator but no such rewards for those who killed their fellow men. It was just as well, he added, that he and his followers had been holding a meeting in North Berwick on the night of the crime, or some of them might have been arrested.[38] Nor was Primmer a lone voice among the clergy of the Established Church. In 1894 the Synod of Glasgow and Ayr met in Glasgow and at the opening service had the opportunity to experience the cathedral's style of worship. It proved too much for one minister who turned to the choir and shouted to them to "cease their interruptions of the worship of God by singing 'Amen' at the close of the prayers." However, "no notice was taken of the reverend gentleman's efforts at reformation."[39]

The Church Service Society (of which 533 ministers were members by 1892) constantly denied any suggestion that it was trying to copy the

---

37. To mark Burns's twenty-five years at the cathedral. He had requested the lectern instead of a personal gift.

38. *Edinburgh Evening News,* February 14, 1891. It later emerged that the culprit had hidden in the cathedral and escaped afterwards by breaking a window. In spite of the reward offered, he was never caught.

39. *Leominster News,* November 2, 1894.

Roman Catholics or Episcopalians. "What they were really doing was restoring the service of the Church of Scotland to its former beauty,"[40] claimed one of the Society's leading figures, Rev. A. K. H. Boyd (1825–99) of St. Andrews, who was once described as carrying out his duties with "archiepiscopal dignity." Yet it is hard to escape the suspicion that, aesthetically at least, such clerics much preferred the style of worship to be found south of the border. Preaching in the cathedral in April 1879 on the first Sunday when the organ was in use, Boyd advocated "a more reverent and cultured ritual" and asked:

> Who that had paced the echoing aisles of the sublime minsters of the South, and reverently joined in a worship worthy them, grown familiar . . . with pealing organ and white-robed choristers, with the chanted psalm and the melodious prayers with their all but inspired felicity, beauty, and majesty, but had turned away with the lingering thought—"Might not the dear old Church, keeping still that Presbyterian government which they believed to be founded on the Word of God, and agreeable thereto, . . . keep more of the beauty of holiness in things outward"?[41]

Worship at Glasgow Cathedral, argued Burns, could be just as "artistic, impressive, as solemnising":

> We are trying to make it such as High-Churchmen, Low-Churchmen, and No-Churchmen may enjoy; and in no other church in Scotland could the attempt be more appropriately made, for when worshiping there we are surrounded by the beautiful, and everything coarse, vulgar, unfinished, out of taste is at variance with the spirit of the place and opposed to the pious aims of those holy men by whom the temple was reared and so fitly adorned.[42]

Here, Burns makes a link between his preferred style of worship and the nature of the building which, in its recently restored guise was, for the first time since the Reformation, a particularly appropriate setting for a more liturgical form of service in which music played a prominent part.[43]

40. *The Scotsman*, May 31, 1883.
41. *Greenock Advertiser*, April 14, 1879.
42. *Herald*, May 21, 1881.
43. For a full account of the nineteenth century restoration, see Macaulay, "Glasgow Cathedral: Liturgical Changes, 1790–1855," in Fawcett, *Glasgow's Great Glass Experiment*, 13–19.

Previously, the building had been divided up for the use of separate congregations: the High Church congregation in the choir, the Barony congregation in the lower church and, from 1648 onwards, the Outer High Church in the western portion of the nave. In 1799 the foundation stone of a new Barony building was laid, though the heritors unfortunately then agreed to lay out a burial ground in the lower church, importing tons of soil for the purpose and creating severe problems of dampness for the whole structure. In 1833 Archibald McLellan, a wealthy benefactor of Glasgow, published his *Essay on the cathedral church of Glasgow* which stimulated the city to tackle urgently needed repairs. Plans were drawn up for an ambitious remodeling of the western front;[44] the clumsily fitted galleries in the quire were taken away and "beautiful stalls and benches in the Cathedral style" substituted. Removal of divisions between choir and nave meant "the eye can now range over in unbroken survey the whole interior from east to west in all its beauty and sublimity."[45] In the next phase between 1855 and 1864 "the windows [were] filled with artistically painted glass at enormous cost" and, although some objected to these being made in Munich and not by local artists, there was no shortage of wealthy donors willing to contribute.[46] The renewed splendor of the cathedral aroused the envy of Glasgow's rival city in the east: in November 1867, the Lord Provost of Edinburgh called a meeting in the City Chambers "for the purpose of considering the propriety and the means of renovating St. Giles' Cathedral in the style of Glasgow Cathedral."[47]

George Stewart Burns was keen to continue the process of beautification of the interior and under the supervision of the leading Glasgow architect John Honeyman (1831–1914) the chancel area was refloored in marble, the central pulpit moved to the side and an ornate Gothic-style reredos of Caen stone and alabaster installed, a gift from Lady Maxwell in memory of her husband, Sir William Maxwell, 10th Baronet of Calderwood. Previously the communion table was of the plainest design, leading one American visitor to comment that "I bet there isn't a merchant in your city who doesn't have a better table than that to eat his dinner from." The installation of a far more ornate new communion table with its carving of the Last Supper, gifted by John Garroway of Rosemount, had the

44. See chapter 13 of the present volume.
45. *Glasgow Herald,* March 17, 1856.
46. See Fairfull-Smith, "The patrons of the Glasgow Cathedral windows," in Fawcett, 67–80.
47. *Aberdeen Press and Journal,* November 6, 1867.

potential to arouse accusations of "idolatry." The tension was defused by an elder. After a service, one of those who had objected to the table came forward to examine it, running his fingers over the carved panel, and someone asked an elder what this man was doing. "Oh," replied the elder with undisguised scorn, "he's tryin' the heids o' the disciples to see if they're as saft as his ain."[48]

Obviously, many other churches saw similar developments in worship styles and church furnishings in this period and it was inevitable that these two closely related trends would become more formally linked. In 1886 the Rev. Professor James Cooper (1846-1922) founded the Aberdeen Ecclesiological Society, followed by a Glasgow Society in 1893, with the aim of studying "the Principles of Christian Worship, and of Church Architecture and the allied Arts which minister thereto", thereby explicitly bringing together ecclesiastical architecture and liturgy. Many members of the new Society were also involved in the Church Service Society and some, including Cooper himself, also joined the "Scoto-Catholic" Scottish Church Society (founded 1892) which held strong doctrinal convictions about the Church of Scotland being part of the universal or "catholic" church.[49] In a chapter entitled "Integrating Some of the Pieces" in his book on the history of Scottish presbyterian worship, Bryan Spinks places all these various initiatives in their wider context, interpreting them as aspects of what he calls the "cultural turn" of the nineteenth-century Romantic Movement which encompassed trends such as Tractarianism in the Church of England, the Gothic revival in architecture and the work of William Morris and the Arts and Crafts Movement.[50]

Dr. Burns joined the Glasgow Ecclesiological Society which held its meetings in various different churches where the members would study the architecture and layout of the building and listen to lectures. At one meeting held at Park Church in February 1894 Burns was in the chair and had to listen to a lecture on "Ecclesiastical Stained Glass" during which the speaker talked of his "sense of pain" at seeing the windows in the cathedral which he thought "could well take up a position in some gaily colored secular building." Unfortunately the report does not record the reaction of the chairman.[51]

48. *Glasgow Herald*, July 14, 1900.
49. See Spinks, *Scottish Presbyterian Worship*, 97-123.
50. Spinks, *Scottish Presbyterian Worship*, 124-154.
51. *Glasgow Herald*, February 13, 1894.

It was not only the building and the style of services which changed significantly during the three decades of Burns's ministry. The nature of the cathedral's parish area was very different by the 1890s following the relocation of the Old College from the High Street to the new Gilmorehill buildings and the consequent loss of scholars who formerly occupied the cathedral's pews, in addition to the movement of some of the more prosperous members of the congregation to the rapidly expanding and more fashionable West End of the city. Burns himself mirrored this development: in 1864 he had acquired Germiston House, a mansion built in 1690 by Robert Dinwiddie, one of the tobacco lords but by 1890 its grounds and outlook had been spoiled by the railway line being built beside it and the minister moved to 3 Westbourne Terrace in Kelvinside. Germiston House was then used as housing for laborers and the study Burns had constructed in the garden was turned into a piggery.[52] In spite of all these changes, Peter Hillis's analysis of nineteenth-century communion rolls leads him to conclude that "the flight to the suburbs did not lead to any sudden decline in [cathedral] membership" and "the congregation continued to be drawn from all sections of society" including a significant number who were of high status.[53]

Burns's period in office also saw a change in the priorities of the minister and session, with various responsibilities being taken over by other agencies. For example, before the Education Act of 1872 parish and sessional schools were run by the churches and the Lennox Charity School and Freeland School came under the jurisdiction of the cathedral's kirk session. Again, the mission church established in the parish area in memory of Burns's predecessor, Dr. Robertson, became a separate charge in its own right, though it was always seen as a church for the poor and many working class churchgoers preferred to attend the cathedral or the Barony instead.[54]

Such developments, perhaps, allowed the minister to focus more on the aesthetic, ritualistic, and musical aspects of the cathedral which appealed to him. His contribution was widely appreciated at the time: he was awarded an honorary Doctor of Divinity degree in 1870 and at the semi-jubilee of his ministry in 1890 received a silver casket containing an address of congratulation expressing the hope that "You may long be

---

52. Germiston House was demolished in 1926.
53. Hillis, "Social Composition," 71.
54. Drummond and Bulloch, *The Church in Late Victorian Scotland*, 194.

spared to continue your ministrations among us." Yet his ministry was drawing towards its end. Henderson hints at "repeated attacks of a sore malady" which, but for the care of his wife, "would have entirely unfitted him for his multifarious duties." When Mrs Burns died in February 1896, he "never fully recovered the cheerfulness and buoyancy which had previously been one of his characteristics"[55] and less than a year later he was laid to rest beside her in the Necropolis, the cause of death being recorded as "apoplexy."

The marble memorial tablet erected in the cathedral in 1899 depicts George Stewart Burns with a benevolent smile that reflects "the sympathetic warmth of his heart, [and] the bright geniality of his social intercourse." Dr. Burns was a man of his time, comfortable in his beliefs, his social position and his civic and ecclesiastical role. In short, he was, in Hillis's words, "the right kind of uncontroversial man."[56]

"A GIANT IN INTELLECT AND ATTAINMENTS": PEARSON MCADAM MUIR

Rev. Dr. Pearson McAdam Muir (1846–1924)

In choosing who should occupy its pulpit, the congregation of Glasgow Cathedral has generally favored continuity, and often the new

---

55. *Arbroath Herald*, January 30, 1896.
56. Hillis, "Social Composition," 51.

incumbent has had some connection with his predecessor. Such was the case with the Rev. Dr. Pearson McAdam Muir who was a friend of Dr. Burns and also had close links with the city of Glasgow. Another son of the manse, he was born at Kirkmabreck, Kircudbright but after the death of his father, Rev. John Muir, when Pearson was twelve years old, his mother moved to Glasgow where he completed his education at the High School and university. One of his childhood friends was the future Unionist Member of Parliament Sir Henry Craik (1846–1927) who recalled that, although neither of them were particularly distinguished in their classes, Muir seemed aware, even as a schoolboy, that his destiny lay in the ministry.

At the age of twenty-four he was inducted to his first charge at Catrine, Ayrshire, which at the time had the status of a chapel of ease and was "at a very low ebb." As there was only one elder connected with it, Muir used to say that he had a very unanimous kirk session. But the young man quickly made his mark and, although he only stayed for about eighteen months, he built up the congregation and raised funds which enabled the church to become a flourishing *quoad sacra* charge.[57] While at Catrine he married Sophia, daughter of the Rev. Dr. Chrystal of Auchinleck, a future Moderator of the General Assembly. In 1872 he was translated to Polmont near Falkirk where he spent "eight happy and fruitful years" before moving to the prestigious charge of Morningside Parish in Edinburgh.

The ecclesiology of McAdam Muir was comparable to that of Burns. He was not only a member but an office bearer of the Church Service Society in which he fulfilled the role of secretary. His praise of Dr. Robert Lee (1804–68)—minister of Old Greyfriars, Edinburgh, and a pioneer of the reforms in worship favored by the Society—as "a brilliant champion" in the "battles of liberty in ritual and doctrine"[58] makes it clear where his own sympathies lay. This stance was quite acceptable at Glasgow Cathedral but elsewhere McAdam Muir found himself caught up in the battles between supporters and opponents of "ritualism" on numerous occasions. In 1880 an attempt had been made to block his call to Morningside by an

---

57. A chapel of ease was a building within the bounds of a parish area where services were held for those who found it difficult to reach the main church premises. The term *quoad sacra* denotes a parish church with full ecclesiastical functions but no civil functions. Numerous churches of this type were opened in the nineteenth century to cater for the need for more church seats within an already existing parish.

58. Henderson, *Dr. McAdam Muir's Ministry*, 41–42.

elder, John Walker, who objected that the call to a new minister should not be sustained until the congregation reversed the "divisive courses" it had pursued "contrary to the present worship and government of the Church of Scotland." Walker particularly deplored the introduction of an "altar" inscribed with the words "This do in Remembrance of Me" and covered with a cloth embroidered IHS and the use of the recently installed organ for concerts, a departure "from the original intention of allowing an organ as an aid merely to the church psalmody." The prospective incumbent was said to be "well aware of said innovations and malpractices" and therefore, by implication, in favor of them. However, the presbytery moderator said he would not "minute or take the slightest notice" of Walker's petition and the call to McAdam Muir went ahead.[59]

Eleven years later, McAdam Muir found himself back in his old church at Polmont as one of the commissioners appointed by the General Assembly to adjudicate on what had become known as "the Polmont Case." The issue was that the minister, Rev. William Ross, had held a service for the pupils of the nearby Blairlodge School, an elite fee-paying establishment, but two elders objected to the fact that it followed an Episcopalian pattern using a service book. Attendances and collections at regular services allegedly began to fall off as a result. The commissioners seem to have handled the matter with tact, aiming to restore harmony in the parish. According to the *Falkirk Herald,* "we understand there was a full and friendly conversation, in which all the Commissioners took part, and that matters were arranged so far that there is every prospect of a speedy and amicable settlement."[60]

Sooner or later McAdam Muir was bound to come up against Pastor Primmer. In 1910 St. Cuthbert's Church, Edinburgh, had let out its hall over several nights for a play about Joan of Arc and Primmer complained to the presbytery about the use of a church hall for "Popish theatricals" at which an image of the Virgin and Child was displayed. This case came before the General Assembly in May 1911 which resolved to set up a committee "to inquire into the law on the subject."[61] Primmer had a certain amount of support but, according to him, the "Romanising conspirators" succeeded in getting themselves placed on the committee with McAdam Muir, "a high Ritualist," in the chair. At the next year's assembly, Muir

---

59. *Edinburgh Evening News,* January 14, 1880.

60. *Falkirk Herald,* July 4, 1890.

61. Primmer, *Life of Jacob Primmer,* 296.

successfully moved that the appeal and petition should be dismissed but Primmer was used to such setbacks: "As regards the result, God will do what we cannot do," he said.[62]

Muir's role in these investigations highlights a major difference between him and his predecessor at the cathedral. While Burns was said to be "lax in his attendance at Presbyteries and Assemblies,"[63] Muir was heavily involved in the bureaucracy of the national church. At various times he served as convener of Glasgow presbytery's Committee on Church Extension, was a member of the General Assembly's Colonial Committee, the Committee on Correspondence with Foreign Churches and the Church Interests Committee, a trustee of Iona Abbey, and much else. This diligence led in due course to his election to the highest office in the Church of Scotland and he served as Moderator of the General Assembly in 1910. The appointment was a matter of great pride for the cathedral and the city of Glasgow and a subscription list opened in the town by several business men raised £500 to "assist him in meeting the heavy extra expenditure he would incur during his tenure of office."[64]

After his moderatorial year Muir had the further honor of being installed as one of the King's Chaplains in Ordinary in Scotland and he continued to play an important role in the General Assembly as convener of the Business Committee, "a post which practically carried with it the official leadership of the Assembly, and consequently of the Church."[65] As such, he was a spokesmen on key ecclesiastical issues of the time, one of these being the gradual move towards reunion of the main presbyterian churches. The nineteenth century had witnessed various divisions within the denominations but in the early twentieth century the churches were beginning to put earlier tensions behind them; the Free and United Presbyterian denominations merged in 1900 to form the United Free (UF) Church which would eventually (in 1929) unite with the Church of Scotland.

The minister of the cathedral was a strong advocate of this process and he used the occasion of his closing moderatorial address to the General Assembly to commend church unity. The coming together of the UF and Established churches in Scotland was still nineteen years in

---

62. Primmer, *Life*, 307.
63. *The Bailie*, October 28, 1874.
64. Henderson, *Dr. McAdam Muir's Ministry*, 32.
65. *Glasgow Herald*, July 14, 1924.

the future, and Muir acknowledged that "the details of possible reunion cannot now be thought of; but this prediction may be hazarded, that if the harmony and goodwill by which the early conferences have been characterized are in anywise continued, brighter days are in store for the religious life of our country."[66] Before then the dark days of World War I would have to be endured, but that, too, provided a further stimulus for the churches to work together.

If Muir had a vision of the future of the Scottish church, he was also greatly interested in its past. A close friend described him as having "a keen historic instinct" and he frequently examined subjects from a historical standpoint in his sermons and lectures. He wrote *The Church of Scotland: a Sketch of its History* published in 1890 as part of a series designed for use in Guilds and Bible classes and took a similar "broad brush" approach in *Religious Writers of England* (1901), which gives potted biographies from the time of the Venerable Bede up to Isaac Watts, William Cowper and John Newton. His pleasure at ministering in a historic building is evident from the chapter detailing the "Monuments and Inscriptions" which he contributed to Eyre-Todd's *Book of Glasgow Cathedral* (1898).

McAdam Muir's various writings and addresses show how being a member of the "ritualist" party did not lessen his respect for his Scottish presbyterian heritage. A series of celebrations took place in May 1905 to mark the 400th anniversary of the birth of John Knox, culminating in a special service in Glasgow Cathedral attended by a vast number of dignitaries, including representatives of the UF, Free and Congregational denominations. Muir's sermon compared Knox the Reformer with Jeremiah the Prophet, both of whom were reluctant to take up their public roles. He reviewed Knox's career and achievements in some detail, and defended his description of the RC mass as "idolatry," reminding the congregation that it was the Thirty-Nine Articles of the Church of England that called masses "blasphemous fables and dangerous deceits." Taking a balanced approach designed to keep both "high" and "low" churchmen on board, Muir remarked that "If we were horrified at the severity of the sayings of Knox, we ought in consistency to be equally horrified by the severity of the sayings of some who were regarded as models of gentleness and culture. . . . It was a time when only the plainest of speaking would draw attention to the magnitude of the evil." The destruction of

---

66. Henderson, *Dr. McAdam Muir's Ministry*, 66.

churches and cathedrals at the time of the Reformation was indeed "a melancholy fact," but the blame lay as much with English invaders as with the reformers. The preacher admitted that "they might not nowadays be able to accept in every detail Knox's opinions" but "how much poorer the country would have been without the Reformation." The message for today, he concluded, was that those present all belonged to the universal church and all were heirs to the Reformation, even if they belonged to different denominations. Thus, McAdam Muir's historical survey ended with a forward look to the time when, he hoped, the Scottish churches could move beyond past divisions.[67]

Muir's most enduring writings saw him engage not only with church history but with the intellectual and theological concerns of his day. Charles Darwin's *Origin of the Species* (1859) and the works of the "higher critics," notably *The Life of Jesus, Critically Examined* by the German theologian David Friedrich Strauss (1808–74), translated into English by George Eliot, presented serious challenges to traditional interpretations of the historicity of the Old and New Testaments. As Principal Caird of Glasgow University told the congregation at the induction of George Stewart Burns to Glasgow Cathedral in June 1865, these were times "of seething thought and unsettled enquiry."[68] Matthew Arnold famously captured the mid-Victorian mood of religious doubt and uncertainty in his poem *Dover Beach*:

> The Sea of Faith
>
> Was once, too, at the full, and round earth's shore
>
> Lay like the folds of a bright girdle furled.
>
> But now I only hear
>
> Its melancholy, long, withdrawing roar . . .

In Scotland, the Free Church scholar William Robertson Smith (1846–94) aroused a great deal of opposition between 1876 and 1880. He was accused of various heretical statements, the main one being that he denied the Mosaic authorship of Deuteronomy. Though narrowly cleared of the charges at the Free Church General Assembly, he continued to expound his theories on the authority of Scripture and was removed from his Chair at the Free Church College in Aberdeen. The rest of his career

---

67. *Glasgow Herald*, May 22, 1905.
68. *Glasgow Herald*, June 23, 1865.

was spent in Cambridge and he died at the age of only forty-eight. Robertson Smith may have lost the battle but ultimately his approach would win the war of ideas in the main Scottish presbyterian denominations. The heresy of one generation becomes the orthodoxy of the next.

McAdam's Muir's views on these questions were first aired in a sermon delivered to the Synod of Lothian and Tweeddale in 1879 entitled "The Witness of Scepticism to Christ" and expanded upon in his 1909 Baird Lectures, published in book form as *Modern Substitutes for Christianity*. Everything in these lectures was based on the assumption stated in the opening sentence: "That there is at present a widespread alienation from the Christian Faith can hardly be denied."[69] With a certain amount of wit, he quotes long-forgotten contemporary opinion formers, or "influencers" as they would now be called, who believed they had "received a revelation to prove that no revelation [by God] has been given."[70] Their objections to Christianity prefigure the views of Richard Dawkins and others today: science has disproved religion; Christianity keeps the masses in ignorance; Christians do not live up to their profession, and so on. Muir reviews the inadequacies of modern substitutes—pantheism, rationalism, humanism—and argues that any good to be found in other religions or philosophical systems ultimately derives from the person of Christ.

> Those views which you hold so strongly, which are to you the most ennobling that have ever been given of God and of religion, where is it that alone they are to be found? In places where Christianity has gone before.[71]

Particular attention is devoted to the critical theologians and Muir comes up with an ingenious line of argument to show that they are not simply to be dismissed as unbelievers. "In the most unexpected quarters," he says, "we find the fascination of Christ remaining. Men . . . defiantly proclaiming that they are not His followers are yet perpetually returning, in what they themselves will confess as their higher moments, to the thought of Him."[72] Muir refers to a contemporary professor at Zurich, Paul Wilhelm Schmiedel (1851–1935), as an example of the connection between skepticism and faith. In Schmiedel's opinion, only nine sayings

---

69. Muir, *Modern Substitutes*, 3.
70. Muir, *Modern Substitutes*, 6.
71. Muir, *Modern Substitutes*, 166.
72. Muir, *Modern Substitutes*, 185.

or "foundation pillars" of Jesus could be taken as genuine; that, says McAdam Muir, is "just enough" for, "having them, I know that Jesus must really have come forward in the way He is said to have done. In a word, I know ... that His Person cannot be referred to the region of myth."[73] Thus, "renouncing so much, [Schmiedel] incontrovertibly establishes so much, incontrovertibly establishes, we may not unreasonably contend, a great deal more than he admits."[74] And so, concludes Muir, modern criticism from Strauss onwards, which at first sight appeared destructive to the Christian faith, helps confirm it and "the Figure of Jesus as a Historical Reality has been more and more endowed with power."[75]

Perhaps the most interesting aspect of these lectures is not so much the validity, or otherwise, of the case McAdam Muir was presenting, but the fact that he was expressing such a tolerant and broad-minded view in an era when even minor differences in doctrine or church practice could still arouse bitter arguments. It is not surprising, therefore, that *Modern Substitutes for Christianity* is his only publication which has stood the test of time, and the book remains in print today.[76]

At the age of sixty-eight, Muir still hoped to contribute more on the national stage and was commissioned to travel to India as a representative of the Church of Scotland, a trip that had to be abandoned because of the Great War. On September 9, 1914 he was due to speak at a special service of intercession in connection with the outbreak of war. He had sat up much of the night preparing his remarks and became seriously ill, losing the power to speak, and a fellow minister had to take his place and read his address.

1915 was consequently an unsettled year for Glasgow Cathedral. In January the minister's leave of absence was extended for a further three months and although assistants were available to cover many of his duties continuity was hard to maintain as changes of personnel were frequent, with several leaving after only a few months in order to serve as army chaplains. Routine running of congregational affairs continued via the well-tried system of committees, with separate groups managing the choir, halls, visitation, clothing society, parish magazine, savings bank, parish mission and Sunday school, all of these activities being under the

73. Muir, *Modern Substitutes*, 182.
74. Muir, *Modern Substitutes*, 183.
75. Muir, *Modern Substitutes*, 184.
76. The full text of the lectures can also be found in pdf form online at: http://clydeserver.com/bairdtrust/node/29

general supervision of the kirk session. But by May there was clearly a feeling that things had drifted on for long enough. While a further three months' leave was granted, a committee was formed "to take into consideration the whole situation" regarding Dr. Muir. By August the committee reported that advice had been sought from two senior doctors who "concurred in the opinion that [Dr. Muir] was quite competent to consider intelligently any proposal put before him." After meeting with presbytery representatives, Muir wrote to the session—whether willingly or otherwise we can only guess—to say that he was unfit to resume his duties and that he desired a successor to be appointed.

If Dr. McAdam Muir was not quite the "jolly good fellow" that *The Bailie* mockingly called Dr. Burns, he does seem to have had, as the Very Reverend Professor George Milligan said in a tribute, "a genial and lovable personality." He once said that working with his assistant ministers had "never brought him the slightest trouble. He let them do what they liked, and they were very obedient!"[77] Session clerk John Henderson is surprisingly forthright in saying that at first his pastoral visits were "short and trying" on account of his "quiet, unassuming manner"; as the years passed, however, it seems "he was soon welcomed with every confidence and heartiness."[78] When it became clear Muir could no longer continue in his post, generous provision was made for his retirement. The kirk session and congregation, supported by the city's Lord Provost and other prominent citizens, subscribed to a scheme with the object of raising £4000 in order to provide an annual income of £400 to Dr. Muir. Not only had the total been secured by the beginning of October but the session had also decided to make an additional contribution of £50 for the first three years. The tone of Dr. Muir's letter of resignation suggests that his ministry had reached an amicable conclusion:

> In all the joys and sorrows of these years I have experienced the most kindly and sympathetic help on all hands, and the effort that has just been made to secure my comfort during my retirement is but the climax of the many kindnesses that have been shown to me alike by Elders and Deacons and every member of the congregation.

Muir lived on until July 1924, continuing to attend the Cathedral on Sundays throughout the short ministry of his successor, James

---

77. *Glasgow Cathedral Parish Magazine,* June 1910, 5.
78. Henderson, *Dr. McAdam Muir's Ministry,* 28.

MacGibbon (1865–1922), formerly of Hamilton, who predeceased him. Muir had known MacGibbon throughout his life, for he was the son of one of Muir's elders at Morningside, and a former assistant to Church Service Society co-founder Cameron Lees (1835–1913)[79] at St. Giles'.

And so, once again, continuity prevailed. The occupants of the pulpit of Glasgow Cathedral from the 1860s until the 1920s displayed a consistent preference for a liturgical form of presbyterian service, steadily putting into practice the vision of cathedral worship first outlined by Dr. Robertson and developed in accordance with the principles of the Church Service Society. Theologically, they remained within the orthodox reformed tradition yet shared a "broad and catholic" outlook which in McAdam Muir's case made him sufficiently open-minded to see certain positives in the findings of the German critics, in this respect anticipating what became known as the "liberal evangelical" position widely shared by Church of Scotland preachers in the twentieth century. All three cathedral ministers moved comfortably in the social circles and organizations appropriate to their status, such as the Trades and Merchant Houses of Glasgow, the Grand Lodge of Freemasons of Scotland and the military; all three were honored with Doctor of Divinity degrees from Glasgow University (Burns in 1870, Muir in 1893 and MacGibbon in 1920). Throughout the period of their ministries, the historic value of the cathedral as a building became more fully recognized by city fathers and citizens alike and the combined efforts of individual donors and public bodies led to the transformation of the interior into a setting worthy of grand civic and religious ceremonies.

It is perhaps fitting to conclude by juxtaposing two descriptions of services at the cathedral, approximately fifty years apart. In his Preface to *Pastoral Counsels,* a collection of Dr. John Robertson's sermons, A. K. H. Boyd gives a picture of a typical Sunday service in the early 1860s for the benefit of readers not familiar with Scottish worship:

> There are no traces of the familiar arrangements of the choir of an English cathedral. There is no organ: no throne: no bishop nor archbishop, as in departed days: no dean, no canons, no choristers in white: not a surplice or stole or hood about the place; far less the cope of older times: no daily service. And the

---

79. Not to be confused with Dr. Robert Lee (1804–68), who pioneered liturgical reforms in worship at Old Greyfriars, Edinburgh. Similar ideas were taken up by the Church Service Society, co-founded in 1865 by Dr. Cameron Lees (1835–1913) of Paisley Abbey and later St. Giles', Edinburgh.

entire staff of the church consists of one minister, with an assistant or two if he choose to have them; and a kirk session of lay elders, that peculiar institution of presbytery. Here, when the bell ceases to ring, no orderly procession of choristers and clergymen enters the ancient place as in ancient days. A single minister, in the black gown and the bands of Puritan origin, issues from the chapter-house, which serves as a vestry, and ascends the pulpit, and calls the congregation (always a crowded one) to join in singing four verses of a psalm. This psalm the minister does not merely announce: he reads the whole passage to be sung. Then a choir of men and women, placed in an ungraceful square box around the pulpit, sing the verses. They sit as they sing; the congregation all sit. A great curtain of crimson, with gold *fleurs-de-lis* is let down to part off the choir from the nave during worship: thus only can a spoken service be generally audible in a place made for a choral one.... I do not fancy that the intelligent Anglican visitor could by possibility have approved or liked the form of worship, or thought it in keeping with the place; but the intelligent visitor who heard Dr. Robertson preach in that choir, would be constrained to confess that a church which makes perhaps too much of the sermon in its worship does succeed, now and then, in giving you such sermons as you do not often hear anywhere else.[80]

Half a century later, on Sunday December 22, 1912, a "Service for the Dedication of the New Roof of the Cathedral" took place in a very different style. There was a lavishly printed order of service which opened with the congregation singing the metrical version of Psalm 122 from the Scottish Psalter ("I joyed when to the house of God, Go up, they said to me") to organ accompaniment, followed by a long formal prayer of adoration, printed in full, beginning "O Lord our God of boundless might and incomprehensible glory, of measureless compassion and infinite love to men" and punctuated on three occasions with "Amen" before concluding with the Lord's Prayer. Two choral settings of psalms followed and an Old Testament reading from I Kings Chapter 8 (Solomon in the Temple). After that, the choir sang Elgar's setting of the "Te Deum," followed by the New Testament reading, a congregational hymn, the recitation of the Apostles' Creed and a prayer of intercession, all of which could be followed word for word in the order of service. A further anthem ("Praise the Lord O my soul" by Goss), prayer and congregational hymn preceded

---

80. Preface to Robertson, *Pastoral Counsels*, xxviii–xxx (condensed).

the sermon. The congregation sang a closing paraphrase and the offering took place at the very end before the benediction, after which the assembled dignitaries processed out of the building to the strains of the concluding organ voluntary. As before, the sermon took central place in this elaborate program, though on this occasion it was more of an address on the history of the cathedral marking "the culmination of another effort to preserve the venerable pile."[81] Appropriately, Dr. McAdam Muir quoted the sermon preached by Dr. Robertson fifty years earlier at the dedication of the great east window, in which he had advocated the reforms in worship "which, now generally accepted, were then regarded as dangerous innovations."[82]

Solomon said of his temple, "behold, the heaven and heaven of heavens cannot contain Thee; how much less this house that I have builded?" (I Kings 8:27). The ministers of Glasgow Cathedral knew it to be so. "No house can contain God," said Robertson—but he added, "that might be a reason against churches altogether. If there are to be churches at all, it is no reason now, any more than in the days of Solomon, why they should not be beautiful."[83]

---

81. Henderson, *Dr. McAdam Muir's Ministry*, 105.
82. Henderson, *Dr. McAdam Muir's Ministry*, 109.
83. Henderson, *Dr. McAdam Muir's Ministry*, 110.

Bibliography

Allen, J. Romilly. *Early Christian Monuments of Scotland*. Edinburgh: Society of Antiquaries, 1903.
Anderson, A. O. et al., *The Chronicle of Melrose*. London: Facsimile Edition, 1936.
———. *Early Sources of Scottish History A.D. 500-1286*. 2 vols, Edinburgh: Oliver & Boyd, 1922.
———. *Scottish Annals from English Chroniclers*. London: David Nutt, 1908.
Anderson, M. O., ed. *A Scottish Chronicle known as the Chronicle of Holyrood*. Edinburgh: Scottish History Society, 1938.
Anderson, W. J. "Ambula Coram Deo: 'The Journal of Bishop Geddes for the year 1790, Part Second.'" *Innes Review* 6 (1955) 131-143.
Annan, Thomas. *The painted windows of Glasgow Cathedral*. Glasgow: Annan, 1867.
[Anon.] *Archaeological and Historical Collections relating to Ayrshire and Galloway*, iv. Edinburgh: Ayrshire and Galloway Archaeological Association, 1884.
[Anon.] *The Faiths of the World. A Concise History of the Great Religious Systems of the World*. Edinburgh: William Blackwood & Sons, 1882.
[Anon.] *Guide to St. Albans Cathedral*. London: HMSO, 1952.
[Anon.] *Miscellany of the Scottish History Society*, ii. Edinburgh: T. & A. Constable, 1904.
[Anon.] *Plans and Elevations of the Proposed Restoration and Additions to Glasgow Cathedral with Explanatory Address by the Local Committee*. Glasgow: J. Hedderwick, 1836.
Arnold-Forster, F. *Studies in Church Dedications*. 3 vols. London: Skeffington & Sons, 1899.
Atkinson, J. C. et al., *Coucher Book of Fountains Abbey*. 2 vols. Manchester: Chetham Society, 1886-1916.
Bain, J. and C. Rogers, eds. *Liber Protocollorum M. Cuthberti Simonis* and *Rental Book of Diocese of Glasgow*. 2 vols. London: Printed for the Grampian Club, 1875.
Bain, J. et al., eds. *Calendar of Documents relating to Scotland*. 5 vols. Edinburgh: H. M. General Register House, 1881-1986.
Ballantine, J. *A Treatise on Painted Glass*. London: Chapman & Hall, 1845.
Barlow, F. *Thomas Becket*. London: Weidenfield & Nicolson, 1986.
Barrell, A. D. M. "The Background to *Cum Universi*: Scoto-papal relations 1159-1192." *Innes Review* 46 (1995) 16-38.
Barrow, G. W. S. *The Anglo-Norman Era in Scottish History*. Oxford: Clarendon Press, 1980.

———. "The Beginnings of Feudalism in Scotland." *Bulletin of the Institute of Historical Research* 29 (1956) 1–31.

———. ed. *The Charters of King David I. The Written Acts of David I King of Scots, 1124–1153, and of his Son Henry Earl of Northumberland, 1139–1152*. Woodbridge: Boydell, 1999.

———. *Regesta Regum Scottorum, i, Acts of Malcolm IV king of Scots 1153–65*. Edinburgh: Edinburgh University Press, 1960.

——— with W. W. Scott. *Regesta Regum Scottorum, ii, The Acts of William I*. Edinburgh: Edinburgh University Press, 1971.

Barrow, J. "Cathedrals, Provosts and Prebends: a comparison of twelfth-century German and English practice." *Journal of Ecclesiastical History* 37 (1986) 536–64.

———. "Hereford bishops and married clergy: c. 1130–1240." *Historical Journal* 60 (1987) 1–8.

Beveridge, D. *Culross and Tulliallan*. 2 vols. Edinburgh: Blackwood & Sons, 1885.

Billings, R. W. and J. H. Burton. *The Baronial and Ecclesiastical Antiquities of Scotland*, iii. Edinburgh: Oliver & Boyd, 1901.

Birch, Walter de Gray. *History of Scottish Seals*, ii. Stirling: Eneas Mackay, 1907.

Blackie, Agnes. *Blackie and Son (1809–1959)*. Glasgow: Blackie & Son, 1959.

Bliss, W. H., ed. *Calendar of Entries in the Papal Registers relating to Great Britain and Ireland: Papal Letters*, i. London, HMSO, 1893.

Boardman, S., J. R. Davies, and E. Williamson. *Saints' Cults in the Celtic World*. Woodbridge: Boydell, 2009.

Boardman, S. and E. Williamson. *The Cult of Saints and the Virgin Mary in Medieval Scotland*. Woodbridge: Boydell, 2010.

Bonar A. A., ed. *The Letters of Samuel Rutherford*. Edinburgh: Oliphant, Anderson & Ferrier, 1894.

Bonnar, Thomas. *Biographical Sketch of George Meikle Kemp*. Edinburgh: Blackwood & Sons, 1892.

Broun, Dauvit. "The Church and the origins of Scottish independence in the twelfth century." *Records of the Scottish Church History Society* 31 (2002) 1–36.

———. *Scottish Independence and the Idea of Britain*. Edinburgh: Edinburgh University Press, 2007.

———. "The Welsh identity of the kingdom of Strathclyde c.900–c.1200." *Innes Review* 55 (2004) 118–180.

Brown, K. M. et al., eds. *Records of the Parliaments of Scotland to 1707*, St Andrews: 2007–2013.

Buchan, John. *The Kirk in Scotland*. Dunbar: Labarum Publications, 1985.

Burrell, Sir William. "A Tour, 1758." National Library of Scotland, MS. 2911, E12.

Burns, C. "Papal gifts to Scottish Monarchs: the Golden Rose and Blessed Sword." *Innes Review* 20 (1969) 150–194.

Burns, C., ed. *Papal Letters to Scotland of Clement VII of Avignon 1378–1394*. Edinburgh: T. & A. Constable [for the Scottish History Society], 1977.

Burns, J. "Popes, Bishops and the Polity of the Church" in P. Linehan, P. and J. Nelson, eds. *The Medieval World*. London: Routledge, 2001.

Burton, J. H. and D. Masson. *Register of the Privy Council of Scotland*, 1st ser., 14 vols. Edinburgh: Scottish Record Publications, 1877–98.

Cabrol, F. and H. Leclerq. *Dictionnaire d'archéologie chretienne et de liturgie*. Paris: Letouzey et Ané, 1907–1953.

Calderwood, D. *The History of the Kirk of Scotland*, ed. T. Thomson. 8 vols. Edinburgh: Wodrow Society, 1842–49.

Cameron, J. K., ed. *The First Book of Discipline*. Edinburgh: St. Andrew Press, 1972.

Canivez, J. M. *Statuta Capitulorum Generalium Ordinis Cisterciensis*. Louvain: Bureau de la Revue, 1933.

Chadwick, Nora K. et al., eds. *Studies in the early British Church*. Cambridge: Cambridge University Press, 1958.

Chalmers, P. MacGregor. "The Shrines of St. Margaret and St. Kentigern." *Proceedings of the Royal Philosophical Society of Glasgow* 34 (1902–3) 315–22.

———. "A Thirteenth Century Tomb in Glasgow Cathedral." *Proceedings of the Royal Philosophical Society of Glasgow* 36 (1904–5) 184–8.

———. *Cathedral Church of Glasgow*. London: Bell's Cathedral series, 1914.

Cheney, C. R. *English Bishops' Chanceries*. Manchester: Manchester University Press, 1950.

Cheyne, A. C. *The Transforming of the Kirk*. Edinburgh: Saint Andrew Press, 1983.

Clanchy, M. T. *Abelard: a Medieval Life*. Oxford: Blackwell, 1997.

Clutton-Brock, A. *Cathedral Church of York*. London: Bell's Cathedral series, 1914.

Cockburn-Hood, T. H. *The Rutherfords of that Ilk*. Edinburgh: Scott & Ferguson, 1884.

Cohn, S. *Popular Protest in Late Medieval English Towns*. Cambridge: Cambridge University Press, 2013.

Collie, James. *Plans, elevations, sections, details & views of the Cathedral of Glasgow*. London: J. Williams, 1835.

Coltart, J. S. *Scottish Church Architecture*. London: Sheldon Press, 1936.

Colvin, Howard. *A Biographical Dictionary of British Architects, 1600–1840*. London: Paul Mellon Centre for Studies in British Art, 1978.

Connal, M. *Diary of Sir Michael Connal*. Glasgow: MacLehose, 1895.

Cook, G. H. *Portrait of St. Albans Cathedral*. London: Phoenix House, 1951.

Cooper, J., ed. *Cartularium Ecclesiae Sancti Nicholai*, ii. Aberdeen: Aberdeen University Press for the New Spalding Club, 1888.

Cowan E. J. and R. A. McDonald. *Alba: Celtic Scotland in the Middle Ages*. East Linton: Tuckwell Press, 2000.

Cowan, I. B. "The Organisation of Secular Cathedral Chapters." *Records of the Scottish Church History Society* 14 (1960–63) 19–47.

———. *The Parishes of Medieval Scotland*. Edinburgh: Scottish Record Society, 1967.

———. "Two Early Taxation Rolls." *Innes Review* 22 (1971) 6–11.

——— and D. E. Easson. *Medieval Religious Houses Scotland*. 2nd ed. London and New York: Longman, 1976.

Cowan, Mairi. *Death, Life and Religious Change in Scottish Towns 1350–1560*. Manchester: Manchester University Press, 2012.

Cowen, Painton. *A Guide to Stained Glass in Britain*. London: Joseph, 1985.

Crawford, B. E., ed. *Church, Chronicle and Learning in Medieval and Early Renaissance Scotland*. Edinburgh: Mercat Press, 1999.

Crawfurd, George. *Lives of Officers of Crown and State in Scotland*. Edinburgh: R. Fleming, 1726.

Crosby, E. U. *Bishop and Chapter in Twelfth-Century England*. Cambridge: Cambridge University Press, 1994.

Crouch, D., ed. *Llandaff Episcopal Acta, 1140–1287*. Cardiff: South Wales Record Society, 1988.

Cruden, Stewart. *Scottish Medieval Churches*. Edinburgh: John Donald, 1986.
Davidson, A. Nevile. *Beginnings but No Ending*. Edinburgh: Edina, 1978.
———. "The Legacy of Leighton." *Society of Friends of Dunblane Cathedral* 10 (1967) Pt. II.
Dawson, Jane. *Scotland Re-Formed, 1488–1587*. Edinburgh: Edinburgh University Press, 2007.
de Paor, Liam. *St. Patrick's World*. Dublin: Four Courts Press, 1993.
Denholm, James. *The History of the City of Glasgow and Suburbs*. Glasgow: A. MacGoun, 1804.
Dennistoun, James, ed. *Cartularium Comitatus de Levenax*. Edinburgh: Maitland Club, 1833.
Dickinson, W. C., ed. John Knox's *History of the Reformation in Scotland*. 2 vols. London: Thomas Nelson, 1949.
Ditchburn, D. "The 'McRoberts Thesis' and Patterns of Sanctity in Late Medieval Scotland" in Boardman and Williamson (eds.) *The Cult of Saints*.
Dixon, C. Scott. "Rural Resistance, the Lutheran Pastor and the Territorial Church" in Brandenburg Ansbach-Kulmbach, 1528–1603" in *The Reformation of the Parishes*.
Donaldson, Gordon. *The Making of the Scottish Prayer Book of 1637*. Edinburgh: Edinburgh University Press, 1954.
———. *Scotland: James V–James VII*. Edinburgh: Oliver & Boyd, 1965.
———. *The Faith of the Scots*. London: Batsford, 1990.
Donnelly, Michael. *Glasgow Stained Glass*. Glasgow: Museums and Art Galleries, 1981.
Dowden, J. *The Bishops of Scotland*. Glasgow: Maclehose, 1912.
———. ed. *The Chartulary of Lindores Abbey*. Edinburgh: Scottish History Society, 1st Series, 1903.
———. "The Inventory of ornaments, jewels, relicks, vestments, service-books etc., belonging to the Cathedral Church of Glasgow in 1432." *Proceedings of the Society of Antiquaries of Scotland* 33 (1899) 280–329.
———. *The Medieval Church in Scotland*. Glasgow: Maclehose, 1910.
Driscoll, Stephen T. *Excavations at Glasgow Cathedral, 1988–1997*. [Durham]: Society for Medieval Archaeology, 2002.
Drummond, Andrew L. and James Bulloch. *The Church in Late Victorian Scotland, 1874–1900*. Edinburgh: Saint Andrew Press, 1980.
Duffy, Eamon. *The Stripping of the Altars: Traditional Religion in England, 1400–1580*. New Haven: Yale University Press, 1992.
Duncan, A. A. M., ed. *Regesta Regum Scottorum, v: the Acts of Robert I*. Edinburgh: Edinburgh University Press, 1988.
———. *Scotland: the Making of the Kingdom*. Edinburgh: Oliver & Boyd, 1975.
———. "Sources and Uses of the Chronicle of Melrose, 1165–1297." In S. Taylor, ed. *Kings, Clerics and Chronicles in Scotland, 500–1297*. Dublin: Four Courts, 2000.
———. "St. Kentigern at Glasgow Cathedral in the twelfth century." In Fawcett, ed. *Medieval Art and Architecture in the Diocese of Glasgow*.
Dunlop, A. I., ed. "Bagimond's Roll. Statement of the Tenths of the Kingdom of Scotland," *Scottish History Society Miscellany, vi*. Edinburgh: Edinburgh University Press [for the Scottish History Society], 1939.
Durkan, J. and J. Kirk. *The University of Glasgow*. Glasgow: University of Glasgow Press, 1977.
Durkan, J. "Glasgow Diocese and the Claims of York." *Innes Review* 50 (1999) 89–101.

———. "The Great Fire at Glasgow Cathedral." *Innes Review* 26 (1975) 89-92.
———. "Notes on Glasgow Cathedral." *Innes Review* 21 (1970) 46-76.
———. *William Turnbull, Bishop of Glasgow*. Glasgow: J. S. Burns [for the Scottish Catholic Historical Committee], 1951.
Edwards, K. *The English Secular Cathedrals in the Middle Ages*. 2nd ed. Manchester: Manchester University Press, 1967.
Eire, Carlos M. N. *Reformations: The Early Modern World, 1450-1650*. New Haven: Yale University Press, 2016.
Estabrook, Carl B. "Ritual, Space, and Authority in Seventeenth-Century English Cathedral Cities." *Journal of Interdisciplinary History* 32 (2002) 593-620.
Eyre-Todd, George. *The Book of Glasgow Cathedral: A History and Description*. Glasgow: Morrison Brothers, 1898.
Fairbairn, Thomas. *Relics of Ancient Architecture and Other Picturesque Scenes in Glasgow*. Glasgow: David Bryce & Son, 1896.
Farmer, D. H. *The Oxford Dictionary of Saints*. 2nd ed. Oxford: Oxford University Press, 1987.
Fawcett, Richard. "The Blackadder Aisle at Glasgow Cathedral: a reconsideration of the architectural evidence for its date." *Proceedings of the Society of Antiquaries* 115 (1987) 277-287.
———. ed. *Glasgow's Great Glass Experiment*. Edinburgh: Historic Scotland, 2003.
———. ed. *Medieval Art and Architecture in the Diocese of Glasgow*. [London]: British Archaeological Association/Historic Scotland, 1998.
———. *Scottish Medieval Churches*. Edinburgh: HMSO, 1985.
Ferguson, P. C. *Medieval Papal Representatives in Scotland 1125-1286*. Edinburgh: Stair Society, 1997.
Fitch, Audrey Beth. *The Search for Salvation: Lay Faith in Scotland 1480-1560*. Edinburgh: Birlinn, 2009.
Fletcher, Sir Banister. *A History of Architecture on the Comparative Method*. 17th ed. London: Athlone Press, 1961.
Forbes, A. P., ed. Jocelin's *Life of St. Kentigern*. In *The Lives of S. Ninian and S. Kentigern*. Edinburgh: The Historians of Scotland Series, v, 1874.
Fraser, W. *Liber S. Marie de Dryburgh*. Edinburgh: Bannatyne Club, 1847.
Gibb, A. *Glasgow: The Making of a City*. London: Croom Helm,1983.
Glasgow Kirk Session Records. National Records of Scotland, CH2/550/1-2.
Glasgow Presbytery Records. National Records of Scotland, CH2/171/1, 2, 31, 32A-B, 33, 35.
Gordon, J. F. S. *Glasghu Facies*, i. Glasgow: John Tweed, 1872.
———. *Scotichronicon*, 3 vols. Glasgow: John Tweed, 1867.
———. *A Vade Mecum to and through the Cathedral of St. Kentigern Glasgow*. Glasgow: W. S. Sime, 1894.
Gough, J. *Itinerary of Edward I*. Paisley: Alexander Gardner, 1900.
Grant, A. and K. J. Stringer, eds. *Medieval Scotland: Crown, Community and Lordship*. Edinburgh: Edinburgh University Press, 1993.
Graham, Michael. *The Uses of Reform: "Godly Discipline" and Popular Behavior in Scotland and Beyond, 1560-1610*. Leiden: Brill, 1996.
Greenway, D. et al., eds. *Tradition and Change: Essays in Honour of Marjorie Chibnall*. Cambridge: Cambridge University Press, 1985.

Greenway, D., ed. *John Le Neve. Fasti Ecclesiae Anglicanae 1066-1300, iv: Salisbury.* London: University of London, Institute of Historical Research, 1991.

Guthrie, Arthur. *Robertson of Irvine: Poet-Preacher.* New York: Thomas Nelson, 1890.

Haig, James, ed. *The Historical Works of Sir James Balfour.* Edinburgh: W. Aitchison, 1824-25.

Hannay, R. K. et al., eds. *Letters of James IV.* Edinburgh: T. & A. Constable, for the Scottish History Society, 1953.

Hamilton Thompson, A. *The English Clergy and their Organisation in the later Middle Ages.* Oxford: Clarendon Press, 1947.

Harrison, F. *York Minster.* London: Methuen, 1927.

Harrison, Martin. *Victorian Stained Glass.* London: Barrie & Jenkins, 1980.

Hartridge, R. A. R. *A History of Vicarages in the Middle Ages.* Cambridge: Cambridge University Press, 1936.

Harvey, C. C. H. and J. Macleod, eds. *Calendar of Writs preserved at Yester House, 1166-1625.* Edinburgh: Scottish Record Society, 1930.

Hay, George. "The Late Medieval Development of the High Kirk of St. Giles, Edinburgh." *Proceedings of the Society of Antiquaries* 107 (1976) 242-260.

Hell, Vera and Helmut. *The Great Pilgrimage of the Middle Ages.* London: Barrie & Rockliff, 1966.

Henderson, G. D. *The Church of Scotland: A Short History.* Edinburgh: Saint Andrew Press, [ND].

Henderson, John. *Dr. Burns's Ministry and Labours in the High Church Parish, 1865-1896.* Glasgow: Printed for Private Circulation, 1901.

———. *Dr. McAdam Muir's Ministry and Labours in the High Church Parish, 1896-1915.* Glasgow: Printed for Private Circulation, 1925.

Hillis, Peter. "The Social Composition of the Cathedral Church of St. Mungo in Late Nineteenth Century Glasgow." *Journal of Scottish Historical Studies* 31 (2011) 46-71.

Holtzmann, W. *Papsturkunden in England,* ii. Berlin: Vandenhoeck & Ruprecht, 1935.

Honeyman, J. *The Age of Glasgow Cathedral,* Glasgow: David Bryce, 1854.

Houfe, Simon. *Sir Albert Richardson: the Professor.* Luton: White Crescent Press, 1980.

Hourlier, Jacques. *Le Chapitre General jusqu'au moment du Grand Schisme.* Paris: Sirey, 1936.

Hunter Blair, F. C., ed. *Charters of the Abbey of Crosraguel.* 2 vols. Edinburgh: Ayrshire and Galloway Archaeological Association, 1886.

Innes, C., ed. *Liber Cartarum Sancte Crucis.* Edinburgh: Bannatyne Club, 1847.

———. ed. *Liber S. Marie de Calchou. Registrum cartarum Abbacie Tironensis de Kelso, 1113-1567.* 2 vols. Edinburgh: Bannatyne Club, 1846.

———. ed. *Liber Sancte Marie de Melros.* 2 vols. Edinburgh: Bannatyne Club, 1837.

———. ed. *Munimenta Alme Universitatis Glasguensis,* 4 vols. Glasgow: Maitland Club, 1854.

———. ed. *Registrum Episcopatus Aberdonensis.* Edinburgh: Maitland and Spalding Clubs, 1845.

———. ed. *Registrum Episcopatus Glasguensis.* 2 vols. Edinburgh: Bannatyne and Maitland Clubs, 1843.

———. ed. *Registrum Monasterii de Passelet.* Edinburgh: Maitland Club, 1832.

———. ed. *Registrum S. Marie de Neubotle.* Edinburgh: Bannatyne Club, 1849.

——— and P. Chambers, eds. *Liber Sancte Thome de Aberbrothoc.* 2 vols. Edinburgh: Bannatyne Club, 1848-1856.

——— et al., eds. *Origines Parochiales Scotiae.* Edinburgh: Bannatyne Club, 1850-1855.

Jackson, Kenneth H. "The Sources for the Life of St. Kentigern." In *Studies in the Early British Church,* ed. Nora K. Chadwick et al. Cambridge: Cambridge University Press, 1958.

Kelly, J. N. D. *The Oxford Dictionary of Popes.* Oxford: Oxford University Press, 1986.

Kirk, J., ed. *The Medieval Church in Scotland.* Edinburgh: Scottish Academic Press, 1995.

———. *The Records of the Synod of Lothian and Tweeddale, 1589-96, 1640-49.* Edinburgh: Stair Society, 1977.

———. *The Second Book of Discipline.* Edinburgh: St. Andrew Press, 2015.

Knight, Charles. *Old England: A Pictorial Museum of Royal, Ecclesiastical, Baronial, Municipal and Popular Antiquities.* London: James Sangster, 1845.

Knott, B. I. "Apologia for Bishop Jocelin." *Innes Review* 66 (2015) 130-143.

Knowles, D. *The Episcopal Colleagues of Archbishop Thomas Becket.* Cambridge: Cambridge University Press, 1951.

———. *The Monastic Order in England.* 2nd ed. Cambridge: Cambridge University Press, 1966.

Laing, D., ed. *The Letters and Journals of Robert Baillie, Principal of the University of Glasgow,* i. Edinburgh: Bannatyne Club, 1841-42.

———. ed. *Original Letters relating to the Ecclesiastical Affairs of Scotland.* 2 vols. Edinburgh: Bannatyne Club, 1851.

———. ed. *The Works of John Knox.* 6 vols. Edinburgh: Bannatyne Club, 1846-64.

Laven, Mary. "Encountering the Counter-Reformation." *Renaissance Quarterly,* 59 (2006) 706-720.

Lawrie, A. C. *Annals of the Reigns of Malcolm and William, Kings of Scotland.* Glasgow: Maclehose, 1910,

———. *Early Scottish Charters.* Glasgow: Maclehose, 1905.

Leach, A. F. *Memorials of Beverley Minster: The Chapter Act Book,* ii. Durham: Andrews & Co. for the Surtees Society, 1903.

Lee, Maurice. *The Road to Revolution: Scotland Under Charles I, 1625-1637.* Urbana and Chicago: University of Illinois Press, 1985.

Lesley, John. *History of Scotland,* Edinburgh: Bannatyne Club, 1830.

Livingstone, M. et al., eds. *Register of the Privy Seal of Scotland.* 8 vols. Edinburgh: HMSO, 1908-82.

Luard, H. R. *Annales Monastici,* iv. London: Rolls Series, 36, 1869.

Lynch, M. *Edinburgh and the Reformation.* Edinburgh: John Donald, 1981.

Lynch, M., ed. *The Scottish Medieval Town.* Edinburgh: John Donald, 1988.

McAleer, J. Philip. "A Unique Facade in Great Britain: the west front of Holyrood Abbey." *Proceedings of the Society of Antiquaries of Scotland* 115 (1985) 263-75.

McCrie, Thomas. *The Story of the Scottish Church.* London: Blackie & Son, 1875.

McNeill, P. G. B. and H. L. MacQueen, eds. *Atlas of Scottish History to 1707.* Edinburgh: The Scottish Medievalists and the Department of Geography, University of Edinburgh. 1996.

McWilliams, Philip. *Paisley Abbey and its remains,* Ph.D diss., University of Glasgow, 1995.

Macaulay, Rev. George. *The Lord's Law and Day: A Review of Dr. Macleod's speech, with criticisms of a sermon preached in the cathedral by Rev. G. S. Burns*. Glasgow: Thomas Murray & Son, 1866.

Macaulay, James. "The Architectural Collaboration Between J. Gillespie Graham and A. W. Pugin." *Architectural History* 27 (1984) 406–420.

———. *Charles Rennie Mackintosh*. New York: W. W. Norton, 2010.

MacCulloch, Diarmaid. *Reformation: Europe's House Divided 1490–1700*. New York: Penguin, 2003.

McFadden, G. J., ed. *An Edition and Translation of the Life of Waldef, Abbot of Melrose, by Jocelin of Furness*. University Microfilms, 1952.

———. "The Life of Waldef and its author Jocelin of Furness." *Innes Review* 6 (1955) 5–13.

MacFarlane, Leslie. "The Primacy of the Scottish Church, 1472–1521." *Innes Review* 20 (1969) 111–129.

MacGeorge, Andrew. *Old Glasgow: The Place and the People*. 3rd ed. Glasgow: Blackie & Son, 1888.

MacGibbon, D. and T. Ross. *Ecclesiastical Architecture of Scotland*, ii. Edinburgh: David Douglas, 1896.

McGurk, F., ed. *Papal Letters to Scotland of Benedict XIII of Avignon 1394–1413*. Edinburgh: T. & A. Constable [for the Scottish History Society], 1977.

McUre, J. *A View of the City of Glasgow*. Glasgow: James Duncan, 1736.

Mackinlay, J. M. *Ancient Church Dedications in Scotland*. Edinburgh: David Douglas, 1914.

McLellan, Archibald. *Essay on the Cathedral Church of Glasgow*. Glasgow: James Brash & Co., 1833.

MacLeod, D. *Servants to St. Mungo: the Church in Sixteenth Century Glasgow*. PhD diss., University of Guelph, 2013.

Macnair, Iain. *Glasgow Cathedral: the Stained Glass Windows*. Glasgow: Society of Friends of Glasgow Cathedral, 2009.

McRoberts, David. "The Death of St. Kentigern." *Innes Review* 24 (1973) 45–50.

———. "Notes on Glasgow Cathedral." *Innes Review* 17 (1966) 40–2.

———. "The Scottish Church and Nationalism in the Fifteenth Century." *Innes Review* 19 (1968) 3–14.

———, ed. *Essays on the Scottish Reformation*. Glasgow: John S. Burns, 1962.

Maidment, J., ed. *Spottiswoode Miscellany*, i. Edinburgh: Spottiswoode Society, 1844.

Makey, Walter. *The Church of the Covenant 1637–51: Revolution and Social Change in Scotland*. Edinburgh: John Donald, 1979.

Maldonado, A. "The Archaeology of Ancrum: Mantle Walls Project Data. Structure Report." Glasgow: University [of Glasgow] School of Humanities, 2012, 10–12.

Marwick, J. D., ed. *Charters and other Documents relating to the City of Glasgow, A.D. 1175–1649*. 2 vols. Edinburgh: Scottish Burgh Records Society, 1894–1906.

———. ed. *Extracts from the Records of the Burgh of Glasgow*, i, 1573–1642. Glasgow: Scottish Burgh Record Society, 1876.

Mays, Deborah, ed. *The Architecture of Scottish Cities*. East Linton: Tuckwell, 1997.

Moorman, J. R. H. *Church Life in England in the Thirteenth Century*. Cambridge: Cambridge University Press, 1955.

Morgan, M. "The Organisation of the Scottish Church in the twelfth century." *Transactions of the Royal Historical Society*, 4th Series, 29 (1947) 135–149.

Morris, C. *The Papal Monarchy: the Western Church from 1050 to 1250*. Oxford: Oxford University Press, 1989.
Muir, Pearson McAdam. *Modern Substitutes for Christianity*. London: Hodder and Stoughton, 1909.
Mullan, D. G. *Episcopacy in Scotland: The History of an Idea, 1560-1638*. Edinburgh: John Donald, 1986.
Napier, M. and M. Russell, eds. Spottiswoode's *History of the Church of Scotland*. 3 vols. Edinburgh: Spottiswoode Society, 1847-51.
Neville, C. J. *Native Lordship in Medieval Scotland. The Earldoms of Strathearn and Lennox c. 1140-1365*. Dublin: Four Courts, 2005.
———. and G. G. Simpson. *Regesta Regum Scottorum, iv, Pt. I: The Acts of Alexander III*. Edinburgh: Edinburgh University Press, 2013.
Nisbet, Alexander. *System of Heraldry*. Edinburgh: William Blackwood, 1816.
Ollivant, S. *The Court of the Official in Pre-Reformation Scotland*. Edinburgh: Stair Society, 1982.
O'Neilly, J. G. and L. E. Tanner. "The Shrine of St. Edward the Confessor." *Archaeologia* 100 (1966) 129-154.
Pagan, James. *History of the Cathedral and See of Glasgow*. Glasgow: Francis Orr, 1856.
Panofsky, Erwin. *Early Netherlandish Painting*. New York: Harper & Row, 1971.
Patrick, D. (ed). *Statutes of the Scottish Church*. Edinburgh: Edinburgh University Press [for the Scottish History Society], 1907.
Paul, G. M., ed. *The Diary of Sir Archibald Johnston of Wariston 1632-1639*. Edinburgh: T. & A. Constable [Scottish History Society], 1911.
Perkins, Jocelin. *Westminster Abbey*, ii. London: Alcuin Club Publications, 1940.
Peterkin, A., ed. *Records of the Kirk of Scotland*. Edinburgh: John Sutherland, 1838.
Pitcairn, R., ed. *Ancient Criminal Trials in Scotland from A. D. 1488 to A. D. 1624*. 3 vols. Edinburgh: Bannatyne Club, 1833
Poole, A. L. *The Obligations of Society in the XIIth and XIIIth centuries*. Oxford: Clarendon Press, 1946.
Potter, K. R., ed. *Gesta Stephani*. Oxford: Clarendon Press, 1976.
Preece, I. W. *Our awin Scottis use: Music in the Scottish Church up to 1603*. Glasgow: Universities of Glasgow and Aberdeen, 2000.
Primmer, J. Boyd. *Life of Jacob Primmer*. Edinburgh: William Bishop, 1916.
Pryde, G. S. *The Burghs of Scotland: A Critical List*. Oxford: Oxford University Press, 1965.
Radford, C. A. R. "The Bishop's Throne in Norwich Cathedral." *The Archaeological Journal* 116 (1961) 115-132.
———. *Official Guide to Glasgow Cathedral*. Edinburgh: HMSO, 1970.
——— and E. L. G. Stones. "The Remains of the Cathedral of Bishop Jocelin at Glasgow (c.1197)." *The Antiquaries Journal* 44 (1964) 220-232.
Raine, J., ed. *Historians of the Church of York*, ii. London: Rolls Series, 1886.
———. *The History and Antiquities of North Durham*. London: Bowyer Nichols & Son, 1852.
Ralston, A. G. *Lauchlan MacLean Watt: Preacher, Poet and Piping Padre*. Glasgow: Society of Friends of Glasgow Cathedral, 2018.
———. *Nevile Davidson: A Life to be Lived*. Eugene, OR: Wipf & Stock, 2019.
Reid, N., ed. *Scotland in the Reign of Alexander III*. Edinburgh: John Donald, 1990.

Renwick, Robert, ed. *Abstracts of Protocols of the Town Clerks of Glasgow.* 11 vols. Glasgow: Carson & Nicol, 1894–1900.

———. *Glasgow Memorials.* Glasgow: Maclehose, 1908.

——— and Sir John Lindsay. *History of Glasgow,* 3 vols. Glasgow: Maclehose, Jackson & Co., 1921–4.

Richardson, J. S. *The Mediaeval Stone Carver in Scotland.* Edinburgh: Edinburgh University Press, 1964.

——— and M. Wood. *Melrose Abbey.* London: HMSO, 1949.

Robertson J., ed. *Concilia Scotiae,* 2 vols. Edinburgh: Bannatyne Club, 1866.

Robertson, John. *Pastoral Counsels: being chapters on Practical and Devotional Subjects.* London: Macmillan, 1867.

Robinson, I. S. *The Papacy 1073-1198.* Cambridge: Cambridge University Press, 1990.

Rollason, D. et al., eds. *Anglo-Norman Durham.* Woodbridge: Boydell, 1994.

Romanes, C. S., ed. *Selections from the records of the regality of Melrose,* i. Edinburgh: T. & A. Constable [Scottish History Society], 1914.

Root, Margaret E. *Dunkeld Cathedral, Perthshire.* Edinburgh: HMSO, 1965.

Rosenwein, Barbara. *Negotiating Space: Power, Restraint and Privileges of Immunity in Early Medieval Europe.* Ithaca: Cornell University Press, 1999.

Row, J. *History of the Kirk of Scotland.* Edinburgh: Wodrow Society, 1842.

Rothes, John, 6th Earl of. *A relation of proceedings concerning the affairs of the Kirk of Scotland, from August 1637 to July 1638.* Edinburgh: Bannatyne Club, 1830.

Rubin, Miri. *Corpus Christi: The Eucharist in Late Medieval Culture.* Cambridge: Cambridge University Press, 1991.

Ruddiman, Thomas and John Sage, eds. *The Works of William Drummond of Hawthornden.* Edinburgh, 1711.

Ryrie, Alec. *The Origins of the Scottish Reformation.* Manchester: Manchester University Press 2006.

Sanderson, Margaret H. B. *Cardinal of Scotland: David Beaton c. 1494-1546.* Edinburgh, John Donald, 1986.

Sandquist, T. A. and M. R. Powicke, eds. *Essays in Medieval History presented to Bertie Wilkinson.* Toronto: Toronto University Press, 1969.

Scott, Geoffrey. *The Architecture of Humanism.* Boston: Houghton Mifflin, 1914.

Scott, H. et al., eds. *Fasti Ecclesiae Scoticanae,* 10 vols. Edinburgh: Oliver & Boyd, 1915–81.

Shead, N. F. "The administration of the diocese of Glasgow in the twelfth and thirteenth centuries." *Scottish Historical Review* 55 (1976) 127–150.

———. "Glasgow: an Ecclesiastical Borough." In Lynch, M., ed. *The Scottish Medieval Town.* Edinburgh: John Donald, 1988.

———. ed. *Scottish Episcopal Acta.* 2 vols. Woodbridge: Boydell [Scottish History Society], 2016, 2020.

——— et al., eds. *Heads of Religious Houses in Scotland from 12th to 16th Centuries,* rev. ed. Edinburgh: Scottish Record Society, New Series 24, 2018 [e-book].

——— et al., eds. *Fasti Ecclesiae Scoticanae Medii Aevi Ad Annum* 1638, 3rd ed. Edinburgh: Scottish Record Society, 2019 [e-book].

Simpson, G. G. and B. Webster. "The Archives of the Medieval Church of Glasgow: an introductory survey." *The Bibliotheck* 3 (1962) 195–201.

Smith, D. C. *Obedience and Prophetic Protest: Social Criticism in the Scottish Church, 1830-1945.* New York: Peter Lang, 1987.

Somerville, R., ed. *Scotia Pontificia: Papal Letters to Scotland before the Pontificate of Innocent III.* Oxford: Clarendon Press, 1982.

Spierling, Karen. *Infant Baptism in Reformation Geneva: The Shaping of a Community,* 1536-1564. Aldershot: Ashgate, 2005.

Spinks, Bryan D. *Scottish Presbyterian Worship.* Edinburgh: Saint Andrew Press, 2020.

Spotswood, J. *History of Church and State in Scotland.* London: printed for R. Royston, bookseller to his most sacred Majesty, 1677.

Stevenson, J. H. and M. Wood. *Scottish Heraldic Seals.* 3 vols. Glasgow: Maclehose, 1940.

Stevenson, David. *The Scottish Revolution 1637-1644: The Triumph of the Covenanters.* Newton Abbot: David & Charles, 1973.

Stones, E. L. G. "The Burials of Medieval Scottish Bishops, with particular reference to the bishops of Glasgow." *Innes Review* 20 (1969) 37-46.

—— and George Hay. "Notes on Glasgow Cathedral." *Innes Review* 18 (1967) 88-98.

——. *Anglo-Scottish Relations* 1174-1328: *Some Selected Documents.* Oxford: Clarendon Press, 1970.

Stringer, K. J. *Regesta Regum Scottorum, iii: The Acts of Alexander II.* Edinburgh, Edinburgh University Press, forthcoming.

Stuart, J. and G. Burnett. *The Exchequer Rolls of Scotland, i.* Edinburgh, H. M. General Register House, 1878.

Summerson, H. "Old and New Bishoprics: Durham and Carlisle." In Rollason, *Anglo-Norman Durham.*

Talbot, Eric J. "An Excavation at the Site of the N. W. Tower of St. Mungo's Cathedral, Glasgow." *Innes Review* 26 (1975) 43-9.

Theiner, A., ed. *Vetera Monumenta Hibernorum et Scotorum Historiam Illustrantia.* Rome: Typis Vaticanis, 1864.

Thomson, J. M. et al. *Register of the Great Seal of Scotland,* 11 vols. Edinburgh: H. M. General Register House, 1882-1914.

Thomson, T. and C. Innes, eds. *Acts of the Parliaments of Scotland,* 12 vols. Edinburgh: 1814-75.

Thomson, T., ed. *The Booke of the Universall Kirk of Scotland: Acts and Proceedings of the General Assemblies of the Kirk of Scotland,* 1560-1618, 3 vols. and appendix. Edinburgh: Bannatyne and Maitland Clubs, 1839-45.

——. *Liber Cartarum Prioratus Sancti Andree in Scotia.* Edinburgh: Bannatyne Club, 1841.

Todd, M. *The Culture of Protestantism in Early Modern Scotland.* New Haven: Yale University Press, 2000.

Topham, John, ed. *Liber Quotidianus Contrarotulatoris Garderobae.* London: J. Nichols [for the Society of Antiquaries of London], 1787.

Tucker, Joanna. *Reading and Shaping Medieval Cartularies.* Woodbridge: Boydell, 2020.

Twemlow, J. A., ed. *Calendar of Papal Registers Relating to Great Britain and Ireland,* Volume 14: 1484-1492. British History Online, www.british-history.ac.uk.

Tyler, J. Jeffery. *Lord of the Sacred City: The Episcopus Exclusus in Late Medieval and Early Modern Germany.* Leiden: Brill, 1999.

Vaassen, Elgin. *Die kgl. Glasmalereianstalt in München 1827-1874.* München/Berlin: Geschichte-Werke-Künstler. 2013.

—— and Peter van Treeck. *Das Görresfenster im Kölner Dom: Geschichte und Wiederherstellung.* In *Kölner Domblatt,* 46,1981.

Vacandard, E. *Vie de Saint Bernard.* Paris: Librairie Victor Lecoffre, 1920.
Waddell, C. "The Two Malachy Offices from Clairvaux." In *Bernard of Clairvaux: Studies presented to Dom Jean Leclercq.* Washington: Cistercian Publications, 1973.
Waddell, J. J. "The Western Towers of Glasgow Cathedral." *Transactions of the Scottish Ecclesiological Society* 6, pt. H, Aberdeen, 1920.
Wade, W. M. *The History of Glasgow, Ancient and Modern.* Paisley: J. Neilson, 1821.
Walsham, Alexandra. *Church Papists: Catholicism, Conformity and Confessional Polemic in Early Modern England.* London: Royal Historical Society, 1993.
Watt, D. E. R. "Bagimond di Vezza and his 'Roll.'" *Scottish Historical Review* 80 (2001) 1–23.
———. *A Biographical Dictionary of Scottish Graduates to A.D. 1410.* Oxford: Clarendon Press, 1977.
———. *Medieval Church Councils in Scotland.* Edinburgh: T. & T. Clark, 2000.
——— et al. *Scotichronicon,* iv. Edinburgh: Mercat Press, 1994.
———. *Series Episcoporum Catholicae Occidentalis,* Series VI, Tomus I, *Ecclesia Scoticana.* Stuttgart: Hiersemann, 1991.
Wedgwood, Alexandra. *A. W. N. Pugin and the Pugin Family.* London: Victoria & Albert Museum, 1985.
Wilson, C. H. *Descriptive catalogue of painted glass Windows in Glasgow Cathedral.* London: Murray, 1865.
Wood-Legh, K. L. *Perpetual Chantries in Britain.* Cambridge: Cambridge University Press, 1965.
Yeoman, P. *Medieval Scotland.* London: Batsford [for Historic Scotland], 1995.

INDEX

Aiken, Emma Butler-Cole, 37
Ainmiller, Max Emanuel, 261–2, 266, 268
Anne, HRH The Princess Royal, 33, 37

Bagimond's Roll, 87
Baillie, Robert, 220–2
Balfour Beatty, 30
Balfour, James, 234–6
Barony, Glasgow, 190–4, 249, 283
Beaton, David, Cardinal, 184–9
Becket, St. Thomas, 81
Begg, James, 285
Benedictine Order, 56, 57
Bilsland, Steven, Lord Bilsland of Kinrara, 12–13, 14, 15, 21, 28
Blackadder, William, Bishop of Glasgow, 110, 137, 145, 152–162, 183–4
Bondington, Bishop William de, 78–80, 82, 83, 92, 164–5
Boyd, A. K. H., 287, 300
Boyd, Zachary, 19
Buchanan, James, 6
Bulloch, James, 5
Burns, G. S., 277–291, 299
Burrell, William, 248

Cameron, Sir D. Y., 8–9
Cameron, John, Bishop of Glasgow, 142, 146, 98. 244
Chalmers, P. Macgregor, 168–170, 178
Charles I, 218–240

Church Service Society, 276, 284, 286–7, 300
Cistercian order, 117–8
Clark, John K., 34, 36
Clonmacnois, 54, 56
Cockburn, J. Hutchison, 7
Cogitosus, 54–6
Collie, James, 149, 177–8, 245, 251
Cooper, James, 289
Cooper, John, 190–4
Cullen, Pat, 35

Dali, Salvador, 32
David I, King of Scotland, 57, 61–74, 76, 88, 93, 96, 99
Davidson, A. Nevile, 3–39, 275
Diack, Alan and Henty, 33–4
Dunbar, Gavin, Archbishop of Glasgow, 184–9

Edward I, King of England, 165–6
Empire Exhibition, Glasgow, 7
Eyre-Todd, George, xxi, 295

Fergus, Thomas, 28
Forbes, Andrew, 35–6

Glasgow Assembly (1638), 218–240
Glasgow Ark, 27, 29
Glasgow Cathedral Annual Festival, 35, 36
Glasgow Cathedral Chapter, 136–143
Glasgow Cathedral Choir Screen and Crossing, 144–151

315

INDEX

Glasgow Cathedral Western Towers, 241–257
Glendinning, Mathew de, 139–141
Graham, J. Gillespie, 252–6
Gray, Robert, 28

Henderson, John, 281
Hepburn, Charles, 20
Herbert, Bishop of Glasgow, 76, 77, 79, 80, 81, 111, 129
Herdman, Robert, 284
Hills, Sir Graham, 39
Honeyman, John, 244, 288

Ingram, Bishop of Glasgow, 90
Innes, Thomas, 10

Jocelin, Bishop of Glasgow, 44–52, 59–60, 70, 74, 76, 81, 87, 97, 103, 104, 111, 112–135
John, Bishop of Glasgow, 87, 90
Johnstone, Archibald, 220

Kemp, G. M., 252–5
Knox, John, 184–5, 189
Königliche Glasmalereianstalt, 258–74

Laing, John, Bishop of Glasgow, 150
Lee, Robert, 292
Lees, Cameron, 300
Love, Robert, 23

Macaulay, George, 283–4
Macaulay, James, 26, 28, 33, 39
MacAskill, Moira, 29
MacFarlane, Sir James, 8
Macleod, Norman, 283
McGlashan, Iain, 34
McLellan, Archibald, 245, 249–54, 288
McLellan, Sir Robin, 39
McLellan, Sadie, 17
Malcolm IV, King of Scotland, 84, 96, 101, 107
Malveisin, William, Bishop of Glasgow, 82
Mandeville, Symon de, 139–40

Margaret, HRH The Princess, 31
Melville, Andrew, 194–5, 199, 219
Milner-White, Eric, 18
Moffat, Robert de, 139–40
Morgan, Edwin, 25
Morris, Jean, 29
Morris, W. J., 21, 26, 34, 37
Mowat, Ronald, 6
Muir, Pearson McAdam, 276, 291–302
Munich Glass, 6, 258–74

National Covenant (1638), 229–30
Noble, A. J., 22

Ogilvie, John, 215

Paton, Joseph, (Baron Maclay), 37
Peace, A. L., 21, 284
Primmer, Jacob, 286, 293–4
Provand's Lordship, 26
Pugin, A. W., 255, 273

Reformation, 181–2, 189–196, 200, 223–4
Richardson, Albert, 12, 15, 16, 19
Rintoul, Jean, 34
Rintoul, Peter, 28, 33
Robertson, John, 277, 302
Rowat, Alexander, 190
Rutherford, Samuel, 227–8

St. Albans, Walter de, 78–9, 83, 88, 91
St. Andrews, 119–121
St. Kentigern (St. Mungo), 43–52, 111, 123–127, 163–171, 200
St. Kentigern Tapestry, 23, 24
St. Mungo Museum of Religious Life, 32, 37
Sarum, Use of, 54, 72–3
Schmiedel, P. W., 297–8
Scottish Church Society, 289
Simson, Cuthbert, 95
Smail, Ian, 36
Smith, W. Robertson, 296–7
Society of Friends of Glasgow Cathedral, 3–40
Spear, Francis, 14

Spottiswoode, Archbishop, 197–217
Stirling-Maxwell, Sir John, 8, 11
Strachan, Douglas, 6

Turnbull, William, Bishop of Glasgow, 99, 109, 146, 244
Turner, John R., 22, 23, 34

Walker, J. W. and Sons, 22
Waltheof, Abbot, 114–6

Wardlaw, Walter de, 137–8
Warr, Charles, 5
Webster, Gordon, 14
Weir, Viscount, 22
Willis and Sons, 21
Wilson, William, 14
Wishart, Robert, Bishop of Glasgow, 173–178

York, Archbishopric of, 77

www.ingramcontent.com/pod-product-compliance
Lightning Source LLC
Chambersburg PA
CBHW050616300426
44112CB00012B/1525